D1030150

Saints of the Americas

Rev. M. A. Habig, O.F.M.

992
HA

OUR SUNDAY VISITOR, INC.
Huntington, Indiana 46750

The Nihil Obstat and Imprimatur are official declarations that a book or pamphlet is free of doctrinal or moral error. No implication is contained therein that those who have granted the Nihil Obstat or Imprimatur agree with the contents, opinions or statements expressed.

Imprimi Potest:
Vitus Duschinsky, O.F.M.
Provincial of St. Louis
Franciscan Fathers

Nihil Obstat:
Rev. Lawrence Gollner
Censor Librorum

Imprimatur:
✠ Leo A. Pursley, D.D.
Bishop of Fort Wayne-South Bend
September 4, 1974

ISBN: 0-87973-880-4
Library of Congress Catalog Card Number: 74-15269

Cover Design by James E. McIlrath

Published, printed and bound in the U.S.A. by
Our Sunday Visitor, Inc.
Noll Plaza
Huntington, Indiana 46750
880

ACKNOWLEDGMENTS

To all, individuals and organizations alike, who have been so generous in helping this author by supplying information and pictures, as well as assisting in other ways, I wish to express my sincere and heartfelt gratitude.

First of all I am indebted to my confrere and friend, Father Achilles Meersman, historian and missionary, formerly in Brazil and now in India, who suggested the writing of this book to me some twenty years ago and supplied me with copies of the articles written in Portuguese by Father A. Thoonsen.

Other confreres to whom I owe special thanks are Father Samuel M. Botero-Restrepo of Medellin, Colombia; Father Fidel de Jesús Chauvet of Mexico City; Father Mark Hegener, manager of the Franciscan Herald Press, Chicago; Father Irenaeus Herscher, librarian of Friedsam Memorial Library, St. Bonaventure University, St. Bonaventure, New York; Father Silvestre Paredes of Mexico City; Father Bernardine Schneider of Tokyo, Japan; Father Antonine Tibesar of Washington, D.C.; Father August Reyling of Quincy, Illinois; and Father Roland J. Burke of Butler, New Jersey.

Likewise, the Claretian Fathers of Chicago; Rev. Thomas F. Egan, S.J., of Auriesville, New York; Rev. Joseph G. Forquer, O.P., of St. Jude's Shrine in Chicago; Rev. Francis J. Litz, C.SS.R., of Philadelphia, Pennsylvania; Rev. Diego Pacheco, S.J., of Nagasaki, Japan; and Rev. John Ryan, S.J., of Baltimore, Maryland.

Also, Sister Marie-Jeanne Beland, C.N.D., of the Marguerite Bourgeoys Center in Montreal; Sister Frances Dolan, C.N.D., of Ridgefield, Connecticut; Sister M. Ellen of Emmitsburg, Maryland; Mother C. Griesedieck, R.S.C.J., of St. Charles, Missouri; Sister Beatrice Leduc, S.G.M., of the Marguerite d'Youville Center in Montreal; Sister Rose Margaret Delaney, S.F.P., of Brooklyn, New York; and Sister Pia, M.S.C., of Columbus Hospital, Chicago.

I would also like to thank Mr. Edmund A. Balcerak of the Extension Society, Chicago; Mr. and Mrs. Robert C. Broderick of Brookfield, Wisconsin; Mr. Paul Delaney, administrator of Huronia Historical Parks, Midland, Ontario, Canada; Mr. Howard Earp of Our Lady of Guadalupe Apostolate, Portland, Oregon; and Miss Jo Williams of Meston Travels, El Paso, Texas.

Lastly, I want to express my appreciation to all employees of Our Sunday Visitor, Inc., who were instrumental in producing this book, and to all others who have helped me in any way but whose names I have not listed.

—M.A.H.

PICTURE CREDITS

The author and publisher acknowledge the following as sources of illustrations appearing in this volume:

Archives of the Franciscan Province of the Sacred Heart, St. Louis, p. 65.
Calendar of Catholic Church Extension Society, Chicago, pp. 35, 86, 189.
Dominican Fathers, St. Pius V Church, Chicago, p. 232.
Franciscan Fathers, Medellin, Colombia, for Berna's drawings of saints and blessed, pp. 136, 137, 165, 171, 173, 177, 181, 245, 250, 253.
Franciscan Missionary Union, Milan, Italy, p. 167.
Franciscan Herald Press, Chicago, pp. 133, 147, 148, 199, 217, 225, 259.
Franciscan Sisters of the Poor, Brooklyn, N.Y., p. 57.
Friedsam Memorial Library, St. Bonaventure, N.Y., p. 125.
George A. Pflaum, Publisher, Dayton, Ohio, p. 77.
James McIlrath drawing, p. 153.
Lateran Museum, Rome, Italy, p. 158.
Louvre, Paris, pp. 111, 259.
Martyrs' Shrine, Auriesville, N.Y., p. 25.
Meston Travels, El Paso, Texas, pp. 277, 327.
Missionary Sisters of St. Peter Claver, St. Louis, p. 194.
NC photo, p. 30.
Our Lady of Guadalupe Apostolate, Portland, Oregon, for Howard G. Earp photo, p. 285.
Religious News Service photos, pp. 204, 239, 259.
Religious of the Sacred Heart, St. Charles, Mo., p. 282.
Old Mission, Santa Barbara, Calif., p. 282.
Reproducta Co., Inc., for copyright portrait, p. 115.
Robert H. Martin photo, p. 310.

INTRODUCTION

THIS book presents for the first time in the English language biographies of all those Americans whose holiness of life has been officially recognized by the Church. By Americans we mean those who spent at least a part of their lives in the Western Hemisphere — all the Americas, North and Central and South. Twenty-two have been canonized, and twenty-three have been beatified.

Of the twenty-two canonized American saints, all except five have been assigned feast days in the new liturgical calendar of the universal Church. Previously only two, St. Rose of Lima and St. Anthony Claret, were listed in the Roman calendar; but when the revision (effective January 1, 1970) was made, fifteen more were added. Eight of these are the Jesuit Martyrs of North America (three of New York and five of Canada). Five, from Mexico, belong to the Martyrs of Nagasaki, Japan (1597). Two are saints of Lima, Peru, namely St. Toribio de Mogrovejo and St. Martin de Porres.

This fact alone is sufficient reason for a book on the "Saints of the Americas." But there are still very many people everywhere who are interested in all the saints.

What the people actually think and feel about the saints became strikingly manifest when the calendar changes were announced on May 9, 1969. The public, of course, was misled by newspaper reports into thinking that a large number of popular saints had been "abolished." Nothing could have been farther from the truth. Some feasts or commemorations of saints in the

Roman missal and breviary, it is true, were suppressed for historical reasons. Others were left to local celebration or were made optional, in order to place greater emphasis on the seasons of the ecclesiastical year. The fact that several feasts of our Lord and our Lady were among those suppressed or restricted was scarcely noticed, as likewise, was the fact that some new feasts were added to the traditional list.

As an editorial in *L'Osservatore Romano* pointed out, "the devotions and local cults are not in the least damaged or put in question, even if the true histories of the lives of some saints are not as exhaustive as some accounts would pretend they are. An unfounded alarm has been created. We hope it will be quickly dissipated. Public opinion has the right to know the reality of the situation — that of a Church adjusting itself to its new world dimensions, without however reneging on the values of a proper devotion, of a healthy cult of local saints."

The chapters of this book are "true histories of the lives of saints." They are not unverifiable legends about vague figures of the distant past, concerning whom we have little or no definite information. We have made every effort to carry out the injunction of Vatican Council II in regard to the readings about the saints in the divine office: "The accounts of martyrdom or the lives of the saints are to accord with the facts of history" (*Constitution on the Sacred Liturgy*, n. 92).

This book, therefore, is not "just another pious work, written for edification." We have left reflection and application to the reader, contenting ourselves with narrating in a simple and readable style the life-stories of the "Saints of the Americas," after having made a careful investigation of the historical facts. The latter, incidentally, are often "stranger than fiction," and in most cases certainly more interesting.

These men and women of the Americas are paragons of true greatness, heroes of holiness, genuine friends of God and benefactors of their fellowmen. Surely, the fact that they have been canonized or beatified should not stand in the way of giving them the place in the history of the New World which they deserve. Good Catholics everywhere, we have no doubt, will be glad to learn about them and will not fail to pay them due veneration.

Clear and beautiful are the numerous statements of Vatican Council II concerning the doctrine and practice of the veneration of the saints.

Not only those who have been formally canonized or beatified by the Church, but all the saints in heaven "establish the whole Church more firmly in holiness. . . .

"They lend nobility to the worship which the Church offers on earth to God. . . .

"They contribute in many ways to the greater upbuilding of the Church on earth. . . .

"They do not cease to intercede with the Father for us. . . .

"They very greatly strengthen our weakness by their brotherly interest" (*Constitution on the Church*, n. 49).

Far from downgrading or denigrating the devotion to the saints, the Council has reiterated in no uncertain terms what the Church has always taught on this subject.

"This most sacred Synod accepts with great devotion the venerable faith of our ancestors regarding this vital fellowship with our brethren who are in heavenly glory" (*Ibid.*, n. 51).

Far from banishing the saints from the church buildings, the sacred liturgy, and the spiritual life of the People of God, both as individuals and as a community, Vatican II has not only restated the pronouncements of previous councils, but has also set forth in a masterful, concise and lucid manner the role which the saints in heaven play in the Church on earth.

The Council calls attention to the union and fellowship of the saints with their pilgrim brethren, the power of their intercession for us with God, the inspiring influence of their example upon us. It points out the correctness, appropriateness and timeliness of the honor we bestow upon the saints by the observance of their feasts, the veneration of their images and the study and imitation of their lives. Yes, the Council exhorts us to have and cherish a deep love of the saints.

"It is supremely fitting, therefore, that we love those friends and fellow heirs of Jesus Christ, who are also our brothers and extraordinary benefactors, that we render due thanks to God for them and 'suppliantly invoke them and have recourse to their prayers, their power and help in obtaining benefits from God through His Son, Jesus Christ, our Lord, who is our sole Redeemer and Savior.' For, by its very nature every genuine testimony of love which we show to those in heaven tends toward and terminates in Christ, who is the 'crown of all saints' " (*Ibid.*, n. 50).

By the veneration and invocation of the saints and devotion to them, is meant of course "the authentic cult of the saints" which "consists, not so much in the multiplying of external acts, but rather in the intensity of our active love. By such love, for our own greater good and that of the Church, we seek from the saints 'example in their way of life, fellowship in their communion, and aid by their intercession' " (*Ibid.*, n. 51).

Hence the Council "urges all concerned to work hard to prevent or correct any abuses, excesses, or defects which may have crept in here and there, and to restore all things to a more ample praise of Christ and of God" *(Ibid.)*.

"At the same time," the Council document adds, "let the people be instructed that our communion with those in heaven, provided that it is understood in the more adequate light of faith, in no way weakens, but conversely, more thoroughly enriches the supreme worship we give to God the Father, through Christ, in the Spirit" *(Ibid.,* n. 51).

To many it will come as a complete surprise that no less than forty-five persons of the New World have been formally canonized or beatified by the Church. Twenty-eight are martyrs "who gave the supreme witness of faith and charity by the shedding of their blood" and whom the Church "has always venerated with special devotion, together with the Blessed Virgin Mary and the holy angels" *(Ibid.,* n. 50). The other seventeen are saints and blessed who "imitated Christ's virginity and poverty more exactly" or "whom the outstanding practice of the Christian virtues and the divine charisms recommended to the pious devotion and imitation of the faithful" *(Ibid.)*.

Seven were founders of religious congregations (the Claretians, Sisters of the Congregation de Notre Dame, the Grey Nuns, Missionary Sisters of the Sacred Heart, Daughters of Charity in the United States, Religious of the Sacred Heart in the United States, Franciscan Sisters of the Poor). Thirty-four were members of religious orders or congregations of men (fourteen Franciscans, thirteen Jesuits, four Dominicans, two Augustinians, one Redemptorist). Two, namely an archbishop and a canon, represent diocesan clergy. Two were members of the laity.

Who may rightly be regarded as saints or blessed of the Americas? Certainly those who were born in any of the countries of the New World, even though they died in some other part of the world. There are nine of these. Secondly, those who were not born in the Western Hemisphere, but died there. These are nineteen in number. And thirdly, those who were neither born nor died in the Americas, but who lived and worked there for some time. There are seventeen such saints and blessed.

We have not included among the "Saints of the Americas" those who merely traveled from Europe to the Far East by way of the Western Hemisphere. Most of these crossed the Atlantic to Mexico and, after remaining there for a short time, continued their voyage across the Pacific. Three were driven by a storm at sea on the coast of Brazil, returned to Europe, and sailed around Africa to the Orient.

The "Saints of the Americas," surely, are very close to all the countries of the New World. Sixteen can be claimed in a special way as its own by Mexico, eight by Canada, eight by the United States, five by Peru (one of these, also by Argentina), four by Brazil (one of these, also by Paraguay), two by Colombia, one by Ecuador, and one by Cuba.

There have been other Americans of outstanding holiness, and some of them are being considered for beatification. It would lead us too far afield if we tried to tell the story of their lives in detail. However, a list of these candidates for sainthood will be found at the end of this book.

"People are looking for prophets," declared Cardinal G. M. Garrone in 1969; "they should be asking for saints. It is less necessary to discover new things in the Church than to become more aware of the newness of the old things, provided that the latter are really God's. . . . The Church feels the need of prophets to point out her way. But it is more necessary for her to feel the need of holiness. She must look to the models who in the course of centuries have recommended themselves to her trust more by holiness than by merely exterior deeds. Then she will have nothing to fear. . . . Then, above all, having established herself permanently in truth, she will draw new hope from it" (*L'Osservatore Romano*, English edition, April 10, 1969, p. 11).

In the Pastoral Letter on the Blessed Virgin Mary, issued by the National Conference of Catholic Bishops (of the United States) on November 21, 1973, we are told: "There is little doubt that we are passing through a period marked by a lack of interest in the saints. Much more is involved here than devotion to the saints, even St. Mary. What is at stake is the reality of the humanity of the risen Jesus. . . . When he was asked about the decline of Marian devotion, the German Jesuit, Father Karl Rahner, declared that the special temptation that affects Christians today, Catholics and Protestants alike, is the temptation to turn the central truths of the faith into abstractions, and abstractions have no need of mothers" and we may add, no need of saints (*Behold Your Mother, Woman of Faith*, n. 85).

This beautiful pastoral has a short Appendix entitled "Mary's Place in American Catholic History." After telling the story of the "Saints of the Americas," it seemed to be not inappropriate to make our book "a double feature" by adding a fuller treatment of the theme of the Pastoral's Appendix as Part II: an account of the extraordinary devotion to our Lady in all the Americas during the past four centuries. Mary Immaculate too, in a very special sense, is one of the "Saints of the Americas."

In our modern age, when the need for genuine holiness is keenly felt, may the "Saints of the Americas" be an inspiration to many and aid them by their intercession to attain the heights of sanctity. May these holy fellow Americans intercede for all of us, and thus help us in the conflict with the powers of darkness, that we too may one day have a share in the perfect and endless happiness which is theirs.

—M.A.H.

CONTENTS

PART II — OUR LADY

All the Americas

Appendices

Part I
SAINTS AND BLESSED

United States

EIGHT saints and blessed have lived and died within the present limits of the United States during the period from 1642 to 1974. Four have been canonized and four beatified. Three saints were Jesuit missionary martyrs. Four blessed were founders of religious communities in the United States. One was the fourth bishop of Philadelphia.

One, Bl. Elizabeth Ann Seton, was a native of the United States. The others came from Bohemia, France, Germany and Italy. One of the latter, St. Frances Xavier Cabrini, became a naturalized United States citizen.

The places where all but one died are Auriesville in New York, Emmitsburg in Maryland, St. Charles in Missouri, Philadelphia in Pennsylvania and Chicago in Illinois.

The feasts of our saints and two of the blessed are observed throughout the United States; on October 19, St. Isaac Jogues and his Companions; on November 13, St. Frances X. Cabrini; on January 4, Bl. Elizabeth Ann Seton; and on January 5, Bl. John N. Neumann. The feasts of the other blessed are limited to certain places and groups.

CHAPTER 1

SAINTS AND BLESSED

United States

St. Isaac Jogues, St. René Goupil and St. John de Lalande

(1642 and 1646) Martyrs of Auriesville, New York

"I DO not know what it is to enter paradise. But this I know, that it is difficult to experience in this world a joy more excessive and more overflowing than that which I felt on my setting foot in New France, and celebrating my first Mass here on the day of the Visitation. I assure you, it was indeed a day of the visitation of the goodness of God and our Lady. I felt as if it were a Christmas day for me, and that I was to be born again to a new life, and a life in God."

These words were written in July, 1636, by a young Jesuit priest who was to become a martyr a decade later and a canonized saint 300 years after his death. They are an excerpt from a letter which Father Isaac Jogues wrote to his "honored mother" in Orléans, France. Earlier that same year he had been ordained a priest. He was now twenty-nine years old.

With four other Jesuits, he had embarked from the French seaport of Dieppe on April 8. They crossed the Atlantic on different ships in a fleet of eight vessels which was taking a new governor, Montmagny, to New France. The latter's predecessor, Samuel de Champlain, had died the previous year. Almost two months later the fleet entered Chaleur Bay, the body of water which separates the present province of Quebec from that of New Brunswick. Another month elapsed before Father Jogues arrived in Quebec.

Champlain had founded Quebec in 1608. It was at his request that the first missionaries in the valley of the St. Lawrence

16

St. Isaac Jogues, missionary to the Iroquois Indians,
was killed with a tomahawk on October 18, 1646.

River came in 1615. They were Father Denis Jamay and three other Franciscans, members of a stricter branch within the order, called Récollets or Recollects. Other Franciscans joined them in the years that followed. Earlier, in 1611, two Jesuits had established themselves in the colony of Acadia (Nova Scotia); and their number was likewise increased. But in 1613 they were driven out by the English.

Already, in 1615, one of the first Franciscans, Father Joseph Le Caron, had begun to do missionary work among the Indians in distant Huronia, the region lying between Nottawasaga Bay and Lake Simcoe in the present province of Ontario. It was here that the Wyandot or Huron Indians lived during the first half of the seventeenth century.

Two other friars were conducted to the Huron mission by Father Le Caron in 1623. One of them, Father Nicholas Viel, and the neophyte Ahautsic became the first martyrs of New France in 1626, when they were thrown into the rapids near Montreal by other Hurons who had accompanied them to the St. Lawrence River.

Previously, in 1619, another Franciscan, Father William Poullain, was captured by the hostile Iroquois Indians and cruelly tortured; but he was saved from being burned to death by some Frenchmen, who exchanged him for several Iroquois captives.

Still another, Father Joseph de la Roche Dallion, a missionary among the Hurons, spent the fall and winter of 1627-1628 among the Indians of the Neutral Nation in the western part of New York, and so became the first priest to visit that state.

Father de la Roche Dallion had come from France in 1625 with five Jesuits who responded to the invitation of the Franciscans to join them in New France and Huronia. One of them was Father Ennemond Massé who had been in Acadia. Another was the future martyr Father John de Brébeuf.

Four years later, however, both Franciscans and Jesuits were expelled from the French colony by the English who seized and held it till it was restored to France in 1632. The Jesuits returned the same year, but the Franciscans were not permitted to go back until 1670.

Among those who came back in 1632 were Fathers Massé and Brébeuf. The next year the mission in Huronia was reestablished. More Jesuits arrived in the years that followed. One such group of new recruits had Father Isaac Jogues as a member.

Born in Orléans, France, on January 10, 1607, Isaac was the son of a prominent official of the city. He was a child of his father's second marriage.

When the boy was baptized in St. Hilary's Church, he received the Old-Testament name Isaac, a favorite one in the family. Soon after his birth, his father died; and his good mother with loving care taught him the science of the saints from childhood.

After graduating from college at the age of seventeen, Isaac entered the Society of Jesus and spent his novitiate year in Rouen. For three years he then studied philosophy at the royal college of La Flèche; and for three years more he was assigned to teaching.

The study of theology and preparation for the priesthood followed. Early in 1636 he was ordained, and he celebrated his first holy Mass in his native city, Orléans, on February 10. Two months later he left for New France.

Father Jogues was not originally destined for the Huron mission, since a sufficient number of fathers had already been assigned. But not long after he had arrived in Quebec, Father Anthony Daniel came with three Huron boys to begin a boarding school for Indian children. The Indians who had accompanied Father Daniel on his trip from Huronia asked that a priest return with them to their country; and Father Jogues was selected to go along with them.

When he arrived in Huronia on August 24, Father Jogues was joyfully welcomed by his five confreres stationed there. They were encountering all kinds of obstacles in their missionary efforts; and to make matters worse, an epidemic broke out.

All the missionaries contracted the disease, and Father Jogues was one of the first (in Father Jogues' case the *Jesuit Relations* identifies the illness only as a violent fever). He grew so ill that he seemed to be near death. Acting as his own surgeon, he applied the remedy of bleeding, and was soon well again.

The first task of the new missionary was to learn the language of the Hurons. His teacher was Father Brébeuf, who had been in the mission previously with the Franciscans. Father Jogues made rapid progress; but the work of converting the Indians was a very difficult one, because of the envy and opposition of their sorcerers. During the epidemic, it is true, the missionaries were able to baptize more than 1,200; but adult converts were few in number.

Things came to a head when the Indians held a council and condemned all the missionaries to death. Father Brébeuf, observing an Indian custom, invited the Hurons to a farewell banquet in the missionaries' cabin. So convincingly did he speak to them about life after death, that the leaders of the Indians changed their mind and left the fathers in peace. Father Brébeuf was adopted into the tribe and made a chief.

19

In 1638 a new mission, St. Joseph II, was established at Tean-austayé, near present-day Hillsdale in Medonté township. Father Brébeuf was in charge with Father Jogues as his assistant. During the first year they baptized seventy-two adults and forty-eight children.

Two years later, Father Charles Garnier and Father Jogues were sent to found another mission among the Petun or Tobacco Indians in the Blue Mountains between Lakes Huron and Ontario, thirty miles to the southwest. They had to make the expedition during winter and traveled on snowshoes, because during the rest of the year these Indians were too busy trading and fishing.

On the way they were deserted by their guides. When they arrived at their destination, they were threatened and ordered to leave. In none of the Indian villages were they allowed to remain more than two days. The journey ended in failure.

The next year Father Garnier made another attempt, and this time he was successful. He founded the Mission of the Apostles; and soon it had nine stations.

During the same winter of 1640, Father Jogues accompanied Father Raymbault on another expedition for a distance of 250 miles, mostly along the north shore of Lake Huron, all the way to the Ottawas at Sault Ste. Marie. The Chippewas (Ojibways) were visiting the Ottawas at that time, and the priests found a gathering of 2,000 Indians.

Though the missionaries were invited to remain, they were not prepared to do so at the time. They planted a huge cross, facing the unconquered west, and returned. The hardships of the journey were too great for Father Jogues' companion, and he died the following year in Quebec.

By the summer of 1642 the missionaries in Huronia were in dire straits. Father Jogues was chosen to go back to Quebec to get new supplies. The journey was a difficult one because it was made by canoe on a series of rivers connected by portages. The latter had to be traversed on foot with the travelers carrying both canoe and baggage on their shoulders. It was also a dangerous journey, because they could easily meet a party of Iroquois, the implacable enemies of the Hurons.

But Father Jogues was ready. He even asked God for the privilege of suffering for the faith. Before leaving Huronia, he paid a visit to our Lord in the mission chapel; and with head bowed down to the ground, he begged for the grace and favor of enduring with love and valor whatever hardships and sufferings might be his.

With a group of eighteen Indians and five Frenchmen, Father

Jogues set out on June 13. Thirty-five days later they were at Trois Riviérès (Three Rivers), north of Montreal. Here and in Quebec the party remained for twenty-five days, transacting business and gathering supplies. On August 1, they commenced the return trip. There were now about forty persons in the company, four of them Frenchmen, including Father Jogues and his lay assistant René Goupil. The latter was a so-called *donné* or oblate, a lay missionary who dedicated his life to the important work of helping the priest in whatever way he could.

René Goupil, whose birthplace was Angers, France, was of the same age as Father Jogues. He had tried to become a Jesuit, but poor health forced him to leave the novitiate. Subsequently he studied surgery; and going to Canada, he offered his services to the missionaries among the Hurons.

On the second day of the journey the travelers were suddenly attacked by Iroquois Indians who were lying in wait for them. Many of the Hurons fled into the woods; but eighteen Hurons, who were Christians or catechumens, and the four Frenchmen were taken prisoners and cruelly maltreated. Three Hurons were killed in the encounter.

St. Isaac Jogues was tortured by the Iroquois when he was their prisoner in 1642.

The Iroquois, who numbered about 25,000 persons, comprised five tribes — Mohawks, Onondagas, Oneidas, Cayugas and Senecas. In the order given, east to west, they lived in the Mohawk valley of the present state of New York, between Schenectady and Lake Erie. The easternmost village of the Mohawks was situated near the present Auriesville.

It was a Mohawk war party who fell upon Father Jogues and his companions. Taking their captives with them, they returned to their villages in eastern New York. They did not reach the first of these until August 18. During the journey they inflicted outrageous tortures on their prisoners.

A year later, on August 5, 1643, Father Jogues wrote a detailed Latin account of his captivity to his provincial superior in France, Father Jean Filleau. One of the reasons why he wrote the letter in Latin was his wish "that this letter may not be too common." He was then a slave in the Auriesville village.

After he was taken prisoner on August 2, writes Father Jogues, ". . . the Mohawks grew fierce, and, assailing me with their fists and with knotty sticks, left me half dead on the ground; and, a little later, . . . they also tore off my nails, and bit with their teeth my two forefingers, causing me incredible pain. They did the same to René Goupil. . . .

"We suffered many hardships on the journey, during which we spent thirty-eight days amid hunger, excessive heat, threats, and blows, in addition to the cruel pains of our wounds, not healed, which had putrefied, so that worms dropped from them. Besides, they even went so far — a savage act — as to tear out in cold blood our hair and beards, and to wound us with their nails, which are extremely sharp, in the most tender and sensitive parts of the body."

On the eighth day, continues Father Jogues, "I, who was the last, and therefore more exposed to these beatings, fell, midway in the journey which we were obliged to make to a hill, on which they had created a stage. I thought that I must die there, because I neither could nor cared to arise. What I suffered is known to One for whose love and cause it is a pleasant and glorious thing to suffer. Finally . . . they ceased beating me, and conducted me, half dead, to the stage — all bleeding from the blows which they had given me, especially in the face. Having come down from it, they loaded me . . . with new blows on the neck and the rest of the body. They burned one of my fingers, and crushed another with their teeth. The others, already bruised and their sinews torn, they so twisted that even at present, although partly healed, they are crippled and deformed."

When they arrived at the first of the Iroquois villages, those who were waiting for them "beat us with sticks, fists, and stones, as before, especially my head, because they hate shaven and short hair. Two nails had been left me. These they tore out with their teeth, and tore off that flesh which is under them, with their very sharp nails, even to the bone."

They then led Father Jogues and René Goupil to the next village, continued to beat them on the way "not only with sticks, but also with iron rods, which they have from the Dutch. . . . René, who was not very nimble, received so many blows, especially in the face, that nothing was seen of him except the whites of his eyes."

Arriving at the second village, they were again taken to a platform and beaten with a great rod. An Algonquin Christian woman who had been enslaved was forced to cut off the thumb of Father Jogues' left hand. "As for René," writes Father Jogues, "they cut off his right thumb at the first joint. I thank God that they left me the one on my right hand, so that by this letter I may pray my fathers and brethren to offer prayers in the Holy Church of God."

On the feast of the Assumption of the Blessed Virgin Mary, they were conducted to still another village, five or six miles distant from the first. There they were struck "especially on the bones of the legs, with what pain may be imagined." On a platform, to which the prisoners were taken, the Indians "threw coals and live ashes on our bare flesh, which for us who were bound, it was difficult to throw off."

For seven days the captives were taken from village to village and tortured in new ways. Finally, on September 29, one of the Iroquois struck René on the head with a tomahawk, causing him to fall on the ground half dead. The barbarian then killed him with two more blows.

"He was not more than thirty-five years of age," writes Father Jogues of René. "He was a man of unusual simplicity and innocence of life, of invincible patience, and very conformable to the will of God. . . . He had consecrated himself, under obedience to the superiors of the Society, in the service of our neophytes and catechumens — to whom with the art of surgery he was of great assistance. . . . A few days before, he had consecrated himself with the vows. . . . The sign of the cross, which he often made on the brows of the children, was the last and true cause of his death." The following spring, Father Jogues found the bones of the martyr on the bank of the river and buried them as best he could.

Father Jogues himself was made a slave and adopted into the Wolf clan. At first he was treated with cruelty, but gradually his master became more kindly disposed to him. He was granted a certain measure of freedom, and he learned much of the Iroquois language. Once he saved a woman and her child from drowning.

Not far distant, at Rensselaerswyck (present-day Albany), the Dutch had a trading post called Fort Orange. As soon as they learned of Father Jogues' captivity, they sought to have him released; but their efforts were in vain.

On July 31, 1643, more than a year after he had fallen into the hands of the Iroquois, Father Jogues was taken along by them to Fort Orange on a trading and fishing trip. The commandant of the fort urged him to escape to a ship which was in the harbor. After some hesitation, Father Jogues succeeded in doing so. He felt that, having learned the Iroquois language, he would be able to return to his captors later as a missionary.

But, when the Indians threatened reprisals, Father Jogues returned to Fort Orange and hid in a barn. The commandant remained firm in his refusal to surrender the priest to the Iroquois. To satisfy them, he offered them a ransom of three hundred livres of gold.

For several days more Father Jogues remained hidden behind some casks in the storehouse. By command of William Kieft, governor of New Netherlands, he was then taken aboard the ship at Albany. He sailed down the Hudson to Manhattan Island, and thence to England. On Christmas eve he arrived on the coast of France.

Everyone welcomed the living martyr with great respect; but Father Jogues was more anxious to avoid the honors bestowed upon him than he had been to escape from the Iroquois. According to canon law, his mutilated hands impeded him from celebrating holy Mass, but Pope Urban VIII granted him a dispensation.

Early in 1644 the missionary returned to New France, and went to Montreal, which had only recently been founded. There, while waiting for an opportunity to go back to Huronia, he ministered to the Indians of the neighborhood.

Strangely enough, the Iroquois at this time sent an embassy to Three Rivers to sue for peace with the French. Father Jogues attended the meeting; and with John Bourdon, the representative of the government, he was sent in May, 1646, as an ambassador to Ossernenon, the principle village of the Iroquois, to confer with their chiefs.

Going by way of Lake Champlain and Lake Orange, they reached their destination and remained for a week to confirm the

Statue of St. Isaac Jogues at the Martyrs' Shrine
in Auriesville, New York.

pact. Then they returned to Quebec. However, Father Jogues left behind a box of religious articles, for he intended to return.

Shortly afterwards he started out, with the *donné* John de Lalande, on his third visit to the Iroquois. John de Lalande was a native of Dieppe, who had offered his services as a lay missionary. Beyond that we know nothing concerning his life, not even the date of his birth.

The Mohawks had a poor crop that year; and soon after the French Embassy had gone back to Quebec, an epidemic broke out among them. The superstitious Indians put the blame for their misfortune on the box which Father Jogues had left at Ossernenon. When they learned that the missionary was on the way back, some members of the Bear clan lay in wait for him two days before he reached the Iroquois villages.

Once more they mishandled him and made him a captive, along with John de Lalande and one Huron guide who did not flee. The other clans tried to protect the prisoners, but the Bears refused to let a council decide their fate. On October 18 they tomahawked Father Jogues as he entered a cabin for a meal to which they had traitorously invited him. Then they cut off his head and put it on one of the palisade poles.

The next day they killed John de Lalande and the Huron guide and threw their beheaded bodies into the river.

Thus did Father Jogues and his assistant win the martyr's crown, on October 18 and 19, 1646, near Auriesville, New York, about forty miles from Albany. A shrine at the site of their martyrdom honors their memory and that of René Goupil, the martyr of 1642.

The cause of these martyrs' beatification and that of the five Jesuit martyrs of Huronia was begun by an informative process in Rouen soon after their death. But it was not until June 21, 1925, that Pope Pius XI beatified them. The same Supreme Pontiff canonized them five years later on June 29. Their feast is celebrated in the United States and Canada on October 19.

Liturgical Prayer

O God, you blessed the first fruits of the faith in the United States of America by the missionary labors and martyrdom of blessed Isaac, René and John. May the harvest of Christians grow daily more abundant in the whole world through the intercession of these saints. Through Jesus Christ, your Son, our Lord, who lives and reigns with you in the unity of the Holy Spirit, God, forever and ever. Amen.

CHAPTER 2
SAINTS AND BLESSED
United States

Bl. Elizabeth Ann Bayley Seton
*(1774-1821) Founder of the Sisters of Charity
in the United States*

Two young Episcopalian women, who went about on their errands of mercy in New York City during the closing years of the eighteenth century, were called "the Protestant Sisters of Charity." In 1797, the year John Adams succeeded George Washington as president of the United States, these two ladies helped found a "Society for the Relief of Poor Widows with Small Children."

Seven years later, one of them was herself a poor widow with five small children, because she had become a Catholic and for this reason was ostracized by her well-to-do relatives and friends. Her name was Mrs. Elizabeth Ann Bayley Seton; and her "soul's friend" was her sister-in-law Rebecca Seton, who died that same year (July, 1804).

On the royal road of the cross Mrs. Elizabeth Seton learned to give herself wholly to the service of God and her neighbor; and God chose her to become the founder, in 1809, of the first religious sisterhood in the United States. She was beatified in 1963 — the first American, born in the United States, to be enrolled among the blessed.

Elizabeth Ann was born in New York City on August 28, 1774, two years before the English colonies in America declared their independence. Her father was Dr. Richard Bayley, a distinguished surgeon, born in Connecticut but educated in England. He was professor of anatomy in King's College in New York, now Columbia University, and also health officer of the Port of New

York. He was also a good Christian of the Episcopalian Church.

Dr. Bayley's wife and Elizabeth's mother was Catherine Charleton, the devout daughter of an Anglican minister of Staten Island. She died when Elizabeth was three years old, leaving her husband and two other young daughters besides Elizabeth. The doctor married a second time; and Elizabeth showed great affection to her stepmother as well as her stepbrothers and stepsisters.

Elizabeth's childhood years coincided with the seven years of the colonies' War of Independence. Her education she received chiefly from her father, who trained her to self-restraint as well as intellectual pursuits, and her notebooks indicate that she took a special interest in religious and historical subjects. She read much and acquired a facility in writing. Her favorite reading was the Scriptures, especially the Book of Psalms; and this practice she kept up throughout her life. Being a very religious girl, she always wore a crucifix around her neck.

At the age of nineteen, on January 25, 1794, Elizabeth married a wealthy young merchant of Scottish descent, William Magee Seton, who was an Episcopalian like herself. During the ten years of their married life, they had five children. Three were girls, Anna Marie who was the oldest, then Catherine and Rebecca the youngest. The oldest boy was William, and the other son Richard.

The three sisters of her husband, Rebecca, Harriet and Cecilia, were very dear friends of Elizabeth. It was Rebecca who accompanied Elizabeth when she visited and brought comfort and aid to the sick and the poor in New York. Harriet and Cecilia later followed her into the Catholic Church.

Because of the war between Great Britain and revolutionary France, which forced the Bank of England to stop specie payments in 1797, the Seton family firm found itself in financial difficulties when Elizabeth's father-in-law died in 1798. Elizabeth shared her young husband's anxieties and aided him with her sound judgment; but the family fortune could not be recovered and business troubles grew worse. The younger Seton became ill as a result; and during a lull in the Napoleonic Wars, following the Peace of Amiens in 1802 between France and England, the doctor advised a sea voyage.

Leaving her four youngest children in the care of Rebecca, and taking along Anna Marie the oldest, Mrs. Seton sailed with her husband on the *Shepherdess*, October 2, 1803. Their destination was Leghorn (Livorno), Italy, the home of the Filicchi brothers, who were business friends of the Seton firm. It was a long voyage, lasting a month and a half.

When they arrived at Leghorn on November 19, they were quarantined for thirty days in the Lazaretto, because it was rumored that there was a yellow fever epidemic in New York. It was a damp and gloomy stone building, and his long detention there probably brought on the death of Mr. Seton. Not long after they were released, he died at Pisa on December 27.

After the death of her husband, Mrs. Seton and her daughter remained in Leghorn for about three months as guests of the Filicchis. Here and in the Catholic churches of Italy which she visited, Elizabeth became acquainted with the Catholic religion.

Her return to New York was delayed by Anna Marie's illness and then her own; and by the time she was ready to go back, she was convinced that the Catholic Church was in truth the only one instituted by Christ. She would have become a Catholic then and there, but was advised to wait until she got back home. "My conversion," wrote Elizabeth Seton, "is due to the fact that I visited a Catholic country."

Antonio Filicchi accompanied Mrs. Seton and her daughter on the return trip. After another long voyage, they reached New York on June 3, 1804. A time of great spiritual perplexity followed for Elizabeth Seton. Dr. Henry Hobart, later an Anglican bishop, had been her friend and adviser; and he now tried in every possible way to dissuade her from becoming a Catholic.

Mr. Filicchi, on the other hand, presented to her the claims of the Catholic Church and arranged an exchange of letters between her and Father John Louis Cheverus, who was subsequently named bishop of Boston (1808). Through Mr. Filicchi, Elizabeth Seton also wrote to Bishop John Carroll of Baltimore. Her favorite prayer at this time was: "If I am right, Thy grace impart still in the right to stay. If I am wrong, oh, teach my heart to find the better way."

To prayer for light, she added fasting. On Ash Wednesday, March 14, 1805, she was received into the Catholic Church by Father Matthew O'Brien, the pastor of St. Peter's Church on Barclay Street, New York. On March 20, she made her first confession, and on the 25th, the feast of the Annunciation, she received her First Communion. "At last," she wrote, "God is mine and I am His."

The step taken by Mrs. Seton raised a storm of protest among her Protestant relatives and friends, most of whom turned against her. Dr. Bayley, her father, had died in 1801. Little of her husband's fortune remained. She had to find a way of gaining a livelihood for herself and her five children.

The young widow, thirty-one years old, undertook the work

Statue of Bl. Elizabeth Ann Bayley Seton (1774–1821).

of a teacher. A Catholic couple, Mr. and Mrs. White, were just then opening a school for boys in the suburbs of New York; and Mrs. Seton joined them. However, the school had to close soon afterwards, because it was unjustly branded as a proselytizing scheme.

Aided by a few faithful friends, Mrs. Seton then opened a boarding house for boys who were attending a school conducted by the Protestant curate of St. Marks.

Rebecca Seton, her sister-in-law, had died not long after Elizabeth had become a Catholic. Cecilia Seton contracted a serious illness in January, 1806, and asked to see the ostracized convert; Elizabeth visited her frequently. When it was learned that Cecilia too wanted to embrace the Catholic faith, Elizabeth was threatened with expulsion from New York by the state legislature. The boarding house too had to be closed.

Mrs. Seton now hoped to find a place of refuge in a convent in Canada, where she could resume her teaching and thus support her three daughters. Her two boys had already been sent by the Filicchis to Georgetown College. Bishop Carroll was not in favor of her plan to go to Canada.

Father William Du Bourg, the rector of St. Mary's Seminary in Baltimore, happened to be visiting in New York. He invited her to establish a school for girls in Baltimore. After the matter had been given due consideration, Mrs. Seton and her three daughters left New York and made the trip to Baltimore by sea on the *Grand Sachem*. They arrived on the feast of Corpus Christi, June 16, 1808. The two boys were transferred from Georgetown to St. Mary's College, near Baltimore.

In a modest brick house on Paca Street, in the shadow of the seminary, Mrs. Seton opened her girls' school in September; and God blessed her work. In New York it had been very difficult for her to satisfy her desire for daily Mass and Communion. Now the chapel of the seminary was next door to her school, and she began to live like a religious.

Since her conversion Mrs. Seton had longed to enter a convent, but her duties toward her five children seemed to stand in the way. Now the fulfillment of her wish did not appear so impractical. She donned a quaint costume, similar to one worn by a certain sisterhood in Italy.

Cecilia Conway of Philadelphia, who had been thinking of becoming a nun in Europe, joined Mrs. Seton in Baltimore. Soon other postulants arrived. Among those who came were Cecilia Seton, now a Catholic, and her sister Harriet who likewise entered the Catholic Church in December, 1809.

31

Father Du Bourg, Mrs. Seton's spiritual director, saw no reason why Mrs. Seton should not establish a religious community and at the same time retain the guardianship of her children. For fifteen years he had been praying for an opportunity of establishing the Daughters of Charity of St. Vincent de Paul in the United States. Why could this not be done through Mrs. Seton and her companions?

The first tentative steps toward the founding of a religious sisterhood were taken in May, 1809. Provisional rules were adopted and a religious garb was chosen. Father Du Bourg was appointed director. On June 2, Mrs. Seton and four companions put on the habit for the first time, "a long black robe with a cape, and a white cap with a crimped border; a black band passed around the head and fastened beneath the chin." The same day, Elizabeth Seton knelt before Archbishop Carroll, and in the presence of many priests pronounced the private vows of poverty, chastity and obedience. The archbishop then appointed her superior of the newly formed community; and thus Mrs. Seton became Mother Seton. The new community was named the Sisters of St. Joseph.

Less than three weeks later, June 21, the "Sisters of St. Joseph" moved to the Valley of St. Joseph at Emmitsburg, some fifty miles from Baltimore. The school building in Paca Street had become too small. Providentially a Virginian convert and seminarian, Mr. Cooper, had offered $10,000 for the establishment of a school for poor children. A farm, situated one half mile from the village of Emmitsburg and two miles from Mt. St. Mary's College, was purchased. The construction of a school building, called the "White House," and of a sisters' residence, the "Stone House," had been going on.

When Mother Seton and her sisters arrived, the Stone House was not as yet ready, so for six weeks they lived in a small log cabin on the mountainside which Father John Dubois, one of their directors, had put at their disposal. They took possession of the Stone House, "the cradle of the community," on July 31; and on February 22, 1810, they were able to open the new free school in the completed White House. Thus was launched the free parochial school system in the United States.

From the beginning it was the intention to make Mother Seton's religious community the first American foundation of the worldwide sisterhood, the Daughters of Charity of St. Vincent de Paul. Bishop Benedict J. Flaget was commissioned in 1810 to procure the rules of these Sisters of Charity in France and to arrange that three French nuns be sent to train Mother Seton's community in the spirit of St. Vincent.

A letter announcing the coming of the three French sisters was received at Emmitsburg; but Napoleon issued orders that they were not to depart from France. However, a copy of the rules was received; and after some modifications had been made, Archbishop Carroll gave his official approval in January, 1812.

Though it was against her will and she still had the care of her children, Mother Seton was once more appointed superior. The following year, on July 19, 1813, Mother Seton and eighteen sisters bound themselves to the religious life by the public vows. Thus was established the first community of the Sisters of Charity in the United States. Its union with the Daughters of Charity of St. Vincent was not effected until 1850.

Mother Seton continued to be the mother superior of the rapidly growing sisterhood until her death. The priest directors were Fathers Du Bourg, David and Dubois, the latter for fifteen years. Father Dubois had previously held the same position for forty Daughters of Charity in France.

During a great part of her religious life Mother Seton experienced great spiritual desolation. But she cheerfully accepted the cross from the hands of God, and thus her soul was more and more purified and united with God. Her writings show that she was all on fire with love of God and zeal for souls.

By the bereavements which fell to her lot, God detached her heart more and more from the things of earth. Harriet Seton died a convert at Emmitsburg in December, 1809; and in April, the following year, Cecilia's life too was cut short. Rebecca, Mother Seton's youngest daughter, died at the age of fourteen; and Anna Marie, her oldest daughter departed from this life as a novice on March 12, 1812, after taking the vows of religion on her deathbed.

Undaunted, Mother Seton guided her community and promoted its work for God and souls in an exemplary manner. In her work of sanctifying souls, she was greatly aided by her perfect sincerity and gracious charm.

In 1814 Mother Seton sent some sisters to take charge of an orphan asylum in Philadelphia, "the first Catholic orphanage in the United States." Another orphanage was opened in New York in 1817. Arrangements were also made for "the first Catholic hospital" in Baltimore, although this hospital was not opened until 1823. At the time of her death, Mother Seton had established twenty communities of her sisters.

It is truly amazing how much she accomplished during the ten and a half years that she lived at Emmitsburg. Besides directing her sisters and training teachers, she visited the poor and the sick in the neighborhood and converted many of them. Most of these were blacks. In addition, with a facile pen, she did a great deal of writing. She prepared textbooks for the classrooms, translated a number of ascetical works from the French as well as a life of St. Vincent de Paul and one of Mlle. Le Gras, and wrote several spiritual treatises of her own. These with her diaries and many letters fill thirteen volumes in the archives of the motherhouse of Emmitsburg.

Elected superior for the third time in 1819, Mother Seton protested that it was the election of the dead. She lived for two more years, and died of a pulmonary infection on January 4, 1821, less than forty-seven years old. She was buried in the cemetery of St. Joseph College at Emmitsburg. Shortly before her death, one of the sisters asked Mother Seton what she considered to have been the greatest grace in her life. She did not have to pause to consider the matter. Her immediate reply was: "The greatest grace of my life was having been led into the Catholic Church."

To Antonio Filicchi, Father Bruté wrote after the death of Mother Seton: "She lived only for her sisters and for the performance of her holy duties. . . . How profound her faith! How tender her piety! How sincere her humility, combined with so great intelligence! How great her goodness and kindness to all!"

Mother Seton was survived by three of her children. Catherine, who was the only one present at her mother's deathbed, lived as a Sister of Charity to the advanced age of ninety. William, the oldest son, became an officer in the United States Navy and died shortly after the Civil War in 1868. The other son, Richard, entered the field of business with the Filicchi family. His death occurred only a few years after that of his mother.

Two sons of Richard Seton became quite famous. Robert Seton (1839-1927) was the first student at the North American College in Rome. In 1902 he returned to Rome as Monsignor Seton, and for twelve years served as unofficial "ambassador" of the American people to the Holy See. The post of archbishop of Chicago was offered to him in 1903, but he declined it; and the same year he was made titular archbishop of Heliopolis. He wrote three published volumes and edited some of the writings of his saintly grandmother.

William Seton (1835-1905), another son of Richard, was admitted to the bar in New York and attained moderate success as an author. He wrote much on the Darwinian theory of evolution, trying to popularize it and to harmonize it with Catholic doctrine.

One of Mother Seton's stepbrothers, Guy Carleton Bayley, had a son who succeeded Martin J. Spalding as Archbishop of Baltimore in 1872. His name was James Roosevelt Bayley (1814-

Bl. Elizabeth Ann Seton, founder of the Sisters of Charity in the United States.

1877). Ordained an Episcopalian minister, he became a Catholic in 1842. He was consecrated first bishop of Newark in 1853 at the age of thirty-nine, and nineteen years later was transferred to the archiepiscopal see of Baltimore.

Archbishop Gibbons of Baltimore in 1880 urged that steps be taken toward the canonization of Mother Seton. Official inquiries were made in Baltimore, and the first results were taken by a special messenger to Rome and placed into the hands of a postulator on June 7, 1911. The closing sessions of the inquiry in Baltimore were held in 1924; and Mother Seton's writings were approved in 1936. Her cause of beatification was formally introduced in 1940.

It was Pope John XXIII who declared Mother Seton "Venerable" on December 18, 1959, and on March 17, 1963, solemnly enrolled her among the blessed.

Today several thousand Sisters of Charity in the United States and in overseas missions, under seven separate obediences, constitute the spiritual progeny of Bl. Elizabeth Ann Bayley Seton. Two offshoots of the Emmitsburg sisterhood were organized into diocesan sisterhoods shortly before the parent community was incorporated into the Daughters of Charity of St. Vincent in 1850. Those of Newark (Convent, New Jersey — S.C.) and Halifax (S.C.) branched off from the one in New York (S.C.), and that of Greensburg (S.C.), from the one in Cincinnati (S.C.). In 1911 the total membership of these sisterhoods was about 6,000.

The original Emmitsburg sisterhood, now known as the Daughters of Charity of St. Vincent de Paul, with general headquarters in Paris, has five provinces in the United States with a total of 2,128 sisters as of the beginning of 1974. The Emittsburg Province, with 680 professed sisters, is represented in seven archdioceses and dioceses.

Liturgical Prayer

Hear our prayer, O God our Savior, and let us learn the spirit of real devotion and charity from blessed Elizabeth Ann, as we joyfully recall her exemplary life. Through Jesus Christ, your Son, our Lord, who lives and reigns with you in the unity of the Holy Spirit, God, forever and ever. Amen.

CHAPTER 3

SAINTS AND BLESSED

United States

Bl. Rose Philippine Duchesne

(1769-1852) 'Woman Who Prays Always'

BEFORE noon on a hot day in June — June 29, 1841, to be exact — four nuns, Religious of the Sacred Heart, arrived at the busy levee of St. Louis, in the Missouri Territory, and boarded a river paddler which was being readied for a trip up the Missouri River.

They did not have far to go to reach the dock, since they came from their convent at Broadway and Soulard Street. Their destination was a Potawatomi Indian mission on Sugar Creek, near the Osage River, in what is now eastern Kansas but was then Indian territory. There they were going to open a school for the Indian children and help the three Jesuit missionaries who had their headquarters at the mission.

One of the nuns was Mother Rose Philippine Duchesne, now in her seventy-second year. Why was she going along? Surely, at her advanced age she would not be able to do any effective pioneer work on the rough frontier. Yet she was supremely happy. Ever since she was a little girl in France, she had aspired to be a missionary to the American Indians. Now at last her wish was to be fulfilled.

Even if she could not do much work, she could still be of some help and she could pray and by her prayers draw God's blessing upon the enterprise. That she prayed much was soon discovered by the Indians; for, they gave her the Potawatomi name of *Quah-kah-ka-num-ad*, Woman-who-prays-always.

The steamboat was scheduled to leave at noon, but there was

Bl. Rose Philippine Duchesne came from France to mid-America in 1818.

a delay of two hours. Bishop Jean-Marie Chanche of Natchez, Mississippi, who had come to see them off, remained and chatted with the nuns in French, telling them about his new diocese which so far had only one priest besides himself. When the steamer's deep-throated whistle blew, he gave the nuns his blessing. He blessed the young black carpenter and handyman, Edmund, from the convent in St. Louis, who would do the heavy work for the nuns. He gave his blessing also to the three priests who were going along: the provincial of the Jesuits, Father Peter Verhaegen; the pastor of St. Charles, Father John Baptist Smedts; and the diocesan priest Father Francis J. Renaud.

The river trip was pleasant, and the steamer passed no less than fifteen towns. The Missouri Territory was becoming populated. On July 4, they had not yet reached Westport Landing, which is now Kansas City. Here they got off the boat, and made a four-day journey toward the south to Sugar Creek by wagon in slow stages.

When they reached the Osage River, they were met by two Indian horsemen who welcomed them and returned posthaste to their village with the news that the travelers were close at hand. Every two miles along the remaining eighteen miles, there was a pair of Indians, mounted on fine horses, who greeted them with a demonstration of their equestrian prowess and gave them directions for the best roads.

One mile from the mission, 500 braves in gala dress were waiting for them and conducted them to the village. In the settlement 700 people assembled to express their gratitude to the nuns for coming to live and work in their midst.

Since the log house which the Indians were building for the nuns was only about half finished, Manope, one of the Indians who lived near the church, vacated his cabin (which measured fifteen feet long by twelve feet wide); here the nuns resided until October 19, when they moved into their primitive home. The church, which had been blessed the previous year, and the convent stood on an eminence about 100 feet above the bottomlands, through which flowed a little stream lined with sugar maples.

The Potawatomis in the settlement had come from northern Indiana; and about half their number, those who lived near the church, were Catholics. The pagans dwelt at some distance in a separate group; but they were gradually being converted to Christianity. Other Indians were in the vicinity, including Kickapoo, Wabash and Osage.

The first Potawatomis had come in 1835 when the United States government began moving the Indians from the eastern states to territory west of the Mississippi. Others followed with a young priest, Father Benjamin-Marie Petit, who died in St. Louis, February 10, 1839. The Jesuits, who had founded a mission among the Kickapoo in 1836, took over the care of the Potawatomis and made their village their center.

The convent into which the nuns moved three months after their arrival was not completed until mid-March, 1842. While the construction work was going on, Mother Duchesne was advised that it would be better for her to spend her days in the church. She practically lived there, spending her time in prayer. It was then that the Indians named her *Quah-kah-ka-num-ad.*

When completed, the log convent was a one-story structure with a loft that was used as a dormitory. Though its inside walls were covered with heavy linen cloth, it was not much better than the cabins of the Indians. The Potawatomis did not have much of this world's goods, and there was a great deal of suffering among them. The nuns visited the sick, besides teaching the children; and whenever she could, Mother Duchesne — old, sickly and feeble though she was — joined them on their errands of mercy.

On the evening of Palm Sunday, Mother Elizabeth Galitzin, official visitor of the American convents of the Society, arrived and remained for two days. She decided that Mother Duchesne should retire to the convent in St. Charles, Missouri. Resigning herself to God's will, she left with Father Verhaegen on June 19 and reached St. Louis exactly one year after she had set out for Sugar Creek. During the last decade of her life "the woman who prayed always" spent her days for the most part in prayer and meditation.

Grenoble, the capital of the province of Dauphiné in south-eastern France, on the border of Italy, was the birthplace of Rose Philippine Duchesne. Born on August 29, 1769, she was the daughter of Pierre-Francois Duchesne and Rose Euphrosine née Périer, both members of prominent families. She was the second of eight children, seven girls and one boy. Her senior sister died when she was nine; four of her sisters and her brother married, while her youngest sister became a Visitation nun.

When her parents married in 1765, her mother received a dowry of one hundred thousand francs, and the third floor of the big Périer house in the Place de San André was allotted to them as their home. Her father was a distinguished lawyer and later played an active part in political life; but he gradually drifted away from the Catholic faith and adopted the radical views which were then current. Her mother, however, was a deeply religious woman who raised her children as faithful Church members.

At the age of three, Rose Philippine had a siege of smallpox which disfigured her face. In later life the scars softened and to a great extent even disappeared.

Uncle Claude, the oldest of her mother's brothers, purchased the old castle and park of Vizille, one of the most magnificent estates of Dauphiné, about twelve miles south of Grenoble, and converted a part of the chateau into a textile factory, reserving the spacious apartments overlooking the park for a residence. As a child, Philippine often visited Vizille with her mother on holidays.

Most of her schooling she received from a private tutor at home. But when she was twelve, she and her sister Josephine went to board in the Visitation convent at Grenoble to prepare for their first Holy Communion. Situated on a hillside, at the foot of the Alps, the convent had been founded by St. Francis de Sales in 1619 as the fourth of the Visitation Order.

When she received her first Holy Communion on Pentecost Sunday, May 19, 1782, Philippine made up her mind to become a Visitation nun and if possible a missionary to the American Indians. When her parents learned that she was thinking of becoming a nun, they recalled her after she had been in the convent school for two years. Philippine continued her studies at home, in the old Périer residence, all of which was now occupied by the Duchesne family.

When she was about nineteen and her parents selected a young man whom they wanted her to marry, Philippine, accompanied by an aunt in whom she confided, went to see the superior of the convent where she had been a pupil. Now that she was there, why could she not stay? The superior acquiesced, and she stayed. Her parents came a few days later, but they were not able to change her mind. However, a year later, when she was to take her first vows, her father objected so vehemently that she remained a novice for four and a half years.

In September, 1792, after the revolutionary government had decreed the suppression of religious orders of women, Philippine had to lay aside her religious habit and return to her family. In the Reign of Terror which followed, 1793-1794, Grenoble did not suffer the unheard of atrocities which were committed in the larger cities, such as Paris, Lyons, Bordeaux, Arras and Nantes. At Grenoble, it is true, two priests were guillotined, while some were imprisoned in the former Visitation convent, and still others went into hiding.

At great risk to herself, Philippine formed an association of Ladies of Mercy for the purpose of giving material and spiritual help to priests, guiding them to the dying, and aiding the sick and the poor. Her uncle Augustin and his wife and daughter were murdered by insurgents in 1793. Her mother and the children were living in a country home which her father had purchased in the town of Grâne. Fugitive priests found a refuge there during the first months of 1793; and one of them was employed as the overseer of the estate and the construction of a textile factory.

After the fall of Robespierre in 1794, Philippine and her associates continued their charitable work as Ladies of Mercy, and for two years she resided in a town on the Drôme River. But she was back at Grâne to nurse her mother during her last illness and was present at her death on June 30, 1797.

When the convent at Grenoble was reopened in 1801, Philippine returned to it with other former nuns. For three years they encountered various difficulties; and in 1804 Mother Superior Barat, who had founded the Society of the Sacred Heart four years earlier, was invited to take over the convent. On December 31 of that year Philippine began her novitiate, and the following year she made her profession.

Her longing to be a missionary was as ardent as ever, and she repeatedly begged the founder for permission to go to the United States with some companions. In 1815 she was chosen secretary general of the Society, and the hope of realizing her wish grew dimmer. However, on January 14, 1817, Bishop William Du Bourg of Louisiana visited Mother Barat and asked her to send some of her nuns to his missionary diocese. She gave her consent. Five nuns were chosen; and Mother Philippine, one of them, was appointed their superior.

In March of the following year they left France and crossed the Atlantic on the sailship *Rebecca*. After a two-months' voyage of storms, calms and a meeting with an Argentinian pirate ship which left them unmolested, they landed in New Orleans, Louisiana, on the feast of the Sacred Heart, May 29, 1818. They were hospitably received by the Ursulines until they could continue their journey to St. Louis on a riverboat. On July 12, they boarded the *Franklin*, and forty days later arrived in St. Louis where, for three weeks, they were the guests of General Bernard Pratte and his wife.

Mother Philippine had expected to make her first foundation there, but she humbly submitted when Bishop Du Bourg took them to St. Charles, Missouri. Here they found a temporary home in the seven-room house of Mrs. Duquette. On September 14, Mother Philippine opened a small boarding school and a day school. The latter was the first free school for girls west of the Mississippi.

When the lease of the Duquette house expired at the end of the following year, Mother Philippine's little community with their boarders moved to St. Ferdinand de Florissant, situated like St. Charles on the Missouri River. Land had been purchased for them; but until the convent could be built the nuns and their students, ten to fifteen persons, lived in a few primitive log cabins of the bishop's farm on a little knoll near the river. The construction of the convent was completed by the end of 1820, and the nearby church the next year.

As other nuns arrived from France and new members were admitted in the United States, other houses could be established. The first one founded from Florissant was the Grand Côteau convent at Opelousa, Louisiana, in 1821. Two nuns from Florissant left for Grand Côteau on August 5 of that year; and the following year Mother Philippine paid the new establishment a visit.

It was her second trip on the Mississippi. She left St. Louis on July 20 and reached Grand Côteau on August 29. The return trip, which she commenced on September 11, lasted eighty days. The *Hecla,* which she boarded at New Orleans, was disabled when it reached Natchez; and this town refused to admit the passengers as a precaution against yellow fever. Mother Duchesne had a fever when she got on the boat. In the home of Mrs. Davis on the opposite bank of the river, she was hospitably received.

The *Cincinnati,* on which she resumed her journey, October 30, ran aground on a sandbank at New Madrid in southeastern Missouri; and she had to tarry there for five days until the water rose sufficiently to free the boat. After spending two days with the Prattes in St. Louis, she went back to Florissant. The following year, the Jesuits from Maryland came to Florissant, and the spiritual guidance that the nuns received from them was a source of great consolation to Mother Duchesne. At this time also some Indian children were taken into the convent boarding school.

In 1825 another convent was founded in Louisiana at St. Michael on the Mississippi River; and though it was done a little too quickly for her, the project received Mother Duchesne's encouragement. Her supervision was not clearly defined, because a new foundation, once it had been established, was directly subject to Mother Barat. However, the convents in Louisiana developed more quickly than those in Missouri.

Two more convents had their beginning in 1827, and these were more directly under Mother Duchesne's guidance. One was the convent in St. Louis, at Soulard and Broadway, which was built through the munificence of John Mullanphy. Connected with it was an academy or boarding school for girls, an orphanage, and a day school, though the last mentioned had to be discontinued in the spring of 1830. The boarders at Florissant were transferred to St. Louis. Mother Duchesne, who had been in charge at Florissant during the past eight years, moved to the St. Louis convent and was its superior for the next seven years.

The second convent opened in 1827 was the one in St. Charles. Once more the Religious of the Sacred Heart occupied the old Duquette house until a new brick building was constructed in 1834-1835. The following year another convent was begun at La Fourche, Louisiana; but it was closed four years later.

Following instructions received from Mother Barat, Mother Duchesne made her third trip on the Mississippi in 1829-1830 to confer with the heads of the houses in Louisiana. Setting out from St. Louis on November 5, she went south on the *Missouri* and visited Grand Côteau, St. Michael and La Fourche. Returning on the *Oregon*, she got only as far as the mouth of the Ohio River on February 2, 1830, and from there traveled to St. Louis by oxcart.

In that year, twelve years after Mother Duchesne and her four companions had come to Missouri, the Society had six convents in the Mississippi valley with sixty-four nuns, of whom fourteen had come from France and fifty had joined them in the new establishments. More than 350 children were being educated in the convent schools.

As early as 1825 Mother Duchesne had asked to be relieved of the burdens of superiorship, but Mother Barat informed her that there was no one to take her place. However, on November 30, 1831, the mother general granted her request. When Bishop Joseph Rosati learned of this, he pleaded with Mother Barat that Mother Duchesne be allowed to continue directing the convent in St. Louis; and so she stayed on.

However, in 1834 Mother Duchesne was transferred from St. Louis to Florissant, where for the next five years she served as superior of the novitiate convent. At this time also her position of leadership of the American houses terminated with the appointment of Mother Eugenie Aude as assistant mother general for America.

Mother Duchesne was quite sick when she returned to St. Louis as a member of that community in October, 1839. She seemed to regain a new lease on life when she was allowed to go to the Sugar Creek Indian mission for about a year in 1841.

She then retired to Florissant, and during the last ten years edified all by her exemplary and prayerful life. When Mother Galitzin visited the Louisiana and Missouri convents in an official capacity in 1841, a convent was founded in New York City, and

Mother Mary Aloysia Hardy went along to take charge. She had been one of the first pupils at Grand Côteau. In 1846 the property in Manhattanville was acquired; and Mother Hardy, who died in 1885, founded other convents in the eastern states.

Thirty-five years after she had come to Missouri, having endured all the hardships of a pioneer, rejoicing to see others reap the fruits of her labors though she herself had patiently and perseveringly suffered many disappointments, Mother Duchesne died a holy death at Florissant. She quietly breathed her last at noon, as the Angelus bell ceased ringing, November 18, 1852.

Father Verhaegen wrote of her: "Eminent in all virtues of life, but especially in humility, she sweetly and calmly departed this life in the odor of sanctity." The cause of her beatification was launched in St. Louis in 1895. The declaration that she had practiced all the virtues in an heroic degree, made in 1935, gave her the title of "Venerable."

On May 12, 1940, Pope Pius XII solemnly beatified Bl. Rose Philippine Duchesne in the Vatican Basilica of St. Peter. Her feast is observed by the Religious of the Sacred Heart on November 17. A beautiful new memorial church in St. Charles, Missouri, enshrines the tomb of "the woman who prayed always."

Liturgical Prayer

O God, you poured into the heart of blessed Philippine the gifts of charity. Through her merits and intercession grant that your faithful may with wholehearted love perform the deeds that are pleasing to you. Through Jesus Christ, your Son, our Lord, who lives and reigns with you in the unity of the Holy Spirit, God, forever and ever. Amen.

CHAPTER 4

SAINTS AND BLESSED

United States

Bl. John N. Neumann

(1811-1860) Bishop of Philadelphia

THE *Europa*, in its day, was regarded as a big ship. It was a three-master, 210 feet long. Loaded to capacity with emigrants, it left Le Havre, France, on April 20, 1836, and entered the harbor of New York six weeks later, on June 2. For another week it was held in quarantine at Staten Island.

During the crossing it had struggled with a raging storm for four days, waited out a calm, and evaded dangerous icebergs. Before it reached New York, its supply of drinking water was almost undrinkable and its scant provisions had almost run out.

One of the emigrants on board was a poor young man of twenty-five. Though he had completed his theological studies, he was still only a cleric in minor orders. Small of stature — only five feet two inches tall — he was shabbily dressed, and he had only a few francs in his pocket. No hat covered his tousled light brown hair — somebody had stolen his hat.

His deep-set eyes were penetrating and serious, but at the same time expressive of kindness, and always ready to light up with a smile. He had hardly any baggage, except a big sack full of prayer books and religious books. A missionary society in Strasbourg had encumbered him with them, thinking they were doing him a favor.

For the sum of eighty francs he had bought the cheapest passage available, which meant that he could place his thin straw mattress and pillow wherever there was a vacant spot on the

crowded deck. His fellow passengers were rough, unfeeling people, who hoped to find a better life in the land of the free and the home of the brave. Their taunts hurt him, but he bore them patiently.

He was a fair sailor, suffering from seasickness only during the first three days; but his sallow complexion seemed to indicate that he was not in the best of health.

On June 9, the feast of Corpus Christi, he was finally permitted to go ashore on Staten Island. He boarded a small steamboat, called *Hercules*, and set foot on lower Manhattan at one in the afternoon. Despite a pouring rain he searched all day for a Catholic church, but found none. That night he stayed in a small inn kept by a Swiss. The next morning he was directed to the nearest church, and the priest in the rectory told him where the bishop's residence was.

When the weary traveler was introduced as John Nepomuk Neumann from Bohemia, the aged bishop welcomed him with open arms. The bishop was John Dubois, now in his seventy-second year. He had been the priest who had greatly assisted Mother Seton at Emmitsburg, Maryland. The third incumbent of the see of New York, he had only thirty-six priests to care for

47

200,000 Catholics living in all of New York State and half of lower New Jersey.

On June 19, Bishop Dubois ordained John Neumann a subdeacon, on the 24th a deacon, and on the 25th a priest. A few days later Father Neumann, wearing a new suit given to him by Father Raffeiner of New York and supplied with travel money by the bishop, was on his way to Buffalo, to a parish comprising 900 square miles in western New York with only one priest, Father Pax.

Father Neumann was born on March 28, 1811 (which was Maundy Thursday that year, not Good Friday as he himself thought), at Prachatitz in Bohemia, the Czech portion of the present Czechoslovakia, but at that time a part of Austria. He was baptized the same day and received the name of John, his patron being Bohemia's St. John Nepomucene, or "of Nepomuk." His father Philip was a Bavarian who had settled in the town in 1802, when Napoleon's armies overran Europe. Two years later Philip's first wife died with her child; and in 1805 he married Agnes Lebis, who became the mother of six children, four girls and two boys. John was the third child; and the other boy, Wenceslaus, was the youngest.

At the age of seven John began his studies at the village school, and soon became a lover of books like his father. He was twelve when he was enrolled as a student at the Gymnasium in nearby Budweis, which was a high school and college. After his graduation in 1831, his mother, who knew that her son felt drawn to the priesthood, encouraged him to apply for admission to the diocesan seminary at Budweis. He was accepted and studied theology there for two years, then moved to the archdiocesan seminary in Prague in 1833, but returned to Budweis to complete his studies in 1835. Because of the heterodox views of some of its professors, the seminary in Prague was not as good as the one in Budweis.

Though ridiculed at Prague, John distinguished himself as a studious seminarian; and at the same time he made rapid progress in the science of the saints. He became versed not only in all the branches of sacred learning, but also in natural sciences, especially botany; and besides mastering Latin, Greek and Hebrew, he learned to speak fluently at least eight modern languages, including various Slavic dialects.

He was now ready for the priesthood, but his reception of the major orders was first postponed because of the illness of the bishop of Budweis and then put off indefinitely because the diocese had a sufficient number of priests in that year (1835).

48

During his seminary days John had read with great interest the quarterly reports of the Missionary Society of St. Leopold, containing accounts of the work being done in the United States by such pioneer priests as Father Frederick Baraga. He longed to follow their example. Why wait at home where he was not needed?

On the morning of February 8, 1836, he left his native Prachatitz to make the long journey to New York. Some parish priests, who were his friends, had raised a meager 200 francs for his travel expenses. Though his good parents knew he wanted to be a missionary, he said good-bye only to his sister Veronica. It would make his leave-taking easier for everybody, he thought. His mother was under the impression that he was making one of his usual visits to Budweis. There he visited the bishop and wrote a farewell letter to his parents.

Leaving Budweis on February 16, he made the trip across Europe on foot, and partly by stagecoach and boat (via Linz, Munich, Strasbourg, Nancy, Paris and Rouen), arriving at Le Havre on April 7. Thirteen days later he set sail for New York on the *Europa.*

After his ordination in New York, Father Neumann devoted himself for four years to the pastoral care of all the outlying places of the parish of Buffalo. He reached his destination by going up the Hudson to Albany on a boat and then continuing westward by rail and a horse-drawn canal-barge. It was July 4 when he reached Rochester, where he stayed a few days to minister to the German-speaking people, and July 12 when he arrived at Buffalo, then no more than a town with one paved street.

Father Pax, the priest in charge, welcomed him and offered him a choice between Buffalo and the country districts. Father Neumann chose the latter, a very difficult assignment. His flock included 300 Catholic Germans and 100 Irish, French and Scots. He was able to speak German and French, became more conversant with English, and even learned Gaelic.

At Williamsville, eight miles northeast of Buffalo, where there was an unfinished stone church, Father Neumann established his headquarters, dismissed an unsatisfactory schoolmaster and temporarily served as teacher, and soon completed the church, which was 115 feet long, 20 wide, and 30 high.

The following year he moved to North Bush (present Kenmore) which had a church of untrimmed logs, and built a two-room log cabin for himself. Here he lived very austerely, subsisting for long periods on bread alone. Seldom did he build a fire; and it seems he only slept three or four hours a night.

Bl. John N. Neumann ministered to pioneers in western New York, 1836-1840.

50

From his headquarters he made frequent journeys on foot in all kinds of weather to points ten or twenty and sometimes forty miles distant, visiting the settlers on their scattered farms and caring for his mission stations. Besides the churches at North Bush and Williamsville he attended other wooden chapels at Cayuga Creek, Lancaster and Eden, the last being thirty miles to the south of Buffalo.

On one occasion he became so exhausted tramping through the forest that he lay down beside a tree trunk and fell fast asleep. He woke to find himself surrounded by Indians in a threatening attitude. Immediately he began to pray; and the Indians, recognizing him as a blackrobe, became friendly. They spread a buffalo skin on the ground, placed the little priest upon it and carried him to his destination.

After some time a friend gave him a horse, which he used to make longer trips; but it was a spirited and cunning animal and Father Neumann had difficulty managing it. Once he came close to suffering injury.

On his journeys he could hear the roar of Niagara Falls. Though the wonders of nature were an inspiration to him, he denied himself the pleasure of visiting the famous cataracts. That seemed to him to be more pleasing to God.

In the summer of 1837 Bishop Dubois, accompanied by Redemptorist Father Prost of Rochester, visited Father Neumann at North Bush and administered the sacrament of confirmation there and in his mission stations. The bishop was surprised to see what the little priest had accomplished in so short a time and commended him highly.

About two years later, Wenceslaus Neumann came from Bohemia to assist his older brother as a lay missionary. His coming was a great consolation to the lone priest, and by his work as a teacher and builder Wenceslaus rendered an invaluable service to him and his flock.

But Father Neumann could not long keep up the strenuous work he was doing. He began to suffer from fevers which lasted as long as three months. At Easter time, 1840, he had a complete breakdown; and after recovering to some extent, he made up his mind to join the Redemptorists. On three occasions during the previous years he had visited their house in Rochester; and Father Prost, who had been stationed there, was now the superior of the Redemptorists in the United States.

On September 4, Father Neumann formally requested Father Prost for admission to the Congregation of the Most Holy Redeemer; twelve days later he received an affirmative reply, which directed him to go to Pittsburgh. Bidding farewell to his beloved missions, he crossed Lake Erie on a crowded steamer in the middle of October. Because of rough weather, the trip of ninety miles across the lake lasted two days. Wenceslaus followed him later and became a Redemptorist lay brother.

Invested with the religious habit by Father Prost on November 29, Father Neumann was the first novice of the Redemptorists in the United States. His novitiate year was an unusual one. He was transferred from place to place and continued his priestly work, especially as a preacher of missions.

From Pittsburgh he went to Baltimore, New York, Rochester, Buffalo, Norwalk and then back to Baltimore by a circuitous route, stopping at Canton and Randolph, Ohio, and at Steubenville, where he was quite ill.

He arrived at Baltimore on December 8, 1841. There, after a retreat of fourteen days, he made his religious profession on January 16, 1842. The decade which followed was a hectic one for the new Redemptorist Father. Though his health was poor practically all the time, he worked hard as a missionary, principally among the Germans, and also held important positions in his religious congregation.

In 1843 he was appointed one of two consultors to the American superior, who was dependent on the provincial of the Belgian province. The next year he was made local superior in Pittsburgh and served in that capacity for three years.

Because of troubles in Europe, the Redemptorists in the United States were placed under the provincial of Austria toward the close of 1847. In February of that year Father Neumann became the head of the American Redemptorists, first as vice-regent and then, in 1848, as vice-provincial as well as local superior in Baltimore. The latter post he retained till 1852.

He was succeeded by a new vice-provincial in 1849, but continued in office as a consultor. As such, he was responsible to a great extent for the opening of a Redemptorist seminary in Cumberland, Maryland.

While in Pittsburgh, Father Neumann also wrote a small as well as a large German catechism and a German Bible history, which were published. He also gathered material for a comprehensive work on theology, which he never completed.

He was rector of St. Alphonsus in Baltimore when the see of Philadelphia became vacant by the appointment of Bishop Francis Patrick Kenrick as archbishop of Baltimore on August 19, 1851. The new archbishop recommended Father Neumann as his successor in Philadelphia, and he was nominated bishop on February 1, 1852. He accepted the appointment only because Pope Pius IX commanded him to do so; and in Baltimore he was consecrated fourth bishop of Philadelphia on Passion Sunday, March 28. For his motto he chose the words of the *Anima Christi:* "Passion of Christ, strengthen me."

In his first pastoral letter, Bishop Neumann wrote:

"To leave those from whom we had experienced for many years the most cordial affection; to enter upon an entirely new sphere of duty; to assume the government of so vast a number of souls, who would look to us to lead them on to our heavenly home — all thus urged us to implore the Lord to remove the chalice from us. We have, however, been compelled to bow in obedience to the successor of St. Peter, knowing that whatsoever he binds on earth shall be bound also in heaven." All his pastoral letters are beautifully written masterpieces.

The same year, the First Plenary Council of Baltimore was held; and though he had just been consecrated, Bishop Neumann occupied an important and conspicuous place among his fellow bishops. He was commissioned to revise his large catechism; and it appeared as an approved textbook of 180 pages in 1853.

The diocese of Philadelphia was at this time the largest in the country, comprising eastern Pennsylvania, western New Jersey, and all of Delaware. Every year Bishop Neumann visited all the larger parishes, and every two years the smaller ones. In the country places he remained for several days, confirming, preaching, hearing confessions, visiting the sick and anointing the dying. Once he walked twenty-five miles and back to confirm one boy. On some of these journeys he was accompanied by his nephew, Father John Berger, son of his sister Catherine, who came to Philadelphia in 1857. Father Berger afterwards wrote the first life of his uncle.

Bishop Neumann was the first in the United States to introduce the Forty Hours Devotion in his diocese; and his example was followed by the other bishops. In 1853 he had a Latin brochure printed containing the prayers and rubrics for the Forty Hours.

In the course of five years, he saw the exterior of Sts. Peter and Paul Cathedral in Philadelphia completed, and fifty churches erected in the diocese. He raised the standard of studies in St. Charles Borromeo Seminary at Ellicott, Maryland, and in 1859 founded a diocesan preparatory seminary. From the beginning he promoted the establishment of parochial schools. There were only two such schools in 1852, but by 1860 they numbered nearly 100.

For the boys he procured as teachers the Christian Brothers, and for the girls various sisterhoods. He helped the Notre Dame Sisters of Munich to become firmly established in the United States; introduced the Holy Cross Sisters of France for an industrial school; and on the advice of Pope Pius IX, in 1855, founded the Sisters of the Third Order of St. Francis, Philadelphia Foundation. The latter now (1974) have four provinces in the United States, with the general motherhouse at Glen Riddle, Pennsylvania, and a total membership of 1,730 professed sisters, working in twenty-three archdioceses and dioceses of the country as well as in Ireland and in Puerto Rico. Bishop Neumann was also a friend of the Colored Oblate Sisters of Baltimore, and by his tact and charity saved them from extinction.

Bishop Neumann was one of the 154 prelates who journeyed to Rome in 1854 to be present at the solemn definition of the dogma of the Immaculate Conception by Pope Pius IX. "I have neither the time nor the ability to describe the solemnity," he wrote in a letter, "but I thank God that among the many graces he has bestowed upon me, he allowed me to see this day in Rome."

The proclamation of the dogma took place in the Vatican Basilica of St. Peter's on December 8; and eight days later Bishop Neumann had a private audience with the Holy Father. He was able to report that in three years the number of children attending parochial schools in his diocese had been increased from 500 to 9,000. With a knowing smile the Supreme Pontiff said to him: "Bishop Neumann of Philadelphia, is not obedience better than sacrifice?"

Before the end of the year Bishop Neumann left Rome, made a pilgrimage to the shrine of Our Lady of Loreto, and then paid a visit to his native town of Prachatitz in Bohemia, where his father was still living. Despite his efforts to make this visit as quietly as possible, he was greeted on arrival with the booming of cannons and the ringing of bells.

Many were the problems and difficulties with which Bishop Neumann had to contend in the administration of his diocese. Among these were those caused by the parish trustees, the Know-Nothing Party and the Nativists. Concerning these matters the bishop issued wise regulations in a diocesan synod which he held in 1855.

The Eighth Provincial Council of Baltimore was held the same year, and at this meeting of the bishops the creation of a new diocese was discussed. Bishop Neumann was in favor of a division of the diocese of Philadelphia and the erection of one at Pottsville; and he offered to go to the latter or another.

Pottsville was not made a diocese, but Bishop Neumann in

1857 received a coadjutor in the person of Bishop James Frederick Wood, a native of Philadelphia, son of a Protestant English merchant and a convert since 1836.

The question of a Pottsville diocese again came up in the Ninth Provincial Council of Baltimore, held in 1858; and Bishop Neumann again asked that he be transferred there, leaving Philadelphia in charge of Bishop Wood. There was some misunderstanding in this matter on the part of certain persons; and Bishop Neumann found it necessary to write a letter to Cardinal Barnabò in which he clarified the situation and declared his complete submission to the will of the Holy Father. Pottsville was never made a diocese.

Though Bishop Neumann had suffered from frequent illnesses, his sudden death, at the age of forty-eight, was wholly unexpected. On January 8, 1860, he went out in the afternoon to attend to some business matters and was walking back when he suffered an apoplectic stroke in front of a private residence. He was carried into the house and laid on the floor with a pillow under his head. There he died at three in the afternoon.

Archbishop Kenrick delivered a beautiful funeral oration in which he extolled the holy life and work of Bishop Neumann. "Each hour, and almost each moment," he said, "his soul communed with God. . . . His soul now communes with the Ambroses, the Augustines, the Gregorys and especially with the sainted Alphonsus whom he imitated so diligently. With them he praises God for the multitude of his mercies and gives him homage." Bishop Neumann was buried in the Redemptorist Church of St. Peter in Philadelphia.

The cause of his beatification was begun in 1886. Ten years later he received the title of "Venerable." In February, 1963, Pope John XXIII issued the proclamation for his beatification, but the ceremony was delayed by the death of Pope John; and Pope Paul VI, soon after the Second Vatican Council had reassembled, beatified him on October 13. The feast of Bl. John N. Neumann is observed on January 5.

Liturgical Prayer

O Lord, graciously hear the prayers we offer to you as we recall the holy life of your blessed confessor-bishop John. Forgive us all our sins through the merits and intercession of him who served you so well on earth. Through Jesus Christ, your Son, our Lord, who lives and reigns with you in the unity of the Holy Spirit, God, forever and ever. Amen.

CHAPTER 5

SAINTS AND BLESSED

United States

Bl. Frances Schervier

(1819-1876) Founder of the Franciscan Sisters of the Poor

Two religious sisters, wearing black veils, long brown dresses, and scapulars on which were sewn conspicuous red crosses with the instruments of the passion of our Lord, got off the train at Fort Wayne, Indiana, on July 2, 1863. One of them was Mother Frances Schervier, small in stature but big of heart, the founder of the Sisters of the Poor of St. Francis who had their motherhouse in Aachen, Germany. The other was Sister Felicitas, one of the first five sisters who had come to Cincinnati in 1858 and was now the superior of the American branch of the sisterhood.

They had come to see Bishop John Henry Luers of Fort Wayne to make arrangements for the founding of a convent in the country town of Hessen Cassel, about eight miles south of the city. The bishop was desirous of having the sisters in his diocese, and it seemed he had a place to offer which would enable Mother Frances to carry out a project dear to her heart.

As an eleven-year-old girl she had wanted to become a Trappistine nun, but later she found that her life's work and that of the congregation she founded lay in the active work of the care of the sick and poor. Nonetheless she always recognized the great spiritual advantages of the contemplative life, and she introduced into some of her communities in Europe and the United States small groups of so-called Recluses. And now she planned to found at Hessen Cassel a convent in which some of the sisters, wearing an ashen-gray habit and called "Sisters of St. Margaret of Cortona,"

*Bl. Frances Schervier sojourned in the United States
in 1863 and again in 1868.*

would lead a semi-cloistered life of prayer, penance, household
duties, and the making of church vestments "for the relief of the
souls in purgatory." Other sisters in the same convent, wearing
the brown habit, would teach the children of the farming community and nurse the sick of the area. Both groups would take their
meals and recreation in common. Later perhaps the sisters would
be able to establish a hospital in Fort Wayne.

The pastor of St. Joseph Church at Hessen Cassel, Father
Jacob Meyer, then took the two sisters to see the one-story, seven-
room frame house near his church, which was to serve as their
convent. "That meant," wrote Mother Frances, "two hours in a
country wagon on roads so bad that we continually invoked our

guardian angel. The pious missionary of the place, a German doctor of divinity, acted as driver, and brought us back to Fort Wayne the next day, where we were most kindly received by the Sisters of Providence. These good sisters overwhelmed us with kindness, and with our hearts full of affection and gratitude we left them" — at midnight to go on by train to another little town in southern Illinois called Teutopolis.

The convent at Hessen Cassel was opened on August 9, and Mother Frances was there again for the occasion. However, during those pioneer days it was not the ideal spot for the double convent that she had been led to think. The sisters encountered various difficulties and reverses. A fire destroyed all but the brick structure of the church in 1864; there were no more candidates for the "Sisters of St. Margaret" after the first three were received, and one of these had to be dismissed. The convent was closed in April, 1866, and the sisters went back to St. Clare's Convent in Cincinnati. There were Sisters of St. Margaret at this house until 1881, when they were incorporated into the regular community.

Teutopolis too was a small country town, but it had a college, St. Joseph College, one of the first Catholic colleges in Illinois. At the request of Bishop Henry Damian Juncker of Alton, Illinois, Franciscans of the German Province of the Holy Cross, having headquarters in Westphalia, had established the center of an American branch at Teutopolis in 1858, the same year in which the first Sisters of the Poor of St. Francis came to Cincinnati. Acceding to the same bishop's wishes, they opened St. Joseph College in this town in 1862 to prepare young men for professional and business careers and also to serve as the diocesan preparatory seminary. At first the household work was done by three hired women and one man. In May, 1863, five Sisters of the Poor of St. Francis consented to take over the kitchen, laundry and cleaning temporarily and began to reside at the college. They remained for three years despite the fact that such work was not on their program except inasmuch as it was an instance of helping the poor.

Mother Frances had met Bishop Juncker in Munich when both were beggars at the offices of the Ludwig's Missionsverein, and she arranged her visit to Teutopolis so it would coincide with his presence there during his confirmation tour.

In a letter which she wrote from Teutopolis on July 6, 1863, she has an interesting account of her trip from Fort Wayne, where she and Sister Felicitas boarded the train at midnight, July 2: "We had to ride on the train all night and through the next day until five o'clock in the afternoon (seventeen hours from Fort Wayne to Teutopolis — a very slow train). Then we had still two hours' ride of a neck-breaking kind (three miles from Effingham to Teutopolis).

"The man who drove the wagon, a farm cart, said once: 'Hold on now tightly, so you'll not fall out. Here is a bad place. Last year a boy fell out of the wagon I was driving and broke his arm.'

"We two had been sitting on chairs, and so did two other passengers in the cart. But I now decided to sit on the floor of the cart, and this proved to be a very good idea; for, the chairs tumbled about dreadfully. We all had a good laugh. I always recommend myself to the dear angels and saints and so, with the help of God, I always get through safely. We arrived here in Teutopolis toward seven o'clock Saturday evening."

First Mother Frances went to the chapel at the college. Her first visit was always to our Lord in the Blessed Sacrament. Then she greeted the sisters briefly, because they still had much work to do, and went to see a novice, Sister Xaveria, who was critically ill of typhoid fever.

"The good child," wrote Mother Frances, "felt that she was going to die and yearned intensely, so I was told, for my arrival. . . . Although she was already quite delirious, at my entrance she sprang out of bed and fell at once on her knees and looked at me with an angelic, unspeakably touching expression. Her clasped hands indicated that she desired me to bless her. I was moved to tears. It was remarkable, for immediately afterwards she lost consciousness completely."

Mother Frances remained with the patient and arranged to have extreme unction administered to her the next morning. Bishop Juncker arrived at midnight and prayed at the bedside of the sick sister in the morning before going to St. Francis Church to administer confirmation. The sister died at eleven o'clock Sunday morning and was buried the next day at eight in the morning. Bishop Juncker celebrated the Requiem Mass ("That good, humble prelate," wrote Mother Frances, "said he would not allow himself to be deprived of doing that . . .") and Father Mathias Hiltermann, the guardian of the friary adjoining the parish church, preached an eloquent sermon.

"Who among you will take the place of this young sister? The Reverend Mother is here in town now and can receive you at once."

Several girls offered to join the sisters that very day, but they were too young to be admitted. In later years the sisters received many applicants from Teutopolis and neighboring places.

Mother Frances added the following significant remarks: "His Lordship [Bishop Juncker] has so many needs of various kinds in his diocese, which he desires to entrust to our Congregation, that I must be very much on my guard in order not to let myself be carried away by sympathy. I pray every day with the sisters for light, counsel and strength. The *Veni Creator* is my favorite prayer, particularly here in America. On the journey too I always felt urged to pray it with great confidence. . . . Tomorrow afternoon I hope to leave here. We have then a night and half a day's ride on the train to Cincinnati, where soon will be held investment and profession."

The daughter of the sixth governor of Ohio, Sarah Worthington Peter, a convert to the Catholic faith, had been instrumental in bringing the Sisters of the Poor of St. Francis to Cincinnati in order to care for the sick and poor among the many German immigrants in the city. When the first sisters arrived in 1858, there was as yet no house that they could occupy. Should they stay or go back to Aachen? Like Father Junípero Serra at San Diego Mission in California less than a century earlier, they made a novena in honor of St. Joseph; and on the fourth day they were offered temporary use of a large building in which they could admit patients. It was the beginning of the first St. Mary's Hospital, the construction of which was begun the same year.

The following year Sarah Peter invited the sisters to her own residence and it became St. Clara's Convent, motherhouse and novitiate. New members joined the sisters there and additional recruits came from Germany; and in 1860 they crossed the Ohio River and founded St. Elizabeth Hospital in Covington, Kentucky. Two years later they made a beginning in Columbus, Ohio (St. Francis Hospital) and also in the east, in Hoboken, New Jersey (St. Mary's Hospital). Mother Frances visited all of these establishments during her three-month sojourn in the United States and rejoiced to see not only the progress that had been made in the preceding five years but also the promise of further expansion in the immediate future. By 1862, a total of thirty-eight sisters had come to the United States from Europe; and including novices and postulants, their membership was now seventy-four.

At Hessen Cassel and Teutopolis the Civil War which was being waged between the North and the South seemed to be far away, but in Cincinnati it was closer. Not only had Mother Frances' sisters been sheltering orphans and mothers with children and caring for sick soldiers in their several hospitals in Ohio, but they also served as nurses at a military hospital on Third Street in Cincinnati for some time in 1862. In the same year, May 12-30, Sister Felicitas and two other sisters and two postulants, together with Sarah Peter, were aboard the Ohio River hospital boat, the *Superior*, which went as far as Pittsburg Landing. At the latter place they went ashore and visited the hospital tents. Early in 1864 the sisters also made visits to the hospital at Camp Chase, five miles from Columbus, where Catholic soldiers welcomed them like angels from heaven.

While Mother Frances was in Cincinnati in mid-July, 1863, Colonel John Morgan and his troops made their raids into southern and eastern Ohio. The Confederates, after crossing the Cumberland River, had turned north through Kentucky. Contrary to orders, Colonel Morgan led his men across the Ohio River, burning and pillaging as they went but bypassing Cincinnati.

Mother Frances was referring to these raids when she wrote to Sister Joanna in Aachen: "You would not like it here, for there is the unrest and danger of war. All the stores are closed. The poor men drill all the day and stay prepared for a hostile attack, as the enemy is roving about, some forty or fifty miles from the city.

"A few months ago it was worse. Then the Most Reverend Archbishop [John B. Purcell] requested our Recluses to pray unceasingly so that the city would be spared. Afterwards the good, pious prelate ascribed the liberation to their prayers and even announced this from the pulpit. . . . We do not have the least fear and are quite happy and cheerful."

Mother Frances planned to make another visit to the United States in 1865, but illness prevented her from making the voyage at the time. However, she did return in 1868 and again remained for four months (May 6 to the end of August). During the five years that had elapsed since her first visit, God had blessed the work of her sisters with a remarkable development and expansion. Five new hospitals were opened, all but one in the eastern part of the United States: St. Francis Hospital in Jersey City, New Jersey, in 1864; St. Peter's Hospital in Brooklyn and St. Francis Home in New York in 1865; St. Mary's Hospital in Quincy, Illinois, in 1866; and St. Michael's Hospital in Newark, New Jersey, in 1867.

In Newark where a beginning was just being made, Mother Frances conversed in French for a long time with Bishop James Roosevelt Bayley and Monsignor Doane who came to see her. "Their conversation did me so much good," she said afterwards. "What must heaven be, if even here on earth there are such excellent souls!" On his part, Monsignor Doane always referred to her afterwards as "one of the uncanonized saints." Mother Frances was now able also to speak a little English.

One of the lay workers at Newark was Mary Flanigan. She was now past forty and had never learned to read. To Mother

61

Frances these were not insurmountable obstacles, and Mary was admitted to the community as Sister Matthia. She served God in his poor as a sister for twenty-seven years more.

In Covington, Kentucky, Mother Frances was delighted to see the hospital taking care of sixty foundlings and orphans. While she was there, a man brought in a black waif that seemed to be near death. It was baptized at once, and Mother Frances was the sponsor. She took the infant into her arms and held "little Francis" close to her heart. It died the next day.

About the middle of July, Mother Frances went to see the new establishment in Quincy, Illinois, St. Mary's Hospital. Because of its isolation from the other houses in the Midwest, Sister Eusebia, the superior, had named it the "Isle of Sanctity." Mother Frances found the hospital to be well-equipped except for the lack of screens, and she directed that they be installed. During her first sojourn in the United States she had suffered much from those "tormenting spirits," the mosquitoes. To her, screens were not an unnecessary expense.

To investigate an offer that had been made for a foundation in St. Louis, Mother Frances traveled from Quincy on a Mississippi River steamboat to "the Gateway of the West." The river was very low, and unhappily the paddler got stuck on a sandbank for about fourteen hours. Most of the time Mother Frances sat in the blazing sun on the deck, explaining the Catholic religion to a lady passenger. Her companion, Sister Antonia, became worried; and by signs she finally succeeded in communicating a message to the lady: use your large hand fan so that Mother Frances will also get the benefit of it.

When Mother Frances bade farewell to the community at St. Clara's Convent in Cincinnati on August 6, she remarked: "This is the last time I shall be among you." And in a last message for the Recluses at this convent, she wrote: "During our voyage it would please me if you would burn a candle before our Blessed Mother, the Star of the Sea — yes, until you hear that we have landed safely. On that day burn a candle in thanksgiving. . . . May you all become saints, dearest sisters; for that, no permission is required."

Mother Frances Schervier was in her fiftieth year when she visited the United States in 1868. She was born on January 3, 1819, in Charlemagne's historic capital of Austrasia, now known as Aachen or Aix-la-Chapelle. This West German city, with a population today of over 150,000, is situated near the Belgian border, some forty miles west of Cologne.

Her father, John Henry Caspar Joseph Schervier, was German, the descendant of a prominent family that traced its ancestors in Aachen back to the thirteenth century; he was the proprietor of a needle factory in the city. His first wife died, after giving birth to a girl, about a year after their wedding. Three years later he married Marie Louise Victoire Migeon, who was a native of France, the youngest daughter of another needle manufacturer in the city of Charleville on the Meuse River. During the latter part of the French Revolution she and her parents had been held in prison.

Frances was the second youngest of seven children. Marie Christine Pauline, the youngest, later joined the sisterhood founded by Frances and died in 1855. Two other sisters of Frances, Marie Louise Jeannette Henriette and Maria Julia Ottilia, died a year after their mother, one in June and the other in July, 1833. Frances' three brothers were: Louis Henry, who married in 1849 and again in 1879; Charles Adolphe, who died as an infant in 1814; and Charles Gerard, who was ordained a priest in 1840 and died in 1861. Maria Elizabeth, the stepsister who was born in 1808 married in 1830 and died in 1840.

Frances was so named when she was baptized because her godfather was Emperor Francis I of Austria. This came about in the following manner. In 1818, three years after the Battle of Waterloo, Aachen was the scene of an important congress attended by the three monarchs of Europe: the Emperor of Austria, King Frederick William III of Prussia and Tsar Alexander I of Russia. Since Napoleon Bonaparte was now safely imprisoned on the South Atlantic island of St. Helena, they agreed to withdraw their armies of occupation from France.

While in Aachen, Emperor Francis paid a visit to the Schervier needle factory to see how these important little household items were made. He wanted to do this incognito, but did not succeed. He received a royal welcome at the factory. Mrs. Schervier, who was looking forward to giving birth to her sixth child, was bold enough to ask the visiting emperor to be its godfather. He graciously consented and named the aged Canon Anthony William Deboeur of Aachen to be his proxy at the child's baptism.

To have an emperor as godfather was an extraordinary distinction; but to Frances, when she attained the use of reason, it had little meaning. Practically speaking, her godfather was the old Canon Deboeur who began to reside with the family. What counted for Frances, even from early childhood, was the privilege of being a loving child of God who could serve her dear Lord in the least of his brethren.

Once, later on, Frances did call attention to her godfather,

63

but then it was only to request an alms for St. John's Kitchen founded by Father Joseph Istas in Aachen during the winter of 1841. Archduke John of Austria was a visitor in Cologne at the time, and she sent a letter to him by special messenger, introducing herself as a godchild of Emperor Francis and asking for a contribution for her poor. Soon afterwards the burgomaster of Aachen received fifty German thaler for Miss Schervier.

"In school [St. Leonard's, a boarding school which Frances attended as a day scholar] I heard," Frances wrote later on, "how our dear Savior had loved the poor and become poor and despised for us. I conceived a special affection for the needy. . . . The sight of my Savior hanging naked on the Cross had touched my heart. I conceived the thought of clothing him in his poor."

She was not yet eleven years old, when she was permitted to receive her First Holy Communion together with her sister Julia Ottilia who was about a year and a half older. It was the feast of St. Francis of Assisi (October 4, 1829) and also that of Our Lady of Victories, her mother's nameday. The whole family received Holy Communion from the hands of Canon Deboeur on this day. A year later Archbishop Ferdinand von Spiegel administered the sacrament of confirmation to Frances.

At this time she was filled with a very strong desire to give her young life to God in the strict penitential order of Trappistines; and it persisted for several years despite the fact that her Father Confessor and another priest advised her to give up the idea. Finally, when the latter told her to renounce this desire at least for a time, she did so while kneeling before a crucifix at home. "It seemed to me," she wrote, "as if I received from the cross an interior manifestation that God had accepted the sacrifice of my will, that I should turn to something else, and devote myself to active pursuits of charity. . . . I felt an ardent desire to serve and love our Lord in the poor, the sick and the miserable. In that solemn moment, moved by divine grace, I offered myself to God for the service of suffering mankind."

Frances was still thinking of becoming a Trappistine nun when her good mother died at the age of fifty-two years, February 22, 1832. "I can truly say," Frances wrote later, "that mother was very virtuous. . . . I now conceived the thought of asking the Blessed Virgin Mary to be my mother, and kneeling, did so with all my heart. Henceforth I daily said a little prayer composed for this purpose. . . . The dear Mother of God assisted me henceforth most maternally."

During the summer of the following year both of Frances' older sisters likewise died. That meant that for the present

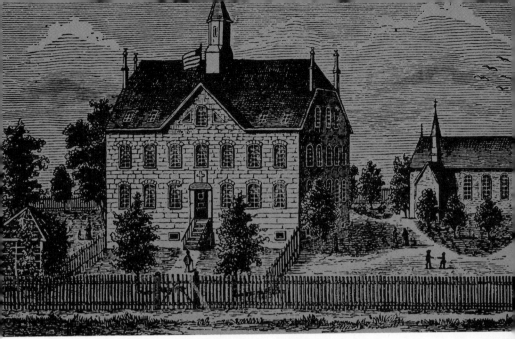

*First buildings of St. Joseph College founded at
Teutopolis, Illinois, in 1862.*

Frances had to give up any plans of joining a religious sisterhood. Although she was only in her fifteenth year the management of the household now devolved upon her.

"In my household duties," wrote Frances, "I always implored the aid of the Blessed Virgin, especially for the direction and care of the servants, which was a rather serious and difficult task for my youthful age. . . . Meanwhile, my younger sister Pauline was sent to Belgium, where she remained at school a year and a half."

At first her father would not allow Frances to attend holy Mass and receive Holy Communion as often as she wanted, nor to go out alone in order to help the poor and sick. But after Pauline, who was only about a year and a half younger, returned from boarding school and was able to take care of some of Frances' duties at home, her father gradually gave her more freedom.

"Now," as she wrote, "was to be fulfilled what for years I had in mind, what I had longed for, waking and sleeping. I could hardly restrain my joy and my gratitude to God. . . . I discerned my Divine Redeemer in the poor and sick as manifestly, as if I had seen him with my very eyes. . . . When I gave food and drink to our Lord in the person of his poor, I always felt an increase of sensible love for him, and was thereby amply repaid for the little privations which I had undergone for the purpose. O how sweet and pure this charity was to me!"

About 1840 several young ladies of Aachen founded a society to help the poor and to nurse the sick in their homes. They asked

Mr. Schervier to allow his daughter Frances to join them and he gave the desired permission. Soon Frances surpassed her associates in her ministrations to the needy and the sick, their souls as well as their bodies; and to obtain the means for assisting the poor she went begging for them among those who were blessed with this world's goods. She began also to take a special interest in the conversion of fallen women.

During the severe winter of 1841, the curate of St. Paul's parish church, Father Joseph Istas, established St. John's Kitchen in a former Dominican priory which was now city property. It provided free meals for all helpless poor people and those families that were really in want. Frances took charge of the project, not only the preparation and distribution of food, but also the collection of necessary funds. Even after Father Istas died in 1843, she continued the good work for about two years.

In St. Nicholas Church, formerly in the hands of the Franciscans, Frances attended the afternoon services on the feast of St. Anthony, June 13, 1844. The sermon preached on this occasion by Father Van den Meulen, director of the Third Order Secular of St. Francis, made such a profound impression on Frances that she decided then and there to become a tertiary, a secular Franciscan. Father Van den Meulen invested her with the scapular and cord on the vigil of the feast of Sts. Peter and Paul. "I regarded it," she wrote, "as a great, undeserved grace of God."

Some of her friends and co-workers followed her example, one of them being Gertrude Frank. The latter told Frances that while she was engaged in prayer God gave her a message: it was the will of God that Frances leave her home and become the founder of a new religious congregation. Bishop John Theodore Laurent later was convinced that Gertrude spoke the truth, but she had a hard time convincing Frances.

During the night of February 26, 1845, Frances' father was stricken with acute pains. She and her two brothers hastened to answer his call for help and saw him collapse and fall to the floor. Frances did not lose her usual presence of mind; she sent Henry to get a doctor, reminded Charles who was now a priest and teacher of religion at the high school of Aachen to give absolution to his father, and then ran to get the parish priest of St. Paul's to administer the last sacraments. When the latter and the doctor arrived, they were both too late. Mr. Schervier was no longer alive.

"The condolence with our affliction," wrote Frances, "was general, for father was a righteous man, and benevolent of heart. Serious affairs remained for us children to settle, but the good Lord disposed all for the best."

It was now possible for Frances to leave home; and that is what she did when Gertrude Frank and three other friends, all of them Franciscan tertiaries, proposed that they band together, form a religious community, and devote themselves wholly to the works of charity. Frances was twenty-six years old, and Gertrude twenty-nine. The other three were: Catharine Daverkosen, thirty-one; Joanna Bruchhaus, twenty-six; and Catharine Lassen, twenty-six. Because there were two Catharines, Miss Daverkosen took the name of Sister Mary. A benefactor rented a house for them for three years: No. 12 beyond St. James' Gate. The five young women moved into the house on October 3, 1845; and that marked the beginning of a new religious congregation, subsequently called the Sisters of the Poor of St. Francis.

Frances still had no thought of becoming a founder despite Gertrude's assurances; and she wanted Sister Mary to be the superior. The others, however, all chose Frances and she had to accept. During the summer of 1849, Frances did succeed in having Sister Mary elected superior, but only for a short time. Bishop Laurent made it clear to Frances that she was opposing the will of God, and she resumed her duties as superior and "founder" before Easter, 1850. Born in Aachen in 1804, Bishop Laurent returned to his native city in 1848 when he was banished by the Masonic party from Luxembourg, where he had been vicar apostolic since 1841. He played an important role in the life of Mother Frances and the development of her religious community, and died at Aachen in 1884.

Urged to do so by Bishop Laurent, Mother Frances compiled a rule and constitutions and submitted them to Cardinal von Geisel, Archbishop of Cologne, for approval. This was granted, after some delay, in July of 1851; and on August 12, the feast of St. Clare, the same year, Mother Frances and her companions who had increased to twenty-three were clothed with the brown religious habit of St. Francis. Thus the new religious congregation called the Sisters of the Poor of St. Francis was formally established. (New and longer constitutions, which were approved by the archbishop of Cologne in 1865, were sent to Rome in 1870 and received a "decree of praise" from Pope Pius IX with suggestions for some changes in twelve articles. The constitutions were fully approved in 1908 by Pope St. Pius X.)

The first ones, besides the poor sick in their homes, to receive the special attention of Mother Frances and her companions were repentant fallen women who needed a place of refuge. They came to the house at St. James' Gate and soon it was overcrowded with them, their total number being about thirty. During the Lent of

1848, Mother Frances made a trip to Holland to collect necessary funds. However, the Good Shepherd Sisters of Angers, France, were able to establish a house in Aachen at this time; and the penitents were turned over to their care in November of that year.

The three years for which the house at St. James' Gate had been rented were drawing to a close, and Mother Frances and her companions had to look for a new home. In January, 1849, the city permitted them to move into the former Dominican priory as nurses of victims of an expected cholera epidemic and then those who were afflicted with smallpox. The sisters attended divine services in a special section of St. Paul's Church.

It was in 1849 that with the consent of her associates Mother Frances introduced into their religious community a small group of so-called Recluses who led a contemplative life while the others devoted themselves to various works of charity. She firmly believed — and others did too — that by their prayers and penances the Recluses brought God's blessings on all the activities of the sisters. Among nine new members admitted in 1849 was Mother Frances' younger sister Pauline, who took the name of Sister Paula. One of the first group, Sister Gertrude Frank, died April 7, 1850.

Residing in the old Dominican house at the pleasure of the city authorities, the sisters took in some sick who were incurables, also some aged people, and once more some fallen women who for some reason could not be admitted elsewhere; and they continued to nurse the sick in their homes and to take care of charity kitchens. But as their number increased they were anxious to acquire a convent and motherhouse of their own. In the summer of 1852, what had once been a Poor Clare monastery and was suppressed in 1803 was offered for sale at the price of 21,000 thaler. Bishop Laurent told them to buy it — but they had no funds and could not even make the necessary loan. They prayed for divine assistance and a loan of 10,000 came from Bonn; they prayed again, and the relative of one of the sisters supplied 8,000 thaler. Mother Frances was able to purchase the old monastery on August 6; and the sisters moved into it in the spring of 1853. Necessary repairs and alterations were made, and new buildings were added later.

In the meantime, Mother Frances had also begun to open branch houses. Sister Paula was sent to Juelich to take charge of a poor house or "inn" already in operation in June, 1850. A house was opened in Bonn in 1851. In the same year two sisters began to spend the day with the female prisoners in the House of Detention in Aachen, and later resided there day and night. A convent and hospital were founded in Burtscheid in 1852. From that time on, in the 1850s and 1860s, numerous new foundations were made and hospitals were established in Germany and the United States.

For a time (about four weeks in 1849) Mother Frances even served as a nurse of Catholic patients in the Protestant hospital at Lennep. At first she was not welcome, but she soon won the esteem and even the affection of the staff and patients. Whenever she heard that a poor criminal had been sentenced to death, she asked the authorities for permission to stay with the prisoner during his last hours. Seven or eight times she passed through this ordeal, spending hours with a condemned person, speaking maternal words of comfort, instilling confidence, arousing contrition, eliciting resignation. On one such occasion in 1855, she wrote after witnessing the execution: "I have just returned from the prison, where two poor sinners were executed today. I am half dead with fatigue and commiseration. Oh, what a grace for the two criminals to have so sincerely converted. What comfort, what help our holy religion offers."

As a successful beggar for Christ's poor, Mother Frances was able to give valuable and timely assistance also to other religious orders and congregations. The help she gave the founder of the Brothers of the Poor of St. Francis was such that she may deservedly be called a co-founder of the brotherhood. Philip Hoever, a teacher in St. Peter's School, Aachen, was so affected by the death of his young wife that he sent his two sons to a Jesuit college and decided to spend the rest of his life in the service of God. He sought the counsel of Mother Frances; and after joining the Third Order Secular of St. Francis, he and three companions took up their abode in a house next to the motherhouse of the sisters in 1857. The latter supplied them with food. In December, 1858, there were twenty-three brothers.

It was Mother Frances who helped them to decide what their special purpose would be — the care and education of neglected boys. It was she who obtained approval for them as the "Brothers of the Poor of St. Francis" from the archbishop of Cologne, and with a donation of 9,000 thaler enabled them to buy a large house and make it a home for boys. She also introduced them to the United States, where they succeeded her sisters in the domestic department of St. Joseph College, Teutopolis, Illinois, for two years (1866-1868) and then established the Mt. Alverno school for boys near Cincinnati. These religious brothers are represented in the archdioceses of Cincinnati, Chicago, Newark, and the dioceses of Davenport and Little Rock.

In the same year in which the Brothers of the Poor were founded (1857), Mother Frances and Bishop John T. Laurent assisted Mother Josepha Koch in the founding of a nursing sisterhood named the Sisters of St. Francis of the Holy Family. By order of the archbishop of Cologne Mother Josepha, a member of the Franciscan Sisters of the Sacred Heart of Eupen, undertook the care of cholera victims in his territory. Afterwards she remained to establish the new sisterhood. At the time of the *Kulturkampf* in 1875, they moved their motherhouse to Louvain, and during World War I to Mayen in Netteltal, diocese of Traves. In 1875 they also made a foundation in the United States in Iowa City. Three years later they moved to Dubuque and eventually became a separate congregation.

Still another Franciscan sisterhood which was founded with the help of Mother Frances is that of the Sisters of St. Francis of Perpetual Adoration (formerly Poor Sisters of St. Francis Seraph of Perpetual Adoration), begun in 1863 at Olpe in Westphalia, Germany, by Mother Mary Teresa Bonzel. In a statement Mother Teresa made May 2, 1887, she recounts how Mother Frances helped give a firm footing to the new sisterhood. Mother Frances herself made a trip to Olpe, and Mother Teresa spent six weeks at Aachen. In person and by letters Mother Frances assisted the new community with instruction and advice. She supplied church goods for their chapel; she had some of the sisters trained in nursing; she helped draw up the constitutions.

Mother Teresa wanted to unite her community at Olpe with that of Mother Frances in Aachen. But Mother Frances told her to go on independently, and if her efforts did not prove successful, the union could take place. At the time of the *Kulturkampf* (1875) the Olpe sisters also made a foundation in the United States, and devoted themselves to educational work as well as nursing. They developed into two provinces (Mishawaka, Indiana, and Colorado Springs, Colorado), with a total membership in 1974 of about 750 sisters. The general motherhouse is still in Olpe, Germany.

In three short but hotly contested wars which followed closely one upon the other during the 1860s, Mother Frances was quick to send her sisters to nurse sick and wounded soldiers. She personally conducted them to the scene of fighting and took part in their work during the war of 1864 which was waged by Prussia and Austria against Denmark over the two duchies of Schleswig and Holstein. At the request of the German Knights of Malta, they went first to Rendsburg and then to Schleswig (Castle Gottorf) and to Flensburg. A total of nineteen sisters served as war nurses; and when the conflict was over, six remained in Flensburg on the border of Denmark to take over the care of the large hospital of the Knights.

During the Austro-Prussian War, June-July, 1866, Mother Frances sent twenty-seven sisters to two hospitals at Langensalza in which there were 400 wounded soldiers and six more to Hessen-Cassel where there were 500 wounded. And during the Franco-Prussian War, 1870-1871, 125 Sisters of the Poor of St. Francis attended about 3,000 wounded German and French soldiers daily during the ten months from July, 1870, to May, 1871.

What renders Mother Frances' tireless charitable activities and extraordinary achievements all the more remarkable is the fact that frequently during her life she suffered from serious illnesses, particularly attacks of asthma. When she returned to Aachen after her second trip to the United States in 1868, her health declined noticeably and by the end of 1869 she had been greatly weakened by her asthmatic condition. In January, 1870, she had to take to bed; for a month she could take nothing except water poured over toasted bread. In April the asthma ceased to plague her, but she was extremely weak. Miss Alwine Kamper of Cologne, a benefactor, offered to take her to Lourdes, and she consented. She arrived in the latter part of May and was carried to the grotto. After drinking some of the miraculous water she immediately felt better and was able to walk. After about twelve days, she seemed to be entirely cured. Mother Frances was convinced it was a miracle.

Mother Frances still had a task to perform. During the last three years of her life she fought bravely to keep her religious congregation alive and active in Germany despite the infamous May Laws of Bismarck's *Kulturkampf,* and she succeeded though some restrictions were placed on the Sisters of the Poor of St. Francis.

From the Decree of the Sacred Congregation of Rites by which the cause of Mother Frances Schervier's beatification and canonization was introduced in Rome (May 9, 1934), we quote the following:

"When the harsh persecutions of the Catholic Church arose, Frances, prepared to be broken but not to bow, resisted valiantly, was victorious, and was permitted to remain in Germany. It is manifestly evident from the acts that all virtues shone forth in her beyond the average. It seems likewise certain that God granted his servant the gift of prophecy, the searching of hearts, and other favors. Broken by her labors and penances, she was suddenly stricken with a grave illness. On December 14, 1876, in her fifty-eighth year, tortured grievously with intense pains, which she nevertheless bore with invincible patience and an admirable fortitude of spirit, she breathed forth her pure soul at Aachen, with the sweet names of Jesus and Mary on her lips." It was the year in which her sisters in the United States observed the one-hundredth anniversary of the independence of their native or adopted country.

During her long term of office as superior general, Mother Frances admitted no less than 815 sisters into her religious congregation; and in the United States, during the eighteen years from 1858 to 1876, the number of those who joined the sisterhood was 272. After the death of the founder, the congregation continued to grow to such an extent that in 1932 it had a total of more than 2,500 sisters in ninety houses. Of the latter, twenty were in the United States; and these formed two so-called provinces, one having its headquarters in Hartwell, near Cincinnati, Ohio, and the other in Warwick, New York.

At their general chapter in 1952 it was decided to divide the congregation into two autonomous sisterhoods: the Sisters of the Poor of St. Francis in Germany and Belgium, with three provinces and about 1,600 sisters in 1974 and their general motherhouse in Aachen, and the Franciscan Sisters of the Poor of the United States with their motherhouse, at that time, at Frascati, near Rome, Italy. Subsequently, the latter, having a membership of about 400 and houses in the United States, Italy and Brazil, merged their two provinces into one group with general headquarters in Brooklyn, New York.

The cause of Mother Frances' beatification having been completed in 1974, she was solemnly beatified by Pope Paul VI in the Vatican Basilica of St. Peter on April 28. Present on this occasion were many of her spiritual daughters from both sides of the Atlantic — about 500 from Germany and Belgium, and about one hundred from the United States. Accompanying the religious pilgrimage of the latter to Rome, Assisi and Aachen — where the body of Bl. Frances Schervier is enshrined in the chapel of the motherhouse — was Father Roland Burke, O.F.M., who had served as vice-postulator for the cause of Mother Frances in the United States since 1940.

Liturgical Prayer

O God, you inspired blessed Frances to strive for perfect charity and so attain your kingdom at the end of her pilgrimage on earth. Strengthen us through her intercession that we may advance rejoicing in the way of love. Through Jesus Christ, your Son, our Lord, who lives and reigns with you in the unity of the Holy Spirit, God, forever and ever. Amen.

CHAPTER 6

SAINTS AND BLESSED

United States

St. Frances Xavier Cabrini

(1850-1917) Founder of the Missionaries of the Sacred Heart

THE *Bourgogne* dropped anchor in the port of New York on March 31, 1889, after a stormy crossing of the Atlantic from Le Havre, France. It was an old and slow ship, but it had made the voyage in eight days. In the steerage there were 1500 Italian immigrants.

On board were also seven Italian sisters wearing simple black dresses and black veils. One of them, the superior of the group, was Mother Frances Xavier Cabrini, a frail little woman, thirty-eight years old. Since childhood she had wanted to become a missionary in China; but Pope Leo XIII had told her to go west, not east, and to work among the Italian immigrants in America.

The seven sisters were standing on the long, icy, windswept dock, looking in vain for someone whom they expected to be there to meet them. They found their way to a shabby hotel near Chinatown and spent the night there in two small, dirty rooms. The next morning they went to see Archbishop Michael Corrigan. He had approved their coming, but now he told them that he had no funds available for a convent and school.

"You might as well board the next ship," he said, "and go back to Italy." Without consulting the archbishop, the Countess Palma di Cesnola, whose maiden name had been Mary Reid, had rented a building on 59th Street which she regarded as suitable for an orphanage; but the archbishop did not approve of the location.

Mother Cabrini did not know this, but she was not daunted by the disheartening words of the archbishop. Presenting her credentials, she replied: "The Holy Father has sent us, and we will stay."

The archbishop was impressed. "You may open a day school," he said, "but no orphanage."

Then he took them to the convent of the Sisters of Charity across the street from the cathedral and requested the superior to give Mother Cabrini and her companions shelter and food.

During the next three weeks, Mother Cabrini prayed for divine assistance, went on begging tours for needed funds, and began teaching the children at St. Joachim's Church. By her humility and tactfulness she gained the archbishop's admiring approval, not only for a day school, but also for an orphanage; she even brought about an accord between him and the countess.

On Palm Sunday Archbishop Corrigan went personally to the convent of the Sisters of Charity and presented to Mother Cabrini the palm branch which he had carried during the procession in the cathedral.

Mother Cabrini and her sisters moved into a temporary convent on White Street on April 21 and then to a day school which was opened on Roosevelt Street. The orphanage was begun on May 3 with a Mass celebrated by the archbishop.

Generous benefactors came to the aid of Mother Cabrini. And when she was praised for the dispatch and determination with which she made her foundations, she smiled and said: "I am merely watching God perform wonders through us."

Letters arrived from Italy, telling her that her presence was needed there to straighten out some difficulties. Accompanied by two Irish postulants, Mother Cabrini left New York on July 20 and returned to Codogno, where she had founded the Missionaries of the Sacred Heart only nine years earlier. Thus she made the first two of her twenty-four crossings of the Atlantic.

The youngest of fifteen children, Maria Francesca was born on July 15, 1850, at Sant' Angelo di Lodi in Lombardy. Her father, Agostino Cabrini, was a hard-working farmer. Her mother, Stella née Oldini, came from Milan. Both gave their numerous progeny the good example of faithful observance of the commandments of God and the Church. Maria Francesca was confirmed when she was seven, and received her First Holy Communion when she reached the age of ten. She took delight in reading the *Annals* of the Society of the Propagation of the Faith and dreamt of becoming a missionary in China.

Everybody in the happy home called her Cecchina — an abbreviation of the diminutive Franceschina. Her sister Rosa, fifteen years older, began to take charge of her when she was thirteen; and like Rosa, Cecchina prepared herself to be a teacher. She received a teacher's certificate when she was eighteen. Two years later, in 1870, both father and mother died.

Francesca applied for admission in a religious sisterhood, but she was told she was not strong enough. She tried another, only to get the same answer. Previously she had become a member of the Third Order Secular of St. Francis, and she faithfully observed its rule of life while continuing her work as a teacher. Her spare time was spent in works of mercy, visiting the poor and teaching catechism.

For two years she taught in a school at nearby Vilardo. An epidemic of smallpox broke out in 1872, and Francesca assisted the victims as much as she could. Then she was asked to improve the situation in an orphanage at Codogno which was in the care of three women who had taken the three vows but had hardly lived like religious. Sister Antonia Tondini, who had donated 30,000 lire for the establishment of the orphanage was in charge; and she was not pleased at all when Francesca joined them.

"Just for two weeks," Monsignor Serrati, the pastor of Codogno, told her. She remained for six years, six very difficult years. She and two of her pupils were invested with a religious habit like that worn by Sister Antonia and her companions — a black dress and a white bonnet. Five other girls joined her later. Three years later Francesca took the vows of the religious life, and, as superior appointed by Monsignor Serrati, received the profession of her seven companions. This amounted to a deposition of Sister Antonia, who proceeded to persecute Sister Francesca during the next three years. In the end, the bishop of Lodi had to suppress the orphanage and convent, but for the sake of peace he allowed Antonia Tondini to keep the house.

To Sister Francesca Bishop Dominic Gelmini of Lodi said: "You wanted to join a missionary sisterhood. With your seven companions you can now found one of your own."

Her reply was: "I will look for a house."

Behind the church at Codogno there was a building which would serve her purposes admirably. It had once been a Franciscan friary, but was suppressed by Napoleon. With 10,000 lire, supplied by Monsignor Serrati, the property was purchased; and here Sister Francesca and her companions established themselves. The day was November 14, 1880. It was the birthday of a new sisterhood, the Missionary Salesians of the Sacred Heart — a name which was definitely changed in 1889 to Missionaries of the Sacred Heart.

The founder was henceforth known as Mother Francesca Saverio Cabrini. She, who was already a spiritual daughter of St. Francis of Assisi, thus added two other saints of the same name to her patrons — St. Francis de Sales and St. Francis Xavier.

After much prayer and study, she wrote a rule of life which received the approbation of the bishop and was accepted by her sisters. She had been like a mistress of novices to them at the former orphanage, and had inspired them with her own missionary ideal.

They were joined by new members, and in 1884 another convent was opened in Milan. Three years later Mother Cabrini went to Rome to found a convent there and to obtain papal approval. Though such approval is usually not granted to a new religious congregation until many years after its establishment, she found kind friends in Rome who encouarged her in her project. Such were the Franciscan minister general, the Dominican master general, and especially Mother Mary of the Passion, founder of the Franciscan Missionaries of Mary.

She also met Bishop John Baptist Scalabrini of Piacenza, who had founded the Missionaries of St. Charles Borromeo or the Scalabrini Fathers. They devoted themselves to the care of Italian immigrants in other lands. He wanted her to undertake the same kind of work.

Mother Cabrini went first to see the Cardinal Vicar of Rome who promptly advised her to return to Codogno. There was no need for another convent in Rome, he said; and the approbation of her rule was a matter which could be considered only at some future date, after her community had grown and developed. Far from being dismayed, Mother Cabrini was bold enough to ask the cardinal to show her rule to the Holy Father himself, Pope Leo XIII; and that surprised the cardinal so much, he did it.

A few days later, the cardinal summoned Mother Cabrini and told her to establish, not one, but two houses in Rome; and when Pope Leo saw the rule, he dispensed with all further formalities and approved it, practically as Mother Cabrini had written it.

The following year Mother Cabrini returned to Rome and had a private audience with Pope Leo. It was then that he told her that she would find the fulfillment of her missionary aspirations, not in China, but in America.

A year later she was on her way to New York. The following year (1890) during her second sojourn of three and a half months in New York, she acquired the former Jesuit novitiate at West Park, Ulster County, New York; and here at the present day is the American novitiate of the Missionaries of the Sacred Heart. In 1891 she made her third voyage to New York, taking with her

*"Saint among the Skyscrapers," a painting of
St. Frances Xavier Cabrini by Robert J. Smith.*

twenty-nine of her sisters. Including seven who had been received in New York, there were now fifty of Mother Cabrini's sisters in the United States.

But it was not merely the United States that made up the America which Pope Leo had given her as the field of labor of her sisters; it comprised all of the Americas. After founding a small hospital, which later became New York's Columbus Hospital,

Mother Cabrini and fourteen of her sisters set sail on October 10 for Nicaragua and opened a school in Granada on December 3. A few days later, when the sisters were driven out of Nicaragua, they found a better place in Panama; and when the revolutionaries forced them to leave Panama, they went to Buenos Aires.

In the spring of 1892 Mother Cabrini returned to the United States, that is, to New Orleans; and with three sisters from New York she made a foundation in this city. By October she was back in Italy, where she remained for nearly two years. She was an irresistible beggar, and even asked Pope Leo XIII for a donation from his private funds. He gave her $1,000.

In 1894 she sailed once more from Genoa to New York; and after seeing Columbus Hospital legally incorporated on March 26, 1895, and formally approved by the State of New York, she entered upon her first tour of South America.

First she visited her sisters in Panama and then sailed down the west coast to Chile, crossed the Andes on the back of a mule in the company of other travelers, and went on to Buenos Aires.

Sending a call to New York for some sisters, she opened an academy in Buenos Aires on March 1, 1896. Subsequently she visited this city on two more occasions, in 1900-1901 and in 1908, and founded two more houses in Argentina. She also established two houses in Brazil, namely in São Paulo (1902) and Rio de Janeiro (1908).

The greater part of 1899 Mother Cabrini spent in the United States, taking over parochial schools in and near New York, Newark, Scranton, Chicago and Denver. In Arlington, New Jersey, she opened an orphanage; and in New York she signed the deed on September 2 for a boarding high school, which was named Mother Cabrini High School.

She then went back to Europe. During this and other visits to Europe she established a number of convents outside of Italy: in Paris, at Brockley in England, in and near Madrid, and at Bilbao in Spain.

The longest uninterrupted period that Mother Cabrini spent in the United States extended from 1902 to 1906. During these years she established schools, orphanages, hospitals in Chicago, Seattle and Los Angeles, and at Burbank, California, a "preventorium" for girls afflicted with tuberculosis.

At the end of 1903 she went to Chicago to found another Columbus Hospital there. She had only $1,000 but collected another $9,000 and purchased the former North Shore Hotel, fronting Lincoln Park, for the sum of $160,000. The sellers tried to cheat her out of a strip of land twenty-five feet wide at one end of the property, but they failed because she personally measured the lot. The contractors too were dishonest. She dismissed them and personally superintended the remodeling of the hotel into a hospital.

Six years later she was in Chicago again to establish an extension of Columbus Hospital on the west side at Vermont Park. Certain people tried to sabotage this project, but Mother Cabrini put a stop to this by bringing patients into the unfinished building.

In the same year (1909), while in Seattle, Mother Cabrini finally took time out to get her naturalization papers as an American citizen and take the oath of allegiance to the United States — something she had intended to do from the outset, but was unable to do because she was too busy.

When the Missionaries of the Sacred Heart observed the twenty-fifth anniversary of their founding in 1906, seventeen years after Mother Cabrini had come to the United States for the first time, she was in California. During that quarter century she had founded no less than fifty convents in eight different countries, and the number of her sisters had increased to almost 1,000. "I have not done it," she said; "God has done it all, and I have merely looked on."

It was an amazing record. Mother Cabrini had indeed succeeded in achieving the impossible. How could a frail, little, sickly woman be as dynamic and resourceful as she was? Intermittently she suffered from fevers which lasted for months. Now and then she had to spend several days in bed. There were times when she seemed to be utterly exhausted. On several occasions she appeared to be near death.

But there was no sickness, no difficulty, no obstacle that could slow down her whirlwind pace. "While I am at work," she said, "I am well. I fall sick the instant I stop working." The reason lay in the fact that she was aflame with a burning love of God and fired with a consuming zeal for the welfare of souls. She wanted to win the whole world for Christ's kingdom on earth. That was the reason, too, why all her activity and travels did not interfere in the least with her life of continual prayer and intimate union with God.

She looked forward, it is true, to the time when she might retire and leave the direction of her sisterhood in other hands. But the opportunity of resigning from her position as mother general never came. In 1910 her admiring and loyal followers entered into a kind of conspiracy with Cardinal Vives y Tuto, prefect of the Sacred Congregation of Religious; and the cardinal disarmed her by saying: "Since you have done such a poor job in governing your sisterhood so far, we will give you another chance."

When Mother Cabrini left Rome in the spring of 1912, she was never again to set foot in her homeland. Early in 1913 she went to Seattle to procure a place for an orphanage; and in the summer she was in New York to establish another orphanage at Dobb's Ferry. In 1914 World War I broke out, and the following year Italy became involved in the conflict. From New York she traveled to Seattle in August, 1915; and by a shrewd business transaction on April 21, 1916, she acquired the Perry Hotel, which eventually became St. Frances Cabrini Hospital.

From Seattle she went to Los Angeles, and then to Chicago, arriving at Columbus Hospital on April 18, 1917. It was quite evident that she could no longer go on as she had been doing. While in South America in 1908, she had contracted malaria; and the fever was sapping her strength now.

However, she attended the spiritual exercises which were begun on July 4. In accordance with the doctor's orders, she was taken occasionally for a drive into the country. In October she bought a farm in Parkridge which would furnish supplies to the hospital. She continued to fail during November; and on the 21st she fainted after receiving Holy Communion in the chapel. She was carried to her room, but was up again later the same day.

The next day, December 22, 1917, she was too ill to get up from bed. Later in the day, she rang the bell at her door. The sisters came running and found her sitting in a wicker chair, blood on her gown and on the handkerchief she was holding to her mouth. She lapsed into unconsciousness, and the doctor was called as well as the priest. The latter gave her absolution and administered the sacrament of the anointing of the sick. Mother Cabrini did not regain consciousness and died peacefully and quietly.

Though a sickly person practically during her whole life, she reached the age of sixty-seven years. She had founded sixty-seven convents of her sisterhood in Europe and the Americas. By 1931 there were eighty foundations. Fourteen years after the death of the founder, two sisters went to China and began to work in the country to which Mother Cabrini had wanted to go as a missionary when she was a child.

Cardinal Mundelein officiated at Mother Cabrini's funeral in Chicago on December 27; and then her body was interred at West Park, New York. From there it was transferred in 1932 to Mother Cabrini High School in upper Manhattan.

The cause of her beatification was begun in Chicago on August 3, 1928. An exception was made to the rule requiring the lapse of fifty years after the death of a servant of God; and in 1937 the declaration was issued that Venerable Mother Cabrini had practiced the virtues in a heroic degree. The following year, a decade after her cause was commenced, she was beatified, the first United States citizen to receive that honor from the Church.

Cardinal Mundelein was present at her beatification; and in a sermon which was broadcast he said:

"I knew Mother Cabrini very well, first in the East, in New York, the place of her first missionary endeavor, later on in Chicago, where she made three different foundations. . . .

"When we comtemplate this frail little woman, in the short space of two-score years, recruiting an army of 4,000 women under the banner of the Sacred Heart of Jesus, dedicated to a life of poverty and self-sacrifice, fired by the enthusiasm of the Crusaders of old, burning with love of their fellowmen, crossing the seas, penetrating into unknown lands, teaching them and their children by word and example to become good Christians and law-abiding citizens, befriending the poor, teaching the ignorant, washing the sick, all without hope of reward or recompense here below — tell me, does not all this fulfill the concept of a noble woman?"

The solemn ceremony of Mother Cabrini's beatification was carried out by Pope Pius XI on November 13, 1938. A little more than five years later, on January 11, 1944, Pope Pius XII signed the decree of her canonization. Because of World War II, the actual ceremony did not take place until 1946. The feast of St. Frances Xavier Cabrini, formerly celebrated on December 22, now is observed in the United States on November 13.

The Missionary Sisters of the Sacred Heart (M.S.C.), who have their general motherhouse in Rome, in 1974 had 391 sisters in the United States, members of one province with houses in seven archdioceses and two dioceses.

Liturgical Prayer

O Lord Jesus Christ, you enkindled the fire of your Sacred Heart in the holy virgin Frances Xavier, so that she might win souls for you in many lands and establish a new religious congregation of women in your Church. Grant that through her intercession we may make our own the dispositions of your Sacred Heart and be worthy of the haven of eternal happiness: you who live and reign with God the Father in the unity of the Holy Spirit, God, forever and ever. Amen.

Part I
SAINTS AND BLESSED

CANADA'S saints and blessed are eight in number. Five canonized saints were Jesuit missionaries of New France who died as martyrs in the southern part of the province of Ontario. They, as well as Bl. Marguerite Bourgeoys, came from France; the other two blessed were natives of the province of Quebec. One of these was a martyr in France during the Revolution in that country. Two blessed were founders of new religious sisterhoods in Canada. The feast of the canonized Jesuit martyrs of North America is observed throughout Canada on the same day as in the United States, October 19.

CHAPTER 7

SAINTS AND BLESSED

Canada

St. John de Brébeuf, St. Anthony Daniel, St. Charles Garnier, St. Gabriel Lalemant and St. Noel Chabanel

(1648 and 1649) Martyrs of Huronia

THE real name of the Huron tribe of American Indians was the Wyandots. "Hurons" was a sobriquet given to them by the French. When, for the first time, one of Champlain's men saw some of these Indians with the furrowed hair of their heads standing up like the bristles of a boar, he exclaimed: "Quelle hure!" What a boar's head!

The Hurons were the original stock from which came their inveterate enemies, the Iroquois, who included five tribes in the present state of New York and were about 25,000 in number. According to Father Brébeuf, the Hurons numbered some 30,000 in 1636; but murderous attacks by the Iroquois and epidemics reduced them to less than 15,000 by the middle of the seventeenth century.

Up to that time the Hurons lived in villages which were situated for the most part in what is now Simcoe County in the Canadian province of Ontario. This region, called Huronia, is located at the southern end of Lake Huron's Georgian Bay. It is, therefore, a part of the Canadian "peninsula" which is bounded by the Great Lakes and extends farther south than Detroit, Michigan.

The first missionary to the Hurons was Father Joseph Le

84

Caron, one of the first Franciscans who came to New France in 1615 at the request of Samuel de Champlain. Because the Hurons were not nomads and had settled permanently in a definite area, it was thought that it would be less difficult to convert them to Christianity. Father Le Caron founded a mission in the Huron village of Ihonatiria in 1615, and remained for about a year.

The Company of One Hundred Associates which controlled New France was interested only in trade, not in establishing settlements and evangelizing the Indians. With Champlain, Father Le Caron returned to France in 1616 to remedy the situation. The monopoly of the Associates was broken; but the new Company of Merchants (the two Huguenot Caen brothers) was no better than the first.

In 1623 Father Le Caron returned to Huronia with Father Nicholas Viel and Brother Gabriel Sagard. For ten months they worked together and compiled a dictionary of the Huron language. With Brother Sagard, Father Le Caron then returned to Quebec, leaving Father Viel in charge of the mission.

Realizing that their work in New France was a task too great for them to carry out alone, the Franciscans invited the Jesuits to come to their aid. With Father Joseph de la Roche Dallion, five Jesuits (three priests and two brothers) arrived in 1625. One of the priests was Father John de Brébeuf. Father Le Caron made another voyage to France the same year, returning the following year with a Franciscan brother and three more Jesuits.

In the summer of 1625, Father Viel, going to the St. Lawrence to make his annual retreat, died a martyr at the Sault au Récollet. His place was taken in Huronia the following year by Father Joseph de la Roche Dallion and the two Jesuits, Father Brébeuf and Father Noué. The latter could not master the language and went back to Quebec. Together the other two continued the missionary work among the Hurons until 1629, except during the winter of 1626-1627, when Father de la Roche Dallion made an expedition to the Neutral Nation in western New York.

Their work was cut short in 1629, when the English seized the colony of New France and expelled both the Franciscans and the Jesuits. Three years later, when New France was given back to France, the Jesuits returned, but the Franciscans were prevented from resuming their work in New France until 1670. The situation in the reestablished colony was improved somewhat, because Cardinal Richelieu supplanted the Company of Merchants with a reorganized Catholic Company of One Hundred Associates.

One of the five Jesuits who arrived in 1632 was Father Anthony Daniel. The following year Father Brébeuf returned with an-

St. John de Brébeuf and four fellow Jesuit
missionaries died as martyrs in Huronia, Canada.

other new missionary. In 1634, their number was augmented by six, and the next year by seven more. Among the eight who arrived in 1636 were Father Isaac Jogues and Father Charles Garnier. These were joined in 1643 by Father Noel Chabanel, and in 1646 by Father Gabriel Lalemant. The six priests named here, with Father Jogues' two assistants, are the eight canonized Jesuit Martyrs of North America. All of them, except Father Jogues and his two companions, died in Huronia between July 4, 1648, and December 8, 1649.

Father John de Brébeuf came from a Norman family which counted Crusaders among its forbears. He was born on March 25, 1593, at Condé-sur-Vine, near Lisieux. After studying the classics, philosophy and moral theology, and devoting two years to each subject, he entered the Jesuit novitiate at Rouen in 1617. He was then twenty-four years old and in poor health, suffering from tuberculosis.

Unable to follow the regular courses of study or even to teach for any length of time, he was sent, after his novitiate of two years, to the recently opened house at Pontoise, where he completed his theological studies privately and leisurely. Four years later, in 1623, on the feast of the Annunciation which was transferred to April 4 that year, the invalid consumptive was ordained a priest at the age of thirty. A remarkable recovery followed, and Father John grew big and strong within a short time.

In 1635 he went to New France for the first time; and, after wintering with the Algonquins, he spent two years in the Huron mission of Ihonatiria, learning the language of the Indians and becoming acquainted with their customs, but not succeeding in winning a single adult convert. Expelled in 1629, he returned to New France in 1633, and the following year went back to Huronia with Father Anthony Daniel and Father Ambrose Davost, to become "the giant apostle of the Hurons." His second sojourn among these Indians lasted fourteen years, not including a year of rest in Quebec.

Father Anthony Daniel, a Norman like Father Brébeuf, was born at Dieppe on May 27, 1601. He had completed his course in rhetoric and philosophy and had begun to study law, when he decided at the age of twenty to become a Jesuit and entered the Society at the Rouen novitiate in 1621. His two-year novitiate was followed by a four-year term of teaching in the local college. He then went to Clermont College in Paris for theology, and in 1621 he was ordained a priest. For a short time he taught the classics once more at the college of Eu and with Father Brébeuf assisted the rector; in 1632 he departed for New France.

Father Charles Garnier was a Parisian, the son of wealthy parents. He was born on May 25, 1605. During his youth, as he himself said, "the Blessed Virgin carried me in her arms." As a student in the College of Clermont, he used the allowance he received from his parents to give relief to prisoners. At the age of nineteen he entered the Society of Jesus; and after his novitiate, he received his training at Clermont College. From 1629 to 1632 he was a teacher at Eu. Ordained a priest in 1635, he offered to go to New France; but his departure was delayed for a year because his aged father, a benefactor of the Jesuits, was reluctant to see him go. The following year he went with Father Isaac Jogues to New France.

Father Gabriel Lalemant, born October 10, 1610, was likewise a Parisian and the nephew of two other prominent missionaries of

New France, Father Charles Lalemant and Father Jerome Lalemant. Father Charles, the novice-master of Fathers Brébeuf, Daniel and Jogues, was in New France during the first period, 1625-1629. Father Jerome, his brother, succeeded Father Brébeuf as the superior of the Huron mission in 1638. At the end of his two-year novitiate, in 1632, Gabriel added a fourth vow to those of the religious life, promising to devote his life, with his superiors' permission, to the work of a missionary. However, his health was weak; and for the next fourteen years, after completing his studies, he was a teacher. For one year he was chaplain of the college of LaFlèche. Then for another year he taught philosophy at Moulins. From 1644 to 1646 he was director of studies at Bourges, and then left for New France and Huronia. A newcomer among the missionaries, he died a martyr less than three years later.

Father Noel Chabanel, the youngest of the martyrs, was born near Mende in southern France on February 2, 1613, and joined the Jesuits in 1630. During an interval of five years between his courses of philosophy and theology, he was engaged in teaching. He arrived in New France on August 15, 1643, after a voyage that lasted three months, and went on to Huronia. . . .

When Father Brébeuf returned to New France in 1633, he wanted to go back to Huronia the same year; but the Hurons who had come to Quebec to trade refused to take him along, because they were frightened by an Ottawa chief who raised objections.

The next year, however, the Hurons were accompanied on their return trip from Quebec by Fathers Brébeuf, Anthony Daniel and Ambrose Davost. On the journey, which usually lasted a month, the missionaries had to suffer much and were robbed and abandoned.

But they finally reached their destination, and the mission was reestablished at Ihonatiria, which now occupied a new site, the present Todd's Point. The Indians built a cabin for the three priests at this place, and Father Brébeuf taught his companions the Huron language. During the first three years, however, they were not able to baptize a single adult.

In 1636 Fathers Daniel and Davost took three Huron children to Quebec to start an Indian school, which never enjoyed success and had to be closed in 1639. Father Daniel returned to Huronia. Other Jesuits joined Father Brébeuf in the meantime, and during these years there was an average of five missionaries. Father Brébeuf had been appointed superior of the mission in 1634.

It was in 1636 also that the missionaries moved from Ihonatiria to Ossossané, and built a chapel of boards, eighty feet in length. They named it Conception Mission. The first adult convert was baptized the following year, and in 1638 there were eighty adult baptisms. In the latter year another mission was founded at Teanaustayé and named for St. Joseph.

Father Jerome Lalemant arrived in August of the same year as the newly appointed superior. He introduced an order of the day for the missionaries, now ten in number; and a central mission, Ste. Marie, was established at some distance from the Indian villages. It had a fort, hospital and cemetery. Father Lalemant was succeeded by Father Paul Ragueneau in 1646.

Thirty miles to the southwest Father Charles Garnier founded the Mission of the Apostles among the Tobacco Indians in 1641. By 1642 the number of missionaries had increased to twenty-four, and the Indians were accepting the faith in increasing numbers. There were now five main missions and thirty stations.

In 1640 the missionaries of Huronia began to make excursions to other tribes during the winter months. Thus Father Brébeuf and a companion traveled to the Neutral Nation who lived in New York, north of Lake Erie, the same Indians who had been visited by Father Joseph de la Roche Dallion sometime in 1626-1627.

They received no welcome; and on the homeward journey, which lasted twenty-five days, Father Brébeuf fell and broke a shoulder blade. The following year he went to Quebec for medical aid; and after a year of rest he returned to Huronia.

The work among the Hurons continued to enjoy a plentiful spiritual harvest; and if a period of peace had continued, the whole tribe might well have been converted. However, the irreconcilable Iroquois were determined to destroy their enemies, the Hurons. Their first attack was made as early as 1642, when they annihilated the village of Kontarea on the outskirts of Huronia. But it was only after the martyrdom of Father Isaac Jogues in the Mohawk village at Auriesville that the Iroquois carried out their design with relentless fury.

Martyrdom of Father Anthony Daniel

On July 4, 1648, the Iroquois suddenly attacked St. Joseph Mission in the village of Teanaustayé. Father Anthony was just finishing the celebration of Mass. Panic ensued in his Indian congregation, but he managed to find his way into their midst and baptized as many catechumens as possible. There were so many that he had to dip his handkerchief in water and administer the sacrament by aspersion. The Iroquois were fast becoming the masters, but Father Daniel gave no thought to escaping.

Remembering some old and sick Indians whom he had prepared for baptism, he went from cabin to cabin, conferring the sacrament on them and encouraging them to remain steadfast.

Going back to the church and finding it filled with Christians, he warned them to take to flight while there was still time. Then he went out to meet the Iroquois. He was immediately surrounded by them, and they showered their arrows upon him. The missionary fell to the ground, pierced in the breast. The invaders stripped his body and threw it into the church, to which they set fire. Satisfied with the havoc they had wrought, they departed.

Martyrdom of Fathers Brébeuf and Lalemant

The following year, on March 16, 1649, the Iroquois returned and attacked the Huron village where Father John de Brébeuf and his young assistant Father Gabriel Lalemant were stationed. The two missionaries were not killed outright but reserved for torture as extreme as any recorded in history.

They were stripped and beaten with sticks all over their bodies, but Father Brébeuf continued to exhort and encourage the Christian captives around him. One of the two priests had his hands cut off. Then the fiends applied hatchets, heated in fire, to their victims, placed red-hot lance blades around their necks, and ignited belts of bark steeped in pitch and tar.

Father Lalemant raised his eyes heavenward, and with sighs begged God for strength and courage; but Father Brébeuf gave no outward sign of the intense pain he was suffering, and he even began to preach to his persecutors as well as the Christian captives. The Iroquois silenced him by gagging his mouth, cutting off his nose and tearing off his lips.

In derision of baptism, they then poured boiling water upon the two priests. Lastly, while the two martyrs were still alive, they slashed large pieces of flesh from their bodies, roasted them, and devoured them. They put an end to these excruciating sufferings of the two Fathers by tearing out their hearts through an opening which they cut above their breasts. These too they ate.

Martyrdom of Father Charles Garnier

During the first week of December, 1649, the Iroquois made

90

Greg. Hnwi. f.

their final raid, this time on the Petun or Tobacco Indians' village of St. John, where Father Charles Garnier had founded a mission in 1641. Learning that the Iroquois were approaching, the village sent out its warriors to meet them. But the wily Iroquois, having extracted this information from some fugitives and knowing that there was no one left to defend the village itself, avoided the force sent against them and in a roundabout way reached the village and suddenly appeared at its gates.

A frenzied orgy of cruelty followed as the invaders mowed down women, children and the aged. Father Charles Garnier, the only priest at the village when the attack was made, hurried from place to place, giving absolution to the Christians and baptizing children and catechumens. He continued to do so until he was shot down by two bullets from a musket fired by one of the Iroquois.

Still breathing, the missionary made three fruitless attempts to crawl to the aid of a wounded man near him. He collapsed and a tomahawk blow, cleaving his skull, put an end to his life. After the departure of the invaders, some surviving neophytes buried the body of their missionary on the site where the church had stood.

Martyrdom of Father Noel Chabanel

When the Iroquois destroyed the Petun village of St. John, Father Noel Chabanel, Father Garnier's assistant, was absent; but he was on the way back to the town with some companions. They were so close to it that they could hear the cries of the poor people as they were being cut down by their bloodthirsty adversaries. Father Noel urged his fellow travelers to run away. He followed them, but soon he was too exhausted to keep up with them.

For a long time it remained uncertain whether he had escaped or had lost his life. Finally it was established as a fact that the missionary had been dispatched, not by an Iroquois, but by an apostate Huron. The wretch himself confessed that he had committed the foul deed out of hatred for the Christian faith. The date given for the martyrdom of Father Chabanel is December 8, 1649, and December 7 for that of Father Garnier.

During the Iroquois attacks in 1648 and 1649, a large number of Huron men were slaughtered and many women and children were carried off as prisoners. There was little left of the fifteen Huron villages and not many of the several thousands of neophytes remained. The missionaries who had not died as martyrs led the survivors to a place of safety near French settlements.

Later the Mission of St. Ignace with Ottawa and Huron villages was established on the north side of the Straits of Mackinac in the present state of Michigan, probably in 1670. Just north of St. Ignace a French fort was constructed in 1673, and a town of French settlers developed near the fort. As in other similar instances of the Church's history, the blood of martyrs became the seed of Christians.

The cause of the five Jesuit martyrs of Huronia as well as the three of Auriesville, New York, was commenced in the archdiocese of Quebec in 1904. Pope Pius XI beatified the eight martyrs in 1925 and canonized them in 1930. All of them are included in the feast of the Jesuit Martyrs of North America, which is observed on October 19.

Mission Sainte-Marie, the central mission from which the Jesuit missionaries attended the Huron villages, has been restored at present-day Midland by the government of Ontario. On a hill overlooking the restored mission stands the Martyrs' Shrine Church, built in 1926. Nearby, at Penetanguishene, is St. Anne's Church, which was built in 1902 in memory of the martyrdom of Fathers Brébeuf and Lalemant. In front of the latter church is a monument to Father Le Caron, first missionary to the Hurons. Relics of three of the Jesuit martyrs of Huronia are in the Chapel of the Congregation of Men on Dauphiné Street in Quebec City.

Liturgical Prayer

O God, you blessed the firstfruits of the faith in Canada by the missionary labors and martyrdom of blessed John, Anthony, Gabriel, Charles and Noel. May the harvest of Christians grow daily more abundant in the whole world through the intercession of these saints. Through Jesus Christ, your Son, our Lord, who lives and reigns with you in the unity of the Holy Spirit, God, forever and ever. Amen.

CHAPTER 8

SAINTS AND BLESSED

Canada

Bl. Marguerite Bourgeoys

(1620-1700) Founder of the Congregation de Notre Dame

THE *St. Nicholas,* an old sailing ship, set out from Nantes, France, to cross the Atlantic Ocean. The day was June 20, 1653. The destination was Ville Marie (the City of Mary), which had been founded about a decade earlier on the St. Lawrence River and is now called Montreal.

On board was forty-year-old Paul de Chomedy de Maisonneuve, founder and governor of Ville Marie, and 108 men whom he was taking to his little colony which had numbered only seventeen persons when he left it the previous year. Among the newcomers were soldiers, bakers, charcoal burners, smiths and shoemakers. They had agreed to remain at Ville Marie for at least five years, their expenses to be paid by the Company of Ladies and Gentlemen of Ville Marie.

There were also about a half dozen women, including a few who were married, several prospective brides, and thirty-three-year-old Marguerite Bourgeoys who was going along to become the teacher of the settlement's children.

They had been at sea for several days, when the leaks which appeared in the old vessel made it evident that it was not seaworthy. Forced to return to the port of St. Nazaire, they learned that the ship was beyond repair. On another ship they set sail once more on July 20, and after a voyage of sixty-three days they finally reached Quebec on September 22. During the crossing illness broke out among the passengers, and eight men died. Though she had no training as a nurse, Marguerite attended the sick with motherly care.

In Quebec the group received a warm welcome. The town was little more than a fort with a few little houses and an Ursuline convent. Among those who were waiting for them was Jeanne Mance, who with a companion had come to Ville Marie with the first colonists in 1642 and had founded a hospital, the Hôtel Dieu. The weary travelers remained at Quebec for a while; then after a further voyage of two weeks up the St. Lawrence, they reached Ville Marie in November.

With Jeanne, Marguerite resided for the present in the governor's house, serving as housekeeper, helping at the hospital, and chaperoning the girls who had come to marry settlers. They were wards of the king who paid their expenses and provided a dowry. Later too Marguerite continued to be a mother to such girls who were sent from France, and she trained them in housekeeping until they were married.

There were only a few children at Ville Marie when Marguerite arrived, but about four years later she opened the first school and eventually she became the founder of the first non-cloistered teaching sisterhood in Canada. Except for three journeys which she made to France to recruit additional co-workers, she remained at Ville Marie until her death almost a half century later. As Maisonneuve may be called the father of Montreal, so Marguerite Bourgeoys deservedly shares with Jeanne Mance the title of mother of the city.

Troyes, France, was her native city, as it was of Jeanne Mance; and Maisonneuve's sister was a cloistered nun in the same city and a close friend of Marguerite. The third of twelve children, Marguerite was born on Good Friday, April 17, 1620, and baptized the same day in the parish church of St. James of the March. Her parents were Abraham Bourgeoys and Guillemette née Garnier.

She was seventeen when her mother died shortly after giving birth to a daughter; and Marguerite became a second mother to the child. The thought of entering a convent had never entered her mind until she was twenty. Taking part in an outdoor procession in honor of Our Lady of the Rosary and passing a statue of the Blessed Virgin standing in the facade of a church, she was deeply moved when the statue seemed to her to be alive and bestowed on her individually a glance that was both sweet and sad. It was a turning point in her life, and she decided to give herself completely to the service of God.

She applied for admission in a Carmelite convent, but her request was not granted. Then she tried to enter a convent of Poor

Clares, but here too she was refused. For the present she contented herself with joining a group of lay women who served as externs for the convent of cloistered nuns in Troyes. After some
time she and two companions formed a little community of teachers and opened a school; but not long afterwards one of her associates married and the other died. The school had to be closed,
and Marguerite once more joined the externs.

From Sister Louise, Maisonneuve's sister, Marguerite
learned about the City of Mary which had been founded on the St.
Lawrence River. On his second voyage to the New World, in 1535,
Jacques Cartier had sailed up the river as far as the Lachine
Rapids, where there was an Indian village called Hochelaga. To
the eminence overlooking the site he gave the name of Mount
Royal or Montreal. Not until 1608 was the fort and town of Quebec
founded by Samuel de Champlain. Little progress was made in
the occupation of the valley of the St. Lawrence River during the
three and a half decades which followed.

The Company of One Hundred Associates, which was in control, included Protestants as well as Catholics; and this circum-
stance did not contribute to a unified effort. The Company was
more interested in exploiting their trading rights and making a
profit than in promoting colonization. The Company of Merchants
which supplanted it in 1616 was not much better; and when Cardinal Richelieu reorganized the One Hundred Associates in 1632,
there was only a slight improvement.

At Champlain's request, four Franciscans arrived in 1615 as
the first missionaries on the St. Lawrence River and among the
Huron Indians. They were subsequently joined by others, and in
1625 by some Jesuits. Four years later both the Franciscans and
the Jesuits were driven out of New France by the English, and
France temporarily lost its New World colony. When it was restored in 1632, only the Jesuits were permitted to return and to
devote themselves primarily to the conversion of the various
tribes of Indians.

About a decade later, however, Father Jean Jacques Olier,
the founder of the Sulpicians, and other zealous Catholics in Paris
organized another company which had for its sole purpose the establishment of a Catholic settlement in New France; and they offered to do this at their own expense. As the Company of Ladies
and Gentlemen of Ville Marie, they received a charter from the
king and were permitted to select their own governor.

They purchased the Island of Montreal from the One
Hundred Associates, and Maisonneuve, a young man of high
ideals who sought no personal gain, was chosen governor. With

96

*Bl. Marguerite Bourgeoys lived in
Montreal, 1653 to 1700.*

his small party of pioneers, he arrived at the foot of Mount Royal on May 18, 1642, and there founded Ville Marie.

It was no more than a small and slow beginning; and in January, 1653, Maisonneuve was back in France to enlist additional colonists. He paid a visit to Sister Louise in Troyes, and told her he was looking for a young woman who would be willing to devote herself to teaching the children of his colony — only one for the present, because there were only a few children. Sister Louise recommended Marguerite Bourgeoys, and after Marguerite had asked the advice of several priests she consented.

After reaching Ville Marie, she taught catechism and trained the king's wards to become good housewives, besides helping at the hospital; but it was not until April 30, 1658, that Marguerite was able to open a school for seven children in a little house of fieldstone, eighteen by twenty-six feet. It had formerly been used as a stable. The bare ground was its floor, and it had a loft reached by an outside ladder. Its windows were covered with oiled paper.

The school was also the home of the teacher, who was now called Sister Bourgeoys. She wore a long black dress and a white kerchief and bonnet. With her lived three little Indian girls who were added to the pupils. On Sundays and holy days Sister Bourgeoys instructed the future brides who continued to come from France.

Soon the school children would increase considerably in number, and additional teachers would be needed. Jeanne Mance also needed more assistants at the Hôtel Dieu. Together the two pioneers left for France in late September, 1658; and in June of the following year, each began the return voyage with three recruits. In Marguerite's care were also a dozen girls, future brides of settlers in Quebec and Montreal. There was also a young man, called Brother Louis, who volunteered to teach the boys at Ville Marie. The party included several Sulpician priests and seven families who were emigrating to New France.

The crossing of the Atlantic on the *St. André* took two months. A violent storm almost wrecked the ship on the way. Sickness broke out among the 200 passengers. Almost all, including Marguerite, were ill for a time; and some of the future brides died. It was October, 1660, when the travelers finally reached Ville Marie.

Some 400 people were now living at the settlement; and it was made a parish, with the Sulpicians in charge. Now that she had a few assistants, Marguerite not only conducted the little day school with an occasional boarder, but also opened a vocational school. She and her fellow teachers began to live like a religious community and to observe a provisional rule of life without, however, taking any vows. The little stone house was their convent as well as their school.

In 1661, since the school was too small, an adjoining house was acquired, and another small house was built for the prospective brides. Several years later, when there were about 100 school children, a new and larger stone house was built for the teachers, boarders and servants. Though the teachers did not bind themselves by the vows, they practiced them.

On May 20, 1669, Bishop Francois de Montmorency Laval, who had come to Quebec as vicar apostolic ten years earlier, recognized Sister Bourgeoys' group as a religious community, the Daughters of the Congregation, with common ownership of the property they held. And he granted them permission to teach throughout New France in whatever place to which they were asked to come.

The following year, Marguerite made her second trip back to France, arriving at La Rochelle at the end of November. This time she obtained the official approval of the king for her congregation and enlisted nine new members.

Taking along a statue of Our Lady of Montaigu, she was back at Ville Marie by September, 1672, almost two years after she had left. France was at war with England at the time; and on the return voyage they had sighted four English men-of-war; but they prayed to our Lady and did not encounter any of the enemy warships.

Sister Bourgeoys and her associates adopted a uniform black dress, with a black belt and veil, and a white linen cornette and kerchief. It was very much like the contemporary peasant dress of Champagne, except that the ends of the veil were tied under the chin.

At Marguerite's request, Bishop Laval in 1676 raised her community to the status of a congregation of secular sisters by authorizing them to take simple vows or promises and to open a novitiate; but he postponed giving them a definite rule until later. They received the name they had chosen, the Congregation de Notre Dame of Montreal.

The community now had some fifteen members; and a number of Canadian girls, including a few Indians, were admitted. A boarding school for girls was opened in 1677, and several small day schools were begun as new settlements were established. The Sulpicians founded an Indian mission on Mount Royal, and the sisters undertook to teach the Indian children, about 100 in number.

A project for which Marguerite had been working for a long time was finally realized when the cornerstone of the little stone church of Notre Dame de Bon Secours was laid in June, 1675, and completed three years later. It was the first stone church in Montreal.

In November, 1679, Mother Marguerite, now in her sixtieth year, set out on her third trip to France. Bishop Laval was in Paris at the time, trying in vain to obtain from the king a decree prohibiting the sale of liquor to the Indians of New France. Taking along the draft of a rule prepared by Abbé Gendret, she wanted to make another attempt to obtain the bishop's approval. Her sisters were now established in five different places, but they had only a provisional rule. It was only her leadership as founder and superior which held them together, and she was beginning to think that a change in superiors was desirable.

Not only did the bishop give her a negative answer, but he also forbade her to recruit any new sisters in France. Disappointed but not disheartened, Mother Marguerite returned to Montreal with a group of prospective brides and the old servant of Maisonneuve who offered his services to her. The founder of Montreal had been recalled in the 1660s and had died at his home in Paris.

On December 6, 1683, a great misfortune befell Mother Marguerite and her sisters, when their new building burned to the ground and two sisters perished in the flames. Temporarily they found lodging in their old houses and at the Hôtel Dieu until a new motherhouse was constructed.

Bishop Laval came to Montreal in 1684 and urged Mother Marguerite to merge her community with the Ursulines in Quebec. But recognizing the need for teachers in the parishes of the colony, she remained firm in her conviction that her sisters should not be bound by the strict enclosure and should take only simple vows.

Bishop Jean Baptiste de Saint Vallier succeeded Bishop Laval in 1685, and he finally consented to Mother Marguerite's repeated request to be relieved of the superiorship. Elections were held in 1693, and Sister Marie Barbier was chosen superior, while Mother Marguerite was made one of the counselors and "admonisher."

During the forty years which had elapsed since her arrival at Ville Marie, she had been engaged in heroic pioneer work. Her sisterhood, now numbering forty members, was established in seven different places, as far distant as Quebec.

The following year, the two stone towers of the fort on Mount Royal were given to the sisters, one serving as their residence and the other as classrooms of their Indian school. These two towers are still standing on the grounds of Montreal College. The Indian school was moved to Sault au Récollet in 1701, and to Lake of Two Mountains in 1720.

At long last, on June 24, 1698, the Congregation de Notre Dame received episcopal approbation for a definite rule which embodied the ideals of its founder. A few days later, the sisters made their profession, taking the four simple vows of poverty, chastity, obedience and commitment to the work of teaching girls. Each received a religious name, that of Mother Marguerite being Sister Marguerite of the Blessed Sacrament. Thus the founder had the happiness of seeing her sisterhood firmly established.

The last years of her life, Mother Bourgeoys spent in retirement and prayer. Not quite eighty years old, she died on January 12, 1700. By her holy life and her many years of unstinted service in the vineyard of the Lord, she had contributed no small measure to the firm establishment of the faith in so-called French Canada.

Regarded as a saint by the grateful settlers in the St. Lawrence valley, she received the title of "Venerable" on December 7, 1878. The official declaration that she had practiced the virtues in an heroic degree was made June 19, 1910; and the solemn ceremony of her beatification by Pope Pius XII took place in Rome on November 12, 1950. Her feast is observed on the anniversary of her death, January 12.

When Bl. Marguerite Bourgeoys died in 1700, her sisterhood had fifty-four members. It continued to grow after her death, and by 1956 it had nearly 4,000 sisters in 262 houses, not only in Canada, but also in the United States, Japan, Honduras, Guatemala and Chile.

The first foundation in the United States was made in 1860; and in 1946 it became a province, with headquarters at the motherhouse and novitiate in Ridgefield, Connecticut. With a membership of 342, this province of the "Sisters of the Congregation de Notre Dame" (C.N.D.), with general headquarters in Montreal, is represented in nine different United States archdioceses and dioceses, and also in Guatemala.

Liturgical Prayer

O Lord, pour out the Spirit of your love upon us. Through the prayers of blessed Marguerite, grant us the grace to spurn earthly things, so that we may seek you alone, O God, with pure hearts. Through Jesus Christ, your Son, our Lord, who lives and reigns with you in the unity of the Holy Spirit, God, forever and ever. Amen.

CHAPTER 9

SAINTS AND BLESSED
Canada

Bl. Marie Marguerite d'Youville
(1701-1771) Founder of the Grey Nuns

IN Montreal, Canada, in 1737, there was a young widow of thirty-six, Madame d'Youville, living alone in her home with her eight-year-old son Charles. Her other son, Francois, had just entered the Sulpician seminary in Quebec. After an unhappy marriage to an unprincipled husband, who died seven years earlier and left her with heavy debts, she had placed herself under the spiritual direction of a saintly Sulpician priest and found solace and strength in a life of total dedication to the practice of her holy religion.

Since she desired to devote the rest of her life to the exercise of the works of mercy, her spiritual director advised her to take poor and helpless people into her home and to provide for their needs. She soon found that this was a project which required the cooperation of others, and she persuaded three other pious young women to join her. The following year, they bound themselves to a life of service to the needy and began to live together.

Through no fault of her own, the bad reputation of Francois, her husband, who had been a swindler and wastrel and drunkard, still clung to the widow d'Youville. The people looked askance at the new and unusual activities in which she and her associates were engaged. Was it not a front to hide the illegal sale of liquor to the Indians, the same business that had been her husband's source of income? Regarding their unfounded suspicion as a fact, they heaped insults on Madame d'Youville and her companions

*Bl. Marie Marguerite d'Youville, a native of
Canada, died at the age of seventy in 1771.*

when they appeared in public and branded them with the opprobrious name of *les Soeurs Grises* — "the Tipsy Sisters."

Undaunted, the four "Tipsy Sisters" continued their charitable work. Their number increased, and eventually they were officially organized as the Sisters of Charity. Popularly they were still known as "les Soeurs Grises," but the name had now become one of respect and admiration. The French word "gris" also means "grey," and, with a sense of humor perhaps, Mother d'Youville had adopted a grey religious habit for her religious congregation. The former "Tipsy Sisters" were now the "Grey Nuns," and the Grey Nuns have won for themselves an enviable reputation as "angels of charity," not only in Canada, but also in other parts of the world.

The eldest of six children, three girls and three boys, Marie Marguerite was the daughter of Christophe Dufrost de Jemmerais and Marie Renée, née Gaultier, the sister of Pierre de la Laverendrye, the discoverer of the Rocky Mountains. She was born on October 15, 1701, at Varennes, near Montreal. Her father died in 1708 when she was seven years old.

Though still a mere child, Marie Marguerite gladly and efficiently undertook to help her mother care for the other children and earn a livelihood for the family. To his bereaved family, the father had left only the house where they lived and a small farm. He had not been able to lay aside anything for the future, and there was no such thing as insurance of any kind. The widow and her little children tilled the soil and raised maize, wheat, beans, potatoes and peas. At least they had enough to eat.

At the school of the Ursulines in Quebec there was a relative among the nuns, and Marie Marguerite went there when she was eleven to receive an education; but after two years she came back. Her mother needed her too much at home. She was tall for her age and looked older than she was. Wasting no time or material or words, she soon displayed a remarkable ability to make a little go a long way, a gift which later on served her in good stead.

After some years the family was able to move from Varennes to Montreal, and Marie Marguerite had more time to devote to social life. She soon became popular among the young people of the capital; and on August 12, 1722, at the age of twenty-one, she married Francois d'Youville, a well-to-do young man who had advantageous connections with the governor-general of New France. They resided in the home of Francois' mother, but the marriage turned out to be an unhappy one.

Despite the fact that her mother-in-law was an envious and domineering person and her husband was a selfish man who showed little regard for her wishes and needs, Marie Marguerite tried hard to make the best of the situation; but all her efforts and patience were in vain. She became the mother of six children, only two of whom, Francois and Charles, reached manhood. Both of them became priests.

Far from becoming embittered by her sorrows and trials, she learned to sanctify them as a member of the Confraternity of the Holy Family; and her crosses became for her a means of drawing closer to Christ. Her constant prayer was: "Lord, make known to me the way I should walk!"

After eight years of married life, her husband died of "acute inflammation of the lungs," which he seems to have brought on himself by his dissipated life. He left her, not only without funds, but with a debt of about 11,000 pounds and the stigma of a bad name. At twenty-nine she was a destitute widow with two little boys. Her house and belongings were sold.

To gain a livelihood for herself and her children, she opened a small shop; and because she was a competent as well as an honest business woman, the store prospered. In a few years she was able not merely to provide for her needs, but also to pay off all her late husband's debts and to give her sons a good education. She even found it possible to give generous aid to the poor.

However, personal service to the needy and the sick was her ideal, and she became a regular visitor at the General Hospital in Montreal which was then in a sad and neglected condition. She looked after the poor sick and aged, alleviated their needs, cleaned their rooms, mended their clothes. On November 21, 1737, she converted her own house into a home for the poor and then enlisted the help of three other noble-minded women. That marked the beginning of a new religious sisterhood — the Grey Nuns.

Many were the difficulties and crosses which the little group encountered during the first years; but relying completely on divine assistance, they persevered in their program no matter how insuperable the obstacles seemed to be. As the widow of the despised d'Youville, Marie Marguerite was not accepted even as a social worker. She and her companions were insulted and pelted with stones in the streets; and they were publicly refused Holy Communion.

Their first house was gutted by fire. They moved to another and were immediately evicted from it. Death thinned their ranks, but others joined them. Eventually the attitude of the people toward them and their work changed, and their true worth was recognized.

By 1745 they were formally established as a religious community of Sisters of Charity; but it was not until they had received the necessary royal sanction in 1753 that Bishop Pontbriand gave his approval on June 15, 1755, to the rule which had been drawn up for them by Father Normant.

The General Hospital of Montreal, founded in 1694 by M. Charon, had been in the care of a brotherhood named for the founder. It was heavily in debt; and to prevent it from going under, the hospital was entrusted to Mother Marie Marguerite and her companions in 1747, though they were still living under a provisional rule.

To save the hospital, M. Bigot, the intendant, with the assent of Bishop Pontbriand, transferred the title to its property to the young community; and Mother Marie Marguerite assumed the entire debt of 49,000 livres. This was a bold undertaking, but the founder had unlimited confidence in God as her Father, a distinguishing mark of her spiritual life.

She even increased the debt by repairing a part and rebuilding the rest of the hospital, and then opening it to the sick of every kind — the incurable, the insane, the aged of both sexes, disabled soldiers, epileptics, lepers and others suffering from contagious diseases, and even foundlings and orphans. No one was excluded. Her foundling home was the first in North America.

To defray the debt, the superior herself spent long hours making clothing for the king's stores and the traders of the upper country. The income received from the sale of these clothes was one of the hospital's chief sources of revenue. At the same time she bought several farms to support 118 needy persons, taught catechism to the farmers' children, introduced closed retreats for women, and helped needy seminarians.

During the Old French and Indian War, the counterpart in the colonies of the Seven Years' War in Europe, 1755-1763, Mother Marie Marguerite, with her sisters, continued her work at the hospital and even increased it. At a great price she ransomed from the Indians an English prisoner whom they were on the point of torturing and she saved a number of fugitives from the Indians' fury. One of the latter, conscious of his debt of gratitude, subsequently prevented the bombardment of the fortress-like hospital.

For Canada the war ended with Wolfe's victory over Montcalm on the plains of Abraham and the capitulation of Quebec in 1760. Bishop Pontbriand withdrew from Quebec to the house of the Sulpicians in Montreal.

Though the Treaty of Paris in 1763, which gave Canada to Great Britain, provided that the Canadians should enjoy "the free exercise of their religion, as far as is permissible under the laws of Great Britain," a persecution of the Church followed. The Franciscans, Jesuits and Sulpicians were forbidden to receive any new members into their ranks.

However, the British permitted thirty-four priests who had been driven out of France to settle in Canada. Twelve of these, who were Sulpicians, founded the College of Montreal in 1767. The previous year, the General Hospital in Montreal was

106

destroyed by fire. Valiant woman that she was, Mother Marie Marguerite accepted the catastrophe as having been permitted by the good Father in heaven. She knelt down with her sisters and prayed the *Te Deum*. The hospital rose again from its ashes, as did the establishment of Mother Bourgeoys' Congregation de Notre Dame which had likewise been consumed by the flames.

This was done despite the fact that at the time of the conquest the hospital was burdened with a big debt on account of the high cost of living and the prevailing unscrupulous corruption. The 100,000 livres which the French government owed the hospital was paid with interest only under Louis XVIII, after Napoleon had met his Waterloo in 1815.

Long before that time Mother Marie Marguerite had gone to her eternal reward. Continuing her ministrations to the sick until she suffered a partial paralysis, she died after a short illness on December 23, 1771, at the age of seventy. All felt sure that a saint had sojourned in their midst.

After the death of the founder, the Grey Nuns spread throughout Canada and into the neighboring United States. Eventually they undertook missionary work among the Eskimos of Alaska, and in China, Africa and Haiti, conducting not only hospitals, but also schools and orphanages.

In the United States the "Sisters of Charity, Grey Nuns" (S.G.M.), with headquarters in Quebec, made their first foundation in 1855. Today (1974) they have a United States province of 140 professed members with a motherhouse at Lexington, Massachusetts. This province is represented in the archdiocese of Boston and four dioceses and has missionaries in Nigeria, West Africa.

The cause of Mother Marie Marguerite's beatification was introduced, and the decree conferring on her the title of "Venerable" was signed April 28, 1890. Good Pope John XXIII beatified her on May 3, 1959.

Liturgical Prayer

O almighty and merciful God, you inflamed blessed Marie Marguerite with such a love of yourself that her wondrous strength of soul led her in the way of perfection in every walk of life. May her merits and prayers bring us grace from heaven to overcome every temptation, for we are conscious of our own frailty and trust solely in your strength. Through Jesus Christ, your Son, our Lord, who lives and reigns with you in the unity of the Holy Spirit, God, forever and ever. Amen.

CHAPTER 10

SAINTS AND BLESSED

Canada

Bl. Andrew Grasset de St. Sauveur

(1758-1792) Canadian Martyr in France

AMONG those who left New France when it became the British Dominion of Canada by the Treaty of Paris, 1763, was a man in his early forties who had held important positions in the government of the French colony, Andrew Grasset de St. Sauveur. With his second wife, Marie-Josephine Quesnel-Fonblanche, now with child, and five little children ranging in age from two to ten, he departed from Montreal early in November of 1764. After a rough voyage, during which they weathered a violent storm lasting sixty hours, they landed safely at Calais, France, on December 9.

Two of the children had the same name as their father. The older of the two, six years old, later became a priest, and was one of the 191 martyrs who were brutally murdered by a mob in the former Carmelite monastery of Paris during the early days of the French Revolution.

Andrew Grasset, Sr., was a young lawyer, twenty-eight years old, when he came to New France in 1749 as secretary to the newly appointed governor, M. de la Jonquière. The following year he was also appointed a member of the Supreme Council. After the death of La Jonquière in 1752, Andrew Grasset, Sr., settled in Montreal, started a business firm, and married Marie-Anne Nolan de la Marque. At the same time he served as the secretary to the governor or mayor of Montreal, M. de Vaudreuil. He retained that position also after Vaudreuil was promoted to the post of governor of New France in 1755.

In the same year, his young wife died; she had been the mother of two daughters, one of whom died in infancy. The following year he married a second time, and five boys were born in their home at the Place du Marche in Montreal. The first was Jacques, born in 1757; and the second, born April 3, 1758, received his father's name Andrew when he was baptized in the old Notre Dame Church which is no longer standing.

About four months after his return to France, Andrew Grasset, Sr., was imprisoned in the Bastille. In September, 1762, three years after the surrender of Quebec, a committee had been appointed to investigate the administration of Governor Vaudreuil; and fifteen months later it issued a verdict, declaring that fifty-five persons associated with him had been guilty of maladministration and corruption. Andrew Grasset, Sr., was one of them. His defense lawyer showed that the charges were false, and the prisoner was released.

Returning to his family at Calais, he once more took up the work of a businessman and was able to provide a good education for his children. Although his imprisonment left a stain on his reputation, he had influential friends in France, and in 1772 he was appointed French consul at Trieste. At this time he gave up his business connections in Calais and established a home for his family at Sens, some sixty miles southeast of Paris.

In 1780 Grasset was promoted to the office of consul in Venice. Two of his sons, Jacques and the younger of the two Andrews, likewise entered the diplomatic service. The latter, referred to as Andrew, Jr., II, at the age of twenty, became chancellor for his father when he moved to Venice. In 1787 he was appointed vice-consul, and in 1789 he succeeded his father as consul.

Meanwhile Andrew, Jr., I, had begun his studies for the priesthood. At the age of twenty-one, while still in minor orders, he received a benefice on August 28, 1779, as "chaplain of the chapel at Saint-Eutrope in Sens." After his ordination to the diaconate, March 20, 1781, he was made a canon of the cathedral, his title being Canon of St.-Pierre, that is, of the altar of St. Peter in the cathedral. His promotion to the priesthood was followed by his appointment as one of the canons and guardians of the cathedral's *Trésor*, the place where its art treasures were kept. This benefice he retained until the Revolution.

The Constituent Assembly, which convened in 1789, enacted the "Civil Constitution of the Clergy" at the end of the following year. Drawn up at the instigation of Jansenist lawyers, it tried to set up a schismatic Church in France, independent of the papacy. It set new boundaries to the dioceses in France, gave all voters the right to nominate parish priests and bishops, ordered the metropolitans to take charge of the canonical installation of their suffragans, and forbade the bishops to seek confirmation in office from the pope. All priests were required to swear that they would abide by the Constitution.

By two briefs, Pope Pius VI condemned the Constitution, and most of the bishops and priests rejected it. A persecution of the clergy followed. On November 29, 1791, the "unsworn" priests were ordered to take an oath of allegiance within a week, under pain of having their allowances stopped and being held as suspects. This was done by the more radical Legislative Assembly which succeeded the Constituent Assembly in October, 1791. The next year, on August 26, it banished the refractory priests from France and declared those who remained to be liable to ten years' imprisonment in France or transportation to Guiana in South America. A decree suppressing all religious orders and congregations whose members took vows had been issued by the Constituent Assembly on February 13, 1790.

With other priests in Sens, Canon Andrew Grasset found a place of refuge in the house of the Eudist Fathers in Paris. It would probably have been safer for him to stay with the members of his family in Sens, but he preferred to remain in the company of fellow priests. Many other priests joined them at the house of the Eudists. They spent their time in religious exercises and recollection, hoping that the evil days would pass and normal conditions would permit them to return to their posts.

However, the situation grew more menacing. One day, the gendarmes entered the house and took all its inmates to the monastery of the Carmelites which had been converted into a prison. There seemed to be no doubt that the prisoners were doomed to death, though the Reign of Terror had not yet begun. They prepared themselves for the sacrifice of their lives by going to confession and by prayer.

At two in the afternoon on September 2, 1792, the church bell of St. Sulpice was rung. In the church a proclamation was announced: "All those who are prisoners in the Carmelite monastery are guilty!" Led by Maillard, a mob, armed with guns, pikes and clubs, rushed to the monastery-prison and began to massacre the priests in cold blood. In the midst of the carnage Maillard bethought himself of giving it some semblance of judicial procedure. He set up a makeshift tribunal, and the prisoners who were still alive were brought before him.

"Are you willing to take the oath of allegiance?" he asked them. One and all replied: "No! My conscience forbids me to do

Baron Francois Gerard's painting of the French Revolution depicts the Paris insurrection of August 10, 1792.

so." A sign from the leader, and they were hustled to the outer stairway near the entrance. Here they were pierced with bayonets, sabers and pikes until all of them were dead. The bodies of some of the martyrs were thrown into a well at one end of the monastery garden; the others were cast into trenches at the four corners of the city.

In this way, three bishops and 188 priests — one of them Bl. Andrew Grasset de St. Sauveur — won the martyr's crown. Pope Pius VI spoke of them as "a choir of martyrs."

Canon Andrew Grasset's father and mother were still living at the time of his glorious death. They lost all their possessions in the Revolution and were reduced to a state of destitution. His father, who had returned to France in 1789, died a ruined man five years later in the Hospice of Incurables. His mother seems to have survived her husband for a short time and ended her days in abject poverty, living and dying in an attic.

Jacques, his oldest brother, who was vice-consul in Hungary in 1793 and subsequently in the Levant, came back to France while the Revolution was still in progress, and later became the author of many books. Andrew, Jr., II, was in Venice during the Revolution, served in the diplomatic service under Napoleon, and retired in 1817 to Sezanne, France.

In some lists of the martyrs of 1792, the name of Grasset appears twice. The second Grasset may have been Canon Andrew Grasset's youngest brother Bernard, who was born in France in 1766; he would have been twenty-four years old. Canon Grasset was thirty-four at the time of his martyrdom.

The cause of beatification of the 191 martyrs was begun on March 14, 1901. Pope Pius XI solemnly beatified them on October 17, 1926. Today, in the crypt of the Carmelite church in Paris, there is a tomb containing some of the bones of the blessed martyrs. Among the names which are inscribed on the plaque which lists the martyrs is the very appropriate one: "Bl. Andrew of Montreal."

In Montreal, the church where Bl. Andrew was baptized has disappeared, but on its site was built the present magnificent Church of Notre Dame. Since December, 1926, an altar in this church honors the memory of Bl. Andrew Grasset de St. Sauveur; and to it come descendants of the early French settlers, as staunch today in their faith as their forbears, to venerate and to invoke the intercession of the blessed martyr who lived as a child for six years in the city of Montreal. In Montreal, the feast of Bl. Andrew Grasset is observed on September 2.

Liturgical Prayer

O God, you rewarded your martyr, blessed Andrew, with the crown of eternal glory for his valiant defense of the faith. Through his merits and example, may we share his crown in heaven by our brave struggle on earth. Through Jesus Christ, your Son, our Lord, who lives and reigns with you in the unity of the Holy Spirit, God, forever and ever. Amen.

Part I
SAINTS AND BLESSED

Cuba

CUBA was still a Spanish possession — Spain's only remaining colony in the New World — when a saint lived and worked there as archbishop of Santiago in the middle of the nineteenth century. He came from Spain and returned to Spain, and died an exile in France. He narrowly escaped becoming a martyr in Cuba. Like the great Spanish saints and missionaries of a former era, St. Anthony Mary Claret was an outstanding apostolic worker at home and abroad. He was also the founder of a new religious congregation, the Claretian Missionaries.

CHAPTER 11
SAINTS AND BLESSED
Cuba

St. Anthony Mary Claret
(1807-1870) Founder of the Claretians

A POOR little archbishop from Spain was one of the last to speak when the discussions on papal infallibility were drawing to a close at the First Vatican Council in 1870. He had no money. He was only five feet, one inch tall.

On his face there was a big scar, the result of an almost deadly wound inflicted on him by a hired assassin in Cuba fourteen years earlier. He had come from France, where he had been an exile since the Spanish Revolution of 1868.

He looked much older than his sixty-two years. A short time before, he had suffered a stroke at one of the sessions of the Council. It happened when he had to listen to the attacks made on papal infallibility by a minority of the 700 prelates, including the cardinal archbishop of Vienna and the bishop of Rottenburg.

As he himself wrote, "The nonsense, and even the blasphemies and heresies which they uttered roused my indignation and zeal to such a pitch that the blood rushed to my head in a cerebral attack." But he returned to the Council sessions as soon as he had recovered sufficiently.

On May 31 he mounted the rostrum to give a brief Latin address. His condition did not permit him to speak at length, and there was no need for it. But what he said was clear and to the point:

"I am here to say that, from long study of Holy Scripture, of a tradition never once ruptured, of the words of the Fathers of the

114

St. Anthony Mary Claret was archbishop of Santiago, Cuba, 1851 to 1857.

Church and the Sacred Councils, from deep meditation on the reasoning of the theologians which for the sake of brevity I shall not cite, I can with full conviction assure you that, in everything touching the sense and forms of the Apostolic Roman Catholic Church, the Supreme Roman Pontiff is infallible. . . ."

He concluded his remarks with these words: "The truth of papal infallibility would be clear to all men if Scripture were understood. And why is it not? For three reasons. The first, as Jesus told St. Teresa, is that men do not really love God. The second is that they lack humility. . . . The third and last is the fact that some do not wish to understand Scripture, simply because they do not wish what is good. Now, with David, I pray, 'May the Lord have mercy on us, bless us, and let his holy countenance shine upon us.' I have spoken."

When the vote was taken in July, he was one of the 451 prelates who voted *placet* (yes). Of the others out of the 601 present, 62 voted *placet juxta modum* (a qualified yes), and 88 *non placet* (no).

The poor little Spanish archbishop, a sick but happy man, returned to France and died two days after the First Vatican Council was adjourned on October 22 because of the Franco-Prussian War. Canonized in 1950, he is now St. Anthony Mary Claret.

Born on Christmas eve, 1807, at Sallent in Catalonia, northern Spain, and baptized on Christmas Day, Antonio was the fifth of the eleven children of Juan Claret and Josepha Clara. Five of the children died before 1825. From his pious parents Antonio received a good Catholic upbringing; and even as a child he gave

115

serious thought to the meaning of "eternity." At the age of ten he received his First Holy Communion.

Since the boy expressed the desire of becoming a priest, his father took him to a priest who began to give him lessons in Latin; but this teacher soon died. Antonio now learned the art of weaving in a small textile mill owned by his parents; and at the age of fifteen or sixteen he took over the direction of the mill. With the employees, he daily prayed the fifteen decades of the Rosary.

At seventeen, he went with his brother Juan to Barcelona to learn all he could about the textile industry as well as drawing, Castilian and French. So deeply did he become engrossed in his work that he no longer thought of becoming a priest, and found it difficult to concentrate on his prayers. Though he became skilled in the manufacture of cloth, he somehow could not bring himself to make a definite choice of such activity as his life's work.

One day, while wading along the beach, he was suddenly swept out to sea by a big wave. He could not swim and would surely have drowned. But he called upon the Mother of God to save him, and she did so by a miracle. He found himself back on the shore, safe and sound. Not even his clothes were wet.

This and other happenings made him lose his interest in the successful business career that beckoned to him. He experienced a longing to become a Carthusian monk. However, a priest to whom he went for advice, counseled him to take up the study of Latin while continuing his factory work. He did this, and in nine months he had mastered Latin to such an extent that he could speak it fluently.

Meanwhile his brother Juan had married the daughter of a man who administered some property of the Bishop of Vich. Hearing about Antonio, the bishop sent for him. The young man, now in his twenty-second year, went to Vich; and the bishop invited him to study at the seminary in that city and offered him lodging in the house of one of the priests.

Antonio still entertained the desire of joining the Carthusians; and less than a year later he was on the way to the monastery at Monte Alegre. When he reached Barcelona, he encountered a severe storm; and unaccountably it made him realize that God wanted him to be a priest engaged in the active ministry. He returned to Vich and gave all his attention to his studies. In the same house where he was staying there was a fellow student who afterwards gained distinction as an author and philosopher — the famous Jaime Luciano Balmes.

While he was a seminarian at Vich, the bloody civil war between the Cristinas and the Carlistas broke out in 1833. One hundred priests were massacred in Madrid by the radicals among the Cristinas. Though he had not as yet completed his studies, Antonio was ordained a priest on June 13, 1835. He received the faculties to preach and hear confession and was sent to his native town to assist the pastor and to complete his studies privately. On October 29, 1837, he succeeded the pastor of Sallent, and for some two years he carried out his new duties in an exemplary manner.

However, his zeal for souls was not satisfied with taking care of a single town; and he received permission to go to Rome and offer his services to the Sacred Congregation of the Propagation of the Faith. Failing to receive a passport, he succeeded in crossing the French border and traveled from Marseilles to Rome by boat.

While making a retreat at Monte Cavallo, he accepted an invitation to join the Jesuits and entered the novitiate on November 2, 1839. In February of the following year, he was stricken with such great pain in his leg that he could no longer walk. The father general of the Jesuits advised him to return to Spain, and by the middle of March he was back in Catalonia. In May he arrived at Viladrau as regent or administrator of the parish, and found that he was entirely cured of his ailment.

Father Claret was a gifted preacher and began to preach missions, which he called "novenas," in other towns. He was transferred from one town to another, until in 1842 he received a letter from Rome appointing him an "apostolic missionary."

During the next seven years he preached missions throughout Catalonia with astounding success. The people came in crowds to listen to "the greatest preacher of his day." His success was due, not to mere natural endowments, but to his holy life, and marvelous cures which he effected, the prophecies which he uttered, and the reading of minds with which he was endowed.

He spent long hours in the confessional, ate very little, slept only a few hours, never accepted any remuneration, and always traveled on foot. At Olot, in 1844, he preached for a whole month, some of his sermons lasting three hours. Twenty-five priests were needed to hear confessions, and every morning three priests were kept busy distributing Holy Communion.

Most of the night he spent praying and writing. As a means to make the fruit of his missions more lasting, he conceived the idea of having his sermons printed; and so he soon became the author of religious books which received wide circulation. His *Camino Recto (The Right Road)* was printed in Catalan at Vich in 1843 as a forty-eight-page booklet, and in a Castilian translation it was reprinted again and again. Over a period of seven years he amplified it into a volume of 500 pages. He lived to see a half million copies of the work distributed in the homes throughout the Iberian peninsula.

The *Camino Recto* was only one of 144 books which Father Claret wrote in the course of his life. In less than a century, 11,000,000 copies of his works, totaling 500,000,000 pages, were printed and distributed or sold. Not a penny did the author keep as profit. During his lifetime he spent $300,000 for Catholic books which were distributed gratis. He wrote: "I consider this one of the greatest alms," that is, the free distribution of good books.

About 1848, with the aid of Canon José Caixal y Estrada, he founded a publishing house, the "Librería Religiosa," and then the "Academia de San Miguel," a loose union of educated Catholics who provided the editing, illustrating and writing of good books. To give the press stability, it was subsequently placed in the care of businessmen.

From the province of Tarragona, where Father Claret was preaching in 1847, the bishop of Vich recalled him to Manresa because of a new Carlist revolt. For a short time he was engaged in giving retreats; but on March 6, 1848, he sailed with the newly consecrated Bishop Codina for the Canary Islands. Until May of the following year, he preached missions on the islands with the same marvelous results as in Catalonia.

Returning to Vich, Father Claret, with the approval of the bishop, gathered a group of young and zealous priests and laid the foundations of the Missionary Sons of the Immaculate Heart of Mary. The founder was then forty-two years old. The age of his associates ranged from twenty-seven to thirty-seven. They made a retreat, and then drafted constitutions. For the present they decided not to take vows, but to live as though they were bound by them, the reason being the anti-clerical attitude of the government. Their work would consist in devoting themselves to the same apostolate of catechizing and preaching in which the founder had been engaged alone until now. Father Claret was chosen as superior.

The first meeting of the new religious congregation was held on July 16, 1849. Less than a month later, Father Claret was notified that he had been chosen archbishop of Santiago on the island of Cuba. He tried to evade the appointment; but when the bishop of Vich wrote to him that he would be resisting the will of God and that, as far as he could, the bishop commanded him to accept the appointment, Father Claret did so in obedience.

During the past two years, a tumor had developed on his leg. He underwent surgery, and after the operation the wound was healed almost instantly. On October 6, 1850, he was consecrated a bishop in the cathedral at Vich; and on December 28, he sailed for Cuba. Before he left, he predicted that his sojourn in Cuba would not extend beyond six years.

What Archbishop Claret accomplished in Cuba during those six years was as spectacular as his preaching in Catalonia. There too he preached missions. Four times he made a pastoral visitation of his entire diocese. He completely transformed the clergy, denounced slavery, and launched an ambitious welfare program.

During his first two pastoral visits he distributed Holy Communion to 300,000 persons and confirmed almost as many; and during the first visitation, 98,217 books were handed out. After that no records were kept of such gifts. A hundred thousand copies of a small catechism, written by the archbishop, were placed in the hands of the people. Nine thousand illegal marriages were rectified, and 40,000 children were thus made legitimate.

By his drastic reforms, Archbishop Claret made enemies among those who refused to amend their lives. They made threats against his life, but these had no effect on him. Twice they attempted, unsuccessfully, to poison him.

At Holguin a hired murderer threw a knife at him, which failed to cut his jugular vein as intended but parted his face from chin to cheekbone; and another knife opened his arm to the bone. He lost a great amount of blood and his salivary glands were severed, but he recovered. His assassin was apprehended but escaped the death penalty because the archbishop interceded for him and even helped him to return to the Canary Islands from which he had come.

After Archbishop Claret had done all he could for his diocese, he asked to be relieved of his charge, but the Holy Father asked him to stay on. However, on March 18, 1857, about six years and one month after his arrival, he received a mandate recalling him to Spain.

On April 12, he embarked from Havana to become Father Confessor to Queen Isabella II in Madrid. Because Pope Pius IX counseled him to accept the appointment, he undertook this important post; but the Holy Father did not accept the archbishop's resignation of the see of Santiago de Cuba until two years later, when he named him titular archbishop of Trajanopolis.

Archbishop Claret entered upon his new duties only under the condition that he need not reside in the palace or be present at court functions, and that he be required to be present only to hear the queen's confession and instruct the *infanta*. He demanded full liberty to preach, to visit hospitals and other welfare institutions, and to do other ministerial work. Much of his time was spent in writing additional books.

On the queen, who received the sacraments frequently, the saintly archbishop exercised a good influence; but he was careful not to become involved in politics. Still there were those who spread wholly unfounded calumnies against him and sought persistently to besmirch his good name. He did not defend himself except when he considered it necessary. Several times secret societies made attempts on his life, from which he emerged unhurt only through a miracle.

In the summer of 1858 the queen made Archbishop Claret director of the Escorial, the vast structure north of Madrid built by Philip II. The Jeronymite custodians had been suppressed and the magnificent complex of buildings was half in ruins and neglected. The archbishop restored them at no extraordinary expense to the crown and introduced a community of priests who lived there and taught in a primary and secondary school.

He also reestablished a seminary at the Escorial in January, 1861. In Madrid itself he greatly improved conditions at the Hospital of Our Lady of Montserrat, and took up his residence there.

When the new United Kingdom of Italy was formed by the rape of the Papal States, the archbishop warned the queen that he would retire from his position as Father Confessor if she gave her approval. Under the pressure of threats, however, the queen finally yielded and recognized King Victor Emmanuel. The archbishop left her on July 17, 1865, and went to Catalonia to give retreats. The queen pleaded with him to return. He went to Rome to see Pope Pius IX. At the request of the Holy Father, he resumed his duties in Madrid after the queen had fulfilled the condition of making a public statement declaring her loyalty to the Holy See.

However, the revolutionary forces in Spain were once more gaining the upper hand. Despite the warnings of the archbishop, the queen was lulled into a false sense of security. She was not prepared for the revolution which broke out in 1868 and she had to flee to Paris. Archbishop Claret accompanied her into exile. The following year he made another journey to Rome, where he had a share in the preparatory work for the First Vatican Council and attended the sessions of the Council.

During the summer of 1870 he returned to France and retired, a very sick man, to Prades where his Missionary Sons of the Immaculate Heart of Mary had a house. Not content with broadcasting the most brazen lies about him, his enemies in Spain insisted on getting him back into the country and sent their emissaries into France to bring him back by force. The ailing archbishop had to leave Prades and seek refuge in the Cistercian monastery at Frontfroide, near Narbonne.

At the beginning of 1868, he had predicted that he had only two years and ten months to live. The end came as he had foretold. The day was October 24, 1870. On his tombstone were inscribed the words of Pope Gregory VIII: "I have loved justice and hated iniquity; therefore, I die in exile." In 1897 his Missionary Sons, the Claretians, had his remains transferred to Vich in Spain.

Seven years after the death of Archbishop Claret, the preliminary investigations for his beatification were begun. In 1899 Pope Leo XIII gave him the title of "Venerable." He was beatified on February 25, 1934, by Pope Pius XI, and canonized on May 7, during the Holy Year of 1950, by Pope Pius XII. His feast is observed on October 23.

The religious congregation which St. Anthony Mary Claret founded in Spain in 1849 grew and established houses, not only in other countries of Europe, but also in America, in Africa and in Asia.

While he was in Cuba, the saint also founded a sisterhood in union with the Servant of God, Mother Antonia Paris, namely the Congregation of Teaching Sisters of Mary Immaculate, also known as Claretian Sisters.

St. Anthony Claret is invoked as a patron of cancer patients. In 1930 Sister Benigna Sibila Alsina was miraculously cured of a cancer near the stomach through the intercession of St. Anthony Claret; and in 1934 the Claretian Sister M. Josephine Marin of Santiago, Cuba, likewise experienced a miraculous cure of breast cancer after having invoked the aid of the saint.

More than a century ago, on September 23, 1859, St. Anthony Claret had a prevision of the great evils which would befall mankind in the twentieth century, including the great wars, the spread of Communism and an inordinate love of pleasure. Though Cuba is now a Communist country, one may perhaps recognize a ray of hope in the fact that one of the saints of the Americas belongs in a special manner to that island country.

Liturgical Prayer

O Lord, hear the prayers we offer you as we recall the apostolic life of your blessed confessor-bishop Anthony. Since we cannot rely on our own merits, let the prayers of this saint who has been pleasing to you be our assistance. Through Jesus Christ, your Son, our Lord, who lives and reigns with you in the unity of the Holy Spirit, God, forever and ever. Amen.

Part I
SAINTS AND BLESSED

Mexico

ALL of Mexico's sixteen saints and blessed, except one, died as martyrs in Japan. The one exception, Bl. Sebastian de Aparicio, came to Mexico only a dozen years after its conquest by Cortez and lived there until the end of the sixteenth century. He was the earliest resident of the New World among those who have been beatified or canonized. Two of the martyrs of Japan were born in Mexico; and one of these, St. Philip of Jesus, was the first native of the Americas eventually to become a canonized saint. Four of the martyrs came from Spain to Mexico in their youth or childhood, one of them as the son of the viceroy of New Spain. The other nine lived and worked in Mexico for some time before going as missionaries to the Philippines and from there to Japan. Six of these were Spaniards, one was a Belgian, and two were Japanese.

CHAPTER 12

SAINTS AND BLESSED

Mexico

St. Philip of Jesus

(1572-1597) First Native Saint of the Americas

WHEN the twenty-six protomartyrs of Japan were executed on Nagasaki's Holy Hill on the morning of February 5, 1597, the first to die for the faith was a native of Mexico, a Franciscan cleric in minor orders about twenty-five years old — St. Philip of Jesus de las Casas.

It was the cross to which he was bound that the two soldiers, armed with lances, approached to begin their bloody work. As Friar Philip (or Felipe) pronounced the holy names of Jesus and Mary, the executioners standing beside him thrust their spears upward into his body from both sides, and his soul winged its flight to the eternal mansion prepared for him.

Felipe was the first-born child of Alonso de las Casas, son of a prominent family of Castile, and Antonia née Martínez, daughter of a tailor in Seville. Shortly after their marriage, they sailed to New Spain and settled in Mexico's southern province of Chiapas, bordering on Guatemala. But they did not remain there long. Having inherited some valuable property in Mexico City, they moved to the capital and established their home in a house on Tiburcio Street, where they had two servants, one in the kitchen and the other in charge of the stable.

Chiapas may have been the birthplace of Felipe, but it is more likely that he was born in Mexico City; and the probable day of his birth was May 1, 1572. (The year 1575, given by some, would make Felipe too young, only fourteen, when he left for Manila to

Albion Ende's painting of St. Philip of Jesus, a native
of Mexico, and one of the protomartyrs of Japan.

shift for himself.) Felipe was not a model as a boy. In fact, he was rather wild, self-willed and easily provoked. He climbed high trees in search of birds' nests, carelessly chased butterflies along a precipice and fought with other boys.

Frequently his mother had to scold him; but she always ended up by saying: "May God make you a saint, Felipe!" When the old black woman in the kitchen, who was often a victim of the youngster's pranks, heard those words, she is said to have remarked: "Felipe, a saint? Not till that old withered fig tree out there in the patio bears fruit." Legend has it that the tree did actually bear fruit when Felipe won the martyr's crown.

Felipe had five brothers and four sisters. His brothers were named Alonso, Matías, Juan, Francisco and Diego. Juan and Francisco entered the Augustinian Order; and Juan went as a missionary to the Philippines where he died a martyr at the hands of the natives in 1609. However, he has not been canonized or beatified like Felipe. María, Ursula, Catalina and Mariana were the names of his sisters.

Sometimes his father, who was a collector of customs and who carried on a profitable trade with the Philippines, took along his oldest son when he traveled to the port of Acapulco. There in the harbor Felipe saw the ships which regularly made the long and daring voyage to and from the islands on the other side of the vast Pacific Ocean.

After completing his primary education, Felipe attended the Colegio Maximo de San Pedro y San Pablo, which was conducted by the Jesuits in Mexico City. One of his teachers was Father Pedro Gutiérrez.

Most of his biographers tell us that he got into bad company and began to lead a scandalous life, causing his parents many a worry and heartache. However, it does not seem that he was quite as wicked as he is represented to have been. He was still in his early teens at this time.

Anyhow, at the age of about fifteen, he became serious-minded enough to apply for admission at the Discalced Franciscans' friary of Santa Barbara in Puebla, and was clothed in their light-brown habit. He did not remain very long. The life of the novices was too strict and austere for him. He took off the coarse habit and left to return to the comfortable home of his parents.

Did he relapse into his former sinful way of life? Some say he did. Anyhow, his parents wanted him to learn a trade; and so it seems they obtained a position for him in a silversmith's shop. Felipe, however, preferred to become a merchant like his father. About two years after he left the Franciscan novitiate in Puebla, he set out for the Philippines to become a trader. No doubt his father supplied him with the funds he needed to make a beginning. He was only seventeen, but he meant to make it a successful venture, possibly also as an agent of his father.

Not too many years ago, the historian L. González Obregón discovered, in the *Archivo General de la Nación* in Mexico City, the log of the Jewish captain of the ship on which Felipe made the voyage to Manila. It begins with the words: "1589. Jesús, María! Book of Antonio Díaz de Cáceres, master of the ship called Nuestra Señora de la Concepción." Then follows a list of the passengers who boarded the vessel on November 28, 1589, and the price each one paid. One of them was: "Felipe de las Casas, 50 ps." The cost of the long voyage was only fifty pesos. Shortly before, his father had made a loan of 8,000 pesos to the government for the purpose of supplying food for the Manila ships.

In Manila the young merchant entered upon his new career with a will and seems to have done very well financially, although some say he wasted all his money in riotous living. In the city he found the same kind of Franciscans as those among whom he had lived for a short time in Puebla, Mexico. Some of them he must have met and known in Mexico. After spending several years in Manila he once more felt drawn to them. He grew weary of the life of a businessman, and his former desire to become a friar and a priest was revived in him.

One biographer says that Felipe made up his mind after the death in Manila of a Portuguese girl with whom he had fallen in love and wished to marry. Be that as it may, Felipe went to the friary of Santa María de los Angeles and asked to be readmitted. His request was granted, and this time he persevered. He made his profession on May 22, 1594, and hence he entered the novitiate the previous year, about three and a half years after coming to Manila.

From the beginning Felipe distinguished himself by his religious fervor and his efforts to atone for the past by rigorous penances. While applying himself diligently to his studies and making rapid progress, he also devoted himself to the care of the sick and helping the poor. By 1596 he was ready for major orders.

The aged Bishop de Salazar had gone back to Spain and died there, and a successor had not arrived. For this reason, and perhaps also because his parents requested it, Friar Felipe received orders from his superiors to return to Mexico for the purpose of being ordained a priest. He embarked on the *San Felipe* at Cavite on July 12, 1596, with Brother Juan Pobre de Zamora.

After two months of slow sailing, the ship encountered such

violent storms that it lost its masts and rudder and was driven on the coast of the Japanese island of Shikoku. Hearing of the vessel's predicament, the local *daimyo* (feudal baron), known as the Lord of Tosa, purposely had the ship brought into shallow water at Hirado, so that it ran aground, and in a few hours began taking water.

Outwardly the *daimyo* welcomed the 200 persons on board; and on October 24 he advised General Landecho who was in command to send two friars and two other Spaniards with gifts to Kyoto for Hideyoshi, the most powerful of the *daimyos*, and to present the gifts through Governor Masuda of that city. Secretly he sent messengers to Masuda and told him to get ready for the confiscation of the ship's rich cargo.

Accordingly Masuda and the scheming *bonze* (Buddhist monk) and doctor Jaquin had an interview with Hideyoshi and persuaded him that the gods had sent him the ship so he could appropriate its cargo and with the proceeds of its sale rebuild the recently destroyed city of Fushimi. Masuda then went to Hirado and brought the cargo on barges to Kyoto by December 2 or 3.

Meanwhile attempts were made through Maeda, the friendly governor of Fushimi, to save the *San Felipe's* cargo. But it was too late. The conspirators had accused the Spaniards of planning to invade Japan, and claimed that the missionaries were merely forerunners of the soldiers who would come to occupy the country. Their proof consisted in the presence on board the *San Felipe* of "many friars and soldiers as well as all kinds of munitions." Hideyoshi believed them and declared: "I will kill all the missionaries and also the Christians."

On December 8, guards were placed at the houses of the Franciscans and Jesuits at Kyoto and Osaka. The two friars who had come to Kyoto with gifts for Hideyoshi were Friar Felipe and Brother John Pobre; and Felipe was in the friary at Kyoto when Father Peter Baptist and his companions were taken prisoner. The original decree for the execution of all the missionaries and Christians in Japan had by that time been limited to twenty-four, and Felipe was on the list of those who were condemned to capital punishment. To the original list of twenty-four names, two more were added on the way to Nagasaki.

Thus Friar Felipe became one of the protomartyrs of Japan, as already related; and he was the first to win the martyr's crown.

Some historians place Hideyoshi's change of mind in regard to the missionaries in Japan on a statement which Landa, the pilot of the *San Felipe*, is supposed to have made when questioned by Masuda. Landa, we are told, declared that the Spaniards "traded with the peoples of the whole world; and if they were well received, they behaved as friends, but if they were treated badly they would seize the land." And when Masuda asked whether it was for this reason that the missionaries came first, the perplexed pilot answered, "Yes." It is not at all certain that Landa spoke these "imprudent words." However, the accusations against the missionaries had already been made some days previously in Kyoto, and achieved their purpose.

When Philip of Jesus was beatified together with the other martyrs of Nagasaki in 1627 (ten years before the death of St. Rose in Lima and forty-one before her beatification) there was a splendid celebration with colorful processions in Mexico. The aged mother of the martyr, who was still living, was given a place of honor beside the viceroy. She died a fortnight later.

In 1629 Bl. Philip of Jesus was declared the patron of Mexico, and permission was granted to celebrate his feast individually. In the archdiocese of Mexico City it was made a feast of the highest rank.

From that time until the so-called "Reform Laws" were enacted which prohibited religious street processions, the procession in honor of Bl. Philip was held annually from the Church of San Francisco el Grande in Calle de Gante to the cathedral in the Zocolo, the great plaza nearby, on the anniversary of his martyrdom which was his feast day. It was one of the most celebrated fiestas in the city.

A new "Capilla de Bienaventurado Felipe de Jesús" was built in the cathedral, and in 1638 some relics of the martyr were placed there in a tomb. Devotion to Bl. Philip spread rapidly throughout Mexico, and a special altar was set aside in his honor in many Franciscan churches.

The Capuchinesses, a branch of the Second Order of St. Francis, erected a church in honor of Bl. Philip in 1673. Together with their monastery, this church was demolished after the passage of the "Reform Laws."

However, after the canonization of St. Philip in 1867, Father Antonio Plancarte y Labastida began, in 1886, to build the "Temple Expiatorio de San Felipe de Jesús" on the Avenida Madero, the former Avenida de San Francisco. It was constructed on the site of two former chapels attached to the old friary of San Francisco, namely the chapel of the Third Order and that of Nuestra Señora de Aranzazú. The cost was $300,000. Many people contributed alms for its completion, and it was dedicated on February 5, 1897. In 1909 it was completely renovated.

Above the high altar is a beautiful painting representing St.

Philip staggering beneath the weight of a cross, with pitying angels in the background. This church is one of the most frequently visited in Mexico City, and one finds a large number of people praying there throughout the day. When the writer visited the church, there was continuous exposition of the Blessed Sacrament on the main altar.

When the centennial of the canonization of the protomartyrs of Japan was observed in 1962, the Catholics of Mexico contributed funds for a monument which was constructed at Nagasaki under the direction of the Jesuits. The monument consists of a chapel, convent, museum and bronze panel. On the panel are twenty-six figures representing the martyrs, with the five Franciscans and three Jesuits in the middle. Behind the panel is a museum of the early Church history of Japan. Adjoining the latter is a chapel built in the Japanese style of architecture and dedicated to St. Philip of Jesus. Special commemorative ceremonies, arranged by both ecclesiastical and civil authorities, were held there on June 8-11.

It is related that, as St. Philip of Jesus hung upon his cross before he was transfixed with two lances, he foretold the destruction of Nagasaki. It is believed that this prophecy found its fulfillment when men of the American Air Corps B-29 dropped atom bomb Number Three on Nagasaki, August 9, 1945.

In 1952 Albion Ende made a beautiful painting of St. Philip of Jesus, portraying him hanging on the cross, and exhibited it in Buffalo and at St. Bonaventure University, St. Bonaventure, New York. He did this "in grateful thanksgiving and in memory of B. M. l/c Harold L. Ende of the *U.S.S. Nashville* and the other 132 brave men killed when a Japanese Kamikaze plane exploded on her deck, December 13, 1944."

Liturgical Prayer

O God, among the first martyrs of Japan, before all others, you bestowed the crown of martyrdom on blessed Philip, fastened to a cross and twice pierced with a lance. Grant to us who rely on him as our intercessor to be crowned with him in heaven. Through Jesus Christ, your Son, our Lord, who lives and reigns with you in the unity of the Holy Spirit, God, forever and ever. Amen.

CHAPTER 13

SAINTS AND BLESSED
Mexico

St. Peter Baptist Blásquez, St. Martin de Aguirre, St. Francis Blanco and St. Francis de San Miguel

(1597) Martyr-Saints of Nagasaki

BESIDES St. Philip of Jesus of Mexico, four others of the pro-tomartyrs of Japan may be counted among the saints of the Americas because they resided for a time in Mexico. They are Father Peter Baptist Blásquez, the leader of the twenty-six canonized martyrs of Nagasaki; Brother Francis de San Miguel, his companion in Mexico, the Philippines and Japan; Father Martin de Aguirre, who followed the other two to Mexico and the Far East; and Father Francis Blanco, the latter's pupil and companion, who was ordained a priest in Mexico.

Born on June 29, 1546, at San Esteban del Valle, about thirty-seven miles from Avila, Spain, St. Peter Baptist was the son of Pedro Blásquez (Villacastín) and María de Blásquez (Herrero). He had four sisters — María, Inez, Francisca and Catalina. A very bright, if not precocious lad, Peter Baptist, after receiving an elementary education, studied Latin and cosmography at Mombeltrán, then attended the Jesuit school at Oropesa, and specialized in organ music and Gregorian chant in Avila. Here he was one of the cathedral's choir boys and also a teacher of his companions.

In 1560, when he was only fifteen years old, he began to study philosophy and theology at the university of Salamanca. Having decided to enter the clerical state, he was ordained a deacon in the cathedral of Avila. Soon afterwards, with the reluctant consent of his parents, he journeyed on foot to Cuesta de la Parra and on June 24, 1568, joined the Alcantarine or Discalced Franciscans in the friary of San Andrés. They were a stricter branch of the Franciscans (Observants), founded only thirteen years earlier by St. Peter of Alcantara, confessor of St. Teresa of Avila.

Some time after completing his novitiate year, he was appointed in 1573 professor of philosophy in the friary of Peñaranda, Salamanca, and subsequently Father Guardian (Superior) first at Cardillejo, near Fontiveros, and then at Mérida, and finally preacher in Toledo. At all the places where he was stationed, Father Peter Baptist distinguished himself as an eloquent preacher of the word of God as well as a strict observer of the rule of St. Francis.

The Alcantarine Province of St. Joseph, to which Father Peter belonged, had opened two friaries in Mexico City and others in the Philippines. Those in the Philippines were organized into the dependent custody of St. Gregory the Great in 1567-1577. Father Peter was still a young man, thirty-five years old, when missionaries were recruited for these establishments in 1580. He asked permission to go along, and his offer was accepted. Both of his parents had died shortly after his religious profession, and also his sister Francisca. María and Inez had both married and were blessed with many children. Catalina died shortly before her brother left Spain.

Father Peter was one of thirty missionaries who gathered at the friary of San Bernardino in Madrid for the departure services held in April, 1581. Archbishop Felipe Lego, the papal nuncio, celebrated a pontifical Mass and then blessed the missionaries in the name of Pope Gregory XIII. Soon afterwards they left Madrid for Seville, and embarked for Mexico. They arrived in Mexico City toward the end of July.

During the next two or more years Father Peter lived and worked in Mexico, not only in the capital but also among the savage Chichimecos who had not as yet accepted Christianity. Father Marcelo de Ribadeniera, who was with him later in Japan, wrote of Father Peter: "In order to sow the divine seed in as many places as possible, the Lord directed him to make a long journey to Michoacán, on foot and barefoot. . . . Moved by fervor and trusting in the Lord, he ventured to enter the land of the Chichimecos, a fierce and barbarous tribe, who inflicted many cruelties on those they captured." Father Peter succeeded in making these Indians his friends, and thus he was able to convert many of them.

*St. Peter Baptist Blásquez and three other Franciscans
among Japan's protomartyrs had previously been in Mexico.*

His sojourn in Mexico was cut short in 1583, when he was named *comisario visitador* (commissary and visitor) of the custody in the Philippines. A commissary and visitor had the task of inspecting the friaries and the life and work of the friars. Father Peter set sail from Acapulco and arrived in Manila in 1584. Manila was then a walled city, with a bishop and a governor, though its population comprised less than 100 Spanish families and about 200 soldiers.

Father Peter was welcomed by Father Juan de Plasencia, who had been elected Father Custodian the previous year, and had distinguished himself as a founder of reductions and a linguist. The Father Visitor confirmed the acts of the chapter which had been held and visited all the Franciscan houses and missions in the Philippines. Then he joined his confreres in the work they were doing so well in the islands.

During his nine years in the Philippines (1584-1593), Father Peter became an outstanding and leading missionary. Mastering the Tagalog language in two years, he was able to preach to the natives in their own tongue and to teach the children in a school founded by Father Plasencia.

In Dilao, a suburb of Manila, there were quite a number of Japanese merchants, some of whom had become Christians. Father Peter began to take a special interest in their welfare in 1587, after a young man by the name of González García joined the friars as a brother. The son of a Portuguese father and an Indian mother in the Goa colony, González had spent some nine years in Japan and spoke Japanese fluently. He proved a great help to Father Peter when he founded a new friary, Santa María de los Angeles, in Dilao, and undertook the spiritual care of the Japanese.

Shortly afterwards, August 25, 1587, the first Dominicans came to Manila, and Father Peter offered them a temporary home in his newly founded friary at Dilao.

The following year, on May 23, Father Peter was elected custodian; and in this capacity, he prepared the way for the erection of the custody into an independent province. Soon after his election, he wrote a letter to King Philip II from the friary of Santa María de los Angeles, dated June 27. In it he begged the king to send additional friars from the Province of St. Joseph and others in Spain to the Philippines, men who were both saintly and learned. Three years later, a group of seventeen Franciscans arrived.

During his administration of three years the first friaries and churches of stone were constructed; and no less than seven new reductions or towns were founded in the provinces of Camarines and Bulacan. At the seaport of Cavite, the hospital of the Holy Spirit was opened on Pentecost Day in 1591 and placed in the care of the Franciscans.

Another hospital was planned by Father Peter at the springs of Los Baños which he had discovered in 1590 near Laguna Bay, about two and a half miles from Manila. Here he established the new friary of San Francisco del Monte. An expert doctor, Brother Francisco de Gata, had found the water of the springs to contain curative powers. This hospital was completed under Father Peter's successor in 1593.

The long-awaited brief of Pope Sixtus V erecting the custody into the Alcantarine Province of St. Gregory finally arrived in Manila in 1591, shortly after Father Peter had been reelected to the office of custodian. Father Peter at once convoked another chapter which met in September of that year and chose Father Pablo de Jesús as first Father Provincial.

Available statistics show that four years later this province had a membership of ninety-five friars, who had the care of forty churches and twenty *visitas* or sub missions. Already in 1583, only five years after the first friars had arrived in the islands, the Franciscans in the Philippines counted 300,000 Christians in their missions.

Two years after the founding of the Province of St. Gregory, Father Peter was chosen to be Spanish ambassador to the court of Hideyoshi, the most powerful *daimyo* in Japan and practically the ruler of the country. But before we go on with the story, it will be well to give a brief biographical sketch of the three saints of the Americas (besides St. Philip of Jesus) who gave their lives for love of God and therefore won the martyr's crown at the same time as St. Peter Baptist.

St. Martin de Aguirre

Father Martin of the Ascension de Aguirre came from the Basque country in northwestern Spain. He was born in 1567 at Vergara de Guipuzcoa, near Pampalona. At the age of eighteen, while a student at the university of Alcalá, he decided to enter the Order of St. Francis in the friary of San Esteban; and on May 17, 1586, the young Martin solemnly and humbly pronounced his vows as a Franciscan.

When Father Peter Ortiz recruited sixty missionaries, apparently in the year 1593, Father Martin who at that time had been a priest for six years, volunteered and was sent to the friary of San Bernardino in Madrid. From there the party set out for Mexico; and here Father Martin remained for a year or so, and taught the arts in the friary of Churubusco.

In 1594 Father Martin went on to Manila, arriving there after Father Peter Baptist had left for Japan. For two years he was a professor of theology in Manila; and in 1596, he and Father Francis Blanco were selected to join Father Peter Baptist in Japan. They augmented the number of Franciscan missionaries in Japan to nine, since three others had been added to the original group of four in September, 1594.

135

St. Martin de Aguirre and St. Francis Blanco had lived in
Mexico before winning the martyr's crown in Japan on February 5, 1597.

St. Francis Blanco

Like Father Martin, Father Francis Blanco hailed from northwestern Spain. He was born in 1571 near Monterey in the province of Galicia. As a student of the university of Salamanca, he became a Franciscan in the Observant Province of St. James at Villalpando.

He was still only a deacon in the friary at Pontevedra, when Father Peter Ortiz enlisted sixteen members of the Province of St. James for his group of sixty new missionaries. He sailed for Mexico with Father Martin de Aguirre; and in the friary of Churubusco, Mexico, he continued his studies under Father Martin. It seems that Father Francis Blanco was ordained a priest in Mexico, although it has also been stated that the ordination took place in Manila. At any rate, Father Francis Blanco completed his studies in the Philippines, to which he went with Father Martin and

136

where Father Martin was his teacher. A young priest, only twenty-five years old, he accompanied Father Martin to Japan in 1596.

St. Francis de San Miguel

The companion of St. Peter Baptist ever since he left Spain was Brother Francis de San Miguel Andrade y Arco. Born in 1543 at Parilla, near Valladolid, Francis became a Franciscan in the Observant Province of the Immaculate Conception in 1560 when he was sixteen years old. Seven years later, he was duly transferred to the Alcantarine Province of St. Joseph.

He was one of the thirty missionaries who arrived in Mexico in July, 1581, and with Father Peter he went to the province of Michoacán and served as his companion and assistant when he worked as a missionary among the Chichimecos. He accompanied Father Peter when he left for the Philippines in 1583. Although he was not a priest, Brother Francis preached the Gospel in the Philippine province of Camarines, and succeeded in converting many of the natives. When Father Peter was appointed Spanish ambassador to Japan in 1593, Brother Francis was selected as one of his three companions. The others were Father Bartholomew Rúiz and Brother González García.

St. Francis de San Miguel, a Franciscan brother, was Bl. Peter Baptist's companion in Mexico and Japan.

137

Like the Philippines, Japan comprises a large number of islands. The four main ones are: Honshu, the largest and situated in the center; Hokkaido, north of it; and Shikoku and Kyushu, to the south, the latter being the most southern.

St. Francis Xavier introduced the Catholic faith into Japan in 1549, and remained in the country until 1551. The work begun by him was continued by fellow Jesuits with remarkable success and in comparative freedom for thirty-seven years until 1587, although from the beginning they had to contend with the determined opposition of the Buddhist *bonzes* who were in control of the cultural life of the country. Near Kyoto, on Honshu Island, the *bonzes* conducted a college with 3,000 students. Shintoism had been limited practically to the two shrines at Ise and Idzumo. There were several sects of Confucian Buddhism, the dominant religion, especially Zen which flourished among the nobility, and Hokke (Lotus) and Jodo (Pure Land) which were common among the ordinary people.

Japan was divided into provinces, at the head of which there were feudal barons, called *daimyos*. By the middle of the fifteenth century, the *daimyos* exercised supreme power in their territories, while the *mikado* (emperor) was reduced to little more than a figurehead. The real rulers were the most powerful among the *daimyos*. Subordinate *daimyos* became their vassals. Since the powerful *daimyos* all tried to gain the upper hand, there was continuous civil war in the middle of the sixteenth century.

However, from 1568 on, the *daimyo* Nobunaga (1533-1582) was in complete control of almost one-half of Japan, that is, thirty out of sixty-six provinces. And since he showed himself favorable to Christianity, the Jesuit missionaries were able to convert many of the Japanese. By 1587 there were over 100,000 Christians in the country.

Nobunaga was succeeded by his principal general Hideyoshi (1582-1598), who had originally been a woodcutter and street sweeper. An ambitious man, he tried not only to gain control of all of Japan but also to conquer Korea. At first he allowed the missionaries to continue their work; but, instigated by the former *bonze* Jaquin, one of his doctors, Hideyoshi issued a decree in 1587 expelling the Jesuits from Japan. Three or four left; but the rest went into hiding, most of them in or near Nagasaki, on Kyushu Island, and tried to minister to their neophytes in secret.

Three years later, Hideyoshi went so far as to send a letter to the Philippines, demanding that he be recognized as ruler of the islands and threatening that his army would invade Luzon if an ambassador was not sent as a sign of submission and friendship. Brother González García translated the letter for Governor Gómez Pérez de Lasmarinas. After giving the matter considerable thought, the governor prepared a reply, saying nothing about submission but offering friendship and favorable conditions of trade. Two envoys were appointed, the Dominican Father John Cobo and Lope de Llano, a layman. Leaving Manila in April, 1592, they presented the reply to Hideyoshi at Nagoya, where he had established his headquarters on account of the war with Korea. Begun earlier in the same year, the war was not going as well as expected. Hideyoshi seemed to be satisfied with the reply from the Philippines; but on the way back, Father Cobo perished in a shipwreck near the island of Taiwan (Formosa).

The death of Father Cobo was not learned until much later. Meanwhile, Harado Kiemon, an envoy of Hideyoshi, arrived in Manila in 1593. He had been sent to accompany Father Cobo, but made the voyage on another ship. Strangely enough, he requested that some Franciscan missionaries be sent to aid the Jesuits in Japan. About the same time Father Cobo's letter, dated October 29, 1592, was received. It expressed the same request and specified that the friars sent should be ten in number.

The Japanese had become acquainted with Franciscans for the first time in 1582-1583, when a ship sailing from Manila to Macao was disabled in a storm and had to enter the port of Hirado, on the west side of Kyushu. On board were Brothers John Pobre Díaz Pardo and Diego Bernal. Brother John, then sixty-eight years old, made a deep and lasting impression on the Japanese — Christians and pagans alike; and in the years that followed, a number of letters were received in Manila, asking that some Franciscans come to Japan.

The governor decided to comply with the request by sending four Franciscans, who were at the same time to serve as official ambassadors. Those chosen were Father Peter Baptist, Father Bartholomew Rúiz, Brother Francis de San Miguel, and Brother González García. The latter was well qualified to be the interpreter. After carrying out their diplomatic mission, the four friars were to remain in Japan as permanent representatives of the governor as well as missionaries.

The ambassadors embarked from Manila on May 30, 1593, on two ships, one a Portuguese frigate and the other Japanese. Fathers Peter and Bartholomew, after a rough voyage, reached Hirado on July 8; but the two brothers entered the port of Nagasaki only on July 18. Hurriedly they joined the two priests; and together they went to see Hideyoshi at Nagoya. Father Peter himself, in a letter of January 7, 1594, relates what took place at Hideyoshi's court.

Seated on his throne, Hideyoshi made a haughty speech, saying among other things: "For the first time in history, all of Japan is firmly in one hand — mine. . . . If the people of Luzon do not recognize me as their lord, then to Luzon I shall send my armies."

Father Peter calmly instructed Brother González to make the following reply:

"Your lordship, our Lord is God and we obey Him and the king who by his authority governs us. By no means, therefore, can we recognize your lordship as the lord of Luzon. Nevertheless, we are ready, as your lordship asked in your letter sent last year to Manila, to conclude a pact of friendship and to promise to observe this pact loyally."

This reply at first provoked a short outburst of anger, but finally the changeable despot was suddenly pleased with it. Father Peter, through Brother González, then made a request: "In confirmation of your lordship's friendship we humbly ask you for permission to stay in Japan and to live among your people according to the rules of our order."

Hideyoshi granted the desired permission and added: "Not only do I allow you to open a house in my country, but I will also contribute to your maintenance."

Lastly, after repeated requests, Hideyoshi directed that a sealed document be drawn up to confirm the pact of friendship.

Father Peter and his three confreres then went to Kyoto on Honshu Island and took up a temporary abode in the small house of a minor official. After a long delay, the land promised by Hideyoshi was given to them; and in 1594 they built a friary and church as well as two fifty-bed hospitals. At the request of Father Peter, additional friars were sent from the Philippines, three in 1594 and two in 1596. The latter were Father Martin de Aguirre and Father Francis Blanco. Two more friaries were established, each with a hospital, one at Nagasaki and a third at Osaka.

The missionary work of the friars, coupled as it was with self-sacrificing charity to the sick and the poor, was blessed with extraordinary success. Many of the neophytes who had grown weak and timid during the persecution returned and contritely begged for forgiveness. Many of the pagans too were attracted by the good example of the friars and asked for baptism. In April, 1596, it was estimated that the number of new converts had risen to 25,000. Hideyoshi was aware of the missionary work of the Franciscans and raised no objections against it at this time.

Brother John Pobre visited his confreres in Japan for three or four months in 1595-1596, and brought back to Manila a glowing account of their work. He also confirmed the report of Father Peter, that the latter had succeeded in persuading Hideyoshi to allow the expelled Jesuits to remain, though he refused to let them preach. But even without preaching, the Jesuits were now able to devote themselves openly to the sacred ministry.

Meanwhile the jealousy and enmity of the *bonzes*, especially Jaquin, were aroused anew. But the spark that started the conflagration of a new persecution was an unfortunate incident. In October, 1596, the richly laden Spanish ship, *San Felipe*, which had set sail from Manila for Mexico, was badly damaged in a storm at sea and was driven in a helpless condition into the port of Hirado. Hideyoshi, who had suffered severe losses during the preceding months because of violent earthquakes, sent an official to take possession of the stranded ship and its cargo.

All kinds of rumors were noised abroad. Hideyoshi was told that there was a large number of missionaries aboard. Actually there were only four Augustinians, one Dominican and two Franciscans, one of whom was Brother John Pobre. The other was the Mexican cleric Philip of Jesus, who was returning home to receive the major orders. Hideyoshi was also informed that on the ship there was a great amount of artillery, numerous guns and other war supplies. These reports and the persistent efforts of Jaquin caused him to look upon all the missionaries as traitors and spies.

On December 8 and again on the eleventh, Hideyoshi issued summary orders for the execution of all the missionaries. Men in high places did all they possibly could to save the missionaries and to show that the accusations against them were wholly unfounded. But Jaquin had gained the upper hand; and on December 30 Hideyoshi condemned to death, by crucifixion, a limited list of six Franciscans and eighteen Japanese. Three of the latter were a Jesuit brother and his two assistant catechists, who were received into the Society of Jesus a few hours before their death. Fifteen were members of the Third Order Secular of St. Francis or the Archconfraternity of the Cord of St. Francis, who had served as catechists, interpreters, helpers and Mass servers of the Franciscan missionaries. Two more tertiaries were added to the group of martyrs on the way to Nagasaki.

Most of those condemned were in Kyoto. A few, including Father Martin de Aguirre and the Jesuit brother Paul Miki and his two assistants, John de Goto and Diego Kisai, were taken prisoner in nearby Osaka; but they too were brought to Kyoto on December 31. On January 3, 1597, the friars were taken to a public place and a part of each one's left ear was cut off. Then they were paraded through the principal streets of Kyoto; and a placard, which was carried along, announced: "These men are being punished because they preached a forbidden religion." A similar parade took place in Osaka the next day, and in Sakai the day after. Then the martyrs were held in Osaka until January 9. The following day they began a journey of twenty-six days to Nagasaki.

On the morning of February 5, the twenty-six martyrs were taken to the low, flat-topped hill of Tateyama overlooking the sea near the city of Nagasaki. Each one was fastened with iron rings and ropes to a cross having an upper and a lower crossbeam. All the crosses were then erected almost simultaneously by being lowered into deep holes and fixed there with earth and stones. The martyrs were then killed with spears by four executioners.

Thus died for the faith Father Peter Baptist and his companions — Father Martin de Aguirre, Father Francis Blanco, Brother Francis de San Miguel, Brother González García, all of whom except the last had lived in Mexico, and the cleric Philip of Jesus, a native of Mexico, together with twenty natives of Japan.

Of the other five Franciscans who were in Japan at the time, four were taken on board a Portuguese ship which was in the harbor of Nagasaki at the time of the execution, and only one was able to escape capture in order to minister to the Japanese Christians. But he too was forced to leave Japan the following October.

Many wonderful things happened at Nagasaki after the death of the martyrs, and Tateyama became known as the "Holy Hill" and a place of pilgrimage. Thirty years after the martyrdom, Pope Urban VIII beatified Father Peter Baptist and his twenty-five companions on July 19, 1627; and on July 10, 1862, Pope Pius IX solemnly canonized them. The feast or memorial of these twenty-six saints is now observed in the Roman calendar as that of St. Paul Miki and companions on February 6. All of Catholic Japan honors them, not only as its protomartyrs, but as its principal patrons. They are the titulars also of the cathedral of Nagasaki.

Liturgical Prayer

O Lord Jesus Christ, it was through the suffering of the cross in imitation of you that the firstfruits of the faith among the people of Japan were sanctified in the blood of the holy martyrs Peter Baptist and his companions. While commemorating their heroic death, may we be spurred on by their example: you who live and reign with the Father in the unity of the Holy Spirit, God, forever and ever. Amen.

CHAPTER 14

SAINTS AND BLESSED

Mexico

Bl. Sebastian de Aparicio

(1502-1600) Pioneer Road Builder of Mexico

ON a sunny day in 1596 Brother Sebastian arrived with his carts and five yoke of oxen at the hacienda of Don Juan de Garcías near Cholula, Mexico. The ninety-four-year-old brother, clothed in the light-blue habit of the Franciscans of Holy Gospel Province, was well-known in this region. For the past twenty years he had been the regular collector of alms for more than 100 friars who resided in the large house of studies at Puebla de los Angeles.

Don Juan was not at home at the time, but his wife, Doña Francisca Méndez Sotomayor, saw the brother coming. She saw him unyoke his oxen and turn them loose. She saw the oxen going toward the cornfields which were almost ripe for harvest. She welcomed Brother Sebastian into the house and set a glass of milk on the table for him, but she was worried.

"Padre," she said, "your oxen are wandering into the cornfields." (The term "padre" was also used sometimes in addressing a lay brother.)

"Do not fear," replied the brother. "They will not break a single stalk and will not eat a single ear of maize. I have given them strict orders not to do any harm to other people's property." And he continued to sip his milk leisurely.

Doña Francisca thought he must be jesting. "Oh, Padre, please stop them. Not only will they do a great deal of damage, they will also overeat and get sick."

Finishing his milk, the brother realized he must convince her.

143

"You do not believe me," he said. "Come, let us go outside. You will see I am not joking."

Just outside the patio, they paused. The oxen were now at a considerable distance from the house. Without raising his voice, Brother Sebastian said: "Capitán, come back here and bring the others with you." Capitán was the leader among the oxen.

"Padre, they are too far away. They cannot hear you."

But, to her great surprise, she saw one of the oxen come trotting toward them; and then the others followed his example.

"Capitán!" said the brother. "Have you and your fellows eaten any of the maize or broken any stalks?"

The ox shook his head just as a speechless person does to say "no."

"I knew you would not disobey me, Capitán. You are a good ox."

As Brother Sebastian held out his sleeve, the ox kissed it. The brother called each of the other oxen by name, and they also kissed the sleeve of his tunic. Then they returned to graze quietly in the fields.

Doña Francisca was dumbfounded. To one of the farmhands she gave instructions to load a generous supply of grain on Brother Sebastian's little carts. When her husband returned home, she told him what had happened. The next morning he went into the fields to examine them. He found the tracks of the oxen, but there was not the slightest sign that the stalks of corn had been touched.

This story was told by Doña Francisca when investigations were instituted for the beatification of Brother Sebastian; and she testified under oath that she was telling the truth.

The incident related is only one of 300 extraordinary happenings and miracles which occurred during the life of Brother Sebastian de Aparicio, whose life span coincided with the entire sixteenth century except its opening year. The son of Juan de Aparicio and Teresa née del Prado, Sebastian was born in 1502 at Gudena in the diocese of Oria, Spain. His parents were very poor, but they gave him something far more precious than any material advantage, namely a good Christian training.

Sebastian was a pious and innocent lad, always respectful and obedient to his parents, whom he loved dearly. To help them in their need, he began at an early age to hire himself out as a shepherd; and at the age of fifteen he left home to work in the employ of others and thus earn some wages for the support of the family.

He began by taking the job of a servant for a wealthy widow

144

in Salamanca; but when he found himself exposed to temptation, he left abruptly. For one year he was the valet of a rich gentleman, and then he became a farmhand for two farmers at San Lucar.

His savings he sent home, and he was able, not only to better the condition of his parents, but also to provide dowries for his sisters so they could contract good marriages. As for himself, Sebastian preferred to lead a celibate life. But he was a handsome young man; and when women of loose morals continued to lay snares for him, he decided to emigrate to the New World.

Sebastian was thirty-one years old when he set sail for Mexico. The year was 1533, only four decades after the discovery of the New World by Christopher Columbus and only a dozen years after the conquest of the Aztec empire by Hernando Cortez. He settled at Puebla de los Angeles where he at first tilled the soil as he had done in Spain. But he soon realized that the colonists were greatly hampered in making headway because of the lack of satisfactory tools as well as roads and transportation which would enable them to bring the produce of their fields to a market. So he started to make plows and carts, and to tame and hitch oxen to the carts; and then he undertook the prodigious task of building a road all the way from Puebla to the port of Vera Cruz, a distance of 196 miles.

Then Sebastian connected Puebla with the capital, Mexico City, by another road of eighty-four miles. Thus the capital was linked with the east coast by a road of 290 miles; and the supplies as well as mail brought by the Spanish galleons from the home country could be transported in ox-drawn carts and wagons from Vera Cruz to Mexico City and the other settlements along the way.

Not satisfied with this remarkable accomplishment, by which he rendered an invaluable service to the new country, Sebastian tackled what was close to being a superhuman enterprise at that time — a road of 466 miles from Mexico City all the way to Zacatecas in the north, a road good enough to permit the hauling of supplies to the silver mines which had been discovered there and of the silver ingots from the mines to the capital. He began this project in 1542 and was able to complete it before 1552.

The modern highway from Mexico City to Zacatecas follows the same route as that of Sebastian's road, with some modifications here and there; and the traveler who makes this trip by automobile cannot but marvel that Sebastian could have done what he did. Nowadays, with bulldozers and other mechanized equipment together with an army of workers, it is comparatively easy

145

to construct a highway; but in the middle of the sixteenth century this work had to be accomplished with simple tools and by manual labor.

What rendered the feat of opening a passable road to Zacatecas all the greater was the fact that there were other obstacles besides those presented by the terrain, namely the presence of the hostile savage Indians called the Chichimecos. But Sebastian somehow managed to gain their confidence and win their friendship; and they proved to be a great help rather than a hindrance. Instinctively they seemed to know that Sebastian had their best interests at heart.

In fact, Sebastian presented to all his contemporaries the unique "believe-it-or-not" spectacle of a layman who was completely free of any selfish motives and was prompted in his extraordinary projects only by Christian charity — a man who literally carried out our Lord's injunction to love God above all things and his neighbor as himself.

Though he sought no personal gain, every project that he undertook seemed to prosper and succeed beyond all expectations. For himself he needed very little — he was content with simple and frugal fare and slept on a single mat. The wealth that he acquired he used to help others who were in need, supplying free transportation of goods in his wagons, lending money without interest, remitting to widows the debts of deceased husbands, ransoming those who were imprisoned for debts, feeding the poor and orphans, and providing dowries for poor girls. The result was that he enjoyed the complete confidence and sincere respect of all, both colonists and natives; and everyone who was in trouble or in need went to him for counsel and aid. When disputes arose, they unhesitatingly left to him the settlement of their quarrels.

When Sebastian completed his self-imposed task of road building in 1552, he was fifty years old. He purchased a large tract of land lying between Tlalnepantla and Azcapotzalco (typical Aztec names of places), just north of Mexico City and not far from the famous shrine of Our Lady of Guadalupe; and there he settled down once more as a farmer and rancher. As before, he was everybody's friend and continued to give aid to all who needed it.

At the age of sixty, Sebastian finally consented to marry a poor maiden, the daughter of some friends of his (who seem to have thought that the old man would die soon and his vast possessions would become their inheritance). But it was a Joseph's marriage; and when his wife died a year later, she was still a virgin. Two years later he entered a similar marriage with another virtuous young woman; but she too died soon afterwards.

Bl. Sebastian de Aparicio built the first roads to Mexico City from Vera Cruz and Zacatecas before 1552.

In 1572, seventy-year-old Sebastian was afflicted with an acute illness which almost caused his death. After his recovery, the experience of having been so close to the judgment seat of God left so deep an impression on him that he decided to give up all earthly possessions and to spend the rest of his days solely in the service of God. He distributed all his goods among the poor, giving the greater part to the Monastery of the Capuchin Poor Clares in Mexico City and offering his own services to this monastery as a servant.

At first he was content with being enrolled in the Third Order Secular of St. Francis; but soon his longing for the religious life became so strong that he went to the large friary of St. Francis, near the cathedral, on June 2, 1573, and begged for admission as a lay brother. Only after another year had passed was the request of the seventy-two-year-old man granted; and he began his novitiate in the friary of Tecali on June 9, 1574.

After his solemn profession on St. Anthony's Day (June 13) of the following year, Brother Sebastian was sent to the big friary at Puebla de los Angeles. Since he had so much experience in the transportation of goods by ox-drawn carts, he was given the task

147

Chapel of San Francisco Church in Puebla, Mexico, where the incorrupt body of Bl. Sebastian is venerated.

of collecting alms for this friary; and for the next twenty-five years, until his death in 1600, Brother Sebastian wandered around as a begging brother throughout the region of Puebla, Cholula, Atlixco, Huejetzingo, Tlaxcala and Huaquechula.

Despite the fact that he spent so much of his time on the road, Brother Sebastian succeeded in living the life of an exemplary and recollected religious as much as and more so than his confreres who spent their time in study and prayer at the friary. The stories told about him may seem to be even more incredible than some of those recounted in the Fioretti of St. Francis of Assisi; but we have the testimony of eyewitnesses who made their depositions under oath when investigations were carried on for the beatification of Brother Sebastian. In Puebla de los Angeles, "the City of

148

the Angels," he came to be known as the Angel of Mexico; for the angels took special care of him when he was on the quest.

Father León de Clary tells us, "The historians of his life relate that these blessed spirits accompanied him in his travels, transported him from one place to another, brought him back to the right path when he had lost his way, sheltered him from the rain and the snow, procured food for him in lonely and desert places, illuminated for him with heavenly light the darkness of the night, and from time to time enlivened his tramp with melodious song." The mention of snow for the region around Puebla seems strange, but there are snow-capped mountain peaks in the area — for instance, Mount Popocatepetl and Mount Ixtaccihuatl.

Because he gathered alms for an exceptionally large friary, Brother Sebastian had to take with him on his trips carts drawn by oxen to carry the corn and other provisions which he received from charitable people. These oxen were so responsive to his wishes that they acted almost like intelligent human beings. They even anticipated his wishes by lying down, getting up, even kneeling and coming to him at the slightest movement of his lips. During the night, after he had set them free, they would graze in the fields; and in the morning they would of their own accord return punctually when Brother Sebastian was ready to move on.

Animals whom others found to be unmanageable offered no resistance to the good brother; and he was able to tame them at once. At times it happened also that he was able to discern the secret thoughts of men and foretell future events.

During his last illness Brother Sebastian was afflicted with almost continuous nausea and vomiting. This prevented him from receiving Holy Viaticum; but the Father Guardian brought the Blessed Sacrament to the sickroom. The holy brother's soul was filled with gratitude and joy. He had himself laid on the bare floor, and there he peacefully and joyfully surrendered his soul into the hands of his Creator. It was on the twenty-fifth day of February in the year 1600, the ninety-eighth year of his life.

So many people came to pay their respects to "the Angel of Mexico" that his remains could not be laid to rest for a considerable time. Today his body can still be seen incorrupt in a glass tomb which occupies a place above and to the rear of the main altar in a large side chapel of the Franciscan church of Puebla, Mexico.

Almost two centuries after his death, that is, on May 27, 1790, Pope Pius VI formally beatified Brother Sebastian. Since then his feast has been observed by the Order of Friars Minor on the day of his death (in leap years, on February 26). In our own day a new interest has been awakened in the cause of Blessed Brother Sebastian's canonization. And Mexico itself is becoming more aware of the debt of gratitude it owes to the memory of its pioneer road builder.

A few years ago *Union,* a newspaper published in Mexico City, paid a glowing tribute to Bl. Sebastian of Aparicio in a full-page illustrated article written by Jesús Pablo Tenorio. Commenting on an announcement of the Secretariat of Public Works that by the end of 1964 Mexico would have a total of 34,176 miles of highways, the author pointed out that 746 of these miles are to a great extent identical with the first passable roads which were built in New Spain (Mexico) in the middle of the sixteenth century by the unselfish and courageous efforts of one man — Bl. Sebastian.

The journalist also called attention to the fact that on one of the busiest streets of Mexico City, at the entrance of the ancient Church of San Francisco on Madero Avenue, just off the Zocolo with its great cathedral and the government buildings, there is a mosaic plaque, placed there by the governmental Department of Colonial Monuments. The text of the inscription on this plaque is as follows: "Blessed Sebastian de Aparicio. Distinguished Franciscan who during the middle third of the sixteenth century introduced into New Spain the very useful method of transportation by means of carts. He became a Franciscan in this place on June 13, 1575."

Bl. Sebastian of Aparicio is honored as a national hero of Mexico, and in other parts of the world he is invoked as a patron of travelers.

Liturgical Prayer

O God, you enabled your confessor, blessed Sebastian, to live in simplicity of heart and you showered upon him heavenly gifts. Through his intercession may we serve you with purity of intention and so obtain the gifts of your grace. Through Jesus Christ, your Son, our Lord, who lives and reigns with you in the unity of the Holy Spirit, God, forever and ever. Amen.

CHAPTER 15

SAINTS AND BLESSED
Mexico

Bl. Richard Trouvé of St. Ann

(1585-1622) A Belgian in Mexico and Japan

A MOST unusual beatification ceremony was carried out in the Basilica of St. Peter on July 6, 1867. On that day Pope Pius IX enrolled among the blessed, not one martyr or a small group, but 205 missionaries and native Christians selected from the 40,000 who died for the faith in Japan during the great persecution which lasted for a quarter century from 1614 to 1640.

Among these were one native of Mexico (New Spain), three colonials of Mexico, and six (a Belgian, two Japanese and three Spaniards) who had resided in Mexico for some time. The Belgian in this group was the Flemish Franciscan priest, Bl. Richard Trouvé of St. Ann, who had twice been a resident of Mexico.

After the crucifixion of St. Peter Baptist and his twenty-five companions on February 5, 1597, the lone Franciscan who had evaded capture and eleven Jesuits managed to remain in the country for nine months; but in October they too were forced to leave.

A year later, on September 16, Japan's dictator Hideyoshi died after a long illness. Before his death, since he had only one six-year-old son, Hideyori, he appointed a council of five regents under the presidency of Tokugawa Ieyasu. (We would invert the two names, since Tokugawa was the family name.) Ieyasu (1542-1616) soon usurped all power and made it quite clear that he aimed at supplanting Hideyori. When the latter reached the age of twenty-two, a civil war began in Japan in November, 1614.

It ended abruptly on June 3 of the next year with the death of Hideyori and his mother; and Ieyasu emerged victorious. The Tokugawa family ruled Japan during the next two and a half centuries, until the revolution of 1867-1868 which restored the power of the emperor. The immediate successor of Ieyasu, who died at the age of seventy-four in 1616, was his son Hitetada. He in turn was followed in 1631 by Iemitsu who ruled until 1651.

The persecution inaugurated by the founder of the Tokugawa dynasty in 1614 was continued by the two *daimyos* who succeeded him until after the Battle of Shimabara in 1638 in which 30,000 Christians were massacred. Japan was then (1640) sealed off from all contact with other countries in the "Sakoku," the closed nation period, which did not come to an end until the nineteenth century.

Even before Hideyoshi's death, in 1598, two Franciscans and several Jesuits had returned to Japan and tried to minister to the Christians in secret. But Ieyasu was anxious to enjoy the benefits of trade with the Philippines and even Mexico, and so he adopted a policy of tolerating the Catholic religion. Since he permitted the missionaries to carry on their work openly, quite a number of Jesuits, Franciscans, Dominicans and Augustinians continued to come to Japan; and for a decade and a half the Church enjoyed comparative peace and made great progress.

Gradually, however, Ieyasu, a practicing Buddhist, changed his attitude toward the Catholic religion and its propagation in Japan. There were various reasons for the change, among them the influence exercised upon him by the enemies of the Catholics, namely the Japanese *bonzes* and Protestant traders from England and Holland. Hidetada, his son, launched a persecution of the Christians in Tokyo in 1613; and the next year Ieyasu published his edict banishing all the missionaries from Japan. While some were forcibly evicted, others succeeded in avoiding capture; and the Church went underground. In the years that followed new missionaries managed to enter the country secretly.

Father Richard Trouvé was one of those expelled in 1614, but he returned to Japan three years later with Father Francis Gálvez. Both became martyrs, and both have been beatified.

Mark Trouvé and his wife Barbara del Forest, Flemings of Han-sur-Heur, in the province of Hainat, Belgium, in 1585 had a son who was named Lambert when he was baptized. They were good Catholics, and they gave Lambert a good Catholic education.

When Lambert was still a child, he was carried away by a wolf. His mother called upon St. Ann for help and begged her to save the boy. Her prayer was answered; and for this reason, later at least, "of St. Ann" was added to his name.

152

The story of Bl. Richard Trouvé's sudden conversion
is told in this drawing by James McIlrath.

Lambert learned the trade of a tailor and, as a young man still in his teens, was a big help to his parents. But he was led into sin by bad companions and fell into the vice of impurity. Every morning and evening, however, he continued to pray the three Hail Marys as he had been taught to do by his mother.

One day he went along with a companion to a house of ill repute. When he got there he, without knowing why, suddenly decided to take his leave. He returned home, prayed the three Hail Marys, and fell asleep. Later during the night he was awakened by a knock on his door. He opened it and was horrified at what he saw — a young man about his own age with a terribly disfigured face.

"Who are you?" he asked.

"Don't you recognize me? I'm your friend, whom you left a few hours ago."

"You look like a demon!" exclaimed Lambert.

"Woe is mine," was the reply. "Stay away from that house where we were a little while ago. Out in the street you'll find my dead body. My soul has been damned. The same would have happened to you, if the Holy Virgin had not protected you because of those three Hail Marys which you say on awakening and retiring. Happy will you be if you heed this warning."

The ghastly visitor disappeared. Lambert rushed outside and

in the street gutter he found the corpse of his friend. Just then he heard the bell of the nearby Franciscan friary ringing as the friars intoned the *Te Deum* at the close of their midnight Matins. Forthwith he went to the friary entrance and pounded on the door. The Father Guardian was summoned by the Brother Porter; and Lambert begged him for admission to the community as a brother candidate without delay. After hearing the applicant's story and finding it to be true, the Father Guardian granted the request.

Legend or fact? It seems to be well-substantiated. The story is narrated by St. Alphonse Liguori, Dom Prosper Gueranger, the Jesuit Father Alphonse Andrade, and even in the learned journal *Archivo Ibero-Americano*.

Anyhow, in 1604 Lambert became Brother Richard in the Franciscan Order, at Nivelle, Flanders, at the age of nineteen, and he served there as porter for a while. In May, 1606, we find him in the Aracoeli friary in Rome. There he met old Brother John Pobre, who had known St. Peter Baptist and had been in Japan several times. He was now in Rome as a messenger and representative of the Philippine Province of St. Gregory. Brother John told Brother Richard the story of the martyrs who were crucified at Nagasaki in 1597 and about the missions which had been resumed in Japan.

"How happy I would be," said Brother Richard, "if I could lay down my life for the salvation of souls, and so atone for my past sins." He meant what he said; and as a step toward the desired goal, he asked and obtained permission from Father General Arcangelo Gualterio of Messina to go to Spain and become a member of the Alcantarine Province of St. Joseph.

A year or two later, he was on his way, with many other new recruits, to Mexico; and after tarrying there for some time, he sailed across the Pacific to Manila in 1609. Before entering the order, Brother Richard had received a good education, and he was mentally gifted. Recognizing his talents, his superiors transferred him to the clerical state in virtue of his vow of obedience. He began his studies for the priesthood at Pangil, in the Philippines; but shortly afterwards he returned to Mexico. So rapidly did he progress in his studies in theology that he was ordained a priest in 1611 while still in Mexico, it seems, although another account says his ordination took place in the Philippines. We are told also that after he was promoted to the priesthood in Mexico, he served as master of novices for a short time.

Once more he made the long voyage across the Pacific to Manila, and in 1612 or 1613 he was sent to Japan. In November, 1614, as a result of Ieyasu's edict of banishment, he had to return to the Philippines. However, in 1617 he was able to reenter Japan with Father Francis Gálvez. For a time he was the only Franciscan priest on Kyushu Island. To escape the priest hunters, he traveled through the mountains, living in caverns and ministering to the Christians in secret. Disguising himself, he visited those who were suffering for the faith in prisons and accompanied the martyrs to the place of execution.

Father Diego de San Francisco, who became his companion after some time, wrote of him: "Father Richard was moved by a great desire of converting souls and of dying as a martyr. And because he was very courageous, he did not miss any opportunity of gaining souls for Christ, even in the midst of the persecution; and whenever possible he was present at the martyrdoms of the Christians, to help them in their final struggle for Christ."

Since Father Richard was a Fleming and his homeland adjoined Holland, he was asked by the Mexican Augustinian Father Bartholomew Gutiérrez and the Dominican Father Diego Collado to make an attempt at liberating the Augustinian Father Peter Manrique de Zúñiga and the Dominican Father Louis Flores, both of whom had lived in Mexico. They had been captured by English pirates and delivered by them to Dutch traders who were holding them as prisoners at Hirado. On October 18, 1620, late in the evening, Father Richard broke into the prison; but, as Father Gutiérrez wrote, "by reason of a misfortune, he failed in his attempt to free the two missionaries and barely escaped capture himself."

The following year, on November 4, after four years of heroic apostolic work, Father Richard was cast into prison at Nagasaki. He had tried to convert an apostate and traitor who was responsible for the arrest of a missionary. Father Richard sought him out and spoke to him. The renegade listened, but as Father Diego Collado wrote, "the seed fell on rocky soil." Instead of repenting, the man sold Father Richard to the persecutors.

A few days later Father Richard, suffering from a high fever, was staying at the home of the Fleites family. The informed priest hunters found him there, dragged him from his sickbed, and took him to the jail at Nagasaki. Mr. and Mrs. Fleites and their daughter were likewise imprisoned and died as martyrs; but only Mrs. Lucy Fleites has been beatified.

In the prison at Nagasaki, Father Richard found two confreres who had been held there for a year. They were Father Peter de Avila and the Mexican colonial, Brother Vincent Ramírez de San José. To prevent them from having contact with the people, all three were moved to the prison at Omura. That increased the number of prisoners at Omura to thirty-one. Besides sixteen Japanese Christians, there were seven Dominicans, six Franciscans and two Jesuits.

During the days of the Great Martyrdom in September, 1622, all of these were put to death, some at Omura on the twelfth, and the others at Nagasaki on the tenth. Those who had been apprehended at Nagasaki — thirteen Christians and eleven missionaries, among them Father Richard — were taken back to that city to be executed together with thirty-two Christians, mostly women and children, prisoners in Nagasaki. On the way, Father Peter de Avila, who had a clear, strong voice, did not cease preaching to the people who had gathered to see the strangely joyful "criminals."

A large area near the sea was prepared, and a crowd of 40,000 gathered to witness the execution. The missionaries and the leaders among the Christians, a total of twenty-five, were condemned to death by a slow fire, the other thirty-one by decapitation. Among the former was the octogenarian, Lucy Fleites, a convert of St. Peter Baptist, and the friend of Father Richard, who distinguished herself by her zeal for the spread of the faith and her encouragement of the other martyrs.

The beheading took place first on a raised scaffold. One by one the heads were placed on a table. Then the others, who had been tied to stakes with kindling wood placed around them at some distance, were slowly burned to death. A few did not die until late at night.

Bl. Richard Trouvé of St. Ann is one of the Franciscan martyrs who are honored in one group designated as Bl. Apollinaris Franco and forty-four companions. They died in Japan between 1617 and 1632. Included among these is the Franciscan tertiary Bl. Lucy Fleites who died at Nagasaki on September 10, 1622, the same day as Bl. Richard. Bl. Apollinaris Franco and two other Franciscans died at Omura two days later. Of these forty-five martyrs, seventeen belonged to the First Order of St. Francis, one to the Third Order Regular, and twenty-seven to the Third Order Secular.

Liturgical Prayer

Almighty God, inspire us by the example of your martyr, blessed Richard, to endure every hardship in this world rather than suffer injury to our souls. Through Jesus Christ, your Son, our Lord, who lives and reigns with you in the unity of the Holy Spirit, God, forever and ever. Amen.

CHAPTER 16

SAINTS AND BLESSED
Mexico

Bl. Peter de Avila and Bl. Vincent Ramírez de San José
(1597-1622) A Spaniard and a Mexican Colonial

IN the harbor of Manila, toward the end of 1619, five Spanish merchants boarded a Chinese ship bound for Japan. They were Diego Palomares, Francisco Barajas, Francisco de Madridejos, Pedro de Avila, and Vicente Ramírez.

On the voyage the captain's suspicions were aroused. He observed them carefully. "They do not behave like other merchants," he thought. "I wonder what they really are. They may be priests."

When they reached Nagasaki, on an inlet of the East China Sea, at the southern end of Kyushu Island, the Chinese captain learned that a priest hunt had been going on since November 13. The *daimyo* Ieyasu had ordered Gonroku, governor of Nagasaki, to arrest all priests in his area. Fearful that he would be accused of smuggling missionaries into Japan but yet not quite sure that his Spanish passengers were anything other than the merchants they claimed to be, the captain placed them under custody in a private house when they disembarked.

They were, in fact, Franciscan missionaries — four priests and one brother. Vicente Ramírez was Brother Vincent de San José. Hearing of their arrival, Father Diego Pardo de San Francisco, superior of the Franciscans in Japan, came to their rescue. He succeeded in having them transferred to the house of two Japanese Christians, Michael and Thomas, both of whom were willing to die if it would save the missionaries.

When the news leaked out that the merchants were mis-

A painting by Japanese artist Luca Hasegawa, commemorating the martyrdom of numerous Christians in Japan.

sionaries, Father Diego went at once to Michael's home; and after some hesitation, he took all five to a safe place. Governor Gonroku was informed of what had happened, but he was not inclined to take great pains in carrying out the orders of Ieyasu concerning the missionaries and their neophytes. However, to protect himself, he directed that an investigation and search be made and imposed light sentences on the Chinese captain and Michael. The former got one year of "street arrest," meaning that he would be under the surveillance of his neighbors during that time, while Michael was subjected to two years of the same.

Two of the rescued missionaries had been residents of Mexico for some time before they went to the Philippines and from there to Japan. They were Father Peter de Avila and Brother Vincent Ramírez.

Father Peter de Avila was born in 1562 at Palomera, Spain. He joined the Franciscans in his native land, and was about fifty-five years old when he encountered some distinguished visitors, namely the Franciscan Bishop-elect Louis Sotelo and the Japanese nobleman Hasekura and their party. Father Sotelo and Hasekura had been sent as ambassadors to the Holy See and to Madrid by one of the stronger *daimyos* of Japan who was more or less independent of Ieyasu, namely Date Masamune of northern Honshu. Father Sotelo and his companions were getting ready to return to Japan, and Father Peter joined them.

They made the voyage to Mexico in 1617 with the annual mid-year fleet, and arrived at Vera Cruz about the beginning of November. For various reasons they were detained in the country and spent the next five months there. When they finally set sail from Acapulco for the Philippines on April 2, 1618, several additional Franciscans went along, and among these was Brother Vincent Ramírez.

Born at Ayamonte, Spain, in 1597, Brother Vincent seems to have emigrated with his parents to Mexico when he was still a boy. At any rate, he was only eighteen years old when he joined the Alcantarine Franciscans in their Mexican Province of San Diego (erected as such in 1599 or 1606). He was clothed with the habit of St. Francis in the friary of Santa Barbara near the city of Puebla de los Angeles. The following year, on October 18, 1616, he made his profession of the vows. Making the voyage across the Pacific with Bishop-elect Sotelo and Father Peter de Avila, he arrived in Manila in the beginning of July, 1618.

Contrary to his will, Bishop-elect Sotelo was detained in Manila until 1622, and Hasekura did not reach Japan until 1620. But, as related, Father Peter and Brother Vincent, disguised as mer-

159

chants, arrived in Japan toward the end of 1619. After they and their three confreres were rescued upon their arrival by Father Diego Pardo, Brother Vincent was assigned to Father Peter de Avila as his companion. Father Peter learned the Japanese language in a very short time; and after a few months Father Diego sent him and Brother Vincent to Nagasaki in order to serve and help the Christians in the neighborhood.

A year late, December 18, 1620, both were discovered and imprisoned. They were betrayed to the authorities by Ochoso, the same apostate whom Father Richard Trouvé afterwards tried to convert. Father Peter, with Brother Vincent, had gone to the house of one Dominic to hear the confessions of the Christians. Ochoso went to the house and finding the two friars there, asked for a little time to prepare himself for confession. This gave the renegade time to report where the two missionaries were staying.

When the soldiers arrived, Father Peter himself opened the door, treated them courteously, and shared a little Spanish Mass wine with them. Father Peter and Brother Vincent were allowed to put on their Franciscan habits and to take along their rosaries. They were tightly bound and thrown into the jail at Nagasaki. Here they languished for almost a year until Father Richard Trouvé, another victim of Ochoso, joined them. With him they were taken to the Omura prison.

In September, 1622, they were brought back to Nagasaki and slowly burned to death in the Great Martyrdom on September 10.

Liturgical Prayer

O God, all-powerful, look down upon our weakness. Since the burden of our sins lies heavy on us, protect us through the intercession of your martyrs, blessed Peter and blessed Vincent, who dwell in the glory of heaven. This we ask of you through our Lord Jesus Christ, your Son, who lives and reigns with you in the unity of the Holy Spirit, God, forever and ever. Amen.

CHAPTER 17

SAINTS AND BLESSED

Mexico

Bl. Peter Manrique de Zúñiga

(1585-1622) Son of the Viceroy of New Spain

THE death penalty had been imposed on any missionary who attempted to enter Japan and on anyone who aided them in making the attempt. Nevertheless, a Japanese ship with two missionaries on board left Manila for a Japanese port in June, 1620. The captain, Joachim Díaz Hiroyama, and his crew of seven sailors were all Japanese Christians; and they were willing to die as martyrs in order to transport the missionaries to their country. To make it possible for them to enter Japan, the missionaries had disguised themselves as merchants. They were the Augustinian Father Peter Manrique de Zúñiga and the Dominican Father Louis Flores.

Captain Hiroyama's ship ran into a storm which drove it first toward the coast of China and then to the island of Formosa (Taiwan). There it was overtaken by English pirates who seized the ship and made its crew and two passengers prisoners. Meeting some Dutch traders who were bound for Japan, the English turned over the prisoners to them.

The Protestant English and the Calvinist Dutch were the enemies of the Catholic Spaniards; and they cooperated with the Japanese authorities in their persecution of the Catholics in Japan. In 1609 the Dutch had been allowed to establish a trading center in the Japanese port of Hirado; and when the first English ship arrived four years later, they too were permitted to set up a similar center at the same place.

The Dutch ship took the prisoners to Hirado; and suspecting that the two Spanish merchants were priests, the traders cast all of them into a prison where they held them for about a year and a half. By torturing the two Spaniards, they tried to make them confess that they were priests. But the latter refused to admit their identity because they did not want to endanger the lives of Captain Hiroyama and his sailors.

Father Richard Trouvé of St. Ann tried to liberate the two missionaries on October 18, 1620, not long after it was learned that they had fallen into the hands of the Dutch; but he did not succeed. At this time or soon thereafter a group of five Japanese Christians made a similar attempt, but they were captured and joined the prisoners.

Finally, on December 8, 1621, Father Peter, realizing that it was useless to conceal the truth any longer, declared himself to be a priest and an Augustinian; and he was taken to another prison on a solitary island. Father Louis remained in the hands of the Dutch until March of the following year, when he likewise admitted that he was a Dominican priest. The Japanese prefect of Hirado then transferred him to the same jail in which Father Peter was being held. The other prisoners — Captain Hiroyama, his seven sailors and the other five Japanese Christians — it seems, were incarcerated in the same place.

On August 15, 1622, about a month before the Great Martyrdom, all of them were moved to the jail in Nagasaki. They arrived there two days later, and spent two more days in the local prison. On the morning of August 19, they were taken to the place of execution near the sea. Father Peter and Father Louis, now wearing their religious habits, and Captain Hiroyama, were tied to stakes and slowly burned to death. The other twelve were beheaded.

Father Peter Manrique de Zúñiga, scion of an eminent noble family of Spain, was born in 1585 in Seville. His parents were Don Alvaro Manrique, Marqués de Villa Manrique, and Doña Teresa de Zúñiga y Manrique. The same year his father was appointed seventh viceroy of New Spain. It may be that little Peter did not accompany his father to Mexico, but was taken there a few years later. The Duke of Medina Sidonia is mentioned as having been his tutor for some time while his father held the office of viceroy.

Don Alvaro's term of office lasted from October 17, 1585, to January 27, 1590; but he and his family apparently remained in Mexico till 1596. Thus Peter may well have spent the first eleven years of his life in Mexico City.

In any event, when he was about nineteen years old, he wanted to become a member of the Augustinian Order. His parents and relatives objected vigorously; but eventually he overcame their opposition, and he received the Augustinian habit at Seville on October 2, 1604.

After his ordination to the priesthood, Father Peter volunteered for work in the Philippines, when Father Diego de Guevara, later bishop of Nueva Cáceres, was in Spain enlisting missionaries for the islands. Again his family protested, but Father Peter won out in the end.

In 1610 Father Peter sailed for Mexico. There he had to remain for a half year before he could board a ship at Acapulco and continue his voyage to Manila. Concerning his sojourn in Mexico we have no details, but there can be no doubt that the zealous young priest was not idle during those six months.

In the Philippines Father Peter devoted himself to missionary work with great success for some six years. But when news arrived from Japan that his confrere, Bl. Fernando Ayala Fernández de San José, had died a martyr in 1617, Father Peter was permitted to go to that country to take the martyr's place.

On his arrival, Father Peter was apprehended at once. But learning that the missionary was the son of the viceroy of New Spain and fearing international complications, Gonroku, the governor of Nagasaki, immediately made secret arrangements for his return to Manila.

Two years later Father Peter made a second attempt to enter Japan, his companion being the Dominican Father Louis Flores. This time he fell into the hands of Dutch Calvinists; and after an imprisonment of about two and a half years in Japan, he was executed at Nagasaki on August 19, 1622, thus winning the martyr's crown at the age of thirty-seven.

Bl. Peter Manrique de Zúñiga is one of the 205 martyrs of Japan who were beatified in 1867. His feast has been observed in Japan, Macao, Seville, and by the Augustinian Order on March 2, and in Mexico City on August 19.

Liturgical Prayer

God, all-powerful, through the intercession of your martyr, blessed Peter, protect our bodies against the dangers of life and keep all rebellious thoughts out of our minds. This we ask through our Lord Jesus Christ, your Son, who lives and reigns with you in the unity of the Holy Spirit, God, forever and ever. Amen.

CHAPTER 18
SAINTS AND BLESSED
Mexico

Bl. Louis Flores

(c. 1570-1622) A Colonial of New Spain in Japan

A NATIVE of Belgium, a national of Spain, a colonial of Mexico (New Spain), a Dominican friar and priest, a missionary in the Philippines, and a martyr in Japan. Such is a brief summary of the life of Bl. Louis Flores, the companion of Bl. Peter Manrique de Zúñiga. Little more is known about him.

He was born of Spanish parents in Antwerp, Belgium, about 1570. His father was a merchant, and Louis followed in his footsteps, taking up the same trade as a young man. He went first to Spain, and then to Mexico where he hoped to become a rich man. However, by the grace of God with which he cooperated, he soon became convinced of the futility of material wealth; and the gold-seeker found something more valuable than worldly goods.

Louis joined the Dominicans in Mexico, was ordained a priest, and for a time held the office of master of novices. At the age of thirty-two, in 1602, he went to the Philippines; and for some seventeen years he devoted himself to missionary work in the islands, especially in Ogachon. For several years he was one of the councilors of the Philippine province of the Dominicans.

Exhausted by his labors in out-of-the-way places, Father Louis retired to Manila to recuperate. News poured in of the persecution raging in Japan and the many martyrdoms of missionaries and their neophytes. Father Louis, though almost fifty years old, asked to be allowed to go to Japan; and permission was granted.

164

Bl. Louis Flores joined the Dominicans in Mexico before undertaking missionary work in the Philippines and Japan.

As related in the life sketch of Bl. Peter Manrique de Zúñiga, Father Louis set out with the Augustinian martyr in 1619. With him, Father Louis fell into the hands, first of English pirates, then Dutch traders, and finally the Japanese persecutors. He gave his life for Christ and so became a martyr at Nagasaki on August 19, 1622, being about fifty-two years old.

Like his companion, Bl. Peter, Bl. Louis Flores is one of the 205 martyrs of Japan beatified in 1867. His feast has been celebrated in Mexico on August 19. The Dominican Order has observed it annually on June 1, when keeping the feast of Bl. Alphonse Navarette and 109 companions, martyrs of Japan. Included among these 110 martyrs, besides Bl. Louis Flores, are twenty-one other members of the Order of Preachers (eleven priests, five novices and five brothers), twenty-four Japanese members of the Third Order of St. Dominic and sixty-four Japanese members of the Confraternity of the Rosary.

Liturgical Prayer

O almighty God, we beg you to grant help to our infirmity through the intercession of your martyr, blessed Louis. As we glory in his triumph, so may we not hesitate to imitate his constancy. This we ask of you through Jesus Christ, your Son, our Lord, who lives and reigns with you in the unity of the Holy Spirit, God, forever and ever. Amen.

165

CHAPTER 19

SAINTS AND BLESSED
Mexico

Bl. Louis Sotelo, Bl. Louis Sasada and Bl. Louis Baba
(1624) Three Martyrs Named Louis

THE *San Juan Bautista*, a proud new ship, was gently swayed by the breeze in the harbor of Uraga, northern Honshu, Japan. The ship was ready to make its maiden voyage across the wide Pacific, to Acapulco, Mexico. Masamune, the *daimyo* of northern Honshu, had the ship built under the direction of General Sebastian Vizcaino, who had been at his court since the summer of 1611 as the ambassador of the Spanish Empire. The general was now on board to return to Mexico; the year was 1613.

On board, too, were two ambassadors of Masamune to the courts of Madrid and Rome — the Franciscan Father Louis Sotelo and Rokuemon Hasekura with thirty Japanese nobles. Father Sotelo, who had a perfect command of the Japanese language, had been a very successful missionary in Japan during the past decade. Only a few months earlier, Masemune had saved the missionary's life by sending a letter to the *daimyo* Ieyasu at Edo (the present Tokyo).

Though Ieyasu was in control of southern Honshu and the greater part of the other Japanese islands, there were still some *daimyos* who were more or less independent. The most powerful among these, Masamune of northern Honshu, had shown himself favorable to Christianity and even exhorted his subjects to become Christians; and the one who was responsible for this to a great extent was Father Sotelo.

A native of Seville, Father Sotelo had gone in 1600, as a young

Bl. Louis Sotelo sojourned in Mexico three different times before he died a martyr in Japan in 1624.

Franciscan priest of twenty-six years, via Mexico, to the Philippines and from there in 1603 to Japan. Now, ten years later, he was taking with him to Mexico two Japanese youths who later would be his companions as martyrs. They were Louis Baba and Louis Sasada.

As his personal servant and cook, Louis Baba was the constant companion of Father Sotelo during his travels and sojourns in Mexico and Europe — a period of five years. Thus with Father Sotelo he was a resident of Mexico for a total of nine and a half months in 1614 and 1617-1618.

Louis Sasada did not go beyond Mexico and remained there until Father Sotelo returned from Europe, and so he resided in Mexico for about four years. When he made the voyage from Japan to Mexico in 1613-1614, he was only thirteen years old. His father, Michael, a pious and esteemed Japanese nobleman, had died a Christian martyr with seven others a short time before, when they were beheaded on August 16, 1613.

It was on October 27 of the same year that the *San Juan Bautista* set sail under the captaincy of Father Sotelo. After a stormy voyage of three months, the sturdy ship entered the harbor of Acapulco, where the ambassadors were given an honorable reception. They remained for four and a half months, and then continued their voyage on another ship which sailed from Vera Cruz on June 10.

Louis Sasada stayed in Mexico to enter the Franciscan Order and study for the priesthood. He became a member of the Province of Sts. Peter and Paul in Michoacán; and, having a keen intellect, he made rapid progress in his studies. He also became a model son of St. Francis, deeply imbibing the spirit of the Poverello.

When Father Sotelo returned more than three years later as bishop-elect of Oshu, northern Honshu, he chose Friar Louis Sasada as his secretary. But they did not depart for the Far East at once, although the *San Juan Bautista* was waiting for them at Acapulco. Bishop-elect Sotelo and Hasekura with his retinue tarried in Mexico for five months, waiting perhaps for more favorable weather. The fact that the governor of Manila was in Mexico at the time and wanted to go along may have been another reason for the delay.

At length the distinguished party embarked on April 2, 1618. Accompanying Father Sotelo, besides Friar Louis Sasada and Father Peter de Avila who had come from Spain with the bishop-elect, were several other Franciscans. One was Father Diego Pardo de San Francisco, subsequently superior in Japan. Another was Brother Vicente de San José, and still another was Brother Bartholomew Laurel Días. All of these, except Father Pardo, are counted among the beatified martyrs of Japan. They reached Manila three months later.

Here all kinds of obstacles blocked Father Sotelo's return to Japan, and he was unavoidably detained in the Philippines for four long years. Hasekura did not continue his voyage back home until 1620, when the *San Juan Bautista* took him back to Sendai, northern Honshu.

In Manila, Friar Louis Sasada completed his studies for the priesthood, his teacher being Father Sotelo himself. He had not yet reached the canonical age, when a special dispensation permitted him to be ordained a priest in Manila.

Finally, during the latter part of 1622, Father Sotelo, disguised as a merchant, was able to board a Chinese ship in the port of Nueva Segovia and sail for Japan. He took along with him, besides Father Louis Sasada, his faithful Japanese servant, Louis Baba, who had been with him ever since he began his journey to Madrid and Rome nine years earlier.

On reaching the coast of Japan near Satsuma in September, the Chinese captain would not permit them to disembark. He had learned of the execution on August 19 of the Christian Japanese ship captain, Joachim Díaz Hiroyama, and his brave crew because they tried to smuggle the Augustinian Father Peter Manrique de Zúñiga and the Dominican Father Louis Flores into the country. The Chinese captain suspected that Father Sotelo and Father Sasada were priests.

Father Diego de San Francisco Pardo de Membrilla, the superior of the Franciscans in Japan, who had succeeded in entering Japan shortly after he arrived in Manila with Father Sotelo in 1618, hearing about the latter's predicament, made an attempt to rescue him and his two companions. He got a rowboat ready, and obtained the help of a dozen strong and faithful rowers. With their aid he planned to board the Chinese ship during the night and to deliver the missionaries out of the hands of the captain. But when the time came, the boat could not be found.

The Chinese captain surrendered his prisoners to the authorities at Nagasaki, and all three were taken to the prison in that city. A few weeks later, after a new prison was opened at Omura, Father Sotelo was moved to it, while Father Louis Sasada and Louis Baba were kept at Nagasaki. Six months later they rejoined Father Sotelo in the Omura jail. Not long afterwards two more missionaries became their companions. They were the Dominican Father Peter Vásquez and Jesuit Father Michael Carvalho.

The imprisonment of Father Sotelo, Father Sasada and Louis Baba lasted almost two years. Father Sotelo received his young companion Louis Baba into the Third Order Secular of St. Francis; and a year later admitted him to profession. Their life in prison was almost like that in a friary.

"Though there are four priests here in jail," wrote Father Sotelo, "we have all that is required to perform our religious exercises and even to celebrate Mass. The Christians at the risk of their lives procure for us all that we need. Therefore, we partake daily of the Table of the Lord, which gives us wonderful consolation and helps us in our privations. The prison is for us, not a prison, but a real palace or delightful garden."

On the feast of St. Louis, King of France, August 25, 1624, the five prisoners were informed that they had been sentenced to death and that the execution was to take place at once. When this news was communicated to them they sang the *Te Deum*.

At ten in the morning, they were taken in two boats to the place of execution at Omura, the three foreign priests in one boat and the two Japanese in another. They were tied to five stakes which had been set up in a half circle: Father Sotelo in the middle, Father Vásquez on one side and Father Carvalho on the other, and Father Sasada and Louis Baba at the ends. The wood piled in front of them was set on fire.

Since Father Sasada and Louis Baba were closer to the flames, the straw ropes which bound them to their stakes were quickly burned through. Both of them went over to Father Sotelo and kneeling before him, asked him for his blessing.

"I bless you," said Father Sotelo, "and may God bless you and give you the fortitude which will obtain for you the crown of eternal life which has been prepared for you."

They returned to their stakes and were soon overcome by the fire and smoke. The next to die were Father Vásquez and Father Carvalho. Father Sotelo suffered longer because he was the farthest removed from the fire. The soldiers put more wood and straw around him. When the straw ropes holding him to the stake were consumed, he fell into the flames.

The books and sacred vestments which the martyrs had used in prison had been taken along by the executioners; and they now threw them on top of Father Sotelo.

After the martyrs had died, the soldiers burned their remains in another fire; and taking the ashes in a boat off shore, they threw them into the sea. Though the people were not permitted to be present at the execution, Matthias, a Japanese Franciscan brother of the Third Order, who had disguised himself as a stable

170

Delayed in Mexico in 1618, Bl. Louis Sotelo, bishop-elect of Oshu, Japan, looks longingly toward the Far East.

boy, was able to be an eyewitness. He reported the details we have briefly narrated.

Father Louis Sotelo, Father Louis Sasada and Louis Baba as well as the other two martyrs were among the 205 who were declared blessed in 1867. The three Franciscans are honored in the order of Friars Minor and in Japan together with Bl. Apollinaris on September 13. Bl. Peter Vásquez is one of the 109 companions of Bl. Alphonse Navarette, and hence his feast has been celebrated by the Dominicans on June 1. Bl. Michael Carvalho is remembered in the calendar of the Society of Jesus on August 25.

Liturgical Prayer

O Lord Jesus Christ, you gave blessed Louis Sotelo and his companions blessed Louis Sasada and blessed Louis Baba the grace to shed their blood in defense of the faith in your name. Through their merits and prayers, may Christian people be strengthened in professing the faith, and may the nations who walk in darkness be led to the light of the Gospel: you who live and reign with the Father in the unity of the Holy Spirit, God, forever and ever. Amen.

CHAPTER 20

SAINTS AND BLESSED

Mexico

Bl. Bartholomew Laurel Días

(c. 1599-1627) A Mexican Colonial and Doctor in Japan

In the novitiate friary of San Francisco at Morelia in Michoacán, Mexico, the following entry was made in the register of professions on October 18, 1617: "The young brother Bartholomew Días or Laurel on this day made his solemn profession according to the Seraphic Rule." Some ten years later a note was added in the margin: "Notice has been received that the saintly Brother Bartholomew with other Franciscans was burned to death by slow fire at Nagasaki on August 17, 1627."

The birthplace of Brother Bartholomew was Puerto Santa María in the province of Cádiz, Spain. Exactly when he emigrated to New Spain, we do not know. Apparently he was still a child when his parents took him to the Spanish colony in the New World. Father Botero tells us that the brother was baptized as an infant at Acapulco in 1599.

As a youth Brother Bartholomew learned the trade of a weaver, and as such was of great help to his parents. When he was about sixteen years old, in 1615, he applied for admission as a brother in a Franciscan friary, either in the Mexican Province of the Holy Gospel or that of Sts. Peter and Paul. His request was granted, but soon afterwards he left for some unknown reason.

The following year he came back and was received as a novice at Morelia in the Province of Sts. Peter and Paul; and after completing his novitiate year, he pronounced his vows as a brother — according to Father Botero, in the friary at Querétaro. During the

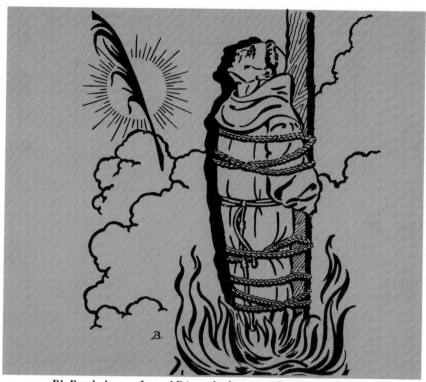

Bl. Bartholomew Laurel Díaz, who became a Franciscan brother in Mexico, won the martyr's crown in Japan in 1627.

next four years, he served as infirmarian, carpenter and maintenance man.

In 1618 Brother Bartholomew went along with Father Sotelo to Manila on the *San Juan Bautista*. Another brother of Mexico, Bl. Vicente Ramírez de San José, and the Japanese cleric Louis Sasada were on the same ship.

During the next five years, Brother Bartholomew nursed the sick in a hospital at Manila. While engaged in this work, he learned in a practical way the art of medicine from the doctors with whom he worked, and he picked up the Japanese language from the Japanese patients whom he attended. Thus he prepared himself for the missions in Japan.

In 1623, Brother Bartholomew went to Japan with three Franciscan priests. All four succeeded in entering the country without being detected. The priests were Father Francis of St. Mary, Father John of St. Philip, and Father Bernard of St. Joseph Osorio. Father Francis had been a missionary in the Philippines since 1606, and he had mastered the Tagalog, Chinese and Japanese languages.

As the companion of Father Francis, Brother Bartholomew proved to be of great help in the priest's apostolic work. In the preliminary investigations for the 205 beatified martyrs of Japan, a witness gave the following testimony:

"The holy lay brother, because he was an expert doctor, could penetrate easily without being recognized into the huts of the poor and help them with his medicines. . . . And in this way he opened the dwellings of the poor people to Father Francis who completed the work begun by the lay brother."

The priest and the brother, assisted by a Japanese catechist of the Third Order of St. Francis, named Anthony of St. Francis, were able to carry out their work in the mountains around Nagasaki and nearby counties for some four years. On the feast of Pentecost, 1627, they were in the house of Gaspar and Mary Vaez. A priest hunter discovered them there on Pentecost Tuesday.

Soldiers were sent immediately to arrest them. The catechist Anthony was not in the house at the time, but he arrived after the soldiers had come. He could have escaped. Instead, he openly declared himself to be a disciple of Father Francis.

The number of those imprisoned was eleven. Besides the priest, brother, catechist and their two hosts, there were six other Japanese Christians, all members of the Third Order of St. Francis.

On August 17, they were taken to the execution grounds. The three Franciscans, Gaspar Vaez, and another Christian who was regarded as a leader were tied to stakes and slowly burned to death. The other six were beheaded.

All eleven were beatified in 1867. They are counted among the forty-four companions of Bl. Apollinaris; and so they are remembered by the Order of Friars Minor on September 13. In Mexico the feast of Bl. Bartholomew Días Laurel is celebrated on the anniversary of his death, August 17.

Liturgical Prayer

O God, in your martyr, blessed Bartholomew, you have given us a shining example of apostolic zeal and fortitude. Through his intercession and merits, grant that we may ever strive to work out our own and our neighbor's salvation. This we ask through Jesus Christ, your Son, our Lord, who lives and reigns with you in the unity of the Holy Spirit, God, forever and ever. Amen.

CHAPTER 21

SAINTS AND BLESSED

Mexico

Bl. Bartholomew Gutiérrez

(1580-1632) A Native of Mexico and Martyr in Japan

THIRTY-FIVE years after the martyrdom of St. Philip of Jesus, another native of Mexico City, born only nine years after St. Philip, likewise died a martyr in Japan after working and suffering in that country as a missionary for fifteen years. He is the Augustinian Bl. Bartholomew Gutiérrez Rodríguez, whose feast is observed in Mexico and Guatemala on March 2 and by his religious brethren on September 2.

Born in Mexico City on September 3, 1580, Bartholomew was the son of Alfonso Gutiérrez and Ana née Rodríguez. The very next day he was baptized in the cathedral of the city.

At the age of sixteen he joined the Hermits of St. Augustine; and the next year, on June 1, 1597, he pronounced his vows. He completed his studies for the priesthood at Yurirapúndaro, and was ordained at Puebla. In 1606, not long after his ordination, the young priest was sent to the Philippines, where he devoted himself to missionary work for some six years.

In 1612, before the persecution began, he was permitted to go to Japan, and was appointed prior of the Augustinians, at Osaka. Two years later he was banished from the country with many other missionaries, and returned to Manila. However, he managed to reenter Japan in 1617; and during the next dozen years he succeeded in evading the priest hunters and reaped a rich harvest of souls.

Often he was in imminent danger of being captured, but

somehow or other he was able to escape his pursuers. Once he was given three days' time in which to flee from Japan. Father Bartholomew spent the three days in giving the catechists intensive instructions and strengthening them in the faith. Taken prisoner, he was confined in a pagan temple because it was thought that the Christians would not visit him there. But they came in great numbers, and the abode of idols became a house of God. Father Bartholomew heard his visitors' confessions and preached the word of God to them. The guard on duty was impressed; he listened, and he himself embraced the Catholic faith.

On another occasion some soldiers were hard on his heels. Father Bartholomew entered a house where he was known, picked up a guitar, and began to play and sing. When the soldiers knocked on the door, the priest himself opened it and invited them to enter. Then he entertained them with his music and singing to such an extent that — strange to say — they forgot why they had come.

At one time the persecutors really had him cornered in a dark place where there were many cobwebs. But seeing the cobwebs, the soldiers did not investigate; and the missionary escaped.

A good Christian woman to whose house Father Bartholomew had come to celebrate holy Mass protected him in a novel way. When the soldiers arrived, she showed no dismay whatever, but treated them with such courtesy and friendliness that they decided not to make a search. Surely, they thought, there is no priest in this house. Another time when he was in a Christian home, Father Bartholomew hid in a clothes closet; and the soldiers failed to find him.

In August, 1629, however, Nagasaki received a new governor, Takenaka Uneme, a cruel man who did everything possible to stamp out all vestiges of the Christian religion. Hasegawa Gonroku, who had been governor for ten years until 1626, was not particularly anxious to persecute the Christians and their priests. He did so only because he had to carry out the instructions of the *daimyo* Hidetada, successor of Ieyasu, in order to keep his job. His immediate successor for three years, Mizuno Kawachi, was worse; but Uneme was the worst. He devised the most dreadful tortures in his feverish endeavor to make the Christians abandon their faith; and some there were who did apostatize.

Betrayed by one of these apostates, Father Bartholomew was finally captured on November 10, 1629, in the village of Kikizu, Arima, and imprisoned at Omura. Before the end of that month, he was joined by four other missionaries who had been arrested. Two of them were Augustinian priests like himself, namely Fa-

176

Bl. Bartholomew Gutiérrez, martyr in Japan, was a native of Mexico and there joined the Augustinians in 1597.

ther Francis of Jesus and Father Vincent Carvalho. Another was a Japanese Jesuit priest, Father Anthony Pinto Ishida. The fourth was a Franciscan, Brother Gabriel of St. Magdalen, who had done excellent work as a physician.

In the Omura prison, the priests were able to offer up the Holy Sacrifice at times and this was a great consolation to all of them. Here, too, they continued their apostolic work, encouraging the Christians who came to see them and making new converts. But after the lapse of two years they were taken to Nagasaki.

In the Nagasaki jail, all five were confined to cramped quarters of only eight square yards; and next to them were fifty-four Christians in an area that measured twenty-four square yards. Numerous attempts were made to make the prisoners renounce their faith, but neither promises of favors nor threats of punishment were able to shake their constancy.

At the beginning of December, 1631, soon after their arrival at Nagasaki, the five missionaries were taken to the hot sulphur springs at Unzen in the mountains near the city. Repeatedly they were immersed in the sulphurous water until the skin all over their bodies was burned by the acid. A doctor was on hand to apply remedies so they could be tortured anew. This barbarous treatment was administered six times a day, and it was kept up for thirty-one days. Then the missionaries were put back into the jail. Here they remained for another eight months.

Finally, the death sentence was pronounced on them and their sufferings came to an end. On September 3, 1632, they were taken to the usual place of execution near the shore, tied to stakes, and slowly burned alive. Thus did Father Bartholomew Gutiérrez Rodríguez of Mexico City win the martyr's crown, together with five other missionaries.

The sixth was added to their number a short time before their death. He was a Japanese priest of the Third Order Regular of St. Francis, Father Jerome Torres. The fact that he had adopted a Portuguese family name seems to indicate that he was a native of Nagasaki or the vicinity.

These six were the last to be included in the list of 205 martyrs of Japan who were solemnly beatified in 1867 by Pope Pius IX. However, they were not the last martyrs. Twenty additional missionaries died for the faith during the two years which followed, 1633 and 1634. With their death, very few were left in Japan; and the end of the first mission period was near. It was not possible to reestablish missions in Japan until the latter part of the nineteenth century.

Liturgical Prayer

O God, you made blessed Bartholomew renowned for zeal in propagating the faith and for martyrdom. Through his example and intercession, may we press forward on the way of your commandments and deserve to win the prize of eternal life. This we ask through Jesus Christ, your Son, our Lord, who lives and reigns with you in the unity of the Holy Spirit, God, forever and ever. Amen.

Part I
SAINTS AND BLESSED

Colombia

NEW Granada was the name by which the Republic of Colombia was known in the sixteenth and seventeenth centuries, when it was the scene of the apostolic labors of two great saints, one of them a missionary to the Indians and the other a missionary among the black slaves who were brought to South America from Africa. The Indian missionary, St. Louis Bertrand, returned to Spain and died there in 1581, the same year in which St. Peter Claver, the Apostle of the Black Slaves, was born.

CHAPTER 22

SAINTS AND BLESSED
Colombia

St. Louis Bertrand
(1526-1581) Apostle of Colombia

EARLY on a winter morning in the year 1541, a fifteen-year-old boy ran away from his home in Valencia, Spain. It was not because he did not like it there or because he had any complaint against his parents. On the contrary, he loved his father and mother very much, and it was hard for him to steal away as he did. But he wanted to be a saint — a saint like St. Alexis and St. Roch, who literally became penniless pilgrims on earth in order to reach their heavenly abode more easily and surely.

In the evening, the parents of the boy received a letter in which he told them that he had gone on a pilgrimage to Compostela. His mother, who was ill, was prostrated with grief. His father immediately went in search of the lad and found him a few miles outside the city.

"Louis, my boy," he pleaded with him. "You are too young to wander about alone; and you have brought such great sorrow upon your sick mother that she is in danger of dying. You must come back home."

"I'm sorry, Father. I thought you would understand why I left the way I did, and not object. I don't want Mother to suffer on my account. I'll go back with you."

The father of the boy called Louis was Juan Beltrán, a notary of Valencia and a very religious man. His forefathers were relatives of the great St. Vincent Ferrer of Valencia, who died in 1418. After the death of his first wife, Juan Beltrán had set out for the

St. Louis Bertrand, a Dominican missionary in northern
South America and the Caribbean Islands, 1562-1569.

Carthusian monastery of Porta Caeli to become a monk. But on
the way, we are told, St. Bruno, the founder of the Carthusians,
and St. Vincent Ferrer appeared to him and assured him that he
was not called to the religious life. He was to become the father of
a saint.

Returning to Valencia, Juan Beltrán married the pious Juana
Angela Exarch, who became the mother of nine children. Her
first-born was the boy Louis, who was baptized at the very font
where St. Vincent had received the sacrament 175 years before.
The day of Louis' birth was January 1, 1626.

Even as a child, Louis began to live like a saint. At the age of eight he started to pray the Little Office of the Blessed Virgin daily. His bed consisted of wooden planks without a mattress. He made the rounds of the hospitals in the city to bring aid and comfort to the poor sick. After his futile attempt to enter upon the life of a pilgrim, he persuaded fifteen other boys to join him in his charitable visits to the hospitals.

For several years, Louis remained in his parental home; and then he tried to run away again; that is, he made secret arrangements for his reception into the Dominican Order at the novitiate of Santo Domingo in Valencia. But on the very day on which Louis was to be clothed in the white habit, his father learned about it. He hurried to the prior, Father Ferran, and dissuaded him from going through with the ceremony. His son, he said, was too young and in such poor health that he would not be able to live as the friars lived.

Once more Louis went back home. But he left his heart at Santo Domingo. After his day's work, he often went to the priory to tend its garden and to spend some time in quiet prayer. Several times he succeeded in concealing himself in a dark corner of the choir so that he might attend the midnight chanting of the divine office by the friars.

When Father Mico succeeded Father Ferran as prior, Louis applied once more for admission to the Order of Preachers. He was now eighteen and a half years old. His request was granted; and on August 26, 1544, his investiture took place.

Soon afterwards his father again tried to convince his son that he did not have the necessary qualifications. Besides poor health, he cited another reason which was indeed a fact. Louis was lacking in those intellectual gifts which were required for a student for the priesthood in the Dominican Order. It would be better if he joined the Carthusians or the Jeronymites.

However, in the presence of Father Mico, Louis told his father that he would rather die than leave the Dominicans; and he made a vow that he would live and die as a follower of St. Dominic. Juan Beltrán finally realized that the step taken by his son was in accordance with God's will and he gave his full consent. A year later, on August 27, Louis made his profession as a Dominican friar.

As a novice, Friar Louis was regarded as a model. Though his demeanor was grave and apparently he had no sense of humor, his kindness and sincerity were so patent that he won the hearts of all who knew him. He would have preferred to continue the life of prayer and self-denial to which he had become attached during his novitiate, but he bravely overcame his repugnance to the studies to which he now had to devote himself.

So diligently did he apply himself that two years later, although he was only in his twenty-second year, he was considered sufficiently prepared for the priesthood. In 1547 he was ordained a priest by the archbishop of Valencia, who was none other than the greathearted and learned Augustinian, St. Thomas of Villanova.

After a lapse of two more years, the young priest, who edified all by the holiness of his life and the exactness with which he performed all his religious exercises, was chosen to be the companion of Father Mico for the founding of a new house at Lombay. There, however, he remained only two months.

Learning of the critical illness of his father, Father Louis returned in 1549 to Valencia just in time to be present at his father's death. After the funeral, he remained in Valencia, and in 1551 he was appointed master of novices and brothers. This office he held during the next six years except for a short journey to Salamanca. He felt the need for a more profound study of theology and obtained permission to go to the famous university in that city. Before he reached his destination, however, a prudent counselor whom he consulted advised him not to carry out his plan.

He returned to Valencia, but he was no longer satisfied with merely training the novices. Quite suddenly he became a famous preacher. Though he was lacking in those natural qualities and talents which are considered essential for a successful career in the pulpit, he somehow made a deep impression on his hearers and exerted a profound influence on their way of living. This can undoubtedly be attributed to the fact that his spoken word was corroborated in a striking manner by the example of his own conduct as well as by his miracles of prophecy and healing.

When a virulent epidemic broke out in Valencia in 1557, the novices were dispersed among several other houses, and Father Louis was assigned as vicar to the priory of Santa Ana at Albayda. The plague lasted three years and decimated the population of Valencia and its environs. While continuing his apostolate in the pulpit, Father Louis also devoted himself to the physical and spiritual care of the pest-stricken with tireless zeal and heroic charity.

With the tenderness of a mother he nursed the sick; and with his own hands he prepared the dead for burial and attended to their interment. Paying no heed to the danger of contracting the disease, he spent all his energies in the exercise of the corporal and spiritual works of mercy. Thus he gave proof that his piety and his love of God and neighbor were genuine. He had advanced far on the road to sanctity.

In one of his sermons, Father Louis boldly denounced the conduct of some noblemen whose lives were a public scandal. Several days later, one of the culprits met Father Louis and his companion and pointed his gun at them. Father Louis made the sign of the cross over the gun and it was transformed instantly into a crucifix. The sinner fell on his knees at the feet of Father Louis and solemnly promised to amend his life. This miracle is the explanation for the picture which shows St. Louis Bertrand holding a crucifix of which the lower part has the shape of the stock or handle of a gun.

The story of what happened in this encounter was broadcast by mouth, and the people came in crowds to listen to the new St. Vincent Ferrer. The largest churches were placed at his disposal, but even these could not accommodate the multitudes who flocked to his sermons. Eventually he was compelled to address his audiences in the public squares of the cities. St. Teresa of Avila (who died in 1582) also heard about the saintly Dominican. As she sought the guidance of the Franciscan St. Peter of Alcantara (who died in 1562), so she asked also the advice of Father Louis Bertrand. She was then engaged in her God-given task of deepening the spiritual life of the Carmelite Order in Spain.

The reply which Father Louis sent to St. Teresa gives us an insight into his character, and it contained a prophecy. "I have received your letter," he wrote, "and since the point on which you ask my advice is of great importance for the honor and glory of God, I thought it best first to pray for light on the subject. This will explain the delay of my answer. But now I say to you, in the name of our Lord Jesus Christ, go on as you have commenced. The Lord will assist you. In His Name, I declare that in fifty years your reform will be one of the most useful and one of the most renowned in the Church of God."

After the epidemic had spent itself, Father Louis and his novices were sent back to Valencia; and the great preacher resumed his former work in his native city. But he did not stay there long. He had already been thinking of going to the New World as a missionary, when two confreres arrived with letters from the master general asking for volunteers to accompany them to the Indies. Father Louis offered to go with them, and his offer was accepted.

Early in 1562, Father Louis set sail from Seville for the Americas. Only seventy years had passed since Columbus discovered the New World. One of the pioneers and defenders of the Indians, the retired Dominican Bishop Bartolomé de las Casas (who died in 1566), was still living in the priory of Atocha in Madrid. But the Dominicans had already established a number of flourishing provinces in Central and South America.

Father Louis and his companions disembarked at the important Caribbean seaport of Cartagena founded in 1533 on the northwestern coast of present-day Colombia, South America, which was then called Nueva Granada. On landing, they went directly to the local priory of St. Joseph for a period of rest and recollection.

Soon afterward Father Louis entered upon his amazing missionary career of about seven years among the Indians in the surrounding areas and the islands of the Caribbean Sea. Endowed with the gift of tongues, as the bull of canonization tells us, he converted the natives by the thousands. It is claimed that he baptized 25,000 of them. He did not remain long in one place, leaving to others the task of continuing the work he began.

Some of the details a historian would like to know concerning his activities have not been recorded. But we do have the names of a number of places he visited. First of all, there was Cartagena itself, where he preached also to the Spanish settlers, though with less fruit than among the Indians. The same is true of other Spanish towns where he sojourned for a short time.

From Cartagena he went into the region to the south, lying between the coast and the Magdalena River, and for several years he preached the faith with great success among the Indians of Tubera. More than 6,000 of them became Christians.

There was, and perhaps there still is, a baptismal register for this region with entries in the handwriting of Father Louis. Other places in this area which were the scene of his missionary labors were Turbaco, Mompós and Teneriffe.

Father Louis then moved eastward beyond the Magdalena River to the Indians of Cipacoa and then northward to those of Paluato, east of Santa Marta. The latter city, on the northern coast of Colombia, had been founded by the Spaniards as early as 1524. The Indians of Paluato refused to listen to Father Louis; but after he had left them and gone toward Santa Marta, some 1,500 of them followed him and begged for baptism. In the mountains of the Sierra Nevada de Santa Marta he continued his evangelization of the Indians.

Father Louis also penetrated into the western part of what is today Venezuela, and made a journey to present-day Panama, which was originally a part of Nueva Granada as well as the later Colombia.

185

From the mainland he also sailed to various islands in the Caribbean and spent a considerable time among the cannibal Caribs. The two principal islands where he carried on his missionary work were those of San Vicente in the Leeward Islands and St. Thomas in the Virgin Islands.

On one of these islands he came close to winning the martyr's palm. In fact, it was only by a miracle that his life was saved. The Caribs had given him a deadly potion to drink. For five days he hovered between life and death. Then the Indians were dismayed to see him vomit small vipers. They made several further attempts to kill him, but could not harm him. Finally they accepted the Christian faith.

In 1569, strange as it may seem, Father Louis wrote to the master general asking permission to return to Spain. Perhaps the reason was poor health; he was never very strong. Possibly it was also the attraction for the contemplative life which he felt as long as he lived. In any case, we can be sure that he made his decision only after praying for light from above.

His brethren in Colombia tried to keep him with them by electing him prior of the monastery at Santa Fé de Bogotá, which is in the interior of the country. He set out for Bogotá, but before he reached the city the permission requested from the general reached him. From Cartagena he sailed for Spain and arrived there on October 18.

One year he spent in retirement at the priory at Valencia. In October, 1570, he was appointed prior of the monastery of San Onofre near Valencia. After the expiration of his term of three years, he served once more as master of novices for three years, and then for three years more (1575-1578) as superior of the house in Valencia.

During these years and until 1580, he was also engaged in preaching the word of God and enjoyed the same remarkable success that had crowned his efforts before he left for South America. But he still felt inclined to give up his work as a preacher and to spend his remaining years exclusively in prayer and contemplation.

At one time, about 1575, he seriously thought of becoming a Carthusian monk. Had his father been right after all? No, it was God's will that he give free rein to his consuming zeal for souls. That was his final decision after prayerfully considering the matter and listening to the advice of his friend and contemporary, the Franciscan Bl. Nicholas Factor.

It will be of interest to add that as a young priest, Bl. Nicholas had left the Observant Franciscans to join the Capuchins; but some years later he returned to the Observants. To his critics, he replied with a smile: "I can but do the will of God. All three branches of the Order of our holy Father St. Francis are holy."

When Father Louis went out to preach, he used to take along several of the novices to give them some practical experience. He told them: "If your preaching makes men lay aside enmities, forgive injuries, avoid scandals and occasions of sin, and reform their conduct, you may say that the seed has fallen on good ground. But to God alone give all the glory and acknowledge yourselves always to be unprofitable servants."

During the last two years of his life, Father Louis was ailing and suffered much from fevers. In 1580, after completing a Lenten series of sermons at Xativa, he went to Valencia to preach in the cathedral. From the pulpit he had to be carried to the Dominican priory in the city, where he lingered on for some time. He predicted that he would die on the feast day of St. Dionysius. On that day the archbishop of Valencia came to minister to him and was present at his death. It was October 9, 1581. Father Louis was fifty-five years and nine months old.

The many miracles which occurred during his lifetime were now followed by others still more numerous. To the present day his body is incorrupt and intact, except for the mutilations inflicted upon it in 1814.

Little more than a quarter century after his death, on June 29, 1608, Pope Paul V beatified Father Louis Bertrand; and on April 12, 1671, Pope Clement X enrolled him among the canonized saints of the Church.

In 1690 Pope Alexander VIII declared him to be the patron of Nueva Granada, that is, the present Republic of Colombia. The feast of St. Louis Bertrand has been observed on October 10 in Colombia, in Valencia, Spain, and in Port-of-Spain, Trinidad; and on October 9, in the Dominican Order, in Chile, and in Venezuela.

Liturgical Prayer

O God, you made your confessor, blessed Louis, an illustrious preacher of the Gospel to save souls and to bring back sinners from the pit of vice to the pathway of virtue. Through his intercession may we be cleansed from all sin and obtain eternal life. Through Jesus Christ, your Son, our Lord, who lives and reigns with you in the unity of the Holy Spirit, God, forever and ever. Amen.

CHAPTER 23
SAINTS AND BLESSED
Colombia

St. Peter Claver

(1581-1654) Slave of the Black Slaves

AT the college of Montesíon in Palma on the Spanish island of Mallorca, in 1605, there were two Jesuits who are now canonized saints. One was an old brother, over seventy, who had been carrying out the duties of a doorkeeper for the past quarter century. He was known for his extraordinary mastery and practice of the science of the saints, though he had never studied theology in a formal way. In fact, he had written some books on the spiritual life. The other was a young scholastic, twenty-four years old, who was taking his course in philosophy at the college.

A deep spiritual friendship developed between the old man and the young man. The scholastic admired the brother's spirit of prayer and penance and tried to follow his example. The brother, on the other hand, recognized the scholastic as one who was capable of heroic sanctity, and gladly gave him instructions in asceticism.

Both were canonized by Pope Leo XIII in 1888. The brother is now St. Alphonsus Rodríguez, and the scholastic is St. Peter Claver.

One day Brother Alfonso said to Pedro Claver: "I cannot tell you my grief at seeing God unknown in the greater part of the world, because there are so few who go to make Him known. Cannot charity cross the seas which have already been charted by greed? Does the love of Christ stir men to seek souls less than the love of the world stirs them to seek riches? If you love the glory of

St. Peter Claver, for thirty-five years the "slave of the slaves" at Cartagena, Colombia, 1615-1650.

God's house, go to the Indies and save these perishing people. Do not wait to be sent under obedience. Be a volunteer!"

Brother Alfonso knew his young friend would do that very thing. Soon afterwards Pedro informed his Father Provincial that he was ready even now to go as a missionary to the colonies in the New World. He was told that the kind of work to which he would be assigned would be decided in due time by his superiors.

"Father Provincial has not given me a very encouraging answer," Pedro told Brother Alfonso.

"Do not feel disappointed," said the brother. "In a few years you will be going to Nueva Granada."

When Pedro Claver completed his philosophy course to take up the study of theology in Barcelona, Brother Alfonso gave him copies of some of his writings on the spiritual life.

Two years later, when a group of missionaries was being recruited from the provinces in Spain for Nueva Granada, Pedro Claver renewed his request; and he was chosen to represent the Province of Aragón in the party which set sail for the Indies in April, 1610.

They landed at Cartagena, Nueva Granada, on the northern coast of what is now Colombia. Pedro Claver went on to Santa Fé de Bogotá to complete his theological studies. Then he was sent to a new house at Tunja for his "tertianship" of spiritual exercises.

In 1615 he was ordained a priest in Cartagena and there celebrated his first holy Mass — the first to do so in that city. Shortly afterward he entered upon a very difficult and fruitful apostolate of thirty-five years among the African slaves who were brought in large numbers to the port of Cartagena.

The son of a Catalonian farmer, Pedro Claver was born at Verdú near Barcelona in 1581. He made his preparatory studies for the priesthood at the university of Barcelona; and after graduating with distinction he received the minor orders. He then decided to become a Jesuit, and was admitted to the novitiate in Tarragona at the age of twenty. After his novitiate, he spent a year in classical studies at Gerona, and was a student of philosophy at Palma for several years.

As a student of theology at Bogotá, he also had other tasks to perform. At various times he served as doorkeeper, sacristan, infirmarian and cook.

After his ordination, he was an assistant for one year to another great missionary, Father Alfonso de Sandoval, who ministered to the African slaves with heroic perseverance for a period of forty years; and so he was introduced to his life's work by one who had learned from long experience.

A report concerning Father Sandoval says of him: "When he heard that a vessel of blacks had come into port, he was immediately covered with a cold sweat and a death-like pallor as he recalled the indescribable work and enervating fatigue required of him on previous similar occasions. He never became accustomed to his work, though he was engaged in it for years."

When Father Peter Claver began his apostolic and charitable career, the slave trade had been in operation for over a century. From the beginning, the Spanish colonists had to contend with a labor problem. The native Indians, who were pressed into service, were for the most part physically unfit for the hard work in the mines and on the plantations, and they were very susceptible to diseases. As early as 1505 African slave labor was introduced into Venezuela.

Before Bartolomé de las Casas was ordained a priest in 1510, he had black slaves working for him. After hearing the Dominican Montesinos preach a sermon in which he condemned the practice, Las Casas freed his slaves and himself became a Dominican friar. In his concern for the Indians, he gave his approval, in 1516, to an arrangement which permitted each colonist to import twelve black slaves provided that the Indians working for him would be freed. It was an unfortunate compromise, and he regretted it later and tried to undo the harm done.

But the slave trade continued and became more widespread. Spaniards were by no means the only ones engaged in it. One of England's national heroes, Sir John Hawkins, played an important role in the shameful traffic. African chiefs were among the worst offenders inasmuch as they sold into slavery their own people and others whom they captured.

The inhuman treatment which the traders gave their human cargo was far worse than that which the slaves received from those who purchased them. On the coasts of Guinea, the Congo and Angola, the dealers bought the slaves from the African chiefs at two to four ecús (crowns) a head, transported them to the New World, and there sold them for 200 crowns each or bartered them for merchandise of equivalent value. They cared not how many perished as a result of the unspeakable conditions in the holds of their ships, where as many as fifty percent died during the voyage of six to seven weeks. They still made a sizable profit.

Because of its location on the Caribbean Sea, Nueva Granada's port of Cartagena, founded in 1533, became one of the principal slave markets in the Americas. Here the ships unloaded the poor slaves, many of them sick or dying, and herded them like cattle into camps or sheds, from which they were taken to the mines or plantations. In Father Peter Claver's day, as many as 1,000 slaves arrived at Cartagena every month, averaging 10,000 per year.

The Church condemned the slave trade and slave labor as a "supreme villainy," but this did not put a stop to it. All that the priests could do was to ameliorate the sad condition of the slaves as much as possible. And not all the masters of the slaves were as cruel and merciless as some of them.

The laws of Spain, recognizing that the slaves were human beings with immortal souls, promoted their Christianization, required that they be free to enter Christian marriages, prohibited the separation of the members of a family, and forbade their seizure once they had gained their freedom. These laws were observed by some, though not all, of the Spanish colonists. But what observance there was, was due in great measure to apostolic men like St. Peter Claver.

By nature Father Peter Claver was shy and lacking in self-confidence. Yet there was nothing timorous or haphazard in the way in which he undertook the task of caring for the bodies and souls of the wretched Africans who were brought to Cartagena. Neither was his enthusiasm something ephemeral. He tackled the problem and carried out his work in an organized, methodical manner; and he persevered in his efforts, despite disheartening setbacks, with unlimited confidence in Divine Providence, irrepressible optimism and disarming humility.

Knowing that he could not do everything alone, he enlisted the help of others who assisted him with money and goods and services. Since the slaves coming from Africa spoke many different and strange dialects, he used a group of seven interpreters. Even then it was difficult to make himself understood, and so he made use of pictures portraying our Lord suffering on the cross, showing white people including the pope and rulers of peoples rejoicing while witnessing the baptism of a black, or depicting the torments of souls condemned for their crimes to hell.

First, however, he tried to win the confidence of the slaves, who were half crazed by suffering and fear, by alleviating their bodily wants. "We must speak to them with our hands," he said, "before we try to do so with our lips." When he heard the signal that a load of slaves was entering the port, he went out on a pilot boat to meet the ship with food and medicines and to come to the aid of those who were in the worst condition. There was not much time for this, because the slaves were immediately taken from the ship and shut up in yards. Here he distributed bread and other food, brandy, lemons, tobacco; and to the sick he gave medicines.

He did not hesitate to care for those who were afflicted with such loathsome diseases that no other person, white or black, would go near them.

Then he began to instruct them, with the help of his interpreters and his pictures, in the truths of Christian faith and morals, both in groups and individually, and thus gradually prepared them for the sacraments of penance and baptism. He tried to make it clear to them that even as slaves they retained their dignity as human beings, and thus he sought to instill in them some degree of self-respect. He drilled them in making the sign of the cross and saying a simple prayer of sorrow for sin and love of God, such as the following: "Jesus Christ, Son of God, you shall be my father and my mother and all my good. I love you very much. I am sorry for having offended you by my sins. O my Lord, I love you much, very much."

When finally he baptized them, he gave the same Christian name to every group of ten catechumens, so they would not forget it and one could recall the name to the other. It is claimed that in the thirty-five years he spent in this work among the slaves he baptized a total of 300,000 persons and yearly he heard more than 5,000 confessions of whites and blacks.

Before the slaves were taken to the mines and plantations, he made a last strong appeal to them to remain steadfast in the faith. They were now children of the Church, and that privilege no one could take from them. Most of them he would not see again, but those who went to places which were not far distant remained the object of his care and solicitude. He visited them in the spring and preached to them, prayed with them, and sang hymns with them. On these occasions he lodged in the quarters of the slaves rather than the haciendas of their masters.

But he did not neglect the owners of the slaves. They too had souls to be saved; and by persuading them to live as good Christians, he also bettered the lot of the slaves. That was much more effective than inveighing against them in public. He pointed out to them that it was for their own temporal and spiritual good to have regard for the physical and spiritual well-being of their slaves. Thus he contributed much to the observance of the laws enacted in behalf of the slaves.

Some heeded his advice and his appeals; others did not. They complained that he was taking up too much of the time when the slaves should have been working. Some fastidious wives declared it was impossible for them to enter the church after the blacks had been there for Mass. And when some of the slaves got themselves into trouble, Father Peter was blamed for it. Sometimes

In 1896 St. Peter Claver was proclaimed patron of all missionary work among blacks throughout the world.

even the ecclesiastical authorities were too willing to listen to his critics. Father Peter did not try to defend himself. "What sort of man must I be," he would say to himself, "that I cannot do a little good without stirring up so much trouble."

On the other hand, when he was praised for the excellent work he was doing on such a grand scale, his reply was: "That is the way it should be. But for me there is nothing but self-indulgence in it. It is due to my enthusiastic and impetuous temperament. If I would not be doing this work, I would be a nuisance to myself and everybody else." And when he was admired for looking after the sick who had the most repulsive diseases, he said: "If being a saint consists in having no taste and having a strong stomach, then perhaps I am one."

One should think that Father Peter had more than enough to do taking care of the slaves, but that was only a part of his activities. In Cartagena there were two hospitals. One was St. Sebastian's for general cases, which was in the care of the Brothers of St. John of God. The other was St. Lazarus, a leper asylum, which also had patients who were afflicted with "St. Anthony's Fire." Twice a week Father Peter visited these hospitals to bring comfort to the patients in their bodily ailments and healing in their spiritual ills. Many a hardened sinner made his peace with God before he died because Father Peter was there to encourage him and pray with him.

Father Peter also visited the prison and prepared condemned criminals to meet their God. Not a single one paid the death penalty who did not have Father Peter at his side during his last hours to absolve him and to pray with him.

He was also the regular Father Confessor of a great many people in Cartagena. Like the Curé of Ars, he is said to have spent as many as fifteen hours in the confessional without interruption.

The vices and disorders of the city, for which the traders and sailors were largely responsible, Father Peter combatted by preaching a mission in the fall of the year, not in a church, but in the public plaza where the four main streets came together.

He was, in fact, not only "the slave of the black slaves," as he called himself, but the apostle of all of Cartagena. The citizens were convinced that divine punishments were more than once averted from them because Father Peter, like another Moses, pleaded for them; and they had no doubt that God confirmed his preaching by the gift of prophecy and other miracles.

The self-denial and self-sacrifice required of Father Peter in a way of life so completely devoted to all the works of mercy was indeed very great. But he was not satisfied with that alone; he added the most rigorous penitential practices and long vigils of prayer in the privacy of his quarters. Toward himself he did not exercise the same fatherly kindness and consideration that he always extended to others.

Toward the end of his missionary career, Father Peter was wrongly accused of not taking proper care in the administration of the sacrament of baptism; and his superior forbade him to do any more baptizing in the future. He submitted humbly and meekly. "It behooves me," he wrote, "always to imitate the example of the ass. When he is evilly spoken of, he is dumb. When he is starved, he is dumb. When he is overloaded, he is dumb. When he is despised and neglected, he is still dumb. He never complains in any circumstances, for he is only an ass. So also must God's servant be."

In 1650 he began to preach the Jubilee among the blacks along the coast. He was then in his sixty-ninth year and so weakened and emaciated by his labors and penances that he had to give up the attempt and retire to his residence. When an epidemic broke out, he was among the first victims. He seemed to be near death and received the last sacraments. Though he recovered and lived for four more years, he was a broken man and to a great extent a neglected invalid.

Brother Nicholas González, his old helper, and Doña Isabella de Urbina, who had made generous contributions of money for his work, remained his faithful friends and did what they could for him. But the young black who was entrusted with the care of the ailing old priest was impatient with him and left him helpless for days.

The pain he endured was almost incessant. He was subject to a trembling in his limbs which made it impossible for him to celebrate Mass. Most of the time he was confined to bed. A few times he had himself carried to a hospital, a dying person, a prisoner, to hear a confession. Once he was even taken to a group of African slaves who had just arrived from a hitherto unknown tribe. An interpreter was found and Father Peter gave them short instructions.

He also managed to drag himself from his bed in the summer of 1654 when Father Diego de Fariña arrived with instructions from the king to continue the work of Father Peter. The old missionary was happy to have a successor and welcomed him with great joy.

Not long afterward he heard the confession of his benefactor, Doña Isabella, and told her it was the last time. On September 6, after attending Mass and receiving Holy Communion, he said to Brother Nicholas: "I am going to die." In the evening of the same day he became very ill and lost consciousness. For two days more he remained in that condition. On the feast of the Nativity of the Blessed Virgin, September 8, 1654, his earthly life ended.

The people of Cartagena, the great as well as the lowly, now vied with each other to do honor to Father Peter Claver. The religious communities all sang Requiem Masses for him. The blacks made arrangements for a special Mass at which the Spanish authorities were present. The vicar general of the diocese officiated at the funeral.

Pope Pius IX beatified Father Peter Claver on July 16, 1850; and Pope Leo XIII canonized him on January 15, 1888. The same Supreme Pontiff, on July 7, 1896, proclaimed St. Peter Claver to be the special heavenly patron of all missionary enterprises among the blacks throughout the world. The feast of St. Peter is observed on September 9.

Liturgical Prayer

O God, you strengthened blessed Peter with remarkable love and patience to help the enslaved blacks in order that you might bring them to a knowledge of your name. May we seek the things that belong to Jesus and in doing so love our neighbor in truth and in deed through the intercession of your saint. Through Jesus Christ, your Son, our Lord, who lives and reigns with you in the unity of the Holy Spirit, God, forever and ever. Amen.

Part I
SAINTS AND BLESSED

Ecuador

IN colonial times, the Republic of Ecuador (the Spanish for "equator") was a part of Peru. The country's patron saint, St. Mariana of Jesus, is almost an exact counterpart of St. Rose of Lima. She was born in Quito one year after the death of St. Rose, and died there at the age of twenty-seven. While St. Rose was canonized in the seventeenth century, it was only in the middle of the twentieth that the name of St. Mariana was added to the Church's roster of canonized saints.

CHAPTER 24

SAINTS AND BLESSED

Ecuador

St. Mariana of Jesus

(1618-1645) The Lily of Quito

QUITO, Ecuador, has been called "the most picturesque city in the world." Though it is only a few miles south of the equator (for which reason the country has been called Ecuador), Quito has an average temperature of 56 degrees Fahrenheit. It lies in a valley high up in the Andes, 9,236 feet above sea level, and is surrounded by snowcapped mountain peaks.

The days, which are warm, and the nights, which are cool, are of equal length. Regularly at six in the morning the sun rises, and it sets at six in the evening. Because of the gentle sunshine and almost daily showers of an hour's duration, flowers abound. Some of the streets are lined with eucalyptus trees; others are steep, dipping toward winding ravines or spanning them with stone viaducts.

From the air Quito looks like "an undulating checkerboard broken by the domes and spires of its many churches." The largest of the churches is that of San Francisco. The city was named San Francisco de Quito when Benalcazar founded it in 1534 on the site of the northern Inca capital. At that time he set aside a plot of ground for a church and friary which were begun by Father Jodoco Ricke, cousin of Charles V and "apostle of Ecuador." The present church's twin Spanish towers were damaged by an earthquake in 1868 and rebuilt in a reduced form.

It took more than a century to build San Francisco; and work on its construction was still in progress when a young *hidalgo* (nobleman) of Toledo, Spain, Captain Jerónimo Zenel Paredes y Flores, arrived in Quito to collect a debt owed to his father. He probably collected the money and sent it to his father, but he himself remained in Quito. He married Mariana Jaramillo de Granobles, daughter of a distinguished Spanish couple who had emigrated to Quito; and he established his home in the spacious parental house on a steep and narrow street facing the Royal Hospital.

It was a big stone house of two stories, built around a patio with galleries upstairs and downstairs. On the ground floor there were six rooms. There was enough room for the three generations living there. Besides they had a house on a big plantation in the country at Cayambe.

Eventually Jerónimo and Mariana became the parents of eight children. The youngest was born on October 31, 1618; and

The sick were the special object of the love of St. Mariana of Jesus Paredes y Flores, "the Lily of Quito."

when baptized on November 22 she received her mother's name Mariana, but was often called by the diminutive, Marianita. She was only about four years old when her father died, and her mother followed him in death not long afterward. Her oldest sister Jerónima, who had married Captain Cosme de Caso before little Mariana was born, henceforth took care of the orphan; and Mariana continued to live with her sister and brother-in-law in the old homestead during the rest of her life.

As a little girl, Marianita had five companions about her own age. Besides her sister Inez, there were Jerónima's three little girls of whom Sebastiana was especially close and dear to her, and a friend, Escolastica. They shared a happy childhood, studying their lessons, learning to dance and sing and play the guitar and other instruments, and becoming proficient in needlework.

All six of them ran away from home on one occasion, after nine-year-old Marianita had listened to a sermon in the Jesuit church about the martyrs who had died in Japan in 1597 and had just been beatified (1627). Marianita had persuaded her companions to join her and become missionaries with her in Japan. The next morning they were found huddled by the roadside a short distance outside the city, shivering a little from the cold of the night, but otherwise safe and sound and easily convinced that they should return home.

Unsuccessful in her endeavor to become a missionary, Marianita made an attempt to become a recluse at the foot of an image of our Lady which stood on the side of the inactive volcano Mount Pichincha. But here too she ran into difficulties, and so she arranged a little convent for herself at home. In Sebastiana she found a kindred soul, and the two of them led very similar lives and were of great help to each other in striving for Christian perfection.

It was at about this time, between the ages of seven and ten, that Marianita was permitted to receive her First Holy Communion, and that she placed herself under the spiritual direction of her confessor Jesuit Father Juan Camacho, and took the vow of perpetual virginity. From early childhood she had shown herself inclined toward a solitary and penitential life. As she grew a little older, her brother-in-law offered to provide the usual dowry for her entry into the convent of the Poor Clares or the Dominican Sisters, but she told him it was God's will that she stay at home.

Accepting the hospitality of an upper room in the old home, Mariana reduced its furnishings to the barest necessities and there spent most of her time in prayer and penitential exercises. Her penances were of such an excessive and extreme nature that one shudders at a mere recital of them; and this phase of her life is undoubtedly something which cannot be held up for imitation. That a frail girl should have survived them even for a few years seems a marvel. In fact, for the last several years of her life, she seems to have subsisted on Holy Communion alone.

Mariana Paredes y Flores changed her name to Mariana de Jesús and wore a black dress and veil. She chose St. Ignatius as her patron, embroidered the monogram of the Holy Name of Jesus on the front of her dress, and considered herself "a daughter of the Company of Jesus."

The Jesuit Fathers who were successively her confessors after Father Camacho were Father Antonio Manosalvas, Father Luis Vásquez, and lastly Father Alonso de Rojas. By an unusual arrangement a Jesuit brother, Hernando de la Cruz, became her spiritual director when Father Vásquez was appointed her confessor. From that time on Brother Hernando held daily conferences with her on spiritual matters.

Mariana's brother Jerónimo was a Franciscan, and so was her cousin Father Lorenzo Fernández; but when Jerónimo made his profession as a friar in 1622, Mariana was only four years old. Both Mariana and Sebastiana were indeed enrolled in the Third Order Secular of St. Francis by the Father Guardian of the Convento de San Francisco on November 6, 1639, and a year and twelve days later both made their profession of the Third Order Rule. Mariana also asked that the Third Order habit be used as her shroud. But she did not use it during life, and the particular kind of spirituality by which she attained perfection was not the Franciscan way but that of St. Ignatius and his Society. She herself said as much.

This, of course, did not prevent her from observing faithfully and exactly the rule of the Third Order, which then required much more than now. In the United States, in our own day, there have been Jesuit Fathers who were the spiritual directors of Franciscan Third Order fraternities.

Each morning she arose at four o'clock to devote an hour and a half to meditation on our Lord's Passion. Then she went to the Jesuit church and there spent the greater part of the morning, beginning with the recitation of the divine office, followed almost daily by confession, then holy Mass and Communion, with a long thanksgiving after Mass, including the praying of the fifteen decades of the Rosary and attendance at another Mass. Noteworthy is the fact that she received Holy Communion every day at a time when this was very rarely done.

About ten o'clock Mariana returned home and ate her meager

"brunch," her only meal, which she reduced more and more. At noon she and Sebastiana took care of the poor and sick who came each day to the door. After aiding as best she could those who needed immediate attention, Mariana went to her room and brought down a big basket filled with loaves of bread which she and Sebastiana distributed to the people as they passed by in a long line. There was something mysterious about this bread. Nobody seemed to know where it came from; and there was always enough of it, no matter how long the line of beggars was.

There were others who were too shamefaced to join the breadline. They came afterwards and did their begging by throwing pebbles at Mariana's window.

In a vacant room on the first floor, Mariana also opened a free clinic for ailing black and Indian children and in an adjoining room she conducted a school for these children.

After praying the canonical hour of Vespers, Mariana spent part of the afternoon doing manual work, weaving and sewing; and the proceeds of her work were given to the poor. Spiritual reading and meditation followed. At ten she took a glass of water instead of supper, and she even denied herself a drink of water sometimes as she recalled the thirst suffered by our Lord on the Cross. The fact that she was suffering from dropsy made Mariana feel thirst more keenly.

More meditation and the reading of the lives of the saints occupied her till after midnight. Then she allowed herself about three hours of sleep or rest on the most uncomfortable bed imaginable. When Father Camacho was her spiritual director, he insisted that she take at least four hours of sleep; but afterward that time was reduced more and more. She also increased her corporal penances, but obeyed when her Father Director commanded her to mitigate them.

Unable to be a missionary in a foreign pagan land, Mariana nevertheless exercised a fruitful apostolate in her own country. Whenever and wherever possible, she endeavored to lead sinners back to God; and her efforts were crowned with remarkable success. By her exhortations and prayers she caused many men and women of all classes to give up a life of sin and to turn to the practice of virtue.

Her influence for good was very great. Very severe toward herself, she was always affable and kind to others. The sick were a special object of her love; and many of them, even some regarded as incurable, she restored to health by making the sign of the cross over them or sprinkling them with holy water. By her prayers she raised at least one dead person to life.

202

Though she had never received more than an elementary education, many, including learned persons, came to visit her and ask her advice and wonder at the extraordinary gifts God had bestowed upon her. Mariana predicted future events, saw distant happenings as if they were taking place before her eyes, and read the secrets of hearts. At prayer she often became oblivious of everything about her and was transported into a state of ecstasy.

The year 1645 was one of great calamities for Ecuador. There were earthquakes, followed by epidemics of measles and diphtheria; and the volcano Pichincha, inactive till then, began to spout hot lava upon the countryside. Two thousand persons lost their lives in the earthquake, and Riobamba was almost entirely destroyed. Quito's population was decimated by the epidemic which carried away 2,000 Spaniards and 10,000 Indians.

From the pulpit of the church of the Jesuits Father Rojas preached an eloquent sermon on the fourth Sunday of Lent. He declared that God was punishing the people for their sins. His discourse reached its climax in an unexpected peroration in which he offered his own life to God if it should be acceptable in exchange for a cessation of the earthquakes and plagues.

Mariana was in her usual place beside the pulpit. She arose and in a clear voice asked God to take her life as a propitiatory offering and to spare that of the priest. From the church she went straight to her home never to leave it again. She was stricken at once with a strange, unidentifiable, lingering sickness. At the same time, the earth tremors stopped and the pestilence began to wane.

For two months Mariana was afflicted with a high fever; she endured a burning thirst; she could hardly breathe; and her whole body was wracked with pain. Frequent blood-lettings did not reduce the fever. Mariana had herself carried from her upstairs room to one on the ground floor. She asked that after her death she be clothed with the Franciscan habit and that the funeral services take place in the Jesuit church. The bishop of Quito came to give her his blessing. Others too visited her, including Father Rojas and Brother Hernando.

On Friday, May 26, 1645, between nine and ten in the evening, as Mariana had foretold, she expired peacefully after receiving the last sacraments and kissing the crucifix. Brother Hernando immediately made a painting of her face. Crowds of people came to pay their last respects.

Catalina, the Indian servant, had poured Mariana's blood, from her many blood-lettings ordered by the physician, into a corner of the patio where there was a nondescript plant. Now the

A painting of St. Mariana of Jesus is carried through the main door of the Vatican Basilica of St. Peter for the canonization ceremonies in 1950.

plant suddenly developed into a flourishing lily with three beautiful flowers. This was regarded as a miracle, and from that time Mariana was called "the Lily of Quito."

During her whole life, Mariana had sought to make atonement for the sins of others by her extraordinary penances. Her last illness and death was likewise an offering made in reparation for sin. In the sermon which he preached at her funeral, Father Rojas declared: "Our country should not only rejoice because this Servant of God has ennobled it with her patronage and today in heaven favors it with her prayers; it should also be moved to eternal thankfulness because it was through her sacrifice that the city was delivered from the fate inflicted on it by the God of vengeance in punishment for its sins."

Mariana de Jesús was only twenty-six years and about seven months old when she died. She was buried temporarily in a vault at the altar of St. Joseph in the Jesuit church; later her body was placed in a tomb at the altar of Our Lady of Loreto; and now it rests beneath the main altar. Steps toward her beatification were taken immediately after her demise, but it was only a century later, in 1754, that her cause was introduced in Rome. Another century passed before her beatification by Pope Pius IX took place in the Vatican Basilica on November 10, 1853. Still another century went by, and Pope Pius XII solemnly canonized her on July 9, 1950. In Ecuador her feast has been observed on June 2, and the Friars Minor and Secular Franciscans honor her by an optional memorial on May 28.

In an audience granted to the Ecuadorian delegations which were present at the canonization, the Holy Father said: "May all those who live today in the full light of devotion to the Most Sacred Heart of Jesus admire the perfection of this innocent victim who, in the dawn of the seventeenth century, already knew how to make reparation the center of her spirituality."

St. Mariana of Jesus is honored as the heavenly patroness of Ecuador. She has also been declared Ecuador's "national heroine." One of the principal decorations conferred by the government of Ecuador is the Order of Mariana de Jesús Paredes y Flores. Postage stamps have been issued in her honor; and her name is given to colleges and other institutions, even to small shops and to buses. The house where she lived, as she had foretold, became a Carmelite convent in 1653 and still is at the present day.

The name of St. Mariana de Jesús has been translated by some into St. Mary Anne of Jesus, but this is an incorrect version. There are two saintly persons with the name of Mary Anne who were contemporaries of St. Mariana and have been beatified. One is Blessed Mary Anne of Jesus who founded a community of Mercederian tertiaries under the jurisdiction of the reformed branch of that religious order and died in 1624; the other is Blessed Mary Anne of Jesus, a Franciscan tertiary who lived from 1557-1620 and, like St. Francis of Assisi, was privileged to have the stigmata.

Liturgical Prayer

O God, you willed that the blessed Mariana, like a lily among thorns, should grow in virginal purity and constant penance amid the enticements of the world. Through her merits and prayers, help us to withdraw from vice and strive for greater perfection. Through Jesus Christ, your Son, our Lord, who lives and reigns with you in the unity of the Holy Spirit, God, forever and ever. Amen.

Part I
SAINTS AND BLESSED

Peru

THE Republic of Peru in South America claims four canonized saints and one blessed as its own. All of them died in that country and their relics are there venerated. Two of them were born in Peru, and the other three came from Spain. For a part of their lives, all five were contemporaries. The period of time during which they lived in Peru comprises less than a century.

St. Rose of Lima is called the first American-born saint inasmuch as she was the first to be canonized. However, St. Philip of Jesus was born in Mexico seventeen years before St. Rose, and hence he was the first native of the Americas to be raised eventually to sainthood. Bl. Roch González, a native of Paraguay, was born ten years before St. Rose.

St. Turibius was the first of the American saints to die in the New World. St. Louis Bertrand died in 1581, the year in which St. Turibius came to Peru; but St. Louis died in Spain.

St. Francis Solano is rightly claimed also by the countries in which he carried on his missionary work among the Indians, namely Argentina and Paraguay.

CHAPTER 25
SAINTS AND BLESSED
Peru

St. Turibius de Mogrovejo
(1538-1606) The Charles Borromeo of Peru

WHEN news was received in Spain of the death in 1575 of the first bishop of Lima, Peru, Archbishop Jerónimo Loaysa, the one chosen to fill the vacant see was a layman then serving as the chief judge of the court of the Inquisition in Granada. His name was Dr. Toribio Alfonso de Mogrovejo y Robles, a doctor of both civil and canon law.

He tried to evade the appointment, pleading that he was neither qualified nor prepared for the office and its burdens. As a youth, it is true, he had entertained the desire of becoming a priest; and though he was now around forty years of age, he had not married. Finally, resigning himself to what he recognized as the will of God, he acquiesced, was ordained a priest and consecrated a bishop, and departed for Peru.

In Lima he became an outstanding prelate and a great saint — a counterpart of his holy contemporary, St. Charles Borromeo of Milan (1538-1584). Like St. Charles, he carried out the decrees of the recent Council of Trent (1545-1563) in his vast New World diocese with admirable diligence and thoroughness.

Toribio was born on November 16, 1538, at Mayorga in the province of León, the second son of the Lord of Mogrovejo (Mogrobejo). His mother's maiden name was Ana de Robles. A pious and studious youth, he overcame all temptations to sin by praying often, avoiding the dangers, and strengthening his will by many acts of self-denial. Daily he prayed the Little Office of the Blessed

St. Turibius Alphonse de Mogrovejo was
archbishop of Lima, Peru, 1580-1606.

Virgin Mary as well as the Rosary; and on Saturdays he fasted in honor of our Lady. At school he usually gave a part of his lunch to some poor person.

One day young Toribio came upon a poor peddler woman who was giving vent by blasphemous utterances to her anger at having lost something from her basket. He approached her and inquired how much the article was worth. Then he gave her enough coins to cover her loss and asked her not to offend God again.

He was thinking of entering a seminary to study for the priesthood when his father died. Regarding it as his task to look after his mother and sisters, he gladly sacrificed his own inheritance to care for his sisters until they were married and his mother was well provided for.

Graduate studies, which he began at Valladolid, he completed at the university of Salamanca, where he was awarded the degree of *Doctor utriusque juris*, the doctorate in both civil and canon

209

law. Then he began to teach law at Salamanca and soon gained a reputation for both his learning and his virtuous life. The attention of King Philip II was called to the young professor, and the king named him chief judge or president of the court of the Inquisition in Granada. During the five years that Dr. Toribio de Mogrovejo held this office, he distinguished himself by unimpeachable integrity and prudence as well as genuine love and concern for the salvation of souls. Not only was he a just judge but also a father and counselor, and a protector of the innocent.

Toribio was about forty years old when the king proposed him for the vacant see of Lima. Like St. Ambrose, he received the minor and major orders, including ordination to the priesthood in quick succession in 1578; but there was an interval of two years before he was consecrated a bishop in Seville by Bishop Cristóbal Rojas y Sandoval.

Peru, which at this time included Ecuador and Bolivia, was still a frontier land, although the viceroy Francisco de Toledo (who returned to Spain in 1581) had given the colony stability by the *Libro de tasas* laws which he promulgated and for which he won the title of "lawgiver of Peru." The first diocese was that of Cuzco, erected in 1538. Lima was made a diocese in 1543, and the Dominican Jerónimo Loaysa Carvajal, bishop of Cartagena since 1537, was transferred to the new see. He remained in charge until his death, twenty-eight years later. It was in 1548 that Lima became an archdiocese, with suffragan sees throughout Hispanic America. Bogotá was raised to the rank of an archdiocese in 1564.

Bidding farewell to his aged mother whom he was not to see again, Archbishop Toribio left Spain in 1580, soon after his consecration, and arrived by ship at Payta, some 600 miles north of Lima, on May 24, 1581. The rest of the journey he made on foot. It was a real missionary tour; for he gave instructions and administered the sacraments in the Spanish settlements and Christian Indian villages along the way. He saw for himself what kind of a land Peru was, its sandy desert-like seashore, its impenetrable forests, and its rugged and high mountains.

Arriving in Lima, he began immediately to correct the objectionable practices which had crept in among many of the Spanish conquistadors and settlers and even some of the clergy. To those who tried to justify themselves by appealing to long-standing customs, the archbishop countered in the words of Tertullian: "Christ calls himself the truth, not custom"; and he resolutely insisted that for a Christian there can be no tampering with the law of God or his justice. Where it was necessary, he did not hesitate to employ the sanction of excommunication, no matter what social posi-

210

tion the culprit had. Eventually, by firmness as well as patience and kindness, he overcame all opposition and was able to eradicate the worst abuses.

To the needy and the sick Archbishop Toribio was a true father and benefactor. Not only did he protect the poor from oppression, but he alleviated their needs with a lavish hand, always careful that his munificent acts of charity were not publicized. Those who shrank from making their indigent condition known publicly were a special object of his care.

There were not a few hospitals in Lima. In colonial times there were eventually no less than ten of them, one having been founded by Archbishop Toribio for poor priests. When he was not away on a journey, the archbishop would visit several hospitals each day to comfort the sick and to administer the sacraments.

At one time, when a pestilence was raging in some parts of his diocese, the archbishop did all he could to relieve the sufferers, depriving himself of the very necessities of life. And since he realized that the plague might well be a punishment from God, he preached repentance and walked in penitential processions. At the same time he personally observed fasts and kept vigils of prayer, begging God to remove the scourge and offering himself as a victim for his flock.

Though his residence was exteriorly a "palace," he lived there like an ascetic. Never was he idle. "Time," he was wont to say, "is not our own. We'll have to give a strict account of it." During the few hours which he allowed himself for sleep and rest, he lay on a bed of bare boards. He added other rigorous penitential practices, chastising his body as did the apostle St. Paul. So far as others were concerned, however, he was always solicitous for their well-being, becoming (like the same apostle) all things to all men.

While giving his fullest attention to all his duties, he did so in constant prayerful union with God. Nevertheless, he set aside certain hours which he spent only in meditation and direct communication with his Lord. Every morning, before celebrating the Holy Sacrifice, he went to confession in order to rid his soul of the least taint of sin. Then he spent a considerable time in preparation for Mass, and afterwards made a long thanksgiving. He always prayed the divine office with great devotion, and sometimes, we are told, angels appeared in visible form to recite the Psalms with him.

Not long after he reached Lima, Archbishop Toribio convoked a provincial council, the third of Lima, summoning to it the bishops of the eleven suffragan sees of the archdiocese. All of them came, except three who were too far away. The council opened on

August 15, 1582, and continued until October of the following year.

It will be of interest to enumerate these dioceses of South America which were established in the sixteenth century. We shall indicate in parentheses the years in which they were erected. They show how rapid was the expansion of the Church all over the continent. Three of the dioceses were in present-day Peru: Cuzco (1538), Arequipa (1577), and Trujillo (1577). The others were Panamá (1521), Nicaragua (1534), Quito in Ecuador (1545), Popayán in Colombia (1546), Asunción in Paraguay (1548), Charcas in Bolivia (1552), Santiago in Chile (1561), and La Imperial in the valley of the Arauco River, Chile (1583). Tucumán in northern Argentina, though made a diocese in 1570, received its first resident bishop only in 1595.

The third council of Lima was concerned especially with the work of civilizing and Christianizing the Indians and with the relation of the Spanish settlers with the Indians. It was decided to have a provincial council every seven years; and Archbishop Toribio presided also over the fourth and fifth councils of Lima in 1591 and 1601. The decrees of these councils are monuments of the archbishop's learning and discretion, and in their day were regarded as models not only throughout Hispanic America, but also in Spain and in Rome.

Archbishop Toribio also made it a rule that a synod be held every two years in his own diocese. During the quarter century of his incumbency, he conducted thirteen such synods. He also founded the first seminary of South America in Lima about 1591.

To provide a greatly needed manual, the archbishop had a Catechism of Christian Doctrine printed in 1583 by Antonio Ricardo. This he did at his own expense, and he saw to it that there was at least one copy in every town. Some have claimed that this was the first book published in South America. However, a catechism was printed in 1577 on a press which the Jesuits introduced at Juli on Lake Titicaca. The first printing press in the New World was the one founded in 1535 by Bishop Juan Zumárraga of Mexico in cooperation with Viceroy Antonio de Mendoza.

Twice Archbishop Toribio made pastoral visitations of every part of his vast diocese; and he commenced a third, but died before completing it. The first visitation lasted seven years, the second four; and the third was in progress for over three years. It is estimated that he traveled 18,000 miles in Peru. Undismayed by dangers, obstacles, or fatigue, he made these difficult journeys on foot or muleback. Often defenseless and alone, he went everywhere, even to places which seemed inaccessible. Besides making an official inspection and administering confirmation, he instructed many new converts and baptized them. In other words, the former doctor of laws became a catechist and a missionary.

Almost to the end of his life, he studied the dialects of the Quechua language because he wanted to converse familiarly with the Indians and teach them Christian doctrine in their own language. Fearlessly he sought out the natives who were wont to flee from the whites or were hostile to them; and by his kindness and goodness he won over a large number.

Riding on a mule at night, he spent the time in mental prayer or prayed the Rosary. Never did he omit holy Mass, even under the most adverse circumstances.

On one occasion, following an unfamiliar path, he came to a frightful precipice. An unknown Indian suddenly showed up, took the archbishop's mule by the bridle, and led it to safety. Before the prelate had a chance to thank him, the Indian disappeared. An angel from heaven had come to his aid in the form of an Indian.

The Indians of Guanacuma tried in vain to transfix him with arrows; and the Chinkakotas lay in ambush, determined to kill him, but were not able to carry out their nefarious design. At Gamalia, the Indians were waging a relentless war against the Christians of the locality and had made disastrous attacks upon them. When the archbishop boldly entered their camp he was met by a volley of arrows, but not a single one so much as grazed him. He succeeded in pacifying the Indians, and later he confirmed them.

When he came to the village of Quives in 1597 to administer the sacrament of confirmation, he was met with an insulting epithet which in the Quechua language meant "Big Nose." Only two little boys and one little girl showed up to receive confirmation, and he gave them the sacrament. The little girl subsequently became St. Rose of Lima.

At Andamarca, in the mountains about 150 miles east of Lima, a group of seventy-two Indian men, seven women, and two boys, came to him and told him they were Christians. A boy dressed in white, they said, had informed them that the archbishop was in the vicinity and had instructed them to bring him the articles which they presented. They were a missal, a breviary and an alb, which had been left with them by a missionary who had made neophytes of them.

While making his third visitation, Archbishop Toribio, now in his sixty-eighth year, contracted a fever at Pacasmayo; but he went on to Guadalupe, Chérrepe and Reque, and in a dying condition reached Saña, 110 miles distant from Lima. He knew that his

213

end was approaching. In fact, he had predicted the time of his death.

Like Father Junípero Serra at the Mission of San Carlos de Borromeo, Archbishop Toribio had himself taken to the church and there he received Holy Viaticum. The anointing of the sick was administered to him later on his deathbed. His heart he bequeathed to the Poor Clare monastery, which his niece had recently founded in Lima, his personal belongings to his servants, and any other funds that were left he bequeathed to the poor.

Over and over again he was heard saying the words of St. Paul: "I desire to be dissolved and to be with Christ." When his last moments came, he asked those about him to chant Psalm 121: "I rejoiced at the things that were said to me; we will go into the house of the Lord." Repeating the words, "Into your hands, O Lord, I commend my spirit," the holy archbishop died on Maundy Thursday, March 23, 1606.

When his body was disinterred a year later and taken to Lima, it was found to be wholly incorrupt, the skin still soft and the joints flexible. Revered as a saint by all — Indians and Spaniards alike — Archbishop Toribio de Mogrovejo continued to help, by his intercession on their behalf in heaven, those who took their recourse to him, sometimes in a miraculous manner.

Pope Innocent XI beatified him in 1679, and Pope Benedict XIII canonized him in 1726. At the request of the Third Plenary Council of Baltimore, the Holy See permitted the celebration of his feast and those of St. Philip of Jesus and St. Francis Solano also in the United States. In the new general calendar of the Church, St. Turibius is remembered on March 23 by an optional commemoration at holy Mass and in Lauds because the Lenten day takes precedence. In Latin America his feast has been observed in the past on April 27.

Among the saints of the Americas St. Toribio represents the bishops and the diocesan clergy. For them especially he is a shining example of priestly zeal and holiness.

Liturgical Prayer

O Lord, guard your Church through the constant protection of your confessor and bishop, blessed Turibius. As pastoral solicitude has made him glorious, so may his intercession make us always fervent in your love. This we ask of you through Jesus Christ, your Son, our Lord, who lives and reigns with you in the unity of the Holy Spirit, God, forever and ever. Amen.

CHAPTER 26

SAINTS AND BLESSED

Peru

St. Francis Solano

(1549-1610) Apostle of Tucumán, Argentina

A YOUNG man, still in his teens, was walking along the Río Aguilar in the province of Córdoba, southern Spain. Suddenly he came upon two men in an open field who were rushing at each other with drawn swords.

"Stop! Stop!" he cried, and ran between them.

Surprised by this interference, the duelists lowered their swords and glared at the youth who had the audacity to mix in their affairs.

"For the sake of God's love, gentlemen," he pleaded with them, "sheathe your swords. One or both of you will surely be wounded or killed if you persist in fighting with such dangerous weapons. And what will be the result? Not merely the loss of life, but eternal ruin. Gentlemen, let there be peace!"

The duelists looked at each other in astonishment, and the young peacemaker won out. They put their swords back into their scabbards.

"Young man," they said. "You are right. We have been fools." They embraced each other in a Spanish hug, and became firm friends.

This is not just a pious story. The incident occurred 400 years ago; and the name of the young man was Francisco Solano. He was born in 1549 at Montilla, a few miles south of Córdoba, in Andalusia, Spain. Baptized on March 10 of that year, he received the name of the Man of Peace, St. Francis of Assisi. His father,

Mateo Sánchez Solano, was the mayor of the city. His mother's maiden name was Ana Jiménez Hidalgo.

Francisco received an excellent education, at first from tutors at home, and then from the Jesuit Fathers who conducted a secondary school in his native city. He was about twenty years old when he joined the Franciscans in the friary at Montilla. Three years later (1572), he was sent to the friary of Nuestra Señora de Loreto, near Seville, to complete his theological studies; and here he was ordained a priest in 1576 at the age of twenty-seven.

There was a famous shrine of our Lady at the Franciscan church in Seville; and since Father Francis had learned to play the violin, he was made director of the church choir. However, after his father's death, which occurred at about this time, his superiors sent him back to Montilla so he could console his sick and sorrowing mother.

Subsequently he was appointed master of novices at Arizafa; and when this novitiate was moved to San Francisco del Monte, the novice-master went to the new location. Later he was made superior of this friary. He soon gained the reputation of being an eloquent preacher, and was invited to preach the word of God in neighboring towns. Noteworthy is the fact that the famous preacher had a special love for children, and they often flocked around him in large groups and walked along with him.

The reason for his success lay not so much in studied oratory as in the holiness of his life. Later on, one of his confreres, Father Juan de Castilla, wrote of Father Francis: "I saw and heard how the pious superior spent each night in prayer, meditation and works of penance; and I marveled very much how such a frail body as his could endure such austerity. In addition, he fasted continuously. His sermons were utterances from another world; and he prayed fervently and perseveringly that the Divine Majesty might not be offended. Never did anyone hear a useless word pass his lips. He spoke only of God. His one desire was to lead as many souls to God as possible."

In 1583 a virulent pestilence broke out in Andalusia. Accompanied by a confrere, Father Francis devoted all his time to the care of the sick, visiting them in their homes, nursing and consoling them, distributing food, and administering the sacraments. When his companion was stricken, he continued alone until he too had to take to his bed. But after he recuperated, he continued his charitable ministrations until the fearful plague ceased.

To avoid the honors which were heaped upon him by the grateful people, Father Francis obtained a transfer to Granada. But for some time he had been longing to do apostolic work in the

St. Francis Solano, Franciscan missionary in Tucumán
(Argentina), 1590-1601, died in Lima, Peru, 1610.

missions and even to suffer martyrdom. He asked to be sent to Morocco; but, just at this time, the Spanish king requested more Franciscan missionaries for the New World, and among those chosen in answer to this call was Father Francis Solano. The mission field to which he was assigned was a difficult one. It was that of Tucumán, the northern part of Argentina, which included a part of the jungle of Gran Chaco, sometimes called the Green Hell.

After crossing the Atlantic, Father Francis and his companion missionaries stopped first on the island of Española or Santo Domingo (Haiti and the Dominican Republic), and then sailed to Cartagena on the northern coast of Colombia. After crossing the Isthmus of Panama on foot, they embarked once more and skirted the Pacific coast of Colombia. In the Gulf of Gorgona or Buenaventura, they encountered a violent storm. The ship was wrecked and 130 passengers were drowned. Father Francis was among those who reached land, after remaining on board as long as he could to help and baptize the black slaves who were on the vessel.

The shore proved to be an inhospitable region. The survivors sought in vain for human beings or for food. Though they were stranded for fifty days, Father Francis retained his accustomed equanimity and prevented the others from yielding to hopelessness. Shortly before Christmas, 1589, a ship arrived from Panama, and they were able to continue their voyage toward Lima. Some distance north of Lima, Father Francis disembarked and walked the rest of the way to the capital of Peru. Here he and his fellow missionaries paused only for a short rest, and then set out on their arduous trek of 1,400 miles across the Andes and south to Tucumán. Steep and lofty mountains had to be scaled, rushing rivers to be traversed, fearful abysses to be crossed. Paths had to be blazed through almost impenetrable forests and across deserted steppes. While snow and ice often made the mountain heights well-nigh impassable, in the valleys below the hot rays of the semitropical sun mercilessly beat down upon the apostolic wanderers. But never did Father Francis relax in his eagerness to reach the land of his desires as soon as possible. Finally he arrived there in the middle of 1590.

Tucumán was first visited by Spanish explorers in 1543. They came by two routes, one from Peru and the other by way of the Río de la Plata. Soon after the conquest of the territory which commenced in 1549, missionaries followed. In 1554 no fewer than fifty-four Franciscans and Dominicans arrived; in 1572 a dozen more joined them, and in 1589 another group of twenty-four. The Franciscan Custody of Tucumán, the equivalent of a small province, was established in 1565. Five years later the territory became a bishopric, but another quarter century elapsed before an orderly diocesan administration could be introduced.

When Father Francis Solano arrived, there were five flourishing mission centers in Tucumán: San Miguel de Tucumán, Santiago del Estero, La Rioja, Nueva Córdoba and Corrientes. But such a center was still lacking in the northeastern section on the boundary of the Gran Chaco, although there was a Franciscan mission at Talavera, or Esteco as the place was called by the Indians. Father Francis was sent to Talavera and given the task of establishing a reduction for the Indians in the region beyond the town.

First the new missionary had to learn the language of the Indians, and he did this in an amazingly short time. Captain Andrés García de Valdes testified: "I gave Padre Solano instructions in the language of the Toconotes, and I consider it an indubitable miracle that he completely mastered the language in less than fourteen days. He preached and taught in this language, heard confessions, and baptized many uncivilized Indians. The remarkable thing about it is that he knew this difficult language much better than many of the Indians."

One of the means that Father Francis used to attract the wild pagan Indians was the music he played on his home-made violin. He had taken his violin along when he set out for the New World, but lost it in the shipwreck in the Gulf of Gorgona. In Tucumán he made a new one of his own with only two strings; but with this makeshift instrument he produced such wondrous music that all who heard it were enthralled by it. Even the most wary among the uncivilized Indians gave him their unlimited confidence and showed him the deepest reverence.

Another marvelous occurrence which made a deep impression on the Indians and had a lasting effect was the uncovering of a spring by Father Francis in the Indian village of Socotonio. Another Indian village which is mentioned as the scene of Father Francis' missionary labors was that of Magdalena. But there were many more. In fact, there were more than fifty such villages in the region of the upper Río Salado (that is, the Río Juramento and its tributary the Río Pasajes) where the Indians settled down at the invitation of Father Francis; and the number of those whom he instructed and baptized ran into many thousands — even hundreds of thousands, according to one biographer.

Once having won over the Toconotes, Father Francis directed his attention to the nomadic Lules Indians who roamed through the region lying between Talavera and the capital, Tucumán. These too he persuaded to settle down about the year 1594, and successfully introduced Christianity among them.

Father Francis even made missionary expeditions into the adjoining Gran Chaco, something that others before him had tried to do in vain; and, as Father Córdoba y Salinas assures us, these too proved successful, though we do not know the number of those who were converted. Paying little attention to his own needs, and satisfied with a few vegetables as food for himself, he sought out the restless and barbaric Indians in their haunts, spoke to them in a friendly way and was understood by them. He knelt down and

219

prayed before them, often with extended arms, played sweet strains on his violin, and sang beautiful hymns for them in his sonorous and melodious voice. And, as Father Córdoba adds, when fatigue and hunger and thirst threatened to gain the upper hand over him, he would turn to the most holy Virgin Mary, carry on a loving conversation with her, and sing joyful songs in her praise and honor.

After five years of intensive missionary work among the Indians, Father Francis was appointed in 1595 as custodian or superior of the entire Custody of Tucumán, which at this time comprised also the territory of Paraguay-La Plata. The latter had been erected into another custody as early as 1538, but during the years from 1575 to 1597 it was joined with that of Tucumán. As superior, it was his duty to visit all the missions; and thus for the next six years he was almost constantly traveling from one mission to another. During the first three years he also visited the Franciscan missions in Paraguay and the La Plata region. That is the historical basis for what one biographer has called "the miraculous hegira of Padre Solano."

Not only the Indian missions but also the Spanish settlements derived great benefit from the visits of Father Francis. Both Indians and Spaniards began to live in a more truly Christian manner as a result of his admonitions. Wherever he could help, he played the part of peacemaker. Once he hurried to the neighborhood of Santiago del Estero, where several tribes were engaged in a bloody conflict. He exhorted the Indian warriors to come to terms, and had the happiness of seeing the war ended then and there.

On another occasion he pacified and converted no less than 9,000 hostile Indians by a single sermon. The Christian natives of the environs of La Rioja had assembled in the church for the services of Maundy Thursday, when a force of unbaptized savages many thousands strong threatened to attack them. Father Francis, who happened to be present, confronted the besiegers. Compellingly he spoke to them of God's punishments and then invited them to abandon the law of hatred and embrace that of love. The result was astounding. Although the Indians belonged to different tribes and spoke different languages, all understood Father Francis and heeded his exhortations. Nine thousand declared themselves ready on the spot to adopt the Christian way of life.

In the canonization bull, Pope Benedict XIII wrote of St. Francis Solano: "While making the sufferings of others his own, and being aflame with the love of God and his neighbor, he was able, through special enlightenment from God, to learn the languages of those peoples, and to preach the faith to them with convincing words. Through the influence of divine grace, he made such a deep impression upon the souls of these wild people that they abandoned their natural barbarity and earnestly vied with one another in hastening to hear the sermons of this holy man; and he instructed and baptized a countless multitude. So much did he win their respect and confidence that they gladly complied with all which previously no one could have induced them to do by force."

After eleven years of missionary work among the Indians of Tucumán and adjoining regions, Father Francis was recalled in 1601 to Lima to take up the duties of the superior of a new *retiro* or house for recollection, namely the friary of Santa María de los Angeles, which is situated outside the city proper among the Andean foothills.

Three years later he made a journey to the coastal city of Trujillo in northern Peru. During his stay of about a year in this city, he prophesied in one of his sermons that it would be destroyed by a devastating earthquake; only the pulpit from which he was preaching would remain standing. This prophecy was fulfilled nine years after his death.

Returning as superior to the friary of Santa María outside Lima, he moved a year later to the Convento de San Francisco, the principal friary in Lima; and there he resided during the last four years of his life. He often left the friary to preach to the people of the city; and the marvelous results he had achieved in his native Andalusia were once more repeated in Peru.

Father Francis was still residing in the friary of Santa María when he preached his famous sermon of 1604 in the marketplace of Lima — a sermon which became one of the city's long-remembered traditions. Before setting out, he prayed for a long time before a crucifix. As he left the friary, he said to the Brother Porter: "Recommend me to the Lord, for today I must render Him an important service."

Business was in full swing when he arrived at the marketplace. Mounting an elevated spot in front of the crowd, he took his crucifix in his hands and with a strong and resonant voice exclaimed:

"Unless you do penance, you will all perish. If God's anger is not appeased, God will destroy this city!" Then, as a biographer reports, "Like living fire the words came from his lips and moved the hearts of his hearers so profoundly that all were deeply affected."

Men and women, young and old, flocked to the churches to go

to confession. There were hardly enough priests in the city to absolve the penitents. Enmities of long standing were patched up, ill-gotten goods were restored, debts were paid, calumnies were recanted, secret sins were confessed. There was such a manifestation of sorrow for past sins, that it could arise only from a sincere and wonderful general reform.

Deeply concerned over the tremendous effect of Father Francis' sermon, the ecclesiastical and secular authorities called the preacher to a judicial investigation to ascertain whether a terrible catastrophe impended. Father Francis gave them a reassuring answer, now that the people had taken his warnings to heart; and the life of the city gradually returned to normal.

The veteran Indian missionary thus became a missionary also to the Spaniards of Peru. He had been preaching in Peru for some nine years, when his health began to decline. He was now in his sixty-second year. Weakened though he was in his body, his soul made higher and higher flights of contemplation until he was called to his reward on July 14, 1610. Immediately after his death he was venerated as a saint in heaven. The highest encomiums were bestowed upon him at his funeral. The Father Provincial of the Jesuits preached the funeral oration and extolled the humble missionary's exalted virtues, his heroic deeds, his numerous miracles and his holy passing.

Clement X, the same pope who had beatified "Rose of St. Mary" of Lima some four years earlier, declared Francis Solano blessed on January 25, 1675; and Pope Benedict XIII canonized him on December 27, 1726. Long before his beatification, Lima requested permission to honor Francis Solano as its patron in 1626. Cartagena in Colombia did the same in 1631; and Santiago in Chile followed suit the next year. In some of the countries of South America the feast of St. Francis Solano has been celebrated in the past on July 24. Formerly, as requested by the bishops, it was observed in the United States. The new calendar of the Order of Friars Minor has an optional memorial on July 14.

Liturgical Prayer

O God, you have led countless American tribes into the bosom of the Church through blessed Francis. By his merits and prayers turn away your anger from our sins and graciously engender reverence for your holy name in those nations who have not yet come to know you. Through Jesus Christ, your Son, our Lord, who lives and reigns with you in the unity of the Holy Spirit, God, forever and ever. Amen.

CHAPTER 27

SAINTS AND BLESSED
Peru

St. Martin de Porres
(1579-1639) The Black Saint of Lima

IN a barber shop in Lima, Peru, at the beginning of the last decade of the sixteenth century, there was a darkskinned twelve-year-old lad who was learning how to cut hair and use a straight razor. He was also being introduced into the art of healing, of blood-letting, and of minor surgical operations. In those days a barber was at the same time a doctor and surgeon, at least for minor cases of illness. The apprentice was a good boy, anxious to learn and to please everybody.

Still, there were some people who insulted him because the color of his skin was black; and they called him a "vile bastard," a "mulatto dog." But the boy, Martin de Porres, did not get angry at all. He rather felt sorry for anyone who had hatred in his heart. His own soul was filled with compassion for all, including animals, who were ill-treated or hungry or sick.

"Yes," Martin would respond, "I am a mulatto dog. But the good God has been very kind to me. He gives me all I need. He has made me a Catholic, and He promises me heaven if I keep His commandments."

Not many years later, as Brother Martin of the Dominican Order, he was to win the respect and admiration of all the people in Lima. They recognized the fact that the humble brother, who was working miracles to help the poor and to cure the sick, was the recipient of extraordinary favors from God and a real saint living in their midst.

Martin, who was born in Lima on December 9, 1579, was indeed a mulatto, the natural son of the Spanish knight of Alcantara, Don Juan de Porres, and a free black woman from Panama whose name was Anna Velásquez. He was baptized in the same church and by the same priest, Father Antonio Polanco, who baptized St. Rose of Lima seven years later.

Don Juan did not like it at all that his two children, Martin and his sister Juana, were as black as their mother. However, when Martin was eight years old, he came forward and acknowledged his fatherhood. He took the boy and his sister and mother to Guayaquil, on the coast of Ecuador, and there provided an elementary education for Martin.

However, when he was appointed governor of Panama, Don Juan abandoned Anna and her two children. Disillusioned but not embittered, Anna returned with her children to Lima. There she tried to raise them as good Catholics, teaching them to avoid everything sinful and to practice the Christian virtues of patience, humility and charity.

Martin was a docile pupil and learned his lessons well. He loved to pray the Rosary and took delight in helping the priests at the Church of St. Lazarus. He carefully avoided bad companions and tried hard not to offend God in any way whatever.

Having noticed that Martin had collected scraps of sailcloth and made a curtain of them, the landlady, Doña Ventura Luna, was curious as to what the boy was doing behind the curtain. She investigated and found him kneeling before a crucifix, praying and weeping. Impressed by the boy's piety, she supplied him with a large piece of cloth which would give him greater privacy for his devotions.

When Martin was twelve years old, his mother apprenticed him to a barber-surgeon in the city, so he could learn a trade and be able to earn a livelihood. For three years he remained with his master and acquired useful knowledge and skill which served him in good stead in later life.

It is not surprising that a youth for whom the things of God and heaven had such an attraction should have a longing to leave the world and its temptations and to dedicate himself wholly to the service of God and his neighbor in a religious community. One day when he was fifteen years old our Lady appeared to him and instructed him to enter the Dominican monastery of the Most Holy Rosary in Lima.

Martin went to the monastery or priory and humbly asked to be admitted as a *donado* (or tertiary brother), and his request was granted.

A painting by Virginia Broderick of St. Martin de Porres, a Dominican brother, who was born and died in Lima, Peru.

Like St. Francis of Assisi, his contemporary and friend, St. Dominic Guzmán founded, besides a religious order of mendicant friars, a so-called third order secular for those who wished to live a more perfect Christian life in their own homes. In the sixteenth century, as in our own day, it was not uncommon for unmarried young men to be received into a Franciscan friary or Dominican priory as members of the third order secular.

Though they took no vows, these tertiary brothers wore the religious habit, attended the community exercises, and lived practically the same life as the friars. Ordinarily the tertiary brother was such only for a number of years during which he was a candidate for the First Order. Then after a year of probation in the novitiate he made his profession as a full-fledged friar. However, some tertiary brothers continued to remain such and to live as religious without vows.

When Martin's father, the proud Don Juan de Porres, heard that his son was a mere *donado*, he was not pleased and wanted Martin to advance without further delay to the status of a Dominican friar of the First Order, the Order of Preachers. But Martin meekly replied: "I am happy and contented to be what I am."

Nine years later, when Brother Martin was twenty-four years old, his superiors of their own accord permitted him to pronounce the vows of poverty, chastity and obedience on June 2, 1603; and thus the tertiary brother became a friar of the Order of Preachers.

By that time Brother Martin had already gained the reputation of being a religious of extraordinary holiness of life. He was a model of obedience, humility, charity and love of God. He imposed upon himself the most rigorous penances. He spent seven hours daily in prayer and meditation, most of them during the night because during the day he was kept busy performing the many tasks assigned to him. Sometimes he was found kneeling before a crucifix in an ecstatic state.

All kinds of miracles were ascribed to him. Some of them occurred in far distant places — in Mexico, in Africa, in China. Brother Martin, it is claimed, was seen in two different places at the same time. Some trees which he planted bore fruit all year round.

Though he had only a rudimentary education, he possessed such expert theological knowledge that learned men, including the archbishop and viceroy, consulted him on difficult questions; and the friars of the priory of the Most Holy Rosary chose him as their spiritual director.

When Brother Martin entered this priory, he was appointed its infirmarian, barber, tailor, wardrobe-keeper and dole distributor. It was the latter job which he loved most since it enabled him to come to the aid of the poor and the sick. Sometimes when sufficient food was not on hand for distribution, it multiplied miraculously in his hands. Many of the sick were suddenly cured when Brother Martin ministered to them.

The African slaves in Lima were the special object of his love and care — not because they were black like himself, but because they were the most neglected and needed help more than others. When a ship with new slaves arrived, he would go to the docks, console the poor victims, tend their wounds, and instruct them in

Christian doctrine and tell them about Christ the Savior who was made a prisoner and nailed to the Cross for the salvation of all men. Once when his priory was in debt, he asked his superior to sell him into slavery and thus to free the house of its indebtedness.

Knowing how selflessly Brother Martin was devoted to helping the needy, the wealthy citizens gave him large sums of money; and he was able to found an orphanage for several hundred children, to which were attached a foundling hospital and other charitable enterprises.

All these activities, however, did not prevent Brother Martin from spending his busy days in an unbroken and intimate union and communion with God. Was he not rendering services to his Lord and Savior himself in the least of his brethren?

He cherished also a very special devotion to his heavenly Mother and Queen. Gladly he rose early to ring the Angelus bell at four in the morning. The altar of our Lady in the church he kept neat and clean and decorated with flowers. Her Rosary he always carried about with him, and whenever he found time he prayed his Ave Marias. Daily he recited the Little Office of the Blessed Virgin Mary.

To a great extent Brother Martin's life resembled that of his friend Bl. John Masías who was living in the priory of St. Mary Magdalen in Lima, and of St. Rose of Lima with whom he was also acquainted. Brother Martin was only six years older than Brother John, and seven years older than Rose.

But we find in the life of Brother Martin a rather unique solicitude also for the well-being of irrational creatures — dogs, cats, even mice and rats. Once, we are told, he raised a dead dog back to life.

At the home of his sister, Juana, who must have held her saintly brother in high esteem, Brother Martin established a refuge and hospital for stray cats and dogs.

For the rats, which had found their way into Lima from the ships coming into the port of Callao, he laid out food, warning them at the same time that they must not touch the granaries. They obeyed him, and so Brother Martin was able to tell the owners of the grain that there was no need to kill them. He had cats and dogs and rats eating out of the same platter that he placed before them.

Brother Martin longed to give his life for Christ as a missionary in some foreign land, preferably Africa. But God had called him to be a missionary and apostle in his native city, where he found more than enough to do for the spread of Christ's kingdom and the welfare of souls. When he alleviated the bodily needs of the poor and sick, he always exhorted them to lead exemplary Christian lives. He was heard to say to them, for instance: "Death is certain, but we know not the time. Then will follow a strict judgment with no other advocate in our behalf than our good works. Hell is terrible; it is horrible; and there is no remedy. Paradise, heaven, oh how wonderful you will be!"

One should not think, however, that Brother Martin had no trials and crosses to bear, no annoying temptations to overcome. But he always retained his composure, remained patient and cheerful, and emerged victorious, with the help of God's grace.

For forty-five years, Brother Martin exercised a profound influence on the citizens of Lima by giving them the example of a life of complete dedication to God and of wholehearted service to the poor and sick. On November 4, 1639, one month before his sixtieth birthday, between eight and nine in the evening, Brother Martin's earthly life came to an end. During his last moments, our Lady once more appeared to him with St. Joseph and other saints, and invited him to go with her to heaven.

All Lima was filled with consternation and sorrow when the news of his passing was announced. Numerous miracles occurred at the time of his demise. His funeral was attended not only by the poor and lowly, but also the rich and the great.

Twenty-five years after his burial, his body was found to be still incorrupt. On the feast of Our Lady of Snows, August 8, 1837, in the Basilica of St. Mary Major in Rome, Pope Gregory XVI solemnly enrolled Brother Martin in the ranks of the blessed. Pope John XXIII canonized him on May 6, 1962.

The feast of St. Martin de Porres has been observed in the past in nearly all the countries of South America on November 5. But the new general calendar of the Church assigns to St. Martin de Porres an optional memorial on November 3. With St. Benedict the Black, he is venerated as the special patron of those who are trying to improve the relations between the various races.

Liturgical Prayer

O God, who exalt the humble, you have transferred your confessor, blessed Martin, to the heavenly kingdom. Grant that, through his merits and intercession, we may so imitate him on earth, that we may merit to be exalted with him in heaven. Through Jesus Christ, your Son, our Lord, who lives and reigns with you in the unity of the Holy Spirit, God, forever and ever. Amen.

CHAPTER 28

SAINTS AND BLESSED

Peru

St. Rose of Lima

(1586-1617) The Peruvian Catherine of Siena

DON Gaspar de Flores was about fifty years old when he settled down in Lima as a member of the viceroy's guard in the year 1580. As a child he had come from Spain to the New World with his parents, or he may have been born soon after their arrival in Puerto Rico. He had a long and varied career as a soldier, mostly in Peru, and always on the side of the lawful government.

Now that the civil wars of Peru had come to an end, he could start thinking of a home. His bride, who was young enough to be his daughter, was María de Oliva, born of Spanish parents in Peru. The couple acquired a roomy house in Lima's Calle de Santo Domingo near the hospital of Espíritu Santo, and raised a big family.

The first child was a girl whom they named Bernardina; the next was a boy, called Hernando or Fernando; and then, on April 20, 1586, was born another girl. About a month later, on Pentecost Sunday, in the Church of San Sebastian, Father Antonio Polanco baptized her and gave her the name of her grandmother Isabel.

Ten other children followed, but it is Isabel who claims our interest. She is known today as St. Rose of Lima, and has been so known ever since 1671 when she became the first native of the New World to be enrolled by the Church among her canonized saints.

Rosa or Rosita was a nickname given to Isabel when she was still a babe in the cradle. Sitting beside her, the Indian maid

Mariana expressed her admiration of the child's loveliness by saying: "Our beautiful baby looks just like a rose!" The mother agreed with the servant, and from that time everybody, except grandmother Isabel (naturally!), called her Rose.

From early childhood Rose began to manifest an extraordinary love of God. She would steal away from her playmates to pray in a quiet spot. With the help of her favorite brother Hernando, who was a year older than she was, Rose built a small leafy bower in the patio where she could pray undisturbed. It was Hernando too who accompanied her when she went to the Church of Santo Domingo.

Once when some mud was thrown on her golden tresses by playmates, and Rose was a little upset about it, Hernando teasingly said to her that a holy girl would not mind a little dirt on her head, and those beautiful locks were only a source of vanity anyway. Rose took the matter so seriously that she got a pair of scissors and cut off her hair.

Rose soon learned to read and write and sing and sew. Her mother gave lessons in reading and writing to other children and also taught Rose; but it was mainly through her own efforts and apparently special divine assistance that Rose quickly learned to read and write. Now she could read the life of St. Catherine of Siena about whom she had heard, and she set herself the task of making her own life as exact a copy of this saint's life as possible.

She was only six years old when she began to fast three times a week, on Wednesdays, Fridays and Saturdays, taking only a morsel of stale bread and a cup of tepid water in the evening. Not many years later she bound herself by vows to abstain from meat and to observe perpetual virginity.

There were seven children in the Flores family when Don Gaspar was appointed superintendent of the silver mines at Quives, in the province of Canta, about fifty miles distant from Lima. The whole family moved to this mining town, which then had a population of 3,000, and lived in a stone house situated on the plaza opposite the church.

The house had only four rooms — two large and two small — for the ten of them, including grandmother Isabel; but the surroundings were pleasant. Not very long after moving to Quives, Rose and Bernardina became ill, and the latter died.

Rose was eleven years old when the saintly Archbishop Toribio de Mogrovejo of Lima visited Quives in 1597, during his last pastoral visitation of his vast diocese; and it was here that St. Toribio administered the sacrament of confirmation to St. Rose. Besides her, there were only two little boys whom Father Francisco González, a Mercederian friar stationed at the church in Quives, was able to present for the sacrament. The Indians of the area had not accepted the Christian faith, and they had no love for the archbishop or the Spaniards.

Three years after they had come to Quives, the Flores family moved back to their house in Lima. Perhaps the mines were no longer productive; at any rate they no longer needed a superintendent. The family was glad to be back in the big house in the capital; and Rose, who was now the oldest girl, helped her parents care for the family which was increased by three more children during the years that followed. She became proficient in needlework and made exquisite lace and embroidered silks, tended the garden and raised beautiful flowers and luscious fruits which she took to the market.

At the same time Rose increased her prayers and penances. Her mother was anxious to arrange an advantageous marriage for her, but after a long struggle Rose finally convinced her that she meant to keep the vow of virginity she had made as a little girl.

At first Rose thought of entering a convent; and when Doña Grimanesa de Mogrovejo, the sister of the archbishop, and others sponsored the founding of a Poor Clare monastery, Rose was invited to join the nuns. But her parents objected, saying they needed the income obtained from the sale of her needlework and flowers.

Later, with the approval of her spiritual adviser, the Dominican Father Velásquez, arrangements were made for her to enter the Augustinian Convent of the Incarnation. Before taking the step, Rose went with Hernando to the altar of Our Lady of the Rosary in the Dominican church for a last visit. She prayed there a long time. Finally Hernando tapped her on the shoulder.

"We must go now," he said.

"I can't get up," replied Rose.

He tried to help her stand up, but she was immovable as a rock. Realizing that this was a sign from heaven, she prayed: "If it is God's will, I will stay at home and not enter the convent."

Now she was able to rise without any difficulty whatever. She returned home, where no one had known of her plans except her bedridden grandmother; and to her she related what had happened. Grandmother Isabel was, of course, glad to have her back; and, incidentally, she too had been calling her Rose ever since Archbishop Toribio had used that name when he confirmed her.

However, at the age of twenty, Rose was received into the Third Order Secular of St. Dominic by Father Velásquez at the altar of Our Lady of the Rosary; and from that time she wore the

Dominican habit and called herself Rosa de Santa María instead of Rosa de Flores.

Rose felt that she had a divine call to live a life of penance in expiation for the offenses committed against God, especially the idolatry of the Indians who refused to embrace Christianity; and she offered up her very severe penitential exercises also in supplication for the conversion of sinners and for the souls in purgatory.

For fourteen years she inflicted such extreme bodily suffering and mortification upon herself that one stands aghast at the account given by her biographers. For us of the modern age this phase of her character and life is simply incomprehensible. We will content ourselves by saying that Rose's excessive penances are not recommended for imitation. However, they put to shame those of our day for whom even slight and ordinary acts of self-denial and penance have become unbearable.

While Rose's penances detached her heart completely from the things of this world and helped her to become an ascetic and mystic of unusual fervor, it was her great love of God and her neighbor that made her a saint. For a time Rose suffered from so-called spiritual aridity, but she persevered in her efforts to please God in all things. Our Lord rewarded her by appearing to her as a child and conversing with her; and our Lady too spoke with her frequently. Her complete absorption in prayer at times reached a state of ecstasy.

The Flores family had some influential and wealthy friends in the family of Don Gonzalo de la Maza, the head of the Commission of Audits in Lima. His wife especially took a solicitous interest in Rose, and it was she no doubt who suggested to her husband that he provide the usual dowry so Rose could enter the Carmelite convent in Lima. Rose was still a novice in the Dominican Third Order at the time. She prayed for light, since the offer seemed inviting to her; and she fell into an ecstasy, after which she never again wavered in her conviction that she was called to become a saint, not as a nun, but in her own home. After a year had elapsed, she made her profession as a Dominican tertiary.

Though she did not enter a convent, she found a substitute in a little hermitage which was built for her in the garden of her parental home. When Rose first asked her mother for this hermitage, she refused; but after Father Lorenzana and the Mazas interceded, she gave in. The little abode measured only five by four feet.

Whenever she could, Rose retired to this quiet spot to pray and to do penance. Daily she prayed the divine office, the Little Office of the Blessed Virgin, the Rosary, and spent much time in contemplative prayer, which for her was above all a prayer of love of God and union with Him.

However, she tried to combine with her life as a recluse also an active apostolate of charity. With her mother's consent, Rose converted one or more rooms of the large house into an infirmary for poor Indian women, and there she lovingly nursed them and instructed them.

Many others came to Rose for help and advice, and her remarkable answers and charitable ministrations were such that people generally regarded her as a saint.

The attention of the Court of the Inquisition was called to the extraordinary life of Rosa de Santa María; and some eminent theologians were appointed to examine her in the presence of her mother and her friend Doña María Uzátegui, the wife of Don Gonzalo de la Maza. They all came to the conclusion that Rose's holiness was genuine and that God had endowed her with infused knowledge on the subjects of ascetical theology and the spiritual life.

It was toward the end of her life that Rose heard the Child Jesus in the arms of Mary say to her: "Rose of My Heart, be My Spouse!" This happened in the Dominican church on Palm Sunday. The sacristan had overlooked giving a blessed palm branch to Rose, and in her disappointment she went to the altar of our Lady to say a prayer of resignation.

Her brother Hernando had a ring made for her, and on Easter Sunday, in a special ceremony, Father Velásquez placed the ring on her finger as an emblem of her "spiritual nuptials." She was now in a special manner "a Bride of Christ."

During the last three years of her life, Rose spent much of her time in the home of the Mazas. She had been invited to become a house guest and to instruct Micaela and Andrea, the two daughters of Don Gonzalo and Doña María. Her mother and Rose herself were pleased with the offer because Rose had just recovered from a serious illness which left her in a weakened condition. What attracted Rose in a special way was the fact that the Maza home had a chapel of its own.

Rose chose a small attic room; and she became a welcome member of the Maza household, obeying Doña María as a mother, and giving lessons to Micaela and Andrea. Her Father Confessor ordered her to mitigate her penitential practices somewhat, and she obeyed; but she did not regain her former strength.

In 1615 news reached Lima that the Dutch pirate, George Spitberg, commanding a squadron of seven ships, had passed through the Straits of Magellan at the southern end of South

America and had ravaged the coast of Chile. He was now on his way to Callao, the port of Lima. The viceroy sent out three warships to meet them, but they suffered a sad defeat at the hands of the intruders. Many people sought refuge in the churches of Lima. Rose too went to the Church of Santo Domingo, determined to defend the Blessed Sacrament with her life.

According to one account, the pirates entered this church, but were so struck with awe and fear when they saw Rose, a radiant figure in white and black, standing in front of the tabernacle, that they forthwith fled back to their ships and abandoned their plan of plundering the city. Rose was hailed as the savior of Lima.

On two other occasions she was credited with saving the city by her prayers and penances, once when the pagan Indians rose in widespread rebellion and threatened to invade Lima, and another time when there were disastrous earthquakes in the vicinity but Lima was spared.

Toward the end of July, 1617, Rose paid her last visit to the home of her parents. Her father, Don Gaspar, was now an old man about ninety years old, confined to his bed and his chair. For the last time Rose also visited her little retreat in the garden where she had spent so many happy solitary hours.

At midnight on August 1, in her attic room at the home of her benefactors, Rose was suddenly afflicted with such acute pains that she cried out for help. In the morning, her Father Confessor, her mother and a doctor were summoned, but the doctor was not able to diagnose her illness. Unwittingly he increased her sufferings by prescribing that the patient drink no water, though her thirst was intense.

Four strong men carried her father, Don Gaspar, in a chair to her bedside. The hardy old soldier broke down and sobbed when he saw the agony which his saintly daughter was enduring with such tranquil patience. He was taken home, strengthened by Rose's consoling words.

Rose's body became rigid and for several weeks she seemed to have a share in the sufferings which Christ endured while hanging on the Cross. Previously she had predicted that she would die on the feast of St. Bartholomew before she reached the age of thirty-two. At eight in the evening of August 23, she said that she would die at midnight. And so it happened. Her last words were: "Jesus, Jesus, be with me!"

The news of Rose's death spread quickly through the city. It was announced that instead of a Requiem Mass, the Mass in honor of All Saints would be offered up at five in the afternoon. The canons of the cathedral served as pallbearers — an honor that was

235

ordinarily conferred only on a deceased archbishop. But the crowd became so unruly that the funeral had to be postponed till the next day.

Rose's body was taken for the night to the chapel of the Dominican novitiate. The following day there was another postponement for the same reason. The third day, the burial took place, quietly and privately, in the cloister of the Dominican priory. Her relics now repose under one of the altars in the Dominican church. A few blocks from this church is her home and the tiny hermitage where she spent many hours in prayer. Here the basilica of St. Rose has been built.

Six years after Rose's death, the cause of her beatification, that is, the preliminary investigation, was begun in Lima. Fifty years after her death, Pope Clement IX issued the bull of her beatification; but the ceremony was not carried out until April 15, 1668, by his successor, Clement X. A year later, on November 3, 1669, this pope declared Blessed Rose of St. Mary to be the patron, not only of Lima and Peru, but of all of Latin America and the Philippines.

The same Supreme Pontiff solemnly canonized Rose two years later in 1671. In the past, since 1727, the feast of St. Rose of Lima has been observed by the Church of the Latin Rite on August 30, but the new general calendar of the Church has transferred her feast to August 23 and given it the rank of an optional memorial for the universal Church. In various places also the feast of the translation of her relics has been celebrated: in Peru on April 20; in Chile on April 22; in Buenos Aires on April 3.

Liturgical Prayer

O almighty God, from whom every good gift comes, it pleased you that blessed Rose should blossom as a flower of purity and patience in the New World under the dew of your heavenly grace. May we also become pleasing enough to draw others to Christ, who lives and reigns with you in the unity of the Holy Spirit, God, forever and ever. Amen.

CHAPTER 29

SAINTS AND BLESSED
Peru

Bl. John Masías
(1585-1645) A Poor Friend of the Poor

IN colonial Peru, during the seventeenth century, there were four saints and one blessed. The latter was the humble Dominican brother John Masías, who spent his life on earth in a remarkably familiar manner with the saints of heaven, particularly the Queen of Heaven, and found the Rosary to be a powerful means of attaining the heights of holiness.

Blessed John Masías was born in 1586 in the Villa de Rivera, Estremadura, Spain. His parents were Pedro Masías de Arcos and Inez Sánchez, decendants of ancient noble families who had been reduced by the fickleness of human riches to a condition of indigence. They were rich in piety, however, and bequeathed to their son Juan (John) a deep longing for sanctity. As a little boy, John preferred to spend his time praying in church rather than playing with other children.

Both parents died when John was about four years old. An uncle then looked after the orphan, but made the boy earn a living for himself as a shepherd. During the long hours he spent herding sheep, John prayed the Rosary and meditated on the mysteries of the Christian faith which are presented to the mind in such a comprehensive manner by this uncomplicated combination of oral and mental prayer.

John soon made it a daily practice to pray the entire Rosary of fifteen decades, not just once but three times — a total of forty-five decades; and he kept up this practice during the rest of his life, over a half century. One complete Rosary he offered up for the conversion of sinners, another for the deliverance of the holy souls from purgatory, and the third for his own spiritual welfare and progress.

While John spent day after day in the open solitary fields, with no living being around him except the sheep which quietly nibbled the grass, it seemed to him that the saints of heaven, especially our Lady and St. John the Apostle, were keeping him company. It was to this St. John, who apparently was his patron saint, that John Masías himself attributed his sudden decision at the age of thirty-four to go to the Spanish colonies in the New World. St. John, he said, appeared to him, assured him that he would always remain his special protector, and instructed him to leave his native land and to make the long journey to Lima, Peru.

The ship on which he embarked from Spain crossed the ocean in forty days and took him to the Colombian port of Cartagena on the northern coast of South America. From here, as John himself related, he traveled on foot or by canoe or boat from one town to the next until he reached Quito in Ecuador. Thence he continued south, walking or riding muleback, to Lima. The journey from Cartagena to Lima lasted four and a half months of actual traveling. However, he interrupted this journey to work for two years on a cattle ranch along the way, in order to earn a little money which would enable him to complete his travels.

In Lima John gave what he had left of his savings to friends and applied for admission as a brother in the priory of Santa María Magdalena, where the rule of St. Dominic was strictly observed. He was thirty-seven years old when he was clothed with the Dominican habit on January 23, 1622.

Brother John entered upon the religious life with such fervor that his self-imposed penances exceeded the bounds of prudence, and the Father Prior had to insist on moderation. The brother had allowed only one hour nightly for sleep, and this in a kneeling posture with his head resting on his bed. As a result he contracted a serious illness and had to undergo a dangerous and painful operation.

While obeying his superior, Brother John continued to live a most austere life to the end of his days. In this matter he shared the views of his close friend and confrere, Brother Martin de Porres.

For more than twenty years Brother John served as the porter of the priory of Santa María Magdalena. This enabled him to become the almoner and friend of the poor and the sick. He soon gained the reputation of being a saint, not only because of his

Bl. John Masías lived in Lima as a Dominican brother
from 1622 to 1645.

wonderful patience and kindness and his inspiring and consoling words, but also because of the remarkable manner in which he obtained needed food and clothing for the destitute, and the cures and other miracles which were attributed to him.

Each day Brother John fed and helped more than 200 persons who came to see him at Santa María Magdalena. Not having the time himself to gather the necessary alms for so many people, he trained or merely gave instructions to a burro which belonged to the priory to go through the city and collect food and clothing. This remarkable animal would go from house to house, and if there was no one on hand to notice him he would knock gently on the door with his foreleg. The pouches slung across his back were usually loaded to capacity when he returned to the priory.

When Brother John learned of a poor family which was too ashamed to beg, he would personally visit their hovel or home and bring them aid. He always added a kind word of good advice and an exhortation to a good life and love of God.

Brother John's confidence in God was unlimited, and always somehow or other he had something that he could give the poor. If there was a shortage, he would hurry to the chapel of Our Lady of the Rosary and tell his heavenly Mother about it. She never failed him.

The fame of Brother John's holiness of life and his charitable ministrations spread to distant cities, to Cuzco, Potosí, Quito and even to Mexico. From all these places he received contributions for his beloved poor.

Busy as he was serving the poor, Brother John still found time to pray his three complete Rosaries every day. Devotion to our Lady played a major role in his religious life and his striving for sanctity. When he spoke of the Virgin Mary, his voice was strikingly expressive of a heartfelt love and tenderness.

Early in the morning on November 4, 1642, our Lady, holding the Child Jesus in her arms, appeared to him while he was absorbed in prayer and offered to place the Holy Child in his hands. The humble brother did not accept the offer because he regarded himself as utterly unworthy. His heavenly visitors were pleased with his humility; and God rewarded it by taking complete possession of his heart and filling his soul with spiritual consolation and graces.

However, God permitted him, like the Curé of Ars, to be troubled and tortured by the evil spirit nightly for twelve years. The good brother was not unduly disturbed and defended himself against Satan's onslaughts by saying: "Jesus Savior, Mary and Joseph, be with me!" And when the Devil fled, Brother John would add: "Coward! Why do you run away when you hear the holy names?"

It was owing to Brother John's efforts that the feast of the Most Holy Name of Mary began to be observed in a special way in

Lima, and the custom was introduced to present to very poor maidens a worthwhile gift (as was done by St. Nicholas) lest they succumb to the temptation of sacrificing their virtue for a price.

One night while Brother John was praying before the statue of our Lady in the Rosary chapel of the church, Lima was shaken by an earthquake. The brother began to tremble with fear. Our Lady spoke to him: "Why are you afraid? Am I not with you?" He regained his tranquillity at once; and afterwards, when there was an earthquake or he was otherwise troubled, he would go to the Rosary chapel where he found peace and calmness.

He had a special devotion to the Blessed Virgin under the title of Nuestra Señora de Belén (Our Lady of Bethlehem); and he asked of her as a special favor that when the time came for him to leave this life his death agony would be a short one.

These intimate details of his life we learn from Brother John himself. He revealed them when he was ordered under obedience by his superior and his Father Confessor, Father Gonzalo García, to relate the favors he had received from God and what his favorite saints — St. John the Evangelist, St. Mary Magdalen, St. Dominic and St. Louis Bertrand — had told him about devotion to our Lady. Brother John declared he had been informed that, through the countless Rosaries he had prayed, as many as 1,400,000 souls had been liberated from purgatory.

Brother John was sixty years old when he died without a struggle on September 17, 1645. He was heard to say: "Our Lord Jesus Christ is here, and so are His most holy Mother, St. Joseph, St. John the Evangelist and other saints." Then he crossed his arms over his breast and expired peacefully after saying: "Into your hands, Lord, I commend my spirit."

The entire city of Lima was saddened by his death. The archbishop and the viceroy were among the many people who attended his funeral. He was beatified in 1837 by Pope Gregory XVI. The feast of Bl. John Masías has been observed annually on October 3 by the Dominicans. On this day they have recited the divine office and offered up holy Mass in his honor.

Liturgical Prayer

Lord Jesus Christ, you are meek and humble of heart. Help us to imitate your confessor, blessed John, an outstanding example of your humility and meekness. May we cast aside the pride of life and serve you at all times. You who live and reign with the Father in the unity of the Holy Spirit, God, forever and ever. Amen.

Part I
SAINTS AND BLESSED

Brazil

Of the four missionary martyrs of Brazil who have been beatified, one died in the Canary Islands but belongs to Brazil inasmuch as he had previously lived and worked there for several years. The other three died as martyrs in what is now the southernmost part of Brazil; but these are rightly claimed also by Paraguay. One of them was a native of Paraguay, and all three were missionaries of the famous Paraguay reductions of the seventeenth century.

SAINTS AND BLESSED
Brazil

Bl. Ignatius Azevedo

(1528-1570) Martyr of Brazil

OFF the coast of the island of Las Palmas in the Canaries, forty Jesuit missionaries who were on board the *Santiago*, a Portuguese merchant ship bound for Brazil, were ruthlessly murdered by the French Huguenot pirate Jacques Sourie on July 15, 1570. The leader of this group of martyrs, Father Ignatius Azevedo, had previously worked in Brazil for about two years; and so he may be counted among the blessed of the Americas.

The oldest son of a noble family, Ignatius was born at Oporto, Portugal, in 1528. His father was Don Emanuel Azevedo; and his mother, Doña Violanta Pereira before her marriage, was a descendant of the lords of Fermedo.

Ignatius received a good education; and after he had completed his studies he was placed by his father in charge of the family estates. Though he did his work well, his heart was not in it. Following the advice of a friend, he made a retreat in Coimbra, and at its conclusion he felt sure that God was calling him to the life of a religious and a priest.

In the meantime Don Emanuel had been arranging a suitable marriage for his first-born son. However, Ignatius eventually overcame the objections of his parents, and with their consent he entered the Society of Jesus at the end of 1548.

Six years later, only twenty-six years old and still a student of theology, he was appointed rector of a new college in Lisbon, named for St. Anthony. Besides directing the work at the college,

Bl. Ignatius Azevedo, S.J., who had sojourned in Brazil, was returning when he died a martyr in the Canaries in 1570.

Ignatius was also engaged in various good works. On one occasion he nursed back to health and converted three men who were in such an advanced stage of a repulsive disease that the hospital nurses refused to touch them.

When St. Ignatius of Loyola died in Rome in 1556 and the provincial superior in Portugal went to the general chapter, Ignatius substituted for him as vice-provincial until he returned. The young Jesuit ex-superior and ex-rector then went to a house of studies to complete his course in theology.

After his ordination to the priesthood, Father Ignatius was sent with a companion to Braga to preach parish missions in that archdiocese. The Dominican archbishop was so pleased with their work that he permitted them to open a house in Braga, and Father Ignatius was appointed its first superior. When the people began to regard him as a saint because of his exemplary life and the miracles which were ascribed to him, Father Ignatius wrote a letter to Father General Laynez humbly asking to be sent to a place where he was not known.

Shortly afterwards Father Laynez died and Father Ignatius was chosen one of two delegates who went along with the provincial to Rome. Here he also served as procurator for the Jesuit missions in the Indies and Brazil. After his election as general, St. Francis Borgia sent Father Ignatius as official visitor to the missions which had been established in Brazil sixteen years earlier. The pioneers were already working among seven native tribes of the country and conducting schools in the Portuguese settlements. After inspecting the work being done and offering his advice, Father Ignatius returned to Rome to make his report. His voyage to and from Brazil and his sojourn in that country lasted three years.

St. Francis Borgia agreed with Father Ignatius' recommendation that more missionaries be sent to Brazil, and directed him to recruit suitable men from the Spanish and Portuguese provinces and to return with them to Brazil as their provincial superior. Father Ignatius enlisted no less than sixty-nine, some of whom were still clerics or novices. After spending five months in religious exercises and making other preparations at Val de Rosal, the party set out on June 5, 1570.

Forty of the missionaries, including Father Ignatius, boarded the *Santiago*, a merchant ship. The other thirty were passengers on a warship, one of a squadron which was under the command of Don Luis Vasconcellos, the governor of Brazil.

Eight days after setting sail, the fleet reached the island of Madeira in the Atlantic Ocean, west of Morocco. Vasconcellos thought it best to remain here for several months to await more favorable winds. But the captain of the *Santiago* wanted to go on to the Canary Islands, farther south, because some of his passengers were anxious to reach them.

This put Father Ignatius into a quandary. Should he and his companions continue the voyage and leave the others to follow later? The Jesuits did not have a house in the Canaries, and it was dangerous for a merchant vessel to travel alone. On the other hand, there was no room for him and his companions on the warships.

Father Ignatius decided to remain on the *Santiago*. He warned his companions that they might meet a corsair, and gave them an address on the glory of martyrdom. The other group of Jesuits he placed under Father Pedro Díaz, appointing him vice-provincial.

Reaching the island of Las Palmas, the *Santiago* stopped first at a place called Third Court, before going on to the town of Las Palmas. On the way the ship was overtaken by a French privateer under the command of the Huguenot pirate Jacques Sourie. Having learned of the *Santiago's* departure for the Canaries and Brazil with a group of Jesuits on board, he had deliberately set out from La Rochelle, France, and gone in chase of it.

The sailors and passengers on the *Santiago* fought bravely to defend themselves against the attackers; and the Jesuits assisted them as much as they could without using weapons or shedding blood. But they were no match against the pirates, who finally boarded their vessel and engaged in a desperate hand-to-hand struggle. After the captain was killed, the survivors surrendered.

Sourie spared the remaining passengers and members of the crew; but, prompted by his hatred of the Catholic religion, he ordered the massacre of all the Jesuits. "Kill them!" shouted Sourie. "Kill these papists who wished to propagate their errors in Brazil!" The pirates profaned the missionaries' church goods and stabbed their crucifix. The Jesuits were first tortured and mutilated and then cruelly dispatched in different ways.

All of the Jesuits accepted martyrdom with heroism and joy — that is, all but one, a coadjutor who was dressed as a cook and whose life was spared that he might serve the pirates. However, there was a youth on board, Juanito by name, a nephew of the captain, who had attached himself to the missionaries with the intention of joining them. He put on a soutane and boldly declared: "I too belong to the Society of Jesus!" Sourie himself cut off his head.

Father Ignatius' last words were: "I am a Catholic and will die for my faith; angels and men are my witnesses." A saber thrust put an end to his life. His body was seen floating on the surface of the water, and near it an image of the Virgin Mary. The latter was recovered.

Of the forty martyrs, two were priests, twelve were professed clerics, nine were novices, sixteen were coadjutors, and one (Juanito) was a layman. Thirty-one of them were Portuguese and nine were Spaniards. Among the latter was Francisco Pérez de Godoy, a nephew of St. Teresa of Avila.

On that same day, July 15, 1570, Francisco appeared to St. Teresa at Avila and announced to her: "Forty martyrs, crowned with garlands of triumph, have winged their way to heaven!" To Don Jerónimo Azevedo, the brother of Father Ignatius, who was far away in the East Indies, it was also revealed that the forty Jesuits had died for the faith.

The beatification of these martyrs took place when their cult was formally approved by Pope Pius IX in 1854. Their feast has been observed annually in Portugal and Brazil on July 15.

Liturgical Prayer

O God, for love of you as well as for the zealous defense of the faith, blessed Ignatius met death at the hands of the impious. We beg you to grant that, being firm in our faith through his intercession, we may ever love you from the depth of our hearts. Through Jesus Christ, your Son, our Lord, who lives and reigns with you in the unity of the Holy Spirit, God, forever and ever. Amen.

SAINTS AND BLESSED

Brazil

Bl. Roch González, Bl. Alphonse Rodríguez and Bl. John de Castillo

(1628) Martyrs of the Paraguay Reductions

THE sixteenth-century Spanish colony of Paraguay, or Paraguay-La Plata, was much more extensive than the present Paraguay, including as it did, also eastern Argentina, Uruguay and southernmost Brazil. In other words, it comprised the entire basin of the Río de la Plata and its large tributaries. The La Plata River, which is really a gulf, is formed by the confluence of the Uruguay and the Paraná rivers. And the Paraguay, which has its source in the Matto Grosso of Brazil, joins the Paraná approximately 150 miles below Asunción. The watershed drained by these rivers is the second largest in the world — an area of one and a half million square miles.

The main settlement in Paraguay-La Plata was Asunción, founded on the feast of the Assumption of Our Lady, August 15, 1537. Although the Port of Santa María de los Buenos Aires had been established the previous year, its settlers were transferred to Asunción in 1541; and Buenos Aires was not founded until June 11, 1580. It was only in 1617 that La Plata and Paraguay became separate provinces and Buenos Aires was made the capital of the former.

Among the first Franciscan missionaries of Paraguay-La Plata the most prominent was Father Luis de Bolaños, whom the Jesuit Father Guevara called "the Giant of the Indian Provinces." For fifty years he traveled over a wide area, gathering the Indians in villages and instructing them in Christian doctrine. Between the years 1580 and 1593, he and his companion Father Alonso de San Buenaventura established no less than eighteen missions or reductions; and when his companion went to Chile in 1593, he placed fifteen of them in the care of the first two Jesuits whom he had invited to Paraguay.

Continuing his work after their arrival until 1620, Father Bolaños founded four more reductions after 1607. In an area that was eighty miles long he built as many as twenty-five churches. He was also the author of the first Guaraní grammar and dictionary as well as the first catechism and prayerbook in that language. They were used in the famous Jesuit reductions of Paraguay, which flourished from 1608 to 1767. Father Bolaños, who died at the age of ninety in 1629, knew Bl. Roch Gonzáles as a boy and later came to his aid when he was almost starving to death as a Jesuit missionary.

The Guaraní Indians of Paraguay belonged to the Caraibes or Ceribs, for whom the Caribbean Sea was named. Paraguay was, in fact, the homeland of these fierce cannibals, who overran and conquered two-thirds of the South American continent, imposing their language and customs on the other aborigenes. These, of course, underwent changes in the course of time. The Caraibes were found all along the mighty Amazon River; and, in canoes which carried eighty to a hundred warriors besides provisions, they invaded the West Indies.

Besides the Guaraní Indians there were in Paraguay-La Plata the Guaycurús, who were predatory nomads but not cannibals. They formed a complicated linguistic family, different from the Tupí of the Guaranís; and they included a large number of tribes having various names, for example the Charruas in Uruguay. They were constantly at war with the Guaranís; and those who were not converted to Christianity remained the implacable enemies of the Spaniards, especially in the territory west of the Paraguay River.

The hardships which the pioneer colonists in Paraguay-La Plata had to endure were perhaps greater than in other parts of South America. And, as Dr. C. E. Chapman writes, "The results obtained (except in the reductions) were the least spectacular of the Spanish conquests in America." But the conquistadors never gave up. Among the early settlers in Asunción were Don Bartolomé González de Villaverde and his wife Doña María de Santa Cruz. One of their sons later served as governor of Asunción, and it seems that another subsequently held the same position. Still another son, to whom they gave the name of Roque or Roch and who was born at Asunción in 1576, became one of the three mis-

249

sionary martyrs of the Americas who were the first to be beatified by the Church.

Even as a youth, Roque González was known for his piety and his desire to become a saint. It is related that, when he was fourteen or fifteen years old, he and three or four like-minded boys left the comforts of home to live as hermits in the wilds as did the early Fathers of the desert. But they were found and brought back before they suffered any harm.

After attending the college which the Jesuits had opened in Asunción a few years previously, Roque was ordained a secular or diocesan priest. He celebrated his first holy Mass on the feast of the Annunciation, March 25, 1599. The ordaining bishop was the Franciscan Fernando de Trejo y Sanabria, first resident bishop of Tucumán, Argentina (1595-1614), who like Roque González was a native of Paraguay, having been born at Asunción in 1554.

For a short time following his ordination Father Roque was engaged in apostolic work among the Indians of Maracayú, above the Jejui River, a tributary of the Paraguay, and in other out-of-

Bl. Roch González, S.J., a missionary of the Paraguay reductions, was a pioneer in southernmost Brazil.

the-way districts. But in 1601, the bishop of Asunción appointed him pastor of the cathedral in the capital, though at the time he was only twenty-five years old. It is interesting to note that this bishop was the Franciscan Martin Ignatius de Loyola, a relative of St. Ignatius and previously a world traveler and missionary in the Far East.

Eight years later, the successor of Bishop Loyola, Reginaldo de Lizzáraga, also a Franciscan, wanted to make Father Roque his vicar general. But Roque was not looking for any promotions. He wanted to be an Indian missionary. With this purpose in mind he joined the Society of Jesus, being received into the order by Father Diego Torres on May 9, 1609.

After a short novitiate of six months, Father Roque was sent to a tribe of hostile Guaycurus in order to conciliate them if possible. It was generally regarded as a foolhardy venture, but Father Roque succeeded in converting the leading chief. The son of this chief was baptized at Asunción in October, 1611.

During the next three years, Father Roque had charge of the reduction of San Ignacio, which had been founded in 1609 in the southern part of present-day Paraguay. In 1613, he baptized over 200 Indians, eighty of them children and 122 adults. The following year he brought together some 600 Indian families to live near Lake Ibera in the eastern part of what is now Argentina, lying between the Paraná and Uruguay, and founded the reduction of Santa Ana. Leaving the latter in the care of his old friend Father Luis Bolaños and another Franciscan, Father Roque then undertook the task of pioneering in the region east of the Uruguay River. This he continued to do during the remaining thirteen years of his life.

After he had prepared himself by prayer, fasting and other penitential exercises, Father Roque entered present-day Uruguay. His eastward progress was blocked by a large number of hostile Charruas (Guaycurús), and so he turned north to explore the banks of the Uruguay River for a considerable distance. Here he founded a mission which he called Concepción in honor of the Immaculate Conception of the Blessed Virgin Mary. Perhaps his reduction was the beginning of the Argentinian city on the west bank of the river, Concepción del Uruguay. Not far from Concepción he founded a second reduction, that of Yaguapoa, which very probably was identical with the mission of San Francisco Xavier. Nearby, it seems he established a third mission, named Candelaria.

In the new missions, Father Roque encountered many difficulties because of famine and small-pox epidemics. At one time there was nothing to eat but decayed manioc tubers. Father Luis de Bolaños, hearing of his predicament, came to his aid with food and clothing. That Father Roque gained great influence over the Indians is shown by the fact that on one occasion, when he met 400 fighting men who were going to attack another tribe, he was able to perusade them to desist and return home.

Conditions had begun to improve in the missions on the Uruguay River by 1626, when Father Roque made a trip to Buenos Aires to obtain from Governor Francisco de Céspedes of the Río de la Plata province the authorization to found new reductions in the region east of the Uruguay, that is in the present Brazilian state of Río Grande do Sul. The governor gave his approval and asked the missionary to explore this hitherto unexplored territory; but he made the mistake of sending along three *regidores* (aldermen or councilmen) for the missions on the Uruguay River. One of them treated the neophytes at the mission of San Francisco Xavier in such a high-handed manner that most of them fled and went back to the wilds. The Jesuit provincial, Father Mastrilli, eventually succeeded in having the *regidores* recalled.

Traveling through Uruguay, Father Roque crossed the Quarai River near Piratiui, and about five miles farther, on the feast of the Finding of the Holy Cross, May 3, 1626, he offered the holy Sacrifice of the Mass for the first time in what is now Río Grande do Sul. Here he founded the mission of San Nicolás.

Father Roque then explored the central portion of this state, extending from Cacequi northwest to Santa María and north from there to Cruz Alta. Having received the help of two young assistants in 1628, he founded two more reductions in this area, that of Asunción near the Ijui River and Todos Santos at Caaró. The two missions were so named because they were begun on the feast of the Assumption, August 15, and on All Saints Day, November 1.

Bl. John de Castillo

Born September 14, 1596, at Belmonte, Spain, John de Castillo received his early education from his grandfather, Alfonso de Castillo, and his mother María Rodríguez de Castillo. John began his higher studies at the university of Alcalá with the intention of becoming a lawyer. However, on March 22, 1614, at the age of seventeen, he entered the Society of Jesus.

Two years later he left Spain for South America with his future fellow missionary, Alphonse Rodríguez. For a time he taught grammar in Chile. After his ordination in 1626, he was sent to the

mission of San Nicolás de Piratiui, which Father Roque had founded on the Uruguay River. Though he was rather sickly by nature, he worked hard and did not even consider taking time out to be cured. Two years later he joined Father Roque in Río Grande do Sul.

Bl. Alphonse Rodríguez

The son of Gonzalo Rodríguez and María née Obnel, Alphonse was born at Zamora, Spain, March 10, 1598. He became a member of the Society of Jesus three days after John de Castillo, and with the latter departed for South America in 1616. There he taught literature for a while, and was ordained a priest in 1623 or 1624. He was known to have been a very pious young man, who had a special devotion to the Passion of Christ and entertained the longing of shedding his blood for the faith. In 1628 he and John de Castillo were assigned to Father Roque as companions in Río Grande do Sul.

The Three Martyrs

After Father Roque had founded and organized the new mission of Asunción, he placed it in the care of Father John de Castillo, and went with Father Alphonse Rodríguez to Caaró to establish the mission of Todos Santos.

Father A. Jaeger, S.J., believes he has determined the exact

253

latitude and longitude where the mission of Todos Santos was located, which place it in Río Grande do Sul, not in Uruguay as some have said.

In the territory where the new missions were established there was a witch doctor, by the name of Nezú, who was filled with hatred of the Christian religion. He captured some Indian children who had been baptized and "dechristianized" them by washing their heads, breasts and backs and scraping their tongues. The other Indians had a superstitious terror of him and his pretended supernatural powers. Not long after the founding of the mission of Todos Santos, the Indian chief Carupé, instigated by Nezú, went to the mission with a band of tribesmen in order to kill the two missionaries. When they arrived, Father Roque happened to be fitting a rope to a bell which he had just suspended above the little church. Following the chief's orders, Maragua, a slave, stole up from behind and with a tomahawk smashed the priest's skull.

Hearing the tumult, Father Alphonse Rodríguez, who was inside the chapel, went to the door. He was seized at once and likewise beaten to death. The chapel was set on fire, and the bodies of the martyrs were thrown into the flames. However, the body of Father Roque was only partially consumed; and the murderers heard a voice issuing from it, warning them of punishments to come. They cut open the corpse, tore out the heart, and transfixed it with an arrow. Then they threw it back into the fire, but it was not burned, merely scorched. The day was November 16, 1628.

Carupé and his followers then went to the mission of Asunción. When Father John de Castillo, who was just getting ready to celebrate Mass, came out of the chapel to see what they wanted, Carupé said to him: "We have come to kill you, just as we have killed the other two at Caaró." Dragging him some distance to an arroyo, they struck him three times with a spade until he was half dead and then crushed the life out of him with two big stones. To complete the work of destruction, they destroyed the image of Nuestra Señora La Conquistadora which was at the mission, profaned the sacred vessels and vestments, and burned the missionary's missal and breviary.

A month later, an expedition of ten Spaniards and almost a thousand Indians arrived to punish the perpetrators of these crimes. They found the pierced heart of Father Roque almost intact. It was sent to the Jesuit Father General in Rome in 1634; but in 1928 it was returned to Buenos Aires, where it is preserved and venerated at the College of San Salvador.

Soon after the death of the martyrs an investigation was set on foot with a view to their beatification. But it was only on January 25, 1934, that Pope Pius XI declared the martyrs blessed. Their feast has been observed by the Jesuits on November 17.

Liturgical Prayer

O God, you adorned with the crown of eternal glory the sufferings which your martyrs, blessed Roch, Alphonse and John, endured for the faith of Christ. Through the intercession of their merits, grant that infidel nations, being freed from the shadow of death, may be led to the path of salvation. Through the same Jesus Christ, your Son, our Lord, who lives and reigns with you in the unity of the Holy Spirit, God, forever and ever. Amen.

Part II
OUR LADY

All the Americas

THE story of the Saints of the Americas would not be complete without a few chapters about our Lady, the Queen of all Saints. In a sense, she is one of the saints of every one of the Americas. She came with the first messengers of the Gospel. She played an important role in the establishment of the Church on both continents.

As the Immaculate Conception, she was officially chosen as the universal patroness of all of Spanish America in the eighteenth century; and in the nineteenth century the United States of America likewise chose Mary Immaculate as its principal patroness.

As the Virgin of Guadalupe, she has been proclaimed the Queen and Mother, not only of Mexico, but also of all the other countries, north and south. Numerous Marian pilgrimage shrines have been erected in all the countries of America. We shall mention some of them; and though the enumeration is not an exhaustive one, the lists offered are representative of the many different countries included under the general name of the Americas. These sanctuaries have been and are striking proof that the New World, no less than the Old World, is in a special manner Mary's Land. She, rather than the conquistadors, conquered it — for her divine Son, Christ, King of the Universe.

CHAPTER 32

OUR LADY

All the Americas

Mary Immaculate

Patroness of the Americas

CHRISTOPHER Columbus accomplished the discovery of the New World under the patronage of our Lady and with the intention of bringing the blessings of Christianity to the pagan aborigines he found there.

Of his three ships, the main one was named *Santa María* or, as some historians claim, *Santa María de la Concepción.* After invoking the protection of Our Lady of La Rábida, Columbus set sail on August 4, 1492, two days after the Franciscan feast of Portiuncula or Our Lady of the Angels. Two months and one week later, on October 12, while singing the *Salve Regina,* he and his men landed on the island of San Salvador in the Bahamas.

Our Lady Comes to the New World

October 12 was the feast of Nuestra Señora del Pilar (Our Lady of the Pillar), a fact which has not hitherto received the attention it deserves. La Virgen del Pilar, so named because the ancient miraculous image of the Blessed Virgin stands on a pillar, has always been the object of special devotion throughout Spain. The celebrated church at Zaragoza where this statue is enshrined is one of the most popular and most frequented of Mary's many sanctuaries in that country.

According to an ancient tradition, the shrine was built by

*Murillo's famous painting of the Immaculate Conception,
now in the Louvre, Paris.*

Santiago (St. James the Apostle) at the wish of the Blessed Virgin herself who, while still alive on earth, appeared to him as he was praying on the bank of the Ebro at Zaragoza; and it was he who set up the statue which is still venerated today in that shrine by thousands of the faithful.

Although the testimony of St. Jerome and of the Mozarabic Office is adduced in favor of the contention that St. James preached the Gospel in Spain, most modern scholars reject this opinion. The oldest written testimony of devotion to Our Lady of the Pillar at Zaragoza, that of Pedro Librana, dates back only to the year 1155. However, Father Fita, the Jesuit scholar, has published data on two Christian tombs at Zaragoza from Roman times on which the Assumption of our Lady into heaven is depicted.

Be that as it may, the shrine of Our Lady of the Pillar is one of the oldest and most famous in Spain. Although the present spacious baroque church, with its half dozen cupolas besides the main and central one, was begun only in 1681, the shrine was well known at the time of Columbus. Pope Callistus III, in 1456, had given his express approval for the devotion to Our Lady of the Pillar.

When Columbus, therefore, set foot on the first land of the New World (which he thought was one of the islands of Cipango or Japan) on the feast of Our Lady of the Pillar, he must have regarded it as an assurance that he was the recipient of our Lady's special protection and, as she had helped to bring the faith to Spain, so she would now also assist the messengers of the Gospel in the newly found world.

To one of the towns established on San Salvador Island Columbus game the name of Concepción. Already at this time the people of Spain distinguished themselves by their ardent devotion to the Immaculate Conception; and in the course of the next three centuries the name *Purísima Concepción* was given to numberless places, rivers, lakes, towns, missions and churches, not only in the Caribbean, in Mexico, and in Central and South America, but also in the southern portion of what is now the United States.

We may well add that in a battle against hostile Indians on the island of Española (Santo Domingo and Haiti) Columbus took recourse to Nuestra Señora de la Merced (Our Lady of Mercy or Ransom) and triumphed in an astounding manner. The first Marian shrine in the New World was then built on Holy Hill in Santo Domingo, the shrine of our Lady of Mercy. Today Our Lady of Mercy is still the special patroness of the Republic of Santo Domingo.

It is especially in the southern portion of what is now the United States extending from Florida to California — the so-called Spanish Borderlands — that we find abundant proof of the pioneers' great devotion to our Lady, especially under her title of the Immaculate Conception. The Spanish explorers, conquistadors and missionaries, particularly in this region, frequently invoked our Lady's aid; and to her intercession they ascribed the success of their hazardous and adventurous enterprises. Not only did they themselves cherish a tender and trustful love of our Lady, but they taught the Indians by word and example to practice a similar childlike devotion to their heavenly Mother.

Ample and definite evidence for these assertions is the fact that of the 200 central Indian missions (not counting sub-missions) which were founded in the Spanish Borderlands during more than two centuries (1570-1793), no less than fifty-one or one-fourth of the total number were dedicated in honor of our Lady and bore Marian names.

Nineteen of these missions were founded in Spanish Florida, which at one time extended as far north as present-day Virginia. Sixteen were established in what is now the State of Texas, thirteen were erected in the present State of New Mexico, and three were founded in Alta California, now the State of California. All of them, except Santa María Mission in Virginia which was begun by the pioneer Jesuits in 1570, were established and staffed by the sons of St. Francis.

These fifty-one missions honored our Lady under various titles and recalled outstanding events in her holy life; but the largest number, thirteen, were named for her Immaculate Conception. Of the others, one recalled the Nativity of the Blessed Virgin, and two the first Christmas in Bethlehem. Four bore the name of Mary's Purification, and five others the name of her Dolors. Two commemorated her sorrowful solitude (Soledad) after the death of her divine Son on Calvary. Five proclaimed her glorious Assumption into heaven.

Of other special titles of our Lady, this rosary of missions, strung across our southern states from ocean to ocean, included four of Our Lady of Guadalupe, three of Our Lady of the Rosary, two of Our Lady of the Angels, one of Our Lady of Refuge, one of Our Lady of Ransom, one of Our Lady of Light and one of the Most Holy Name of Mary.

In addition, six others were simply called missions of St. Mary or our Lady. Two other missions, while not named for our

Lady, had special shrines of the Blessed Virgin Mary, namely the Nombre de Dios (Name of God) Mission near St. Augustine, which was also a shrine of Our Lady the Nursing Mother of Happy Delivery, and the San Carlos Mission at Carmel, California, which had a shrine of Our Lady of Bethlehem. Both of these shrines have been restored.

Besides the fifty-one missions for the Indians, at least nine churches and chapels in the Spanish settlements of this territory were likewise named for our Lady. In St. Augustine, Florida, there was the friary and church of the Immaculate Conception. In Santa Fe, New Mexico, there were no less than five Marian churches and chapels: the parish church of Our Lady of the Assumption, the chapel of Our Lady of the Conquest attached to the parish church, the Rosario chapel, the chapel of our Lady of Guadalupe, and the church of Our Lady of Light. The others were Santa María de Galves friary and church at Pensacola, Florida, the church of Our Lady of the Pillar (or of Guadalupe) first at Bucareli (Midway), and then at Nacogdoches, Texas, and the church of Nuestra Señora la Reina de los Angeles de Portiuncula (Our Lady Queen of the Angels of Portiuncula) at Los Angeles, California. Not included are the presidio chapels, for instance, that of Our Lady of the Pillar at Adaes, present-day Robeline, Louisiana.

In the missions and settlements of the Spanish Borderlands more than 1,500 missionaries labored during the colonial period; and under Mary's patronage their heroic efforts were crowned with remarkable success in many instances, at least as long as they remained in these parts.

About the middle of the seventeenth century some 30,000 converted Indians were living in the Florida missions.

In New Mexico, according to Bandelier, there were as many as 25,000 Indians in the sixteenth and seventeenth centuries; and the greater number of these were led into the Catholic fold, though vestiges of pagan customs remained and still exist among them today. In California the missionaries had the greatest success. By 1832 they had baptized 87,787 Indians; and 16,864 Christian Indians were living in that year in the twenty-one missions.

There can be no doubt that the missionaries of our Spanish Borderlands consistently cherished and inculcated a deep devotion to the Immaculate Virgin Mary. Father Junípero Serra, the Father of California, especially distinguished himself by such devotion. As soon as he felt certain that it was his vocation to be a missionary in the New World, he chose as one of his patrons for its fulfillment the Immaculate Mother of God.

Stopping at Puerto Rico on his way to Mexico, he and his companions sought shelter at the Hermitage of the Immaculate Conception; and immediately after landing on that island they prayed the Franciscan Crown of seven decades and chanted the *Tota Pulchra*.

In those early difficult days at Mission San Diego, California, he turned for help to "our heavenly and most pure Superioress"; and to her intercession he ascribed his and his companions' deliverance when hostile Indians attacked the mission on August 15, 1769, a month after it had been founded.

To the Father Guardian of San Fernando College in Mexico City he wrote: "I beg all of them [the friars at the college] to commend us to God, and to pray for the conversion of these poor pagans to our holy Catholic Faith. . . . I beg them to say a *Salve* to our heavenly and most pure Superioress, in thanksgiving for having preserved us on the feast of her Assumption, and that at the same time she may continue in her same gracious service. I had [an image of] her in one hand and of her divine crucified Son in the other, when the arrows were pouring in upon us; and believe me, with such defensive armor, although I am so great a sinner, it was equally good not to have to die or to face death."

As Father Maynard Geiger, O.F.M., the biographer of Father Serra, writes, "From Spain to Puerto Rico, from Mexico to San Diego and Monterey, the refrain of Fray Junípero Serra appeared to be: 'Thou are all fair, O Mary, and the original stain is not in thee!' "

During California's first land expedition in 1769, Father Crespi named a now extinct lake, on the present site of Santa Barbara, Laguna de la Concepción (Lake of the Conception). To a small Indian village in the western part of Santa Barbara County he likewise gave the name of the Immaculate Conception. He wrote: "I gave it the sweet name of Concepción de María Santísima." Similarly, one of the four *rancherias* attached to Mission San Diego was called Purísima Concepción.

Father Francisco Garcés, Franciscan contemporary of Father Serra in the missions of Pimería Alta, traveled all over Arizona and into California carrying no other baggage save his breviary, an extra tunic, a picture of our Lady, and another of a condemned soul which seems to have been on the reverse side. When he encountered Indians, he instructed them in Christian doctrine, including the last things of man, and explained his pictures. The Indians always showed a lively interest in the picture of our Lady.

A century earlier, the Jesuit pioneer in Pimería Alta, Father Eusebio Francisco Kino, asked for statues of "Jesus of Nazareth

263

and Our Lady of Sorrows" because it was to them that he attributed the success of his missionary labors and travels. To his now famous memoirs he gave the title: *The Celestial Favors of Jesus, the Most Holy Mary, and the Most Glorious Apostle of the Indies, Experienced in . . . Unknown North America.*

In 1776 two missionaries of New Mexico, Father Silvestre Vélez de Escalante of Zuñi and Father Francisco Atanasio Domínguez explored Colorado and Utah for the purpose of finding a connecting route to the new missions on the California coast. On September 21 they reached a river on the eastern side of the Wasatch Mountains divide in Utah, later on called Strawberry Creek and now dammed to form Strawberry Reservoir. To the valley of this river they gave the name Valle de la Purísima.

From Utah Lake they turned south, and because of the winter weather they had to return to Zuñi. On the way back they forded the Colorado River in southernmost Utah near the place where it enters Arizona. This ford, now known as "the Crossing of the Padres," they named La Purísima Concepción de la Virgen on November 7, 1776.

It was not uncommon among the Spaniards and their Indian charges to give the name of Mary Immaculate also to persons. The Franciscan who, in November of 1595, offered up the holy Sacrifice of the Mass on California soil for the first time (only thirty years after the founding of St. Augustine, Florida), had the name of Father Francisco de la Concepción. He was the chaplain of Cermeño's ship *San Agustín*, and the place where he celebrated Mass was near San Francisco at what is now called Drake's Bay.

The baptismal registers of Mission Santa Barbara for 1786-1858 reveal the fact that the name of Mary in some form or other was conferred on 1,166 children and adults, men and women alike, which total represents about one-fourth of those baptized. Of these, fifteen had the name of María de la Concepción or simply Concepción.

Perhaps the most convincing evidence that the padres fostered devotion to Mary Immaculate among their neophytes in our Spanish Borderlands is found in the beautiful prayers and hymns which they taught the Indians.

A favorite greeting and prayer among the Spaniards everywhere, in their colonies and missions as well as their homeland, was the so-called *Alabado*. The most common form of this prayer is the following short form:

"Alabado sea el Santísimo Sacramento del Altar! Bendita sea la limpia y purísima Concepción de Nuestra Señora María Santísima sin mancha de pecado original!" (Praised be the most Holy

Sacrament of the Altar! Blessed be the stainless and most pure Conception of our Lady Mary, most holy, free from the taint of original sin!)

In the missions of our entire Southwest, the Indians learned to sing the *Alabado* in a longer form at services in church, just as we sing (or used to sing) the Psalm *Laudate* after Benediction, and also at other times, for instance when they met a missionary on the road. This form of the *Alabado* had three stanzas. The first gave praise to the Blessed Sacrament. The second extolled the Immaculate Conception. The third was in honor of St. Joseph. The first two verses are as follows:

Alabado y ensalzado
Sea el Divino Sacramento,
En quien Dios oculto asiste,
De las almas et sustento.

Y la limpia Concepción
De la Reina de los cielos,
Que, quedando Virgen pura,
Es Madre del Verbo Eterno.

The following is a literal translation: "Praised and exalted be the Divine Sacrament, in which God is present in a hidden manner and offers Himself as the Food of souls! Praised also be the Immaculate Conception of the Queen of Heaven, who, while remaining a pure Virgin, became the Mother of the Eternal Word!"

In his *Mission Music of California*, Father Owen da Silva offers the following free translation in verse:

Lift your heart in joy and exalt Him
In the Blessed Sacrament all Holy,
Where the Lord, his glory veiling,
Comforts souls true and lowly.

Laud the glorious Conception
Of the Queen in God's Kingdom Supernal,
Who remaining Virgin stainless,
Bore for men the Word Eternal.

The missionaries in California also taught the Christian Indians to have often on their lips the words: "Amar a Dios!" (Love

God!) and "Ave María Purísima!" (Hail Mary, most Pure!) They exhorted their neophytes to rise in the morning with the greeting: "Ave María Purísima del Refugio!" (Hail most Pure Mary of Refuge!)

The Morning Hymn and especially the Evening Hymn, which were sung in all the California missions, honored and invoked Mary Immaculate in a touching manner. In the Morning Hymn the picture of the woman of the Protoevangelium was presented to the neophytes in these words:

The cunning serpent writhes and coils in pains;
Lest it do harm, thou fetterest it with chains.

In the Evening Hymn we find these tender words of greeting:

Hail Mary, blessed of God and full of grace,
The Lord is with thee, purest of our race!

Blessed art thou, Dove of purest, spotless white,
Only woman never touched by sin's chill blight!

With one voice earth and heaven thee acclaim
As Queen, God's Mother, Virgin free from stain!

So shall it be; forever sound our strain!
With one voice earth and heaven thee acclaim.

The most beautiful Marian hymn sung in the missions of our Southwest is the one which celebrated the Assumption of the Immaculate Mother of God into heaven. It was written by Venerable Father Antonio Margil, apostle of Texas and all of New Spain; and Father Serra sang it with his neophytes at Mission San Carlos, California, during the octave of the Assumption shortly before he died on August 28, 1784.

For a long time the writer searched in vain for a copy of this hymn. Father Felipe Cueto, then provincial of the Franciscan Province of Jalisco in Mexico and now bishop of a new diocese adjoining the archdiocese of Mexico City, came to the rescue. The hymn is still being sung in the friary of the former Apostolic College of Our Lady of Guadalupe in Zacatecas. It is difficult to render the musical Spanish into English, but we have attempted a literal as well as readable translation in verse. The hymn consists

266

of fourteen stanzas and a chorus. The latter follows first and then the stanzas:

Ascend, ascend, ascend
O Virgin, to your throne above!
Ascend, ascend, ascend,
Enjoy forever your reign of love!

Pray, who is she who from this earth
Takes leave and quickly mounts so high?
'Tis Mary, Queen, who like the dawn
Lights up the glowing morning sky.

Rejoice, you citizens of heaven,
Angelic choirs in vast array!
God's Mother welcome to your home,
At Mary's feet your homage lay.

You princes of the court of God,
Pry open wide the gates of gold,
Asunder tear concealing veils,
Let all her coming home behold.

The fields and forests, rocky cliffs,
The earth and water, fiery flame,
The sun and moon and shining stars,
Our Queen in unison acclaim.

Our hearts are filled with hope and peace;
She leaves this vale of tears and pains,
Obtains for us who tarry here
The help of Heaven, where she reigns.

As Esther pleaded with her king
And saved her people doomed to woe,
So Mary prays to her dear Son,
For us begs pardon here below.

As Judith bravely overcame
Proud Holofernes' foolish boasts,
So Mary helps us conquer all
Assaults of wily Satan's hosts.

God's Mother reigning now in heaven,
We know it also is your will
To be to each returning child
An Advocate and Mother still.

Partaking of the Bridegroom's feast,
Let fall for us some little crumbs,
That we may share your happiness.
Remember us, poor little ones.

We greet you, Mother, and our Queen.
We raise to you a suppliant hand.
We pray to you with firmest trust,
In this our tearful exile land.

In heaven's bliss forget us not;
Our humble, fervent prayers hear
And make us faithful, strong and true,
The while our enemy is near.

That all the world may be your own,
With love of God cause hearts to burn,
From earthly ties our weak wills wean,
For heaven's treasures make us yearn.

Our Queen and Mother merciful,
We turn to you with tears and sighs,
Afflicted all with miseries,
We beg you, Lady, hear our cries.

Fair Heaven's Queen, farewell to you,
Until in heaven we too shall be
And join you there and happy see
And praise you through eternity.

Patroness of the Spanish Empire

Little wonder, therefore, that as early as 1644 Pope Innocent X permitted the feast of the Conception of the Blessed Virgin Mary to be made a holy day of obligation throughout Spain and its worldwide possessions. It was only in 1708, under Pope Clement XI, that this feast became such for the whole Church.

The next step was the formal choice of Mary Immaculate as the principal and universal patroness of Spain and all its colonies, which included the southern part of the United States from coast to coast. It was in 1760 that Pope Clement XIII gave his official approval to this choice; and the following year he granted permission to make use of the office and Mass of the Immaculate Conception which was then used among the Franciscans. These liturgical formulas clearly taught and extolled Mary's singular privilege of the Immaculate Conception.

Beginning in 1767, the office and Mass of the Immaculate Conception was sanctioned for use not only on the feast itself, but also on every Saturday of the year except in Advent and Lent.

Another grant in the same year permitted the insertion in the Litany of Loreto, throughout the Spanish realm, of the invocation: "Mater Immaculata, ora pro nobis!" (Mother Immaculate, pray for us!)

A symbol as well as instance of the Spaniard's devotion to Mary Immaculate are the beautiful paintings of the Immaculate Conception by the famous artist, Bartolomé Esteban Murillo (1617-1682). *El Maestro,* as Murillo was called, made numerous paintings of the Immaculate Conception. The most famous, which is now in the Louvre, represents the Blessed Virgin surrounded by cherubs and standing upon a crescent, her hands folded on her breast and her eyes turned upward. Similar to it is Murillo's painting of the Assumption of our Lady, also in the Louvre. The spirit which animated Murillo is indicated by the fact that he never began a religious painting without prayer or penance. The pupils of the art school which he founded always greeted each other with the words of the *Alabado* (short form) whenever they met.

New France

Not only in Hispanic America, however, but also in the French and English colonies of North America, the early missionaries honored Mary Immaculate in a striking manner. The well-known Jesuit missionary, Jacques Marquette, for instance, distinguished himself by a special devotion to the Immaculate Conception. When he accompanied Joliet on the exploration trip of the Mississippi as far as the Arkansas River in 1673, he placed the expedition under the protection of Mary Immaculate. The mission which he began among the Illinois Indians near Starved Rock in 1676 (and which later was also the scene of the missionary labors of the Franciscans, Fathers La Ribourde, Membré and Hennepin), he likewise named for the Immaculate Conception of

269

St. Mary. According to Father Dablon, he also gave the name of River of the Immaculate Conception to the Father of Waters.

In a *History of the Devotion to the Blessed Virgin Mary in North America* (that is, the United States and Canada), written in 1862 by the Rev. Xavier Donald MacLeod and published apparently for the first time in 1880, we are told that St. Isaac Jogues dedicated the present State of New York to the Immaculate Conception, and that there was a mission of the Immaculate Conception among the Senecas of New York.

It was to the intercession of our Lady that Father Joseph Bressani, S.J., ascribed his deliverance from the Iroquois in 1644. Although he did not win the crown of martyrdom, as did St. Isaac Jogues in 1646 at Auriesville, New York, Father Bressani was taken prisoner and tortured by the Iroquois on three different occasions. During the thirteen years that he served as a missionary in the Great Lakes region, he is said to have converted 12,000 Indians. When the Hollanders of New York ransomed him in 1644 for the sum of about seventy-five dollars, he wrote:

"I sang my 'When Israel went out of Egypt' (Psalm 113) on the 19th of August — one of the days within the octave of the Assumption of the Virgin, who was my deliverer — after I had been a captive in the country of the Iroquois for four months, a small matter in comparison with what my sins deserved" (*Jesuit Relations*, vol. 39, pp. 78-79).

In the Abenaki Mission on the Kennebec River in Maine, at the time that Father Sebastian Rasle, S.J., was there (he died a martyr in 1724), there were, besides the mission church, two chapels. One was dedicated to the Guardian Angel of the tribe, and the other to our most holy Mother, Mary Immaculate. The latter stood on the path to the cultivated fields, and here the Indians offered prayers when they went to plant or to gather the harvest.

The English Colonies

Before the days of Henry VIII, England had been known as Our Lady's Dower (or Dowry). One of the American colonies was named Maryland in honor of the English Queen, but to the Catholics who came to this colony it was the land of Mary Immaculate, the new dowry of our Lady. In his book, *Our Land and Our Lady*, Daniel Sargent writes:

"At first, it is true, instead of becoming Our Lady's Dower, Transatlantic England became quite the opposite. . . . Yet strangely enough into this anti-Marial stronghold was inserted a

270

Marial colony. . . . In 1634 the *Ark* and the *Dove* arrived in the bay which the Spaniards a hundred years before had christened the Bay of the Mother of God — Chesapeake Bay. They were the ships of Lord Baltimore, though he was dead. With them was one of his sons, Leonard. . . . The colony was given a name. It was Maryland. The name in the minds of the Catholics recalled Our Lady, but officially it was but a compliment to Henrietta María, Queen of England. Thus Our Lady did enter into the English colonies, but not ostentatiously — 'as still as dew that falleth on the grass.' "

What Sargent has written so beautifully, however, does not tell the complete story. The American colony of Maryland was begun, not merely as the land of Mary, but in a special manner as the land and dowry of Mary Immaculate.

While crossing the Atlantic, the *Ark* and the *Dove* encountered a fearful storm. The pinnace of the *Ark* was lost. Abandoned to the wild waves, the ship was hopelessly tossed about and seemed to be doomed to certain shipwreck. Then the Catholics on the *Ark* prayed to Mary Immaculate for deliverance; and on this occasion the Jesuit Father Andrew White reminded the Blessed Mother that it was their intention to consecrate their future home in the New World to her, the Immaculate Conception, as her new dowry. Mary Immaculate, Star of the Sea, saved the ship and led it safely into the harbor of her new dowry.

In Father White's *Relatio itineris in Marilandiam* (Relation of the Journey to Maryland) we find the words: "propositum hujus itineris esse . . . dotem alteram Immaculatae Virgini Matri consecrare" (it was the aim of this journey . . . to consecrate another dowry to the Immaculate Virgin Mother). Though we have no documentary record of the fact, we may take for granted that Father White and the Catholic colonists kept their promise after they landed in Maryland, and consecrated their new home to Mary the ever Blessed Virgin and Mother of God under the title of the Immaculate Conception.

Noteworthy also is what we read of a certain William Bretton, who in circa 1650 gave a grant of land in the new colony of Maryland for a church "in honor of almighty God and the ever Immaculate Virgin Mary."

Patroness of the United States

For a large part of the present United States, comprising as it does the Spanish Borderlands, it was but a rededication of the country to the Immaculate Conception when, in 1846, eight and a

271

half years before Pope Pius IX defined the dogma of the Immaculate Conception, the bishops gathered in the Sixth Provincial Council of Baltimore and officially chose Mary Immaculate as the special patroness of the United States.

In 1846 the United States already included the former Spanish Florida, comprising the seven states of Virginia, the two Carolinas, Alabama, Mississippi, Georgia and Florida — the latter having become a state the previous year. Also included was Texas, which had been annexed and granted statehood in 1845. In the same year the War with Mexico began, and two years later resulted in the cession of the six states of New Mexico, Arizona (increased by the Gadsden Purchase in 1853), Colorado, Utah, Nevada and California.

It was on May 10, 1846, the Fourth Sunday after Easter, that Archbishop Samuel Eccleston and twenty-two bishops were gathered in the Cathedral of the Assumption of our Lady in Baltimore for the opening of the first session of the Sixth Provincial Council of Baltimore.

The ecclesiastical province of Baltimore at this time comprised the entire United States, and hence the Sixth Provincial Council was able to issue decrees for the entire country.

On May 13, at nine in the morning, the bishops gathered for the third private meeting of the Council in the residence of the archbishop and under his chairmanship. At this meeting they adopted a decree by which they chose the Blessed Virgin Mary, conceived without sin, as Patroness of the United States of America. Translated from the Latin, the decree reads as follows:

"With enthusiastic acclaim and with unanimous approval and consent, the Fathers [of the Council] have chosen the Blessed Virgin Mary, conceived without sin, as the Patroness of the United States of America without, however, adding the obligation of hearing Mass and abstaining from servile work on the feast of the Conception of Blessed Mary. And, therefore, they decided that the Supreme Pontiff be asked humbly to transfer the solemnity, unless the feast fall on a Sunday, to the nearest Sunday, on which both private and solemn Masses may be celebrated of the feast thus transferred, and the vesper office of the same feast may be recited."

John Gilmary Shea tells us that it was "to gratify a pious desire pervading the whole United States" that "the Fathers of the Council petitioned the Sovereign Pontiff to ratify their choice of the Blessed Virgin Mary, conceived without sin, as Patroness of the United States, and to transfer the solemnization of the feast to the following Sunday."

In the fourth private meeting of the Council, held on May 15, the bishops agreed to ask the Holy See for permission, in all the dioceses of the country, to add the word "Immaculate" in the orations and preface of the divine office and Mass of the Conception of Mary; and also to add in the Litany of the Blessed Virgin the invocation: "Queen, conceived without sin, pray for us."

The latter favors were granted first, by Pope Pius IX, in an audience on September 13, 1846, and announced by the Sacred Congregation of Propaganda (to which the Church in the United States was subject at that time) in a decree published two days later. When the Sixth Provincial Council of Baltimore met, the ruling Pontiff was Gregory IX. He died on June 1 of that year and was succeeded by Pius IX on June 16.

The choice of our Lady in her Immaculate Conception as Patroness of the United States was approved by Pope Pius IX in an audience on February 7, 1847; and this approval was announced in a decree of Propaganda dated July 2 of the same year. This decree and the one of the previous year bear the signature of Cardinal Fransoni.

Two more decrees issued by the Congregation of Sacred Rites on April 10, 1848, contained replies to questions which had arisen. (1) The Mass of the Immaculate Conception, transferred to Sunday, had the *Gloria* and *Credo* and at the end the Gospel of the Sunday; and if the Mass were sung, it had a commemoration only of the Sunday, but if it were a private Mass it had commemorations also of other feasts observed on that day. (2) The obligation of reciting the vespers of the divine office was satisfied by priests by attendance at the vespers of the Immaculate Conception on the Sunday to which the feast was transferred.

The decree by which the bishops of the United States chose the Immaculate Conception as the Patroness of the country was signed by Archbishop Samuel Eccleston of Baltimore, chairman of the Council, and twenty-two other bishops. Three of the latter were coadjutor bishops (Louisville, New York and Boston), one an administrator (Detroit), and one a vicar apostolic (Texas). Besides the latter, there were twenty-one bishops and one archbishop, each one representing a diocese except that New York had two bishops at the Council. The dioceses formed the one ecclesiastical province of Baltimore, which consisted of the following: Baltimore, Boston, Charleston, Chicago, Cincinnati, Detroit, Dubuque, Hartford, Little Rock, Louisville, Milwaukee, Mobile, Nashville, Natchez, New Orleans, New York, Philadelphia, Pittsburgh, Richmond, St. Louis, Texas and Vincennes.

The request of the American bishops for permission to add

the word "Immaculate" in the orations and preface for the feast of the Conception of the Blessed Virgin requires some explanation. The feast of the Conception of Mary was celebrated in some places as early as the thirteenth century, but the texts used did not clearly teach the doctrine of the Immaculate Conception. This was done in the office *Sicut lilium* and the Mass *Egredimini* of Leonard of Nogarolis, which received the approval of Sixtus IV in 1477 and which contained the same oration we have today for the feast of the Immaculate Conception. When Pius V revised the Roman breviary in 1568, the office and Mass of Nogarolis were dropped (although the Franciscans were allowed to retain them), and the office of the Nativity of the Blessed Virgin was substituted, the word "Conception" being used instead of "Nativity."

When the American bishops asked for permission to add the word "Immaculate," they anticipated and perhaps influenced a step taken by Pope Pius IX a year after he granted their petition. On September 30, 1847, this pope authorized for the diocese of Rome a new office and Mass proper to the feast of the Immaculate Conception which explicitly taught the doctrine of Mary's Immaculate Conception. Two years later, he extended the new office and Mass to the universal Church.

On December 8, 1854, eight years and four months after the American bishops had chosen Mary Immaculate as the Patroness of the United States, Pope Pius IX solemnly declared the Immaculate Conception of the Blessed Virgin Mary to be an article of faith.

Numerous petitions for the definition of this doctrine had poured in during the preceding years, and Pope Pius IX had written the encyclical *Ubi primum*, in which he asked the bishops of the world: (1) how great was the devotion of the faithful to the Immaculate Conception and how great their desire for the definition of this doctrine; and (2) what was the opinion and desire of the bishops themselves. In other words, the pope consulted the bishops.

The American bishops, assembled in the Seventh Provincial Council of Baltimore, May 5-13, 1849, had given a favorable reply to both questions (decrees I and II, on May 12), informing the Holy Father that the faithful in the United States had a great devotion to the Immaculate Conception, and they, the bishops, would be pleased if the Holy Father declared the doctrine of the Immaculate Conception to be an article of faith.

The documents in which are recorded all the facts mentioned concerning the Sixth and Seventh Councils of Baltimore are contained in volume three of the so-called *Collectio Lacensis*, a collection of the acts and decrees of the councils of the bishops of North America and Great Britain from 1789 to 1869, published by Herder at Freiburg in Breisgau in 1875.

Noteworthy is the fact that among these documents there is one which tells us that Bishop Carroll had chosen the Blessed Virgin as patroness of the diocese of Baltimore at the time he was made bishop. The document in question has the minutes of the fifth session, on November 10, 1791, of the Diocesan Synod of Baltimore, which was really the first national synod of the United States.

In his *History of Devotion to the Blessed Virgin Mary in North America*, MacLeod tells us that in 1862 more than 800 churches in North America (the United States and Canada) were dedicated to the Blessed Virgin Mary and of this number 145 were named for the Immaculate Conception.

Another count made by Father Maynard Geiger, O.F.M., in 1943 showed that out of 4,817 churches and institutions in the United States, dedicated to the Blessed Virgin Mary, 637 honored the Immaculate Conception.

Very fittingly the beloved poet-priest of the South, Father Abram J. Ryan, wrote one of his most beautiful poems in Baltimore on the night of December 8, 1880. It opens with these verses:

Fell the snow on the festival's vigil
And surpliced the city in white.
I wonder who wove the pure flakelets;
Ask the Virgin, or God, or the night.

It fitted the Feast: 'twas a symbol,
And earth wore the surplice at morn,
As pure as the vale's stainless lily
For Mary, the sinlessly born;

For Mary, conceived in all sinlessness.
And the sun, thro' the clouds of the East,
With the brightest and fairest of flashes,
Fringed the surplice of white for the Feast.

And round the horizon hung cloudlets,
Pure stoles to be worn by the Feast,
While the earth and the heavens were waiting
For the beautiful Mass of the priest.

A magnificent monument and worthy symbol of the choice of the Immaculate Conception as patroness of the United States is the National Shrine in Washington, D. C. The cornerstone was laid by Cardinal Gibbons in 1920. By 1931 the north crypt, containing the beautiful lower church, was completed.

Then followed a long halt because of the Depression and World War II. After the bishops of the country had made an appeal for needed funds in 1953, the construction of the exterior superstructure was begun in the summer of 1955. The 39,000,000 Catholics of the United States responded generously; and the Knights of Columbus donated 1,000,000 dollars for the bell tower. After four years of building, the exterior of the church and the tower were complete, but most of the interior work still remained to be done. The National Shrine of the Immaculate Conception was solemnly dedicated on November 20, 1959.

Romanesque-Byzantine in design, the Shrine has a massive stone cupola roofed with polychrome tile — blue, red, gold and white. This cupola is 108 feet in diameter at its base; and the cross which surmounts it rises 237 feet into the sky. The interior height of the dome is 159 feet; and the diameter of the interior is 89 feet. Between the interior and exterior domes, an electronic carillon, the gift of Cardinal Stritch of Chicago, has been installed. The great dome surmounting the crossing of the nave and the transepts, and the smaller domes over the nave are brought together with the massive walls by triumphal arches resting on mighty pillars.

Like the dome, the campanile, called the Knight's Tower, is an outstanding landmark in the nation's capital. Including the elevation on which it stands, it is only a few feet lower than the Washington monument. Rising to a height of 329 feet, it is four feet higher than the famous campanile of St. Mark's in Venice.

With an outside length of 459 feet and a width of 240 feet at its widest point, the Shrine is the largest Catholic church in the United States and the seventh largest in the world. It has a seating capacity of 3,000 and, including standing room, a total capacity of 6,000. Built like the great cathedrals of Europe, the Shrine has no skeleton of steel beams. In fact, it does not contain any structural steel, but is constructed entirely of masonry, brick and stone and tile. More than 350 carloads of limestone, 60,000 cubic feet of granite, and more than 10,000,000 common bricks were used in the construction of the edifice.

Dominating the outside wall of the apse (north side) is a huge

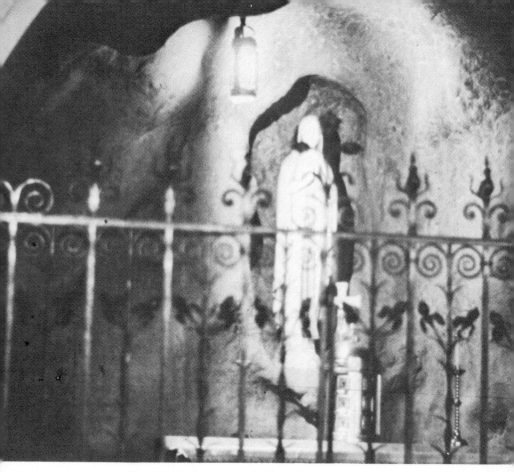

*Chapel in the lower church of the National Shrine of the
Immaculate Conception, Washington, D.C.*

statue of Mary Immaculate, Queen of the Universe, sculptured by
Ivan Mestrovich. The impressive facade, framing the front entrance (south side) includes a heroic statue of Mary Immaculate
with two kneeling angels paying her honor. This too is the work of
Mestrovich. The tympanum over the main entrance, depicting the
Annunciation in bold relief, and other carved symbols and ikons
develop the theme of Mary the Virgin, Mother of Christ the Redeemer.

On the exterior of the Shrine are 137 separate pieces of carved
sculpture. Besides numerous statues, there are more than forty
relief figures and a score of Scriptural inscriptions. On the east
porch is depicted the arrival of the first Catholic settlers in Maryland in 1634 and the consecration of their new home to the Immaculate Conception as her new dowry. The stone tympanum on the
outer west wall depicts Blessed Elizabeth Ann Seton as engaged
in teaching at Emmitsburg, Maryland. On the west porch there is

a statue of St. Frances Xavier Cabrini, the first American citizen to be canonized.

Covering the entire interior wall of the upper apse (north side) is a huge colorful mosaic of Christ the King. The work of John de Rosen, it was completed in time for the dedication. Probably it is the largest single mosaic in the world, or at least the largest image of our Lord in this art form. The sanctuary is so large that it can easily accommodate the more than 250 bishops of the United States with a chair and kneeling bench for each of them.

Though there has been a decline in the devotion of some Catholics of the United States to their heavenly mother and patroness, Mary Immaculate (because they have been misled by so-called progressives), the following beautiful prayer-poem by an anonymous author still expresses the sentiments of the majority:

Patroness of our dear land,
Maiden Mother pure,
Dangers aid us to withstand,
Victory insure.

By your crown of stars,
In the night-blue sky,
Bless old glory's gleaming stars,
Keep them ever high.

Red is for your Mother heart,
White is for your grace,
Blue is for your mantle's art,
Turn to us your face.

Lady Queen Immaculate,
Guard our nation's shores,
Mother, Friend be with us yet,
Always we are yours.

CHAPTER 33

OUR LADY

All the Americas

La Conquistadora

Mary's Conquest of the Latin Americas

M ARY has always been and still is the Queen of the Apostles, the Queen of missions and missionaries. Through the centuries she has played a leading role in the spreading of Christ's kingdom to the farthest ends of the earth.

In one of his ten Rosary encyclicals, *Adjutricem populi* (September 5, 1895), Pope Leo XIII declared: "It is no exaggeration to say that it is chiefly under Mary's patronage and by her aid that the doctrine and laws of the Gospel have spread so rapidly in spite of immense obstacles and difficulties, among all nations and across continents, inaugurating everywhere a new order of justice and peace. . . . It is above all at times and in places where faith has grown lamentably languid through indifference, or has been weakened by the pernicious scourge of heresy and error, that the pitying aid of the august Virgin has made itself felt. At such times men eminent in holiness and apostolic zeal, guided by her suggestions and relying on her assistance, have arisen to thrust back the onslaughts of the wicked and to lead souls to the holiness of Christian life."

Well known is the antiphon found in the Common of the divine office for feasts of the Blessed Virgin Mary: "Rejoice, Virgin Mary, you alone have destroyed heresy in the whole world." Well known, too, is the invocation: "Queen of the Apostles, pray for us!"

As the editor of *Catholic Missions* wrote in May, 1919, "Mary,

Our Lady of Altagracia, one of the first Madonnas brought to the New World, enshrined in a large new church in the Dominican Republic.

Queen of Apostles, is no mere empty title. She was in the midst of the Apostles in Jerusalem in the first days of Christianity, their counseling Mother. And wherever, today, modern apostles are laboring to bring pagan souls to the Cross of Christ, Mary, too, is both their Queen and Mother. The best expression of our love and devotion to our Blessed Mother is, then, to bring her souls, souls from the darkness of paganism to the light of faith."

In the decree on the Mission Activity of the Church (no. 42), Vatican Council II hailed our Lady as Queen of Apostles and, together with all the faithful, turned prayerfully to her as the one who causes the labors of the heralds of the Gospel to bear abundant fruit: "Knowing that it is God who makes his Kingdom come on earth, they (the Council Fathers and the Supreme Pontiff) pour forth their prayers together with all the Christian faithful, that through the intercession of the Virgin Mary, Queen of Apostles, the nations may be led to the knowledge of the truth as soon as possible (1 Timothy 2:4) and that the splendor of God which brightens the face of Jesus Christ may shine upon all men through the Holy Spirit (Corinthians 4:6)."

That the Mother of God, assumed and enthroned in heaven, continues to take a hand in the extension of her divine Son's kingdom on earth, has been perhaps nowhere more strikingly manifest than in the Spanish and Portuguese world empires of the so-called colonial era, the sixteenth, seventeenth and eighteenth centuries.

The apostolic men who went out from Spain and Portugal in such great numbers during these centuries to preach the Gospel to the pagan natives and to extend Christ's kingdom to the farthest ends of the earth placed their bold ventures under Mary's protection, and with her aid they overcame what seemed to be insuperable obstacles.

Sometimes our Lady intervened perceptibly in their behalf and assisted their missionary efforts in a remarkable and extraordinary manner. Everywhere, too, the missionaries fostered a filial love of Mary among their neophytes, and countless shrines and churches were built in the newly conquered lands and dedicated in honor of our Lady under her many titles.

The Conquest of Mexico

Hernando Cortés and his soldiers, despite their faults, were much devoted to our Lady. The military standard which Cortés unfurled on the coast of Vera Cruz in 1519 was adorned with an image of Mary. And, as Bernal Díaz del Castillo tells us, in every chapel which he erected he placed a crucifix and an image of our Lady. To Tabasco he gave the name "Santa María de Victoria."

A characteristic mark of the pioneer missionaries among the Aztecs was their tender devotion to our Lady. Though they were careful to distinguish between the adoration given to God alone and the veneration paid to the Mother of God and our heavenly Mother, they fostered the devotion they themselves practiced also among their converts from the beginning.

To the Indians the devotion and the prayers to "Santa María" had a special appeal. The first prayers which the missionaries taught the Indians were not only the *Credo* and the *Pater*, but also the *Ave María* and the *Salve Regina*.

Not counting the priests who served as chaplains in the army of Cortés, we must recognize Brother Peter of Ghent and two other Flemish Franciscans who arrived in 1523 as the first missionaries to the Indians of New Spain. They were followed the next year by the so-called twelve Apostles of Mexico, Father Martin of Valencia and his companions. The success of these pioneers was truly remarkable.

Brother Peter of Ghent wrote to his Belgian confreres on June 27, 1529: "With my companions, I have baptized more than 200,000 persons in this province of Mexico. There have been so many that it is not possible for me to give an exact figure. Sometimes we baptized 14,000 on one day, other times 10,000 or 8,000."

To the Father Commissary General Matthias Weynssen, Father Martin of Valencia reported on June 12, 1531: "Without exaggeration we can say that up to the present we have baptized more than a million Indians, each one of us more than 100,000."

Concerning the devotion of the first Indian neophytes to our Lady, Bishop-elect Zumárraga in 1531 informed the Franciscan chapter at Toulouse that the Indian boys who were attending the school founded for them by the Franciscans "rise at midnight for Matins and recite the entire Office of Our Lady, to whom they have a very special devotion."

All this occurred before the apparitions of Our Lady of Guadalupe. However, after our Lady had appeared as an Indian maiden to Juan Diego in December, 1531, the number of Indians who embraced the Christian faith increased by leaps and bounds, so much so that many find it difficult to accept the totals which are recorded by reliable witnesses.

In his *History of the Indians of New Spain* which he completed in 1541, Motolinia offers several estimates of the total number of Indians who were baptized during the fifteen years from 1521 to 1536. He tells us that in 1536 there were sixty Franciscans in New Spain (twenty of them recent arrivals, and hence not included in his computations as ministers of the sacraments), and that previously there had been forty others who either died or returned to Spain. In addition there were some secular priests, Dominicans (who came in 1526), and Augustinians (who arrived in 1533). The total number of Indians baptized by these missionaries, says Motolinia, was from 5,000,000 to 9,000,000. Robert Ricard, the eminent historian of early Mexico, writes that even the 9,000,000 figure "is not inadmissible."

If we limit the total to 5,000,000, and allow about 1,000,000 for the period before the apparitions of Our Lady of Guadalupe (according to Father Martin of Valencia's report), we are still confronted with the amazing total of about 4,000,000 Indian converts for the five years following the apparitions. This figure must be doubled by those who accept the total of 9,000,000 new members entering the Church.

This very fact may be regarded as a confirmation of the authenticity of the apparitions of Our Lady of Guadalupe. These apparitions must have had a tremendous impact on the natives of New Spain and promoted their Christianization as nothing else did. Significant is the fact that Motolinia, at the end of his computations of the number of those who were baptized, writes: "We know, for instance, by actual count, that during the past Lent of the year 1536, in the province of Tepeyacac more than 60,000 souls received baptism." The province of Tepeyacac or Tepeyac was the one in which the apparitions of our Lady occurred.

Our Lady of Guadalupe

Did our Lady really appear to Juan Diego in 1531? Why are Zumárraga and Motolinia silent in their writings concerning the Virgin of Guadalupe? In reply, one can ask the question: Are they silent? In a letter to Cortés, Zumárraga wrote: "Your Lordship may please tell the Lady Marquis (Doña Juana de Zúñiga) that I want to give to the cathedral the name of the Immaculate Conception of the Mother of God, because on that day God and His Mother willed to make this gift to this land you conquered." The gift from God and His Mother to the land of Mexico may have been the principal apparition and the miracle of the picture of Our Lady of Guadalupe on December 12, 1531. It may also have been the receipt on December 7, the same year, of news from Vera Cruz that the two royal governors of the second *audiencia* (royal tribunal or provincial high court) had arrived from Spain to put an end to the abuses of the governors of the first *audiencia*.

Motolinia, likewise, may have had Juan Diego and Tepeyac in mind when he wrote: "Many of these Indian converts have seen and told about diverse revelations and visions. In view of the sincerity and simplicity with which they relate them, these seem to be true. But because they could be the opposite, and also because many would not believe me, I do not record them, neither affirming nor denying them."

At most, this remark and Zumárraga's letter are only vague references; but for this vagueness or, if you wish, silence, Father Fidel de Jesús Chauvet, who has made a thorough study of the Guadalupe question, offers an adequate explanation. He writes: "Sooner than expected, great opposition arose against the new image. Some missionary priests, noticing the great concourse of Indians to the chapel, suspected that there could be some sort of trick of the natives themselves, or even some scheme of the devil; for, they argued, that already before, on the same Tepeyac Hill, had been venerated the pagan goddess called 'Tonantsin,' 'our mother.' "

One could have argued with equal or even more cogency that for this very reason our Lady chose Tepeyac as the place of her apparitions and of her chapel. At any rate, the current opposition sufficiently explains the prudent silence of both Zumárraga and Motolinia. God and our Lady would eventually demonstrate that the miracles of Tepeyac were genuine by the good results and further miracles which would accrue from the veneration of Our Lady of Guadalupe.

To say that there is no historical record of the apparition of Our Lady of Guadalupe until the latter half of the seventeenth century is not correct. There is, for instance, the *Información* compiled in 1556 by Archbishop Montúfar for the proceedings against Father Bustamente who is said to have denied the supernatural origin of the Guadalupe image.

Above all, there is the detailed and straightforward account of the apparitions of Our Lady of Guadalupe written in the Nahuatl language by the well-educated Indian Antonio Valeriano who died in 1605. An alumnus of the College of Tlaltelolco (northern suburb of Mexico City, a short distance south of Tepeyac), Valeriano served as professor and rector of the institution and was governor of the Indians of Mexico City for thirty-five years. His account, which has all the earmarks of being a faithful and trustworthy one, was translated into Spanish by Don Luis Becerra Tanco and published in 1675, if not already in 1665. Though

284

Miraculous painting of Our Lady of Guadalupe, patroness of Mexico and Queen of the Americas.

made available in Spanish in the seventeenth century, Valeriano's account belongs to the previous century.

Valeriano relates how our Lady appeared to the Indian Juan Diego four times on December 9, 10, 11 and 12, 1531, and once, on December 12, to his sick uncle Juan Bernardino, who was cured. On the last day, our Lady told Juan Diego to gather some roses, which ordinarily did not grow on Tepeyac Hill at that time of the year. After arranging them in the Indian's rough mantle, she told him to carry them to Bishop Zumárraga as the proof he had requested.

When the Indian unfolded his mantle before the bishop, it was the miraculously painted image of Our Lady of Guadalupe that fascinated him rather than the miraculous roses. Venerating the image as an object from heaven, the bishop placed it first in his private oratory, and then, as news of the miracle spread throughout the entire region, in the main church or cathedral. Without delay a chapel was built on Tepeyac Hill, as our Lady had requested; and the image was carried in solemn procession to its first temporary shrine. Thus Valeriano's account ends. According to Jesuit Father Mariano Cuevas, church historian of Mexico, it took only fifteen days to build the temporary chapel, and the transfer of the picture of Our Lady of Guadalupe took place on the day after Christmas.

Valeriano must have been born just about the time that the apparitions took place or at least shortly afterwards. He tells the story as a careful historian does, meticulously recording dates, places, and names. One cannot read his narrative without gaining the impression that it is not merely a pious legend but a record of facts and events. Let me quote a few excerpts from the introduction and the account of the first apparition:

"It was the year 1531 A.D., the tenth year plus nearly four months of the dominion of the Spaniards in this city of Mexico (Cuatemoc surrendered to Cortés, August 13, 1521). The war was over and the holy Gospel had begun to flourish in this nation.

"Early Saturday morning, before the burst of dawn, on the ninth day of December, a poor plebian Indian, lowly and guileless, was coming from the town where he lived (it is said he was a resident of Tolpetlac) to the church of Santiago el Mayor (the Apostle St. James the Elder), the patron saint of Spain. This church is located in the borough of Tlatelolco, a mission settlement of the Franciscan friars (established shortly after the arrival of the "Twelve Apostles" in 1524, and the place where the College of Santa Cruz was opened for Indian boys in 1536). He was coming to attend the Mass of the Virgin Mary (the votive Mass in honor of the Immaculate Conception which the Franciscans were permitted to celebrate on Saturdays).

"This Indian was one of those who had recently been converted to our holy Catholic faith. He went by the name of Juan, given to him in holy baptism, and by the surname of Diego. He was a native, they say, of the town of Quautitlan, a town four leagues north of this city (of Mexico), a Mexican by birth, and married to an Indian woman whose name was María Lucia and who was of the same station in life as he.

"At the break of day Juan Diego reached the foot of a little hill called Tepeyacac. This name signifies 'summit or pointed top of the highlands,' because the top of the hill rises above the rest of the hills that surround the valley and lake wherein lies the city of Mexico, to which this hill is the nearest. Today, however, it is called Our Lady of Guadalupe. . . .

"On top of the hill and in a cluster of rocks which overlook the plain on the shore of the lake, the Indian heard a sweet and pleasing song. As he reported later, it seemed to come from a multitude and variety of little birds, singing in sweet unison and harmony, the choirs answering one another with singular accord and the high mountains which rise above the little hill redoubling and repeating the echo.

"Raising his eyes to the place from which he thought the song came, he beheld there a white and luminous cloud and around it a beautiful rainbow of different colors. . . .

"Still deep in rapture, the singing having ceased, Juan Diego heard someone calling him by name. The voice was like that of a woman, sweet and soft. It emanated from the brilliant cloud and told him to approach. In all haste he went up the slope of the hillock and drew near.

"In the center of the bright light Juan Diego beheld a most beautiful woman, very similar to the figure which is seen today on the blessed Image and which answers the verbal description the Indian gave it before anyone could have copied or seen it. Her garment, he said, was so brilliant that its splendor, shining on the rough rocks which topped the little hill, made these rocks appear like precious stones, polished and transparent. . . .

"The Lady, of a gentle and pleasing mien, said to him in the Mexican language: 'My son, Juan Diego, whom I love and esteem as my dear little child (this is the way of expressing oneself in Mexican), where are you going?'

" 'Noble and dear Lady,' replied the Indian, 'I am going to the town of Tlatelolco, in order to attend the Mass which the ministers and representatives of God show to us.'

"On hearing this, Mary Most Holy spoke thus to him: 'Know, my dearest son, that I am the ever-Virgin Mary, the Mother of the true God, who is the Author of life, who is the Creator of all things and Lord of heaven and earth, and who is present in all places. It is my wish that a church be built for me in this place. Here, as merciful Mother to yourself and to your people, I will manifest my loving mercy and compassion for the natives, for those who love and seek me, for all who solicit my aid and call upon me in their needs and afflictions. Here I will listen to their tears and prayers and will give them consolation and comfort. In order that my wish may be realized, you must go to the city of Mexico and to the palace of the bishop residing there (Bishop-elect Juan de Zumárraga who arrived in Mexico in 1528, returned to Spain in 1532, and there received episcopal consecration in 1532). Say to him that I am sending you and that I wish a church to be built in this place and dedicated to my name. Tell him what you have seen and heard. You may be sure that I will be grateful to you for what you do for me in the matter I am entrusting to you and that I will reward and exalt you for it. My son, you have heard my wish. Go now in peace. Remember that I will repay you for your trouble and zeal and that in this matter you will have every possible assistance.'

"Prostrating himself on the ground, the Indian replied: 'As your lowly servant, most noble Lady and dear Mistress, I shall carry out your command. Farewell!'" (Translation by Father Francis Borgia Steck, O.F.M.)

And Juan Diego, after suffering several rebuffs and seeing the beautiful Lady three more times, did become Mary's faithful messenger.

Today, the Basilica of Our Lady of Guadalupe, standing at the foot of Tepeyac Hill, is comparable to the shrines of Our Lady at Lourdes and Fatima. Countless miracles have been attributed to the intercession of the Virgin of Guadalupe. Benedict XIV (1740-1758) made her the National Patroness of Mexico and approved a special Mass and office for her annual feast on December 12 (a feast which is now observed also throughout the United States). Leo XIII proclaimed her Queen of the Mexican people and directed that her image be crowned in his name, a ceremony which was carried out in 1895. Pius X, in 1910, declared Our Lady of Guadalupe to be the Patroness of all of Latin America. Pius XII renewed the papal coronation of the miraculous picture of Our Lady of Guadalupe and made her the Queen of all the Americas.

On this occasion (October 12, 1945) the Holy Father broadcast a radio message to Mexico in which he said: "Since that historical

288

event (the presentation by Juan Diego of the miraculous painting to Bishop Zumárraga in 1531) the complete conversion of the natives was a fact. And what is more, there will always be a banner, a fortress against which all wraths and all tempests will make their onslaughts in vain. One of the basic pillars of the faith in Mexico and in all America has been firmly established. . . . Today, we place anew on your temples the crown (the golden crown has been suspended just above the miraculous picture) which puts forever under your powerful protection the purity and the integrity of the holy faith in Mexico and on the entire American continent (both continents). For, we are certain that as long as you are acknowledged as the Queen and Mother, America and Mexico will be saved."

I will never forget my first visit to the Basilica of Guadalupe in the 1930s. One of the periodic persecutions which have afflicted the Church in Mexico was drawing to a close at the time. Priests were not permitted to wear clerical garb in public, and some of the churches were still closed. I had put on a gray suit and a shirt with a tie to enter the country. The Guadalupe shrine was one church which the enemies of the Church had not dared to touch. I was deeply moved, seeing Indians who had come from a great distance, carrying heavy sacks of bricks on their backs in order to do penance for their sins, now crossing the plaza in front of the basilica on their knees. I was about to enter the church (and remove my hat), when a well-dressed gentleman came out and, pointing to my hat, told me to take it off. He no doubt thought I was another of those non-Catholic gringo tourists.

On another visit in the 1940s, I witnessed the consecration of a bishop in the great basilica. It was crowded with people. An orator preached an eloquent sermon to them in Spanish. That is, I thought it had been the sermon, when he knelt down to say a prayer. But then he started again, and I found that he had merely completed the introduction and was now delivering the sermon proper. Mexicans love lengthy discourses and listen to them attentively.

To me one of the most convincing proofs that the painting of Our Lady of Guadalupe is a miraculous image is the fact that its canvas consists of such frail, unsuitable material, a cloth resembling burlap. Scientists and artists, after examining it, have declared that it was humanly impossible to produce such a painting on such a canvas. A further phenomenon for which there is no satisfactory natural explanation, is the fact that a painting on this kind of a canvas has remained intact for some four and a half centuries.

A note about the word "Guadalupe." In Extremadura, Spain, there is another shrine of Our Lady of Guadalupe, this one antedating the one in Mexico. Valeriano tells us that our Lady said to Juan Bernardino, the uncle of Juan Diego, that she wished her image to be called "Santa María de Guadalupe." Becerra Tanco points out that in the Nahuatl tongue "Guadalupe" would be pronounced "Tecoatalope"; and he suggests that our Lady really said "Tequetlanopeuh," meaning "what happened on top of the rocks," and to the Spaniards this sounded very much like "Guadalupe," a name with which they were familiar. Thus "Our Lady of What Happened on Tepeyac Hill" received the name "Our Lady of Guadalupe."

It is well also to point out that the choice of Our Lady of Guadalupe as Queen of Mexico and all the Americas did not supplant the previous choice of Mary Immaculate as Patroness of all of Spanish America and of the United States of America. They are one and the same. As Father Fidel de Jesús Chauvet writes: "This image (of Our Lady of Guadalupe) depicts our Lady in her Immaculate Conception, according to the traditional norms followed by Christian painters. These, from ancient times, whenever they wanted to represent the Immaculate Conception, were wont to paint her alone, without the Infant Child, folded hands before her and the half moon as a footstool. And as such our Blessed Mother wanted her image to be sketched on the Indian's mantle before the bishop's eyes as a most certain proof that she herself was behind those wonderful events. Would it be too much to say that the Blessed Mother wanted to reward the good bishop in this way for his great efforts to honor her under this special title? Hence it would seem logical that our Blessed Lady would send no other proof of her wishes than that of her own heavenly depicted image."

Besides the Basilica of Our Lady of Guadalupe near Mexico City, there are many other churches and chapels of Our Lady of Guadalupe all over Mexico. Practically every church has at least a copy of the original picture. In every church that he visited in Mexico — and there were many — the writer did find such a picture on a side altar or at least in a place of honor.

There are, moreover, numerous churches and chapels in Mexico which have been dedicated in honor of our Lady under one of her many other beautiful titles. Some of them are likewise famous places of pilgrimage. A count made of the places in Mexico bearing our Lady's name revealed the fact that there are no less than 1,756 cities and towns which have a Marian name: 221 are called Santa María, 229 Concepción or Purísima, 154 Soledad, 109

Dolores, 70 Jesús María, 54 Natividad and 49 are known by the name of Candelaria.

Our Lady of Refuge

Of the other titles, besides that of Our Lady of Guadalupe, under which our Lady is honored in Mexico, there is one, namely Nuestra Señora del Refugio (Our Lady of Refuge), which deserves special mention in connection with Mary's spiritual conquest of the land.

The original painting of Our Lady of Refuge was made by an unknown artist at Frascati in Italy more than 200 years ago. A Jesuit Father was wont to take the painting with him when he preached parish missions among the faithful in Italy. Later another Jesuit missionary took the painting along with him to Mexico.

There — so the story runs — the Blessed Virgin spoke to him, instructing him to give the painting to the Franciscan missionaries and indicating that she wished the latter to spread the devotion to Our Lady of Refuge throughout New Spain. The Jesuit Father accordingly brought the painting to the Apostolic College at Guadalupe near Zacatecas in northern Mexico, and here it is still venerated in the Franciscan church at the present day.

Like the other Apostolic or Mission Colleges in Spanish America — the first of which was founded at Querétaro in 1683 — that of Zacatecas, which was established in 1703, had a twofold purpose: (1) missionary work among the Indians, especially on the northern frontier of New Spain, and (2) the preaching of parish missions among the faithful in the Christian towns and cities of Mexico.

The missionaries of the College of Our Lady of Guadalupe always carried copies of the painting of Our Lady of Refuge on their preaching tours through Mexico and thus they propagated the devotion to our Lady under this title throughout the land. Usually traveling in groups of four or five, they would remain for as long as a month in one town for the purpose of preaching a mission. One of the four weeks was a novena in honor of Our Lady of Refuge.

When the missionaries arrived at a town, they were met by the local clergy and people. They unrolled a painting of Our Lady of Refuge, which was then carried in solemn procession to the parish church. In Mexican towns, even those of some size, there is ordinarily only one parish church which is in the care of diocesan

*A painting of Our Lady of Refuge, in the library
of the Old Mission, Santa Barbara, California.*

priests, although there may be several other churches where
priests belonging to a religious order minister to the people.

In the course of time, there were many towns in Mexico, each
of which had four paintings of Our Lady of Refuge. The town was
divided into four parts; and in each a painting of Our Lady of Refuge made the rounds from house to house, remaining in each
house for one day. That day was a great feast day for the home

which was privileged to have the picture. The members of the household and visiting neighbors stayed up all night to pray the Rosary and sing songs in honor of our Lady. This custom is still observed in some places.

In the towns where they preached the missions, the missionaries also erected the Confraternity of Our Lady of Refuge; and it is a remarkable fact that not only the women but also the men for the most part remained faithful members of this confraternity. The members meet every Sunday and spend some time in prayer and song in honor of Our Lady of Refuge. The headquarters of this confraternity are at the Church of St. Sebastian in Guadalajara.

A beautiful custom is the one called "mañanitas," the morning greeting to Our Lady of Refuge. When a person celebrates a feast day in Mexico, it is customary for his friends to go to his home early in the morning and to greet and felicitate him with song and music. Similarly the people greet Our Lady of Refuge early in the morning with song and music.

Many beautiful songs in honor of Our Lady of Refuge have been written. A leader sings the verses and all those present join in the chorus which is repeated after each verse. Thus the fruits of a mission preached by the missionaries of the Zacatecas College were perpetuated for a long time.

Paintings of Our Lady of Refuge were carried also by those missionaries of the College who were engaged in missionary work among the Indians in northern Mexico and in the southwestern part of the present United States (Texas and California). There is such a painting still in the library of Old Mission Santa Barbara in California. It represents our Lady holding the Divine Infant in her arms, both wearing crowns. It had belonged to Fray Francisco García Diego y Moreno, who came from the College of Zacatecas and was the first bishop of the Californias (1840-1846). He placed his vast diocese, including both the present state of California and the Mexican peninsula of Baja (or Lower) California, under the special patronage of Our Lady of Refuge.

Of other shrines of our Lady in Mexico I will briefly mention only one, that of Our Lady of Celaya. I happened to visit San Francisco Church in Celaya, Mexico, where she is enshrined, at the time that a novena was being observed in her honor. The life-size statue of the Blessed Mother had been placed on a pedestal in the center of the church where the nave and the transept cross. It bore a mantle which extended far to both sides and to the rear, forming a kind of tent. All day long people came to pay Mary a visit while kneeling beneath her symbolic mantle.

The following is a fairly complete list of shrines of the Virgin Mary in Mexico and the titles under which she is venerated. It has been compiled from several lists having different captions and classifications and enumerating all the Marian shrines of Hispanic America. These were presented by the Instituto de Cultura Hispanica to the IV Mariological and the XI Marian International Congresses, held at Santo Domingo in the Dominican Republic in March, 1965. N. S. stands for Nuestra Señora (Our Lady).

N. S. de Guadalupe
N. S. de las Aguas
N. S. de los Angeles
N. S. de la Asunción
N. S. de la Aurora
N. S. de la Bala
N. S. del Buen Viaje
N. S. de Bufa
N. S. de la Candelaria
N. S. de Celaya
N. S. de la Cruz
N. S. de la Defensa
N. S. de los Dolores
N. S. de la Encina
N. S. de la Escalera
N. S. de la Esperanza, at Jácona
N. S. de los Gozos
N. S. de Guanajuato
N. S. de Guapulo
La Virgen Hallada
N. S. de Izamal
N. S. de los Lagos
N. S. de la Laguna
N. S. de Loreto
N. S. de la Luz, at Salvatierra and León
N. S. de la Macana
N. S. de Ocotlán
N. S. de la Piedad
N. S. de la Presentación
N. S. del Pueblito
N. S. de la Raíz
N. S. del Rayo, in Guadalajara
N. S. del Refugio
N. S. del Remedio
N. S. del Roble, in Monterrey

N. S. del Rosario
N. S. del Sagrario
N. S. de la Salud, at Pátzcuaro
N. S. de San Juan de Lagos, in Guadalajara
N. S. de Santa Anita
N. S. de la Soledad
N. S. de Talpa
N. S. de los Terceros de León
N. S. de Tlatenango
N. S. de Zacatecas
N. S. de Zape
N. S. de Zapopan

La Misionera — Our Lady of the Miracle

In Lima, Peru, "the City of the Kings" — so named because it was founded on the feast of Epiphany, January 18, 1535 — there is an ancient statue of our Lady which is held in great veneration under the title of "Our Lady of the Miracle." The distinction of a papal coronation was conferred on it in July of 1953. Since then this shrine has become known also outside of Peru, and devotion to Our Lady of the Miracle has spread to other countries of the world.

The statue represents our Lady with her hands folded in prayer. It is clothed in rich garments, and is crowned with a beautiful and precious coronet, surmounted by a cross. A large halo of twelve stars encircles both countenance and crown.

One of the first images of our Lady to be brought from the Old World to the New World, it was carried to Peru more than 400 years ago by Father Marcos de Niza and his eleven Franciscan companions, who arrived with Benalcazar at Coaque on the coast of what is now Ecuador in June, 1531, the same year in which the apparitions of Our Lady of Guadalupe took place in Mexico. At this time, it must be remembered, Peru included (besides the present Republic of Peru) also Ecuador and Bolivia. In 1534, the year Quito was founded, the Franciscans opened a friary in that city, and it served as the headquarters of their missionary activity in all of Peru until 1545.

The little statue of our Lady which they had brought along, they called "La Misionera." Through Mary's intercession and protection they hoped to succeed in making good Christians of the Indians of the former Inca empire.

One such expedition was the one to the mountain city of Cuzco, 11,000 feet up in the Andes, southeast of Lima, the center of the pagan religion of the Incas. Here La Misionera performed her first miracle. Attacked by the Indians, the missionaries and their companions sought refuge in a native hut. The Indians set fire to its straw roof, and the Spaniards were in imminent peril of their lives. It was then that the statue of La Misionera, without any human intervention, left its place inside the hut and hovered over the burning house. The fire ceased at once, and all inside were saved. In thanksgiving for this miraculous escape, the Spaniards erected on the spot a church called "Del Triunfo."

Pizarro formally founded the Spanish city of Cuzco in March, 1534; and the same year, Father Pedro Portugués constructed a small Franciscan friary on a hill close to the city.

The following year, in January, 1535, Pizarro located his capital where Lima is now situated. Present on this occasion was Father Franciso de la Cruz, one of the twelve pioneer Franciscans; and by November, there were three Franciscans in Lima. The following year Pizarro set aside a site for a Franciscan friary, the same where San Francisco de Lima now stands, facing the same plaza as the cathedral.

It was not until 1545, however, that Father Francisco de Santana was named guardian or superior of Lima. After he had erected a little church and friary in 1546, Franciscan headquarters were transferred from Quito to Lima. It was no doubt at this time that the statue of La Misionera was likewise taken from Quito to Lima and placed in the first Franciscan church there.

After the pacification of Peru in 1548, a large number of friars came from Spain and Mexico, and a larger friary and church were built in Lima. At the time that St. Francis Solano died in the friary of San Francisco, in 1610, La Misionera stood in a niche of the facade of the church. No special veneration was paid to the statue by the people of Lima, except by a poor woman who often paused before it to say a prayer.

One day the statue spoke these words to the woman: "You alone. my daughter, among all the people of Lima, visit me and pray to me. One day I will reward you."

The happy woman confided her secret to the saintly Brother Juan Gómez, the same who cared for St. Francis Solano in his last illness and who is credited with many miracles. The good brother often remarked: "Lima does not know what a great treasure it possesses in this miraculous image, but it will soon find out."

So it happened during the year before Brother Juan's death. On November 27, 1630, there was a bullfight in the main plaza where the church of San Francisco stands. A large part of the citizenry was enjoying the show, when suddenly a violent earthquake

296

*Our Lady with the Child Jesus, from an old
illuminated English manuscript.*

shook the city. To the terrified crowd it seemed that they would all perish. But those who stood near the Franciscan church saw the statue move in the direction of the Blessed Sacrament while holding its hands in a suppliant gesture, and the earthquake stopped as abruptly as it had started.

Several hours later, the friars of the "convento," Brother Gómez among them, gathered before the statue to express their gratitude. As they were kneeling in front of the church, they witnessed a second miracle. The statue turned again to its former position and graciously smiled upon the friars.

From that time on, the statue of La Misionera has been honored under the title of Our Lady of the Miracle, a name similar to that of another image in Lima which is greatly venerated, the one known as Our Lord of the Miracle.

Not long after the two miracles mentioned, a magnificent shrine was constructed for the statue of our Lady. Some two centuries later, in 1835, a disastrous fire completely destroyed the shrine and all its treasures; but, by another miracle, the statue of Our Lady of the Miracle was left wholly intact and unharmed by the flames.

Today devotion to Our Lady of the Miracle is becoming more widespread than ever before. But it is the title under which this little statue was venerated during its first century in Peru, that of La Misionera, which has a special significance for us. It is a variation of another title bestowed upon our Lady elsewhere in Spanish America, that of "La Conquistadora," "the Conqueror."

There are, of course, many other Marian shrines in Peru, some of them dating back to the early days. Thus, the first Dominicans who were with Pizarro also carried a statue of our Lady to Lima and placed it in their church of the Queen of the Most Holy Rosary.

In 1585 Spanish troops in Peru were rescued in a marvelous manner from the attacks of pagan Indians when our Lady appeared in the air above them. The entire province of Peru was officially placed under the special protection of the Virgin Mary in 1643 by Philip IV of Spain.

Worthy of special mention is the famous shrine of Our Lady of Copacabana in Bolivia, on the shores of Lake Titicaca, the highest lake in the world. It is frequented by pilgrims from both Peru and Bolivia, and may be regarded as a national shrine of both countries.

Before 1534, this place had been an outpost of the Inca empire and the site of pagan shrines. In 1583 an Indian of Copacabana, Tito Yupauqui, having seen and admired the statues of our Lady in the churches of La Paz, after several unsuccessful attempts, succeeded in fashioning a statue of fair workmanship. This statue was placed in a chapel, and soon the chapel became a celebrated shrine.

Many miracles have been attributed to the intercession of Our Lady of Copacabana, whose feast is observed annually on August 6. In 1925 the statue was solemnly crowned. Previously, in the course of time, it had been adorned with precious jewels. There was a great uprising of the Indians in 1781, but they did not touch the "Camarin" or chapel of Our Lady of Copacabana.

We append the list of Mary's shrines and titles in Peru, compiled in the same way as the one for Mexico. The first is the title under which the Blessed Virgin Mary is officially recognized as the national patroness of the Republic of Peru.

N. S. de la Merced
N. S. de Aguasanta, at San Miguel de Piura
N. S. de la Almudena
N. S. de Altagracia
N. S. de los Angeles
N. S. de la Antiqua, in Cuzco
N. S. del Arco
N. S. de la Asunción, in Juli and Cuzco
N. S. de la Cabeza
N. S. de la Candelaria, in Cuzco
N. S. del Carmen, in Cuzco
N. S. de Cocharcas
N. S. del Consuelo
N. S. de Copacabana, in Lima
N. S. de Chapi
N. S. de los Desamparados
N. S. de los Dolores
Virgen de Guadalupe, in Trujillo
Virgen Immaculada
N. S. de las Lagunas
N. S. de Loreto
N. S. de Lourdes
N. S. de las Mercedes, in Lima
Virgen del Milagro, in Lima
N. S. de la Misericordia
N. S. de las Nieves
N. S. de la O, in Lima
N. S. de las Penas
N. S. del Pilar

N. S. de Pomata, in Cuzco
N. S. de la Portera
N. S. del Prado
N. S. de la Puerta
N. S. de la Quiquijana
N. S. de los Remedios
N. S. del Rosario, in Lima
N. S. Santa María de Wonken
N. S. de la Soledad
N. S. de Vallehermoso, in Arequipa
Virgen de la Victoria

Latin America

Though it is not possible to present a comprehensive survey, it will be well to add a few pertinent facts concerning some of the other countries of Spanish and Portuguese America.

Devotion to Our Lady of Bethlehem was brought to the New World from Portugal. Principally responsible for this were the Bethlehemites, a religious order of nursing and teaching brothers, who were founded in Guatemala City in the mid-seventeenth century by Venerable Pedro de Betancourt (Bethencourt), better known simply as Brother Peter.

For more than a century and a half this brotherhood rendered excellent service in its hospitals and schools which were established in Mexico, Central America, South America and the Canary Islands. In imitation of their saintly founder, these brothers everywhere promoted devotion to the Blessed Virgin Mary, especially under the title of Our Lady of Bethlehem.

An image of Our Lady of Mercy or Ransom (Merced) was carried into Guatemala by Bartholomew de Olmedo; and it became famous as "La Conquistadora." Through the efforts of the Mercederian Friars, Our Lady of Mercy was subsequently proclaimed the patroness of Guatemala. Her statue was solemnly crowned in 1625.

In the Republic of San Salvador there is an ancient statue of Our Lady of Peace which was greatly instrumental in bringing about the pacification of the country. It is still venerated in the church of San Miguel.

One of the missionaries of Paraguay, Father Caballero, always carried an image of our Lady with him. Several times, through Mary's protection, he escaped unscathed when hostile Indians attempted to take his life. With the aid of Mary's picture, he was able to win numerous converts among the natives of the land. Asunción, the capital of Paraguay, was named for the Assumption of our Lady into heaven.

When Valdivia, the conqueror of Chile, advanced into the country at the head of his cavaliers, he had with him a little image of the Blessed Virgin Mary which occupied a place in front of his saddle. Though his private life was far from blameless, he was reconciled with God and his duty before his untimely death. The little statue which had been his companion on his journeys in Flanders, Italy, Peru and Chile, was placed above the main altar in the church of San Francisco, on the Alameda, in Santiago, Chile. At Concepción, Chile, so named in honor of Mary's Immaculate Conception, there is a unique pilgrimage shrine of our Lady which has a rock-drawn figure of the Mother of God which was discovered by a child in the eighteenth century.

The first missionaries to Brazil were the Portuguese Franciscans who came in the beginning of the sixteenth century. In the course of time they established two provinces of their order, giving to one of them the name of the Immaculate Conception. They were followed by Jesuits, Carmelites, Benedictines, Oratorians, in that order; and these also built many churches in Mary's honor. In fact, during the first three centuries almost all the churches and parishes of Brazil had Mary as their principal patroness.

Many are the shrines of the Blessed Virgin in Brazil. Noteworthy is the one of Our Lady of Aparecida at Guaratinguetá in the State of São Paulo and those at Bahía, Pernambuco, Patatininga and Victoria.

The first church at Guaratinguetá which enshrined the little statue of our Lady found by three fishermen in the Río Paraiba and called Nossa Senhora de Aparecida, was blessed in 1745. It was enlarged a century later; and today it has been supplanted by one of the largest churches in the world. The new church can accommodate 15,000 persons. The plaza in front of it is large enough for a vast throng of 200,000.

Franciscan Brother Pedro Palacios, who came to Brazil in 1558, built a shrine in honor of our Lady on a hill overlooking the town of Victoria and placed in the chapel a statue known as Nossa Senhora de Penha, Our Lady of the Rock. Shrine and statue are still there and are still visited by the faithful.

For twelve years Brother Pedro exercised the wholesome influence of a saint upon both colonists and Indians by his holy life, his works of charity among the poor and sick, and his educational work. As the famous Jesuit missionary Father Anchieta testified, Brother Pedro concluded his holy life by a holy death, May 3, 1570.

301

His body was laid to rest in the chapel he had built; but later it was exhumed and transferred to the Franciscan church in Victoria. His cause of beatification was introduced in 1611.

Father Joseph Anchieta was himself a devout client of our Lady. In her honor he wrote a Latin poem of 4,500 verses.

Another Jesuit missionary of Brazil, Father Gabriel Malagrida, always had an image of our Lady with him when he preached missions. He called Mary "the hope and protection" of his missionary work. At the close of his missions, he always conducted a procession in which his image of the Blessed Virgin was carried about. It is still venerated as "Our Lady of Missions."

Similar examples of devotion to our Lady in Latin America could be multiplied many times. In fact, it would require several volumes to tell the story with any degree of completeness. We have selected mainly instances in which it is apparent that our Lady's aid was sought and obtained for the purpose of leading the natives of America into the fold of Christ. It has been our aim to present definite and direct proofs that Mary has truly been La Conquistadora in the southern Americas.

We must content ourselves with adding to the list of our Lady's shrines and titles in Mexico and Peru those for the other countries of Latin America. The first mentioned in each case is the shrine of the National Patroness of that country.

ARGENTINA

N. S. de Lujan
N. S. del Buen Viaje, at Mendoza
N. S. de Carrodilla
N. S. de la Consolación, at Sumampa
N. S. de Guadalupe, at Santa Fé
N. S. del Incendio
N. S. de Itati, at Corrientes
N. S. de Lourdes
N. S. de la Merced, in Buenos Aires
Virgen del Milagro, at Santa Fé
N. S. de la Paz
N. S. de la Reconquista
N. S. de Río Blanco, at Jujuy
N. S. del Rosario, at San Luis de Cuyo and Córdoba
N.S. de Tolumba
N.S. del Valle, at Catamarca
N.S. Yayepu

BOLIVIA

N. S. de Copacabana
N. S. de Apumalla
N. S. de Arami
N. S. de la Asunción, at Chaguaya
N. S. de la Bella, at Arani
N. S. de la Candelaria, at Potosí and Coroico
N. S. de Colpa
N. S. de Cotoca, at Chochabamba
N. S. de Guadalupe, at Sucre
N. S. de la Gracia, at Pucararami
N. S. de Lourdes
N. S. de las Mercedes, at Potosí
N. S. de la Natalidad, at Chirca
N. S. de la Paz
N. S. de las Peñas de Guarina
N. S. de los Remedios, in La Paz
N. S. del Rosario, at Tomina
N. S. del Socavon, at Oruro
N. S. de Surumi, at Chaponta
N. S. del Villar, at Cochabamba

BRAZIL

N. S. de la Aparecida, at Guaratinguetá
N. S. de Ayuda, in Bahía
N. S. de Brotas, in Bahía
N. S. del Buen Suceso
N. S. del Buen Viaje, in Río de Janeiro
N. S. de la Candelaria, in Bahía
N. S. del Carmen de la Legua, at Concepción de Praca
N. S. de Copacabana
N. S. del Destierro, in Bahía
N. S. de la Fé, in Bahía
N. S. de la Gracia, in Bahía
N. S. de Iguape
N. S. de Lourdes
N. S. de las Maravillas, in Bahía
N. S. de los Mares, in Bahía
N. S. de las Misiones
N. S. de Montserrat, in Santos
N. S. de Nazaret, in Pontal, Pará and Bahía

N. S. de la Palma, in Bahía
N. S. de la Paz, in Bahía
N. S. de la Peña, at Barra (Victoria)
N. S. del Pilar
N. S. de la Pluma, in Río de Janeiro
N. S. de la Puerta del Cielo, in Bahía
N. S. de la Purificación, at Sergipe
N. S. del Rocio, at Paranagua
Virgen de San Lucas, in Bahía
N. S. Santa María de Wonken
N. S. del Socorro, in Pará
N. S. de la Victorias, in Bahía and Río de Janeiro

CHILE

N. S. de los Angeles
N. S. de Andacollo, at La Serena
N. S. de Arauco
N. S. de la Asunción
N. S. de la Candelaria, at San Francisco de Copiapó
N. S. del Carmen
N. S. del Carmen de la Tirana
N. S. de la Estampa
N. S. de la Legua, at Osorno
N. S. de Loreto, at Tierra Amrilla
N. S. de Lourdes
N. S. de la Merced, in Santiago
Virgen del Milagro, or del Boldo, at Concepción
N. S. de las Nieves, at Concepción
N. S. Santa María de Wonken, in Santiago
N. S. del Valle, at Santa Rosa del Valle
N. S. de la Viñita, in Santiago

COLOMBIA

N. S. del Rosario de Chiquinquira
N. S. de las Aguas
N. S. de la Altagracia
N. S. del Amparo, at Chivavita
N. S. de los Andes, at Popayan
N. S. de la Antigua
N. S. de Belén

N. S. del Camp
N. S. de la Candelaria
N. S. del Carmen
N. S. de los Dolores
Virgen de Guadalupe
Virgen Inmaculada N. S. de las Lajas, at Pasto
N. S. de la Merced
N. S. de las Mercedes, at Nátaga
N. S. del Milagro
N. S. de la O
N. S. de Otenga
N. S. de la Peña
N. S. de la Pobreza
N. S. de la Popa de Galera, in Cartagena
N. S. del Refugio
N. S. de los Remedios, at Cali
N. S. del Rosario, in Pasto
N. S. de la Salud
N. S. Santa María de Wonken
N. S. de Sopetran
N. S. de Topo
N. S. de Valvanera

COSTA RICA

N. S. de los Angeles
N. S. del Rescate
N. S. de Ujarraz

CUBA

N. S. de la Caridad del Cobre
N. S. de Bayamo
N. S. de los Dolores
N. S. de la Regla, in Havana
Virgen de Guadalupe
N. S. de las Nieves

DOMINICAN REPUBLIC

N. S. de la Altagracia

N. S. de Aguasanta
N. S. de Boya
N. S. de las Mercedes, in Santo Domingo

ECUADOR

N. S. de la Merced
N. S. de Aguasanta, at Baños
N. S. del Amparo
N. S. de los Angeles
N. S. de la Azucena
N. S. de la Borradora
N. S. del Buen Suceso
N. S. de Chilla
N. S. de Cicalpa
N. S. del Cinto
N. S. del Cisne
N. S. de la Consolación
N. S. de Coya
La Dolorosa
N. S. de la Elevación
N. S. de la Escalera
N. S. del Extasis
Virgen de Guadalupe
N. S. de Guanico
N. S. de Guapulo
N. S. de Intax
N. S. de Loreto
N. S. de Lourdes
N. S. de la Luz
N. S. de Macas
N. S. de la Merced
N. S. de Molinos
N. S. de Montserrat
N. S. de Natalidad
La Niña María
N. S. de la Nube
N. S. de la Paz
N. S. de la Pena
La Peregrina
N. S. de Pungala
Virgen del Quinche

EL SALVADOR

N. S. de la Paz

GUATEMALA

N. S. del Rosario
N. S. de la Ascunción
N. S. de Belén
N. S. de los Dolores
N. S. del Rosario
N. S. Santa María de Wonken

HONDURAS

N. S. de Suyapa
N. S. de la Merced
Virgen de la Medalla Milagrosa
N. S. de los Remedios

NICARAGUA

N. S. de la Asunción del Viejo

PANAMA

La Inmaculada Concepción
N. S. de Hool

PARAGUAY

N. S. de la Asunción
N. S. de Belén
N. S. de Caacupe
N. S. de Capiata
N. S. de Fatima
Virgen de las Gracias
María Auxiliadora
Virgen de las Mercedes

N. S. de los Milagros
N. S. del Perpetuo Socorro
N. S. de los Remedios
N. S. del Rosario
N. S. de Tariquea

PUERTO RICO

N. S. de la Divina Providencia
N. S. de Montserrat

URUGUAY

N. S. de Lujan
N. S. de los Treinta y Tres, at Villa Vieja

VENEZUELA

N. S. de Coromoto
N. S. de Altagracia
N. S. de Ayapa
N. S. de Belén, at Toroto and Tumeremo
N. S. de la Caridad
La Concepción de Burburota
La Concepción de Caroni
N. S. de Chiquinquira
N. S. de la Consolación
N. S. de Copacabana
N. S. de la Corteza
Divina Pastora, at Araguaimujo and Corumo
N. S. de los Dolores
N. S. del Espejo
N. S. de Lourdes
N. S. de la Merced
N. S. del Pilar
N. S. del Rosario, at Guasipat
N. S. Santa María de los Angeles del Guacharo
N. S. Santa María de Guana
N. S. Santa María de Wonken
N. S. de Tachira
N. S. de los Valencianos
N. S. del Valle, on Isla Santa Margarita

CHAPTER 34

OUR LADY

All the Americas

Our Lady of the Conquest

Mary's Triumph in the Northern Americas

THE spiritual triumph of our Lady in the New World was not confined to the Latin American countries. The United States and Canada were likewise brought under her domain. Not only in Guatemala, but also in Santa Fe, New Mexico, at her earliest shrine north of Mexico, and at Father Junípero Serra's Mission San Carlos in California she was acclaimed as La Conquistadora. Numerous missions, churches and shrines, named and dedicated in honor of our Lady, sprang up throughout the northern Americas. This part of the Western Hemisphere, too, Mary has won for the kingdom of Christ, her Son.

Our Lady of the Conquest in Santa Fe

The oldest statue of our Lady venerated in the United States today is that of Our Lady of the Rosary, also called La Conquistadora or Our Lady of the Conquest, which is kept in the Lady Chapel of the cathedral of St. Francis of Assisi in Santa Fe, New Mexico. The old adobe chapel was left standing and joined to the new edifice when the present cathedral was built by the well-known Archbishop Lamy in 1869-1886. Since the chapel was completed in 1718, it is the oldest existing shrine of our Lady in the United States today. Although the cathedral has undergone alterations in recent years the old chapel still adjoins the enlarged sanctuary on the left side.

309

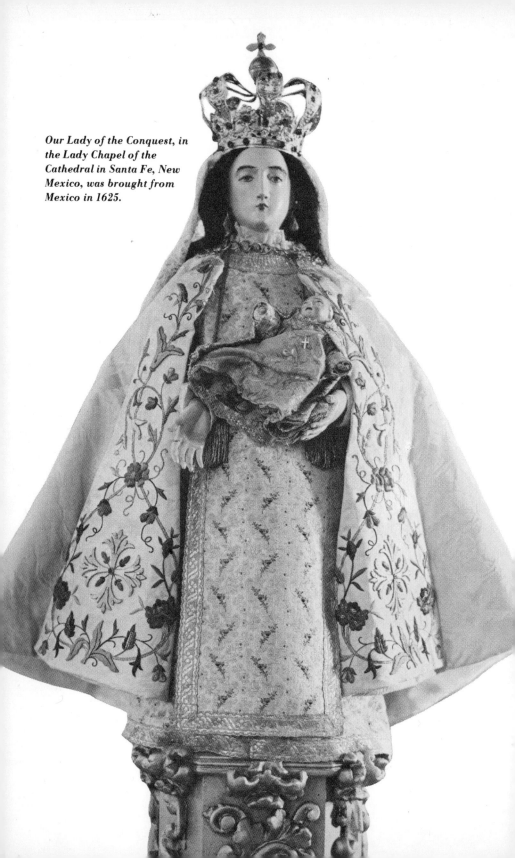

Our Lady of the Conquest, in the Lady Chapel of the Cathedral in Santa Fe, New Mexico, was brought from Mexico in 1625.

The little statue of Our Lady of the Conquest is only twenty-eight inches tall. It is clothed in rich garments, bears a jewelled crown on its head, and has a figure of the Child Jesus in its arms. Originally it was an image of Our Lady of the Assumption, without the mantle and without the Infant; and as such it was brought from Mexico to the parish church of the Assumption in Santa Fe by Father Benavides in 1625.

About 1655, when the Confraternity of the Rosary was established at the parish church in Santa Fe, the statue of Our Lady of the Assumption was converted into one representing Our Lady of the Rosary, with the added title of La Conquistadora. The latter had reference to the aid which our Lady had given the Spanish missionaries and settlers in winning the so-called Province of Nuevo Mexico, comprising present-day New Mexico and northern Arizona, for the kingdom of Christ on earth.

At the time of the Great Pueblo Revolt in 1680, when twenty-one Franciscan missionaries won the crown of martyrdom, the Spaniards who escaped carried the statue of Our Lady of the Conquest with them to the area just below present-day El Paso, Texas.

However, when Vargas reconquered New Mexico in 1692-1693, he brought Our Lady of the Conquest back to Santa Fe. In fact, the bloodless reconquest of New Mexico was attributed to the intercession and protection of Our Lady of the Conquest. In thanksgiving and in fulfillment of a vow, Vargas at this time built Rosario Chapel about a mile west of the plaza of Santa Fe.

A new parish church, dedicated to St. Francis, was built and completed in 1717; and the following year the present Lady Chapel was completed as the special shrine of Our Lady of the Conquest. At the present day an annual procession is still held in which La Conquistadora is carried to the Rosario Chapel and later back to the Lady Chapel in the cathedral. The original Rosario Chapel of 1692 was replaced by a new one in 1807, and an addition was built in 1914.

If the venerable shrine of Our Lady of the Conquest were better known, as it deserves to be, it would surely become a famous place of pilgrimage, not merely for the people of New Mexico for whom it is such, but also for the entire United States.

Our Lady of the Conquest in California

Another shrine of La Conquistadora or Our Lady of the Conquest, dating from the year 1770, is at Mission San Carlos Bor-

311

romeo, near the village of Carmel, California. From 1581 to 1640 the crowns of Spain and Portugal were united; and it was probably during this period that the devotion to Our Lady of Bethlehem spread from her famous shrine near Lisbon to Spain and its colonies. When New Spain decided to plant the cross at Monterey in California, the archbishop of Mexico City gave Gálvez a statue of Our Lady of Bethlehem. Unable to accompany the expedition, Gálvez sent the statue in 1769 to Monterey by ship, giving it the additional title of La Conquistadora.

The ship which carried the statue to California was the *San Antonio*, the same which brought relief at the critical moment to Father Junípero Serra and the others who had come to San Diego by land from Lower California. All except Father Serra were ready at the time to abandon the project of occupying Upper California. Until the summer of 1770, the statue remained at San Diego. Then it was taken on the *San Antonio*, with Father Serra on board, to Monterey, the place chosen as the capital of the new province.

Here the Mission of San Carlos was founded in that year, and the statue was placed in the first temporary mission chapel. The following year, 1771, both mission and shrine were moved to the present site near Carmel. After the secularization of the mission in 1840, the statue passed into private hands. A century later, in 1944, it was enshrined again in the restored mission church. San Carlos Mission, therefore, the old mission where the saintly client of our Lady, Father Junípero Serra, lies buried, is once more the shrine of Our Lady of Bethlehem, La Conquistadora.

First Church of the Immaculate Conception

The first church and the first religious house in the present territory of the United States, dedicated to and named for the Immaculate Conception, were the Franciscan church and friary established at St. Augustine, Florida, in 1584, less than two decades after the founding of this the oldest city in the States. The first structures were but rude shelters, made of poles and palm leaves and having thatched roofs.

Three times both the church and the friary were destroyed by fire, twice by the invading English; but each time they were rebuilt. Only the fourth friary and church, completed after 1755, were constructed with a kind of stone called *coquina*, consisting of broken shells which in the course of time became cemented with shell lime. The Spaniards quarried it on a nearby island.

312

Standing at the southern end of the town, the Franciscan friary with its church were connected by a stone seawall about a mile long with Fort San Marcos which was built at the northern end.

In the seventeenth century the Friary of the Immaculate Conception served as the headquarters of forty-four mission centers in present-day Florida and Georgia. It became the first novitiate in the United States in 1607, when seven candidates were received here into the Franciscan Order; and in 1612 it was made the chief friary of the first religious province in the United States, the Franciscan Province of Santa Elena, which included Florida and Cuba.

Five years later, Father Luis Gerónimo de Oré, a native of Peru, came to Cuba as the official visitor of the province and its missions. Among the friars who then resided in the friary at Havana, which was also named for the Immaculate Conception, was a very old retired missionary, Father Francisco Marrón. He had been a missionary in Peru, in Guatemala, in Mexico, and in Florida. Father Oré had an interview with the veteran missionary, who was now confined to bed; and from him the Father Visitor learned much about the martyrs of Guale (present-day Georgia), Father Pedro de Corpa and four confreres, who were killed by the Indians in 1597. At the time, Father Marrón had been in St. Augustine as the superior of all the missionaries in Spanish Florida. At the end, Father Oré asked him: "Father, how long have you worn the habit of our holy Father St. Francis?"

"For more than eighty years," replied the old friar.

"And how old are you now?"

"I am over a hundred years old."

Not long afterwards Father Marrón died, and Father Oré himself conducted the obsequies.

It was probably in 1590 that Father Marrón went to Florida for the first time. He was the superior of Immaculate Conception Friary at St. Augustine in 1592. However, by 1594 he had made a trip back to Cuba; for, in that year he accompanied Governor Avendaño to Florida, arriving at St. Augustine on June 16. During the next three years he served as parish priest of the frontier town as well as superior of the friary and all the friars in Florida. After the signature of the secular priest Father Escobar de Sambrana, pastor during the first half of 1594, those of Father Marrón are the first in the extant baptismal registers of the parish of St. Augustine, the oldest in the United States.

These are some interesting facts we know about just one of the many friars who lived in the Friary of the Immaculate Conception at St. Augustine and many more who served as missionaries in the missions among the Indians. Up to the time that the friary and its church ceased to exist as such (when Florida was ceded to England in 1763), more than 500 Franciscans had labored in the missions of Spanish Florida, some of them for many years.

In 1763 the British made the former friary a barracks for their troops. The Spaniards regained Florida in 1784 and kept it until the United States acquired it in 1821. However, the Franciscans were not permitted to come back during the second Spanish period.

The United States built St. Francis Barracks on the foundations of the friary and church, and a part of the friary walls are still standing today. The old part of the present cathedral of St. Augustine was not built until 1791-1797, after the return of the Spaniards in 1784. Old Fort San Marcos, now a national monument, is still for the most part in the condition in which the Spaniards left it.

The Shrine of Our Lady in St. Augustine

Half a league, or one and one-fourth miles, north of the old fortified town of St. Augustine, Florida, there was in 1728 an Indian mission town called Nombre de Dios (Name of God), with a stone church which was constructed in that year to replace an earlier one which had been looted by the English. Of the forty-four mission centers founded in Spanish Florida, only a few were constructed of stone or *coquina;* the others were built of wood or of poles and palm leaves.

The stone church at Nombre de Dios was not only a mission church but also a shrine of our Lady. Early in the seventeenth century — we do not know the exact date, but it was about the same time that La Conquistadora was taken to Santa Fe, New Mexico — the church of Nombre de Dios became a Marian shrine when a little statue of Nuestra Señora de la Leche y Buen Parto (Our Nursing Mother of Happy Delivery) was placed in it. At that time the church was still merely a wooden or palm structure.

The devotion to our Lady as the Nursing Mother of the Infant Jesus and Patroness of Christian Mothers can be traced to the earliest times. One of the few drawings of our Lady found on the walls of the second-century Roman catacombs represents her as nursing the Child Jesus; and since then this subject has been a favorite among artists.

It was in Madrid, Spain, in 1598, that the devotion to Nuestra

314

Our Lady the Nursing Mother of Happy Delivery (Nuestra Señora de la Leche) is venerated in a small chapel at St. Augustine, Florida.

Señora de la Leche y Buen Parto came into prominence. A devout couple rescued a statue having this title from irreverent hands and gave it a place of honor in their home. Some time later, when the mother and her unborn child were in almost certain danger of death, the father appealed to Nuestra Señora de Buen Parto. Our Lady heard his prayer in a remarkable way, and granted his wife a happy delivery.

The grateful couple then propagated the devotion by telling other families of the great favor they had received through Mary's powerful intercession. So well-known did the devotion become in a short time that King Philip III of Spain had a special shrine built for the statue of Nuestra Señora de la Leche. The original chapel and statue in San Luis Church in Madrid were destroyed when the Communists set fire to the chapel during the Spanish Civil War on May 13, 1937.

Colonists from Spain had brought the devotion to Nuestra Señora de la Leche to the New World at an early date. Thus a Franciscan friary and church at Matanzas in Cuba was dedicated to our Lady under this title. It is not surprising, therefore, that the devotion was introduced also into Florida and a statue was taken to the new colony about a half century after it was founded. According to tradition, the spot where the 1728 shrine (second stone church) of our Lady stood was the same where the first holy Mass was offered in 1565.

Reaching the harbor of what is now St. Augustine on August 28 of that year, Don Pedro Menéndez de Avilés named the place for the saint of the day, San Agustín. After a week of reconnoitering, he entered the harbor on September 6, and officially landed on September 8, the feast day of the Nativity of Our Lady. Father López de Mendoza, one of the chaplains of the expedition, then offered up the Mass of the feast. The traditional site of these historic events lies along Ocean Street in present-day St. Augustine. It is marked by a rustic altar, by a small restored shrine of Our Lady Nursing Mother, by a large and beautiful new shrine church, and by a very high cross.

The Nombre de Dios Mission is first mentioned as a Franciscan mission in a report of 1596. Six years later, three other Indian towns in the vicinity were attended from it. Father Pedro Bermejo was the resident missionary, and it may have been he who procured a statue of Nuestra Señora de la Leche and placed it in his church.

In 1665 the English buccaneer David invaded and sacked the town of St. Augustine, and probably also destroyed the mission and shrine at Nombre de Dios. Afterwards it was rebuilt a little farther north of St. Augustine.

Again the mission and shrine were very likely destroyed by fire when ex-governor Moore of South Carolina and Colonel Robert Daniel, unable to capture the fort at St. Augustine, burned the town on October 22, 1702. This time the church and shrine at Nombre de Dios were reconstructed of *coquina*.

In 1728 a raiding party of English settlers from Georgia and their Indian allies, under the command of Colonel Palmer, appeared before the gates of St. Augustine. Unable to take the town, they attacked and burned the nearby Indian village of Nombre de Dios. They looted its church and friary and carried off everything of value, including priestly vestments, sacred vessels, and votive offerings at the shrine of our Lady. Many of the Christian Indians were killed or carried off into captivity. The two Franciscan missionaries who were residing at this mission were fired upon but succeeded in making their escape.

One of the English soldiers took the figure of the Infant Jesus from the arms of the statue of Nuestra Señora de la Leche and brought it to Colonel Palmer. The latter rebuked the man and his fellows for what they had done and told them that in time they would suffer for their irreverent act. Strangely enough, Palmer failed to take his own counsel, and threw the tiny statue of the

Child Jesus on the ground. Eight years later, it is said, Palmer himself lost his life on that very spot. Probably it was twelve years later, when Oglethorpe unsuccessfully besieged St. Augustine in 1740.

After the enemy left, the Spanish governor ordered the church and friary at Nombre de Dios to be demolished, lest it be used as a stronghold by the enemy. The stone shrine of our Lady, built only a few years previously, was blown up by gunpowder and only the ruins remained.

However, the Indian town of Nombre de Dios and its shrine of our Lady did not cease to exist. They were moved within "a musket shot" of the Castillo de San Marcos, the fort which stood at the northern end of the town of St. Augustine. By October 5, the same year, a new church and shrine of *coquina* had been built outside the north walls of St. Augustine. This we learn from a letter written at the time. The letter describes the mission church as being the best among those which were in Indian villages. Its walls were constructed of lime and stone, although its roof was of palm. The reason why this was made an outstanding church, says the letter, was the fact that in it was venerated the statue of Nuestra Señora de la Leche.

When the Spaniards left in 1763 and Florida became a British possession, the mission church and shrine of Nuestra Señora de la Leche were destroyed or fell into ruins. During the second Spanish period, 1783 to 1821, it was probably restored; but nothing was left of it in 1873, when Bishop Verot rebuilt the shrine. The very next year, it was blown down in a storm.

The present little shrine chapel was erected in 1915-1918 by Bishop Curley. It was restored and furnished as a chapel in 1925 by Mrs. Hardin in memory of her husband, General Martin D. Hardin. None of the furnishings are older than the building itself, but it has a replica of the old statue of Our Lady Nursing Mother.

The old city gate of St. Augustine is still standing. It was called Puerta de la Leche, not as an entrance into the town, but as an exit from the town to the shrine of our Lady.

In recent years the shrine of Nuestra Señora de la Leche y Buen Parto has attracted more and more attention. Some years ago the director of the shrine stated that it "has been the center of devotion of thousands of mothers and mothers-to-be. Those who were able have journeyed with their husbands to kneel before the altar of our Lady's chapel to ask for the multiple blessings of motherhood for themselves and the protection of Christ's Mother for their families.

"Every year other thousands write to the Father Director

asking that their names be placed on our Lady's altar and that they be remembered in the Masses and prayers at the Shrine. The files of the Shrine Office are filled with letters of thanksgiving from grateful mothers who lovingly point out the miraculous things which our Lady has accomplished for them."

First Immaculate Conception Mission

Four hundred mounted soldiers and ten wagons, under the command of Governor Manuel de Silva Nieto, rode out of Santa Fe, New Mexico, on June 23, 1629. It was a most unusual expedition inasmuch as its purpose was not to conquer new territory but simply to conduct three Franciscan missionaries to the Seven Cities of Cibola in the western part of the present state of New Mexico, for the sole purpose of establishing the very first mission in United States territory to be dedicated to the Immaculate Conception.

The three missionaries were Father Roque Figueredo, Father Agustín de Cuellar, and Father Francisco de la Madre de Dios. Only twenty days previously, they had arrived from Mexico in the company of twenty-seven other Franciscans, led by Father Estéban de Perea.

When the imposing army arrived at the Zuñi pueblo of Hawikuh, the principal one of the Seven Cities, an adobe house was purchased from the Indians for the poor and humble messengers of the Gospel. Thus was established the Mission of La Concepción de Hawikuh.

Almost a century before, in May of 1539, the first white man to enter this territory, Father Marcos de Niza, had seen Hawikuh from a distance. He was deeply impressed by its terraced apartment building of several stories, brightly reflecting the golden light of the setting sun. After Estéban, his black companion, had imprudently gone ahead and had been killed by the Zuñis, the exploring missionary (who had been a pioneer in Peru) returned to Mexico City to report what he had found.

Coronado came the following year, and gave the name of Granada to the pueblo of Hawikuh. He entered it on July 7 only after a hotly contested battle with the natives. The Zuñis engaged in the fight after they had put their women and children on top of nearby Taaiyalone or Thunder Mountain. The name Zuñis was given to these Indians by Espejo in 1583.

When Don Juan de Oñate arrived in 1598, he assigned the province of the Zuñis to Father Andrés Corchado, but the lone

318

missionary was able to gain only a few if any converts among these proud and stubborn Indians.

After Governor Silva Nieto and his formidable army departed from Hawikuh, the Zuñis rebelled against the three missionaries dwelling among them. Learning of this unexpected turn of events, the governor and his cavalry returned. This somehow seemed to break down their opposition — or was it Mary Immaculate, patroness of the mission, who finally won them over? The first baptism was administered on August 28, 1629, and the missionaries probably began at once to construct an adobe church, naming it for La Purísima Concepción.

Much of the story of this mission is recorded in the twenty-seven Spanish inscriptions which were carved into the rocky cliff of El Morro, thirty-five miles east of present-day Zuñi. El Morro, now called Inscription Rock, is a national monument. After Governor Silva Nieto had taken the three missionaries to Hawikuh in 1629, he passed El Morro and there left a record of the expedition in the following inscription: "The captain general of the province of New Mexico, for the king our ruler, passed by here on his return from the towns of Zuñis on July 29, 1629; and he pacified them in answer to the petition they made, asking for his favor as vassals of his majesty, and they pledged their allegiance anew. All of this he did with clemency, zeal, and prudence, as a most Christian, . . . a most extraordinary, and gallant soldier of lasting and lauded memory."

Recalled by the rebellion of the Zuñis against their missionaries, the governor once more passed El Morro and this time added, in poetical form, the inscription:

"Here . . . governor
"Don Francisco Manuel de Silva Nieto
"Whose indubitable arm and valor
"Have overcome the impossible,
"With the wagons of the king, our master,
"A thing he alone put into effect,
"Ninth of August, Sixteen hundred and twenty-nine,
"That it might be heard, I pass on to the Zuñis,
"And I have brought the faith."

Though it was not due exclusively to Governor Silva Nieto, the fact is that after his second visit the missionaries had considerable success in winning the Zuñis for the faith. Not only did they build Mission Concepción at Hawikuh, but in the same year

319

View of the top portion of a typical terraced Pueblo Indian village of New Mexico.

they established two other missions in nearby towns, one at Kechipauan and the other at Halona.

At Kechipauan, which was situated on top of a mesa east of Ojo Caliente, they constructed a stone church with massive walls. These were still standing, eight to fourteen feet high, in 1930. At Halona, the mission was also dedicated to our Lady and named Nuestra Señora de la Candelaria. Modern Zuñi occupies a part of the site of ancient Halona which stood on both sides of the Zuñi River. A large mound of earth on the south side of the river, opposite Zuñi, is all that remains of the former pueblo.

The missionary at La Concepción Mission in Hawikuh in 1632 was Father Francisco de Letrado. On Sunday, February 22, he went outside and urged the Indians to come to Mass. Instead of heeding his exhortation, the Indians shot him to death with arrows.

Five days later, a group of Zuñis from Hawikuh also murdered Father Martín de Arvide, who was on his way to the Hopis (or Moquis). Fearful of punishment at the hands of the Spaniards, the Zuñis abandoned Hawikuh and fled to Thunder Mountain.

An inscription on the face of El Morro, signed by a soldier

whose name was Lujan, tells us that a small force was sent from Santa Fe to punish the murderers: "They passed on March 23, 1632, to avenge the death of Father Letrado." Arriving at the village, they found it deserted, and there was nothing they could do against the fugitives on Thunder Mountain.

Three years later, the Zuñis came down from the mountain and occupied their pueblo once more; and in 1642 a missionary again took residence among them.

In 1672 Father Pedro de Avila y Ayala was stationed at Hawikuh and Father Juan de Galdo at Halona. On October 7 of that year a band of Apache or Navajo warriors fell upon the pueblo of Hawikuh, killed the missionary and many of the Zuñis, and then burned the church. The next day Father Juan de Galdo came and gave Christian burial to his martyred confrere.

It is not certain that the mission church at Hawikuh was rebuilt after 1672; but if it was, the mission was again destroyed at the time of the great rebellion of the Pueblo Indians of New Mexico and northern Arizona in 1680. Hawikuh was abandoned from that time on.

This, however, does not mark the end of La Concepción Mission. When Vargas reconquered New Mexico in 1692, he induced the Zuñis of former Hawikuh and Halona, which were then in ruins, to come down from Thunder Mountain — to which they had retreated twelve years before — and to build a new pueblo (what is today called Zuñi) partly on the site of Halona.

In this new pueblo a mission was established in 1699, and like the one at Hawikuh it was named for the Immaculate Conception — La Limpia Concepción. Later it was also known as Nuestra Señora de Guadalupe.

The church of this Zuñi mission was still incomplete in 1703, when the Indians again fled to Thunder Mountain after several Spanish soldiers had been killed in their village. It was completed in 1705, when these Indians were persuaded to return. From that time Franciscan missionaries continued their work in the Zuñi mission until they were expelled from New Mexico in 1823.

According to a report made in 1750 by Father Andrés Varo, superior of all the New Mexico missions, Zuñi was then the largest of the pueblos with a population of 2,000, and the resident missionary was Father Juan Hernández.

Today there is a new and modern Franciscan mission and school in Zuñi, built of brick. In accordance with the wishes of a benefactor, the new mission was named for St. Anthony.

When the writer visited Zuñi in October, 1937, the tumbledown but picturesque ruins of the former mission church were still standing in the pueblo, although the roof had fallen in long ago; in 1969 he learned that archeologists had begun an investigation of the old ruins.

For more than two centuries, the ruins of La Purísima Concepción church at Hawikuh remained standing. However, in 1894, a section of the old wall was removed by the Indians of Ojo Caliente who used the ancient adobes to construct houses for themselves. An expedition from the Museum of the American Indian in New York City, headed by Frederick W. Hodge, went to Hawikuh in 1919. What remained of Hawikuh had been covered by the drifting sands, but the workers excavated several feet of the walls of both the church and the friary. Charred pieces of wood which they found confirmed the report that both church and friary had been destroyed by fire. The skeleton which they uncovered beneath the adobe altar of the church may well have been the remains of the martyred priest, Father Avila y Ayala, who was killed by the Apaches in 1672.

In October, 1937, the writer found only a few very low crumbling walls of the Hawikuh mission still recognizable. Fragments of Indian pottery lying scattered on the adjoining hill indicated that here had once stood the pueblo of Hawikuh — the pueblo in which was built the first mission of the Immaculate Conception within the present territory of the United States.

La Purísima Concepción at Quarai

The honor of being the earliest mission in the United States to be dedicated to the Immaculate Conception must be shared by the Hawikuh mission with another that was built in New Mexico about the same time, namely the large stone mission of La Purísima Concepción at Quarai or Cuarac, just a little north of the geographic center of the state.

Quarai was one of the five Saline pueblos, so called because of the salt and alkali lagoons which lay to the east. These pueblos have also been called "The Cities That Died of Fear." By 1680 all of them had been abandoned because of the numerous attacks made upon them by the Apaches and the constant threat of such attacks.

Modern Mountainair, New Mexico, which has an elevation of 6,520 feet, is in the center of this territory. Quarai lay eight miles north; Tajique, twenty miles north; Chilili, thirty miles north; Abó, twelve miles southwest; and Gran Quivira or Tabirá, twenty-four miles south. The ruins of the latter are now a na-

322

tional monument, while those of Abó and Quarai are state monuments.

Quarai is situated one mile west of Punta de Agua, in the Estancia Valley, at the foot of the Manzano Mountains which reach a height of 10,600 feet. Manzano means apple tree; and the apple orchard ten miles north of Quarai is the oldest in the United States and probably belonged to the mission of that pueblo.

Work for the preservation of the Quarai ruins was carried on from May, 1934, to September 1, 1940, through the cooperation of the Department of Agriculture and the United States Forest Service. The CCC provided a crew of twenty men in the beginning, and in 1939 the WPA supplied twenty-five men. During the repairs a large movable scaffold, fifty feet high and thirty feet long, was used.

The repairs purposely did not go beyond the evidences for reconstruction. Had this been delayed for many more years, the walls of the mission church would have collapsed. Now, however, the main walls still stand almost forty feet high. These walls, which are about four feet thick, are built of blocks of dark red and brown sandstone, one to four inches thick and about one foot square.

The entire church has a paved floor, consisting of dressed flags of sandstone with smoothed top surfaces, and averaging twenty-four by eighteen inches. The length of the church in the interior is one hundred feet. Its width is fifty feet at the transepts and twenty-seven feet in the body of the nave. The front facade has two towers.

This mission ruin is one of the most striking landmarks of the Southwest. Lummis, in 1913, described it in these words: "An edifice in ruins, it is true, but so tall, so solemn, so dominant of that strange, lonely landscape so out of place in that land of adobe box huts, as to be simply overpowering. On the Rhine it would be a great superlative, in the wilderness of the Manzano it is a miracle."

Edgar L. Hewett, who presents a detailed account of this mission in *Mission Monuments of New Mexico*, writes: "Europe may boast of its castle ruins and California of its missions, but one will seek vainly elsewhere in the United States to find ruins more appealing, more redolent of romance and wonder than Quarai on a summer's day."

The conversion of the Tigua pueblo of Quarai and the building of its imposing church of La Purísima Concepción was the work of Father Estéban Perea, the superior of all the New Mexico missions from 1617 to 1621 and again from 1629 to 1630.

After this veteran missionary had brought thirty new missionaries from Mexico in 1628-1629, he went to Quarai and served as its missionary for about a decade. He supervised the building of La Purísima Concepción church during the first three years of his stay in Quarai. Afterwards he returned to his former mission of Sandía, and there he died and was buried.

The successor of Father Perea at Quarai seems to have been Father Juan de Salas, who likewise held the office of superior of all the friars in New Mexico for two terms, 1630 to 1632 and 1638 to 1641. Two letters written by him establish the fact that he was at Quarai in September, 1643. It was Father Juan de Salas, who, with Father Diego López, in 1629, made the long journey to the Jumanos Indians in Texas, more than a hundred leagues to the east. They made this trip after a delegation of Jumanos came all the way to Santa Fe to beg for missionaries and told the amazing story of the numerous appearances among them of the Lady in Blue.

The Lady in Blue was none other than the saintly nun, Mother Mary of Jesus, abbess of the Conceptionist Poor Clare Convent of La Purísima Concepción at Agreda in Spain, who died in 1665. She is known also for her remarkable four-volume work on the life of the Blessed Virgin Mary, entitled *City of God*.

In an inexplicable manner — by an apparent miracle of bilocation — she visited various Indian tribes of the Southwest about 500 times between 1620 and 1631, instructing them in Christian doctrine, preparing them for baptism, and urging them to go in search of the Franciscan missionaries of New Mexico.

Unable to remain in the country of the Jumanos, Father Juan de Salas and his companion induced many of these Indians to come to Quarai and to settle among the Christian Indians of that pueblo.

The missionary at Quarai in 1659 was Father Gerónimo de la Llana. After serving this mission for many years he died there and was buried in the church of La Purísima Concepción. A century later his remains were unearthed and taken to Santa Fe.

Despite repeated Apache attacks, Quarai was still flourishing in 1669. By 1671, some of the Indians of this pueblo had begun to move elsewhere as a number of them were married at El Paso del Norte (Juárez, Mexico). In 1674, others if not most or all of the Quarai Indians joined those at Tajique, twelve miles to the north. Certain it is that by 1680 the pueblo and mission of Quarai had been completely deserted. This was done despite the fact that Quarai had been a walled town, as has been proved by the School of American Archaeology.

*Father Marcos de Niza saw "the Seven Cities of Cibola," the
Zuñi pueblos in western New Mexico, from a distance, in 1539.*

Between 1675 and 1680 Tajique, too, was abandoned. Many of its Indians, including those from the former Quarai pueblo, went to the mission of San Antonio de Isleta, twelve miles south of Albuquerque. The Indians of Isleta, then numbering about 2,000 did not take part in the rebellion of 1680; and the Spaniards found a place of refuge there. However, before the retreating Governor Otermín arrived at Isleta on August 27, its Indians had joined the ranks of the rebels, probably because of their fear of reprisals from the latter.

The following year, during his attempted reconquest of New Mexico, Governor Otermín captured San Antonio de Isleta without a battle and took some 400 willing Indians, many of them from former Quarai, to Isleta del Sur on the Mexican side of the Rio Grande below El Paso. Because of a change in the course of the Rio Grande which took place in the nineteenth century, Isleta, Mexico, became Isleta, Texas. Long after the founding of Isleta del Sur, the local Indians, when asked where they hailed from, would point to the north and say that their forefathers came from Quarai.

Oldest Church of Mary Immaculate

On the feast of the Immaculate Conception, December 8, 1755, there was great rejoicing at Mission Nuestra Señora de la Purísima Concepción de Acuña, two and a half miles south of San Antonio's Alamo (which was then Mission San Antonio de Valero). The beautiful new stone church, begun many years before and half finished by 1745, had now been completed; and on this day it was solemnly dedicated. It was built of dressed blocks of stone and good mortar. It had a majestic dome and twin towers with bells. Its length was eighty-nine feet and its width twenty-two feet.

This beautiful church has never fallen into ruins, and today it still stands intact, just as it was built more than 200 years ago. Not only is it the oldest church of the Immaculate Conception in the present United States, but it is also the oldest edifice of its kind, the oldest unchanged and unrestored stone church, in the entire country.

Originally Mission Concepción had been founded in 1716 in the principal village of the Ainay Indians, one of the Tejas tribes of eastern Texas, near Douglass, Nacogdoches County. Three years later it was temporarily abandoned because of a war with France which had a post at Natchitoches, Louisiana. But in 1721 the mission was reestablished at its former site by the Marquis de Aguayo.

After the nearby Presidio de los Tejas was suppressed in 1729, the mission (that is, its movable property such as church furnishings and some cattle and farm tools) was moved first to the Colorado River near Austin in 1730, and the following year to its present site on the San Antonio River, halfway between the Alamo and Mission San José y San Miguel de Aguayo (founded in 1720 by Venerable Father Antonio Margil). The still extant marriage register of the mission, which is kept in the archives of San Antonio's Cathedral of San Fernando, tells us that Mission Concepción was established at its present site on March 5, 1731.

Some two months later about 300 Coahuiltecan Indians of various tribes in southwestern Texas had been gathered at Mission Concepción, and the first rude temporary structures had been built. In 1739 a virulent epidemic reduced the mission Indians from 250 to 120. Some died and some fled. But in December, 1740, their number had again increased to 210. It was only then that the first permanent buildings could be constructed.

By 1745, a two-story friary, a house for three Spanish soldiers, and a granary had been built, all of them of stone. These and various workshops and the huts of the mission Indians stood within a rectangle surrounded by a stone wall to protect the mission against attacks by Apaches and Comanches. The tufa stone, with which the mission was built, was quarried close by.

Facing west and the San Antonio River (about one-fourth of a mile distant), the stone church, which was then building and was

*The church of Mission Nuestra
Señora de la Purísima Concepción,
dedicated December 8, 1755, is still
standing in San Antonio, Texas.*

completed ten years later, stood in the eastern part of the mission compound. Its walls are about four feet thick. Only the outside and inside facing of the walls is of cut blocks of stone; the space between is filled with rocks and adobe. The facade of the church was covered with "flower work," that is, decorative geometric designs in color.

At the base of the south tower was a chapel which served as a baptistery. In the other tower was a chapel dedicated to St. Michael. Besides the main altar in the sanctuary, there were and are side altars in the arms of the transept. The acoustics in the church are so perfect that they have been compared with those of the Mormon Temple in Salt Lake City, Utah.

Adjoining the sanctuary is the sacristy, measuring sixty-one feet on all four sides. The floor above the sacristy, which is of a later date, may well have been used as an infirmary.

Behind the church, forming a part of the east wall, once stood the granary, which was about fifty feet long and twenty-four feet wide. It had a flat wooden roof, covered with adobe and plaster.

Next to the south tower of the church, the building of a new friary was begun after the church was completed. By 1762 it was a one-story building of stone, fronted by open arches, with three private rooms for two missionaries and a guest, several offices, and space for storage. Extending westward from the southern end of the friary was a large hall in which were the looms for weaving cotton and woolen fabrics as well as two storerooms.

By 1789 the friary had a second story of one room. In the same year the Indian dwellings, which had been of adobe previously, were also of stone. They were built along the longer southern and northern walls. None of these dwellings, nor the walls, nor the granary have survived.

A branch of the irrigation ditch, connected with the San Antonio River, flowed across the plaza. There were two main gates, defended by two bronze eight-ounce cannons, each weighing eighty-three pounds. A third gate was added by 1789, the north wall being the only one without a gate.

Outside the square was the fenced and irrigated mission farm, about two miles long, and an orchard with a stone fence around it. In 1762 the mission farm produced 1,280 bushels of corn. At some distance from the compound was the mission ranch with 610 head of cattle and 2,200 sheep in 1762. It had several stone houses for the Indian cowboys and shepherds.

In 1773 the missionaries of the Franciscan College of Zacatecas took charge of Mission Concepción because those of Querétaro who had been at the mission since its founding were needed in Pimería Alta, comprising northern Mexico and southern Arizona.

By that time the number of mission Indians had been greatly reduced; and five years later, when the mission's unbranded cattle (almost all of them) were declared government property, the mission was no longer able to take care of a large number of Indians.

The number of Indians baptized at the mission from 1731 to 1762 was 792. The marriage record, with entries from 1733 to 1790, has 249 entries.

In 1794, Mission Concepción was secularized in a modified form, and some of the farmland was distributed among the thirty-eight remaining Christian Indians. However, it continued to be served as a sub-mission by the missionary who resided at Mission San José at least until 1819. Final and complete secularization did not take place until 1824.

Three decades of neglect followed; but from 1856 until 1911, the Brothers of Mary at St. Mary's College in San Antonio (now a university) were the owners of the mission; and the church was used again.

Before the Brothers of Mary took charge of the mission church, it had been used as a stable. In 1850, after it had been made fit for divine services once more, it was rededicated in honor of Nuestra Señora de Lourdes; and, of course, Our Lady of Lourdes is the Immaculate Conception. After the church had been renovated a second time, Bishop John C. Neraz again rededicated it in 1887. The building of St. John Seminary next to the old mission was begun in 1919.

Today the church of Mission Concepción belongs to the Archdiocese of San Antonio. Holy Mass is celebrated in the church on Sundays. Many pilgrims and tourists visit it as well as the other old San Antonio missions, the Alamo, San José (a state and national historic site), San Juan Capistrano, and San Francisco de la Espada, throughout the year.

Our Lady of the Cape

We may not leave Canada out of the picture. Nor do we have any reason for doing so. Well known are Canada's pilgrimage shrines of St. Anne de Beaupré and of the Oratory of St. Joseph in Montreal. But shrines of our Lady are by no means lacking. The most famous of these is the National Marian Pilgrimage Shrine of Our Lady of the Cape.

Cap-de-la-Madeleine (Cape of Magdalene) is a beautiful spot

*Our Lady of the Cape is a statue of the Blessed Virgin at the
Canadian national pilgrimage shrine of Cap-de-la-Madeleine
halfway between Montreal and Quebec.*

on the St. Lawrence River, near Trois Riviérès (Three Rivers), about halfway between Montreal and Quebec. A little stone church built here in 1714 — the oldest in Canada preserved in its original form, just as the church of Mission Concepción in Texas is the oldest in the United States — became the first shrine chapel of Our Lady of the Cape in 1888.

For 175 years this little church had served as a parish church. Father Luc Desilets, the curé of Cap-de-la-Madeleine (1864-1888), promised in 1879 to dedicate the old church to the Queen of the Rosary if she would help him to get from the other side of the river (the south bank) the stone needed for a new and larger parish church.

In mid-March of that year occurred the miracle of the ice-bridge, which lasted long enough to allow the construction material to be carted across the river. With this material was built the new parish church (present-day St. Madelein's Oratory); and on June 22, 1888, the old church was dedicated in honor of the Queen of the Rosary.

On that day another miracle took place. A beautiful statue of our Lady, which had been given to the parish in 1854 on the occasion of the proclamation of the dogma of the Immaculate Conception, had been placed on the high altar of the old chapel. On the day of its dedication as a Marian shrine, three reliable witnesses saw the face of the statue come alive for about ten minutes, the lowered eyes opening wide and gazing over their heads with grave tenderness.

The witnesses were Father Luc Desilets, the Franciscan Father Frederic Janssoone of Ghyvelde (whose cause of beatification has been introduced in Rome), and Pierre Lacroix who was a cripple.

Since that time the chapel of the Queen of the Rosary at Cap-de-la-Madeleine has become justly famous as a pilgrimage shrine. Those who have prayed here to our Lady have received numerous temporal and especially spiritual favors. By authority of Pope Pius X, Our Lady of the Cape was crowned Queen of Canada in 1904, in the presence of the apostolic delegate, all the archbishops, and most of the bishops of the country. Five years later, the First Plenary Council of Quebec recognized the Cap-de-la-Madeleine shrine as the national shrine of our Lady.

During the Marian Year of 1954, which was also the golden jubilee of the first crowning of the statue, a national Marian congress was held at Cap-de-la-Madeleine and Our Lady of the Cape was officially crowned anew as Queen of Canada. On the feast of the Assumption, August 15, in the presence of half a hundred cardinals, archbishops and bishops, the papal legate Cardinal Valeri placed on the Madonna's head a new and precious crown, the gift of Catholics all over the American continent.

The following year, the building of a new and large Rosary Basilica was begun. It was completed seven years later. Previously an annex, a wooden structure, had been added to the old chapel in 1714. The parish church was converted into St. Madeleine's Oratory after another parish church had been built elsewhere in the town.

Many other buildings have been erected on the grounds of the shrine; the Monastery of the Oblate Fathers (Oblates of Mary Immaculate), to whom the care of the shrine was committed in 1902, with a guest house for priest visitors and a convent for the housekeeping Sisters of the Holy Family; the Perpetual Adoration Chapel and Convent of the cloistered nuns called Servants of Jesus and Mary; a pavilion for outdoor Masses; the Marian exhibition; the Marian bookshop and souvenir store; a restaurant on the banks of the St. Lawrence River; Madonna House for sick pilgrims; Pilgrim's Hotel, overlookimg little St. Mary's Lake. There is also an outdoor Way of the Cross of which the Fourteenth Station is an exact replica of the Holy Sepulcher in Jerusalem.

Pilgrimage retreats are held for as many as 500 persons who can be accommodated overnight at the shrine and nearby hotels. From May to October pilgrimages coming from far and near are made to Cap-de-la-Madeleine. During this period Mass is offered up at seven different times daily. Every evening there is an impressive torchlight procession which wends its way from the Old Shrine to St. Mary's Lake, each pilgrim holding a candle with a paper shield to light the way. At the lake, living tableaux are presented on a Gospel scene or on one of Mary's apparitions. On Sundays the devotion of the Way of the Cross is conducted publicly at the outdoor Stations. A Rosary Procession is also held at the outdoor Way of the Rosary, followed by Benediction.

Other shrines of our Lady in Canada, besides the one at Cap-de-la-Madeleine, are at the following places:

Montreal — Notre-Dame-de-Bonsecours, founded before 1670; the present church was built in 1771.

Montreal — Notre Dame Church, built in 1829.

Montreal — Mary Queen of the World Church, which resembles the Basilica of St. Peter in Vatican City.

Rigaud — Notre-Dame-de-Lourdes Shrine, founded in 1874.

Lachute (fifty miles northwest of Montreal, on Highway 8) — Notre-Dame-de-Lourdes Shrine, in the care of the Franciscans.

Quebec City — Basilica of Notre Dame, built in 1650, and for many years the cathedral of the diocese of Quebec which comprised all of New France.

Carleton (overlooking Chaleur Bay) — Notre Dame Oratory, a diocesan shrine since 1959.

Lac Bouchette (on Highway 19) — Shrine of Our Lady of Lourdes and St. Anthony, in the care of Capuchin Franciscans.

(We append a list of pilgrimage shrines of our Lady in the United States, which we have compiled with the help of the Marian Center at St. Boniface Church in San Francisco, California. There are no doubt other Marian shrines that could well be added to our list.)

ALABAMA

1. Cullman:
   Ave Maria Grotto
   St. Bernard's Abbey

ARKANSAS

2. Winslow:
   Our Lady of the Ozarks

CALIFORNIA

3. Carmel:
   Our Lady of Bethlehem
   Mission of San Carlos
4. Los Angeles:
   Our Lady Queen of Angels
   Old Spanish Plaza Church
   100 Sunset Boulevard
5. Riverside:
   Our Lady of Guadalupe
   2858 Ninth Street
6. San Francisco:
   Marian Center and Library
   135 Golden Gate Avenue

7. San Francisco:
   Our Lady of Fatima (Russian Icon)
   20th and Lake Streets
8. San Francisco:
   Mission Dolores (or San Francisco)
   16th and Dolores Streets
9. Santa Clara:
   Our Lady Refuge of Sinners
   Mission Santa Clara Church
10. Soledad:
    Mission Nuestra Señora de la Soledad
11. Wrightswood:
    Our Lady of the Snows

COLORADO

12. U.S. Air Force Academy:
    Our Lady of the Skies

CONNECTICUT

13. Litchfield:
    Our Lady of Lourdes
    St. Louis de Montfort Seminary
14. New Canaan:
    Our Lady Star of the East
15. Putnam:
    Our Lady of Siluva
    Immaculate Conception Convent
    R.F.D. 2

DISTRICT OF COLUMBIA

16. Washington (Brookland):
    Ave Maria Portico
    Portiuncula Chapel
    Lourdes Grotto
    Tomb of the Blessed Virgin
    Franciscan Monastery
    1400 Quincy Street, N.E.
17. Washington (Brookland):
    National Shrine of the Immaculate Conception
    Catholic University of America

FLORIDA

18. St. Augustine:
    Nuestra Señora de la Leche y Buen Parto
    (Our Nursing Mother of Happy Delivery)

ILLINOIS

19. Belleville:
    Our Lady of the Snows
    Route 460 (between Belleville and East
    St. Louis, eight miles from downtown St.
    Louis, Missouri)

20. Chicago:
    Basilica of Our Lady of Sorrows
    5121 West Jackson Boulevard

21. Chicago:
    National Shrine of the Immaculate Heart of Mary
    St. Francis of Assisi Church
    813 West Roosevelt Road

22. Chicago:
    Our Lady of Good Counsel
    3528 S. Hermitage Avenue

23. Downers Grove:
    National Scapular Center
    Aylesford Retreat House
    Route 60 at Cass Avenue

24. Geneva:
    National Shrine of Our Lady of the Sacred Heart
    719 Batavia Avenue

25. Lemont:
    Mary Help of Christians
    St. Mary's Seminary

26. North Riverside:
    Mother of Mothers

27. Oak Brook:
    Portiuncula Shrine
    St. Francis Retreat

INDIANA

28. Cedar Lake:
    Our Lady of Lourdes Retreat House
    Stella Maris Retreat House
29. Notre Dame:
    Our Lady of Lourdes
    Notre Dame University Campus
30. St. Mary-of-the-Woods:
    Our Lady of Providence Queen of the Home
31. Valparaiso:
    Seven Dolors of the Blessed Virgin Mary
    R.F.D. 4, P.O. Box 367

KENTUCKY

32. Covington:
    Cathedral Basilica of the Assumption
    Madison Avenue
33. Covington:
    Grotto of Our Lady of Lourdes
    St. Aloysius Church
    Bakewell and Ninth Streets
34. Hazard:
    Mother of Good Counsel Shrine
    Kentucky Mountain Apostolate
    Mission Center

LOUISIANA

35. New Orleans:
    Our Lady of Prompt Succor
    Ursuline Convent
    2536 State Street

MAINE

36. Bar Harbor:
    Our Lady of Fatima
37. Kennebunkport:
    Grotto of Mary Immaculate

MARYLAND

38. Baltimore:
    Minor Basilica of the Assumption
    Cathedral and Mulberry Streets
39. Baltimore:
    Cathedral of Mary Our Queen

MASSACHUSETTS

40. Attleboro:
    Our Lady of La Salette
41. Boston:
    Our Lady of Good Voyage Chapel
42. Boston:
    Our Lady of the Railways Chapel
    South Station Railroad Terminal
43. Boston:
    Our Lady Queen of the Apostles
    Daughters of St. Paul
    50 St. Paul's Avenue, Jamaica Plains
44. Boston:
    Our Lady of Lourdes Chapel
    698 Beacon Street
45. Boston:
    Lourdes Bureau
    Representatives of Lourdes, France
    27 Isabella Street
46. East Boston:
    Don Orione Madonna Shrine
    111 Orient Avenue
47. East Boston:
    Our Lady of the Airways Chapel
    Logan Airport
48. Framingham:
    International Shrine of Our Lady of
    Health, Happiness and Peace
    Route 9, Salem End Road and Gates Avenue
49. Gloucester:
    Our Lady of Good Voyage
50. Holliston:
    Our Lady of Fatima

51. Ipswich:
    Our Lady of La Salette
52. New Bedford:
    Shrine of Our Lady
    572 Pleasant Street
53. Roxbury:
    Basilica of Our Lady of Perpetual Help
    1545 Tremont Street
54. Stockbridge:
    Our Lady of the Council
    Marian Fathers' Monastery

MICHIGAN

55. Copper Harbor:
    Our Lady of the Pines
    Northern Keweenaw County
56. De Witt:
    Portiuncula in the Pines Retreat House
    East Main Street
57. Jackson:
    Queen of the Miraculous Medal
    Michigan Miraculous Medal Shrine
58. Mio:
    Our Lady of the Woods

MINNESOTA

59. Cold Spring:
    Assumption Chapel
    Near St. Cloud
60. Minneapolis:
    Basilica of St. Mary
    Hennepin Avenue and 16th Street

MISSOURI

61. Carthage:
    Our Lady of the Ozarks
62. Conception:
    Basilica of the Immaculate Conception

63. Eureka:
    Our Lady of Czestochowa
    St. Joseph Hill Infirmary
64. Jefferson City:
    Our Lady of La Salette
    La Salette Seminary
    Swift's Highway, Box 306
65. Perryville:
    Our Lady of the Miraculous Medal
    Church of the Assumption
    320 West St. Joseph Street
66. Portage des Sioux:
    Our Lady of the Rivers
    In the Mississippi River
67. St. Louis:
    Our Lady of Perpetual Help
    St. Alphonsus (Rock) Church
    Grand Boulevard and Finney Avenue
68. Starkenburg:
    Our Lady of Sorrows
    Near Rhineland, Missouri

NEW HAMPSHIRE

69. Bretton Woods:
    Our Lady of the Mountains
    Route 320, at the foot of Mt. Washington
70. Colebrook:
    Our Lady of Grace
71. Enfield:
    Our Lady of La Salette
72. Jaffrey Center:
    Our Lady Queen of Peace
73. Pittsfield:
    Our Lady of the Smile
    St. Anthony Retreat House
    Monastery Hill

NEW JERSEY

74. Summit:
    Our Lady of the Rosary
    Dominican Sisters' Convent

75. Washington:
Ave Maria Institute
Blue Army Headquarters

NEW MEXICO

76. Galisteo:
Our Lady of the Assumption
Santa Cruz Church
22 miles south of Santa Fe
77. Jemez Springs:
Mary Mother of Priests
Via Coeli
78. Rincon:
Our Lady of All Nations
P.O. Box 290
79. San Juan:
Our Lady of Lourdes
Rio Arriba County
80. Santa Fe:
Our Lady of the Conquest
Lady Chapel of St. Francis Cathedral

NEW YORK

81. Auriesville:
Our Lady of the Martyrs and
Notre Dame de Foy
National Shrine of the Jesuit Martyrs
82. Bay Shore:
Our Lady Queen of All Hearts
Montfort Fathers
83. Brooklyn:
Regina Pacis Votive Shrine
1230 Sixty-fifth Street
84. Brooklyn:
Grotto of Our Lady of Lourdes
Aberdeen Street and Broadway
85. Essex:
Our Lady of Hope
86. Graymoor:
Our Lady of the Atonement
Near Garrison

87. Lackawanna:
Basilica of Our Lady of Victory

88. Lewiston:
Our Lady of Fatima
Seminary of Barnabite Fathers

89. Maryknoll:
Our Lady of Maryknoll
Near Ossining

90. New Lebanon:
Lourdes Grotto

91. New York City:
Church of Notre Dame
114th Street and Morningside Drive

92. New York City:
Our Lady of Pellevoisin
Church of St. Paul
113 East 117th Street

NORTH DAKOTA

93. Powers Lake
Our Lady of the Prairies

OHIO

94. Carey:
Our Lady of Consolation

95. Dayton:
Our Lady of the Library
University of Dayton
Marian Library

96. Euclid:
Our Lady of Lourdes Grotto
Sisters of the Most Holy Trinity
21320 Euclid Avenue

97. Maywood:
Our Sorrowful Mother
Off Route 2, near Flat Rock

OREGON

98. Crooked Finger:
    Our Lady of Lourdes
99. Portland:
    Sanctuary of Our Sorrowful Mother
    Sandy Boulevard and N.E. 85th Street

PENNSYLVANIA

100. Germantown:
     Our Lady of the Miraculous Medal
     449 East Locust Avenue
101. Loretto:
     Our Lady of the Alleghenies
     Prince Gallitzin Chapel

TEXAS

102. San Antonio:
     Nuestra Señora de la Purísima Concepción
     de Acuña Mission
     Mission Road
103. San Juan:
     Our Lady of San Juan of the Valley
     P.O. Box 10, Lower Rio Grande River
104. Socorro:
     La Purísima Mission
     Route 80 near El Paso

WISCONSIN

105. Burlington:
     Portiuncula Shrine
     St. Francis Seminary
106. Dickyville:
     Grotto of Our Lady
107. Hubertus:
     Mary Help of the Christians
     Holy Hill on Route 83

108. Kenosha:
     Our Lady of Fatima
     Marytown, 8000 39th Avenue
109. Madison:
     Our Lady of the Green Scapular
     5001 Schofield Street
110. Milwaukee:
     Our Lady of the Rosary of Fatima
     Dominican Sisters of the Perpetual Rosary
     217 North 68th Street
111. New Franken:
     Our Lady of Good Help Chapel
     Crippled Children's Home
     Near Green Bay

Note: As this book goes to press, we learn that the Church of the Immaculate Conception in Allentown, Pennsylvania, was chosen on March 19, 1974, by a national committee in the United States, to be the National Center of Our Lady of Guadalupe, Mother of the Americas; and the reasons for this selection were made known to the bishops of the country in an April 24th communique from the pastor of the Allentown church, Msgr. David Thompson. The date of the dedication was set for October 5, 1974. Besides Allentown, there are in the United States no less than 495 other locations that have churches, chapels or shrines where the reproductions of the miraculous painting of Our Lady of Guadalupe are publicly venerated (cf. *A Handbook on Guadalupe,* pp. 130-132, published in 1974 at Marytown, 8000 39th Ave., Kenosha, Wisconsin 53141).

APPENDICES

BEFORE the Suez Canal was completed in 1869, missionaries from Europe traveled to the Far East by way of Mexico or around Africa. Thus many of those who died as martyrs and have been beatified visited the New World. A list of these is added in the following pages, as well as three rosters of saints and blessed of the Americas showing the religious orders and congregations to which they belonged, listing those who were natives of the Americas, and indicating when their feasts are observed in the course of the year. Finally, we have appended a list of Americans, besides those who have already been beatified, whose cause for canonization has advanced to some stage either in Vatican City or in the dioceses in which they lived or died.

Appendix I

Blessed Who Visited
the New World

OF the sixty-three saints and blessed mentioned in Father Botero's *Los Sesenta y Tres Santos Americanos* (published in 1956), twenty-four are included who merely visited the New World, that is, traveled to their destination in the Far East by way of the Western Hemisphere. In accordance with the norm we have adopted for *Saints of the Americas*, they have not received biographical sketches in this book. However, it does seem well to list them in an appendix.

Since Father Botero's book was published in 1956, it does not, of course, have biographies of Bl. Marie d'Youville, Bl. Elizabeth Ann Seton, Bl. John N. Neumann and Bl. Frances Schervier, who were beatified after that date; but it missed Bl. Marguerite Bourgeoys and Bl. Andrew Grasset. These six account for the fact that we have forty-five American saints and blessed, instead of the thirty-nine which remain after subtracting twenty-four from sixty-three.

In the roster which follows, it should be noted that there are three who, so far as we could ascertain, did not visit the New World, as Father Botero says. (These are marked by an asterisk.) Hence there are only twenty of whom it can be said that they journeyed from Europe to the Far East via the Americas. All of them became martyrs — seventeen of them in Japan, two in China, and one in Tonkin (now North Vietnam). The seventeen martyrs of Japan belong to the 205 who were beatified by Pope Pius IX on July 6, 1867.

We have arranged our list of these martyrs according to their religious affiliation and the date of their death. There may be others whose names can be added, but we have restricted ourselves to Father Botero's list.

Augustinians (three)

Bl. Ferdinand of St. Joseph Ayala Fernandez. Born 1575 at Ballesteros, Spain. Went to the Philippines by way of Mexico in

1603, and from there to Japan in 1605. Was beheaded at Omura, June 1, 1617. Feast in Augustinian Order on June 3 and at Ciudad Real, Spain, on June 1. (The feastdays mentioned here and for the martyrs whose names follow were those observed before the revision of the Roman as well as local and special calendars.)

Bl. Vincent of St. Anthony Carvalho. Born at Alfama, Portugal. Went to the Philippines via Mexico in 1621, and from there to Japan in 1623. Was burned alive at Nagasaki on September 3, 1632. Feast in the Augustinian Order on March 2.

Bl. Francis of Jesus de Ortega. Born at Villa Medina, Spain. Went to the Philippines via Mexico in 1621 (with Bl. Vincent Carvalho), and from there to Japan in 1623. Was burned alive at Nagasaki on September 3, 1632. Feast in the Augustinian Order on March 2.

Dominicans (nine)

Bl. Francis de Morales. Born October 14, 1567, in Madrid, Spain. Went to the Philippines via Mexico in 1598, and from there to Japan. Was burned alive at Nagasaki in the Great Martyrdom, September 10, 1622. Feast in the Dominican Order on June 1, and in Madrid on September 10.

Bl. Alphonse de Mena. Born at Logroño, Spain. Went to the Philippines via Mexico with his uncle Bl. Alphonse Navarette, and from there to Japan in 1611. Was burned alive at Nagasaki in the Great Martyrdom, September 10, 1622. Feast in the Dominican Order on June 1 and in Salamanca on March 23.

Bl. Joseph of St. Hyacinth. Born at Villareal de Salvanés near Madrid, Spain. Went to the Philippines via Mexico, and from there to Japan. Was burned alive at Nagasaki in the Great Martyrdom, September 10, 1622. Feast in the Dominican Order on June 1.

Bl. Hyacinth Orfanel. Born at Llana near Valencia, Spain. Went to the Philippines via Mexico, and from there to Japan. Was burned alive at Nagasaki in the Great Martyrdom, September 10, 1622. Feast in the Dominican Order on June 1, and at Totosa, Spain, on September 10.

Bl. Thomas of the Holy Spirit de Zumárraga. Born 1575 in Victoria, Spain. Went to the Philippines via Mexico in 1601, and from there to Japan. Was burned alive at Omura (with two Dominican novices and three Franciscans, one of the latter being Bl. Apollinaris Franco) on September 12, 1622, in the Great Martyrdom. Feast in the Dominican Order on June 1, and in Victoria, Spain on September 13.

346

Bl. Peter Vásquez. Born at Verín, Galicia, Spain. Went to the Philippines via Mexico in 1613, and from there to Japan in 1621. Was burned alive at Omura (with Franciscan Bl. Louis Sotelo and companions) on August 25, 1624. Feast in the Dominican Order on June 1.

Bl. Francis de Fernandez de Capillas. Born 1605 at Baguerim de Campos, Spain. Went to the Philippines via Mexico in 1631, and from there to China in 1642. Was beheaded in the Chinese province of Fukien on January 15, 1649. Beatified May 2, 1909. Feast in the Dominican Order and at Palena, Spain, on January 15, and in Valladolid, Spain, on January 2. He is called "the protomartyr of China" inasmuch as he was the first of China's martyrs to be beatified. The first martyrs, eight in number, died in 1339 at Ili in the province of Sinkiang.

Bl. Francis Serrano y Frias. Born in 1695 in Spain, he went to the Philippines via Mexico, and from there to Fukien Province, China. While in prison at Foochow, he was nominated titular bishop of Tipasa. He was strangled on October 20, 1749. Beatified on April 18, 1893. Feast at Seville, Spain, on October 29, and in the Dominican Order on May 27, as one of the four companions of Bl. Peter Saenz (Sanz), martyrs in China.

Bl. Dominic Henares. Born December 19, 1775, at Baén, Spain. Went to the Philippines via Mexico, and from there to Tonkin (North Vietnam). In 1803 he was consecrated titular bishop of Fez (Father Botero says he was named bishop but not consecrated), as coadjutor to Bl. Ignatius Delgado, Vicar Apostolic of Tonkin. Was beheaded at Nam Dinh on June 25, 1838. Beatified May 27, 1900. Feast in the Dominican Order on July 11, as one of the twenty-five companions of Bl. Ignatius Delgado (thirteen members of the Order of Preachers and twelve of the Dominican Third Order).

Franciscans (eight)

Bl. John of St. Martha, priest. Born 1578 at Pradas, Tarragona, Spain. Went to the Philippines via Mexico in 1605, and from there to Japan in 1607. Expelled from Japan in 1614, he returned a few hours later on a small boat. Was beheaded at Kyoto on August 16, 1618. Feast in the Franciscan Order on September 13, as one of the forty-four companions of Bl. Apollinaris Franco, martyrs in Japan. (All the other beatified Franciscan martyrs of Japan, whose names follow, are also included among the forty-four companions of Bl. Apollinaris.)

Bl. Apollinaris Franco, priest. Born c. 1575 at Aguilar de Campo, Spain. Went with fifty companions to Mexico in 1600, and thence to the Philippines with forty Franciscans and forty Dominicans in 1601. Arrived in Japan in 1606. Burned to death at Omura on September 13, 1622, in the Great Martyrdom. Feast on September 13 (O.F.M.).

*Bl. Paul (Diego) of St. Clare, brother. Born in Japan, and hence did not visit the New World. One of six Christians who assisted Bl. Apollinaris. While in prison, he was admitted to the Order of Friars Minor, and a year later pronounced his vows. Burned to death at Omura on September 13, 1622. Feast on September 13 (O.F.M.).

Bl. Francis Gálvez, priest. Born 1567 at Utiel, Spain. Went to the Philippines via Mexico in 1601 and from there to Japan in 1606. Expelled in 1614, he returned in 1616-1618 via Malacca and Macao. Was burned to death at Shinagawa, south of Tokyo, on December 4, 1623. Feast on September 13 (O.F.M.).

*Bl. Martin Gómez, Franciscan tertiary. Born in Japan. Adopted a Spanish family name. Never visited the New World. One of the six Japanese Christians who were beheaded on August 17, 1627, when Bl. Brother Bartholomew Laurel Días was burned alive at Nagasaki. Feast on September 13 (O.F.M.). There was another Franciscan martyr of Japan, Father Louis Gómez Palomino, who went from Spain to the Philippines via Mexico, and from there to Japan in 1598 and again in 1601. He died a martyr at Tokyo on June 6, 1634, but has not been beatified.

*Bl. Dominic Doxigo or of Nagasaki, Franciscan tertiary. (*Doxigo* is Japanese for "catechist.") Born in Japan. Never visited the New World. One of the six Japanese Christians who were beheaded at Nagasaki on August 17, 1627. Feast on September 13 (O.F.M.). There was another Bl. Dominic of St. Francis, a Japanese who made his profession as a brother of the Order of Friars Minor while in prison and died a martyr at Nagasaki on September 8, 1628. Feast on September 13 (O.F.M.).

Bl. Francis of St. Mary, priest. Born in Mancha, Spain. He went to the Philippines via Mexico in 1605, and from there to Japan in 1623. There Brother Bartholomew Laurel Días was his companion. Burned to death at Nagasaki on August 17, 1627. Feast on September 13 (O.F.M.).

Bl. Gabriel of St. Magdalen Tarazona y Rodríguez, brother and physician. Born at Fonseca, Spain. Went to the Philippines via Mexico in 1611, and from there to Japan in 1612. Died a martyr at Nagasaki on September 3, 1632. Feast on September 13, (O.F.M.).

Bl. Charles Spinola, priest. Born at Prague, his father being the Italian Count of Spinola, then in the Austrian service. His first attempt to reach Japan by the African route to the Far East around the Cape of Good Hope failed when his ship was driven by a storm onto the coast of Brazil in 1599. The second time, 1599-1602, he succeeded. Arrested in 1618, he was burned to death at Nagasaki on September 10, 1633, in the Great Martyrdom. Feast, with seven other martyrs of Japan, in the Society of Jesus, on September 25.

Bl. Jerome of the Angels, priest. Born at Castrogiovanni, Sicily. Went to Japan with Bl. Charles Spinola in 1599-1602. Apparently he accompanied Bl. Charles on his first as well as second attempt to reach the Far East. Arrested in August, 1623, in Tokyo, he was burned alive on December 4 of that year. Feast in Japan and in the Society of Jesus on December 4, and at Piazza, Sicily, on December 5.

Bl. Didacus (Diogo, Diego) Carvalho, priest. Born 1578 in Coimbra, Portugal. He seems to have accompanied Bl. Charles Spinola on his first and second attempts to reach the Far East in 1599-1602. Went to Japan in 1609, was expelled in 1614, and returned in 1615. Arrested with nine companions, he was twice immersed in icy water until he died, February 22, 1624. Feast in Japan, Macao and the Society of Jesus on February 25.

Appendix II

Saints and Blessed of the Americas According to Their Religious Affiliation

Augustinians (O.S.A.): Bl. Peter Manrique de Zúñiga, Bl. Bartholomew Gutiérrez Rodríguez.

Claretians (C.M.F.): St. Anthony Mary Claret.

Congregation de Notre Dame (C.N.D.): Bl. Marguerite Bourgeoys.

Daughters of Charity (D.C.): Bl. Elizabeth Ann Seton.

Diocesan Clergy: St. Turibius de Mogrovejo, Bl. Andrew Grasset de St. Sauveur.

Dominicans (O.P.): St. Louis Bertrand, St. Martin de Porres, Bl. John Masías, Bl. Louis Flores.

Franciscans (O.F.M.): St. Philip of Jesus, St. Peter Baptist Blásquez, St. Martin de Aguirre, St. Francis Blanco, St. Francis de San Miguel, St. Francis Solano, Bl. Sebastian de Aparicio, Bl. Peter de Avila, Bl. Vincent Ramírez de San José, Bl. Richard Trouvé of St. Ann, Bl. Louis Sotelo, Bl. Louis Sasada, Bl. Louis Baba, Bl. Bartholomew Laurel Días.

Franciscan Sisters of the Poor: Bl. Frances Schervier.

Jesuits (S.J.): St. Isaac Jogues, St. René Goupil, St. John de Lalande, St. John Brébeuf, St. Anthony Daniel, St. Gabriel Lalemant, St. Charles Garnier, St. Noel Chabanel, St. Peter Claver, St. Ignatius Azevedo, Bl. Roch González, Bl. John de Castillo, Bl. Alphonse Rodríguez.

Laity: St. Mariana of Jesus, St. Rose of Lima.

Missionary Sisters of the Sacred Heart (M.S.C.): St. Frances X. Cabrini.

Redemptorists (C.SS.R.): Bl. John N. Neumann.

Sisters of Charity or Grey Nuns (S.G.M.): Bl. Marie Marguerite d'Youville.

Society of the Sacred Heart (R.S.C.J.): Bl. Rose Philippine Duchesne.

Appendix III

Calendar of the Saints and Blessed of the Americas[1]

January 4[2] .... Bl. Elizabeth Ann Seton
January 5 .... Bl. John N. Neumann
January 12 .... Bl. Marguerite Bourgeoys
February 6 .... St. Peter Baptist Blásquez[3]
February 6 .... St. Martin de Aguirre[3]
February 6 .... St. Francis Blanco[3]
February 6 .... St. Francis de San Miguel[3]
February 6 .... St. Philip of Jesus[3]
February 25 .... Bl. Sebastian de Aparicio
March 2 .... Bl. Peter Manrique de Zúñiga
March 23 .... St. Toribio de Mogrovejo
May 28 .... St. Mariana of Jesus
June 1 .... Bl. Louis Flores[4]
July 14 .... St. Francis Solano
July 15 .... Bl. Ignatius Azevedo
August 23 .... St. Rose of Lima
September 2 .... Bl. Andrew Grasset
September 2 .... Bl. Bartholomew Gutiérrez
September 9 .... St. Peter Claver
September 13 .... Bl. Richard Trouvé[5]
September 13 .... Bl. Peter de Avila[5]
September 13 .... Bl. Vincent Ramírez[5]
September 13 .... Bl. Louis Sotelo[5]
September 13 .... Bl. Louis Sasada[5]
September 13 .... Bl. Louis Baba[5]
September 13 .... Bl. Bartholomew Laurel Días[5]
October 3 .... Bl. John Masías
October 9 .... St. Louis Bertrand
October 16 ....Bl. Marie Marguerite d'Youville
October 19[6] .... St. Isaac Jogues
October 19 .... St. John de Brébeuf
October 19 .... St. Anthony Daniel
October 19 .... St. Charles Garnier
October 19 .... St. Gabriel Lalemant
October 19 .... St. Noel Chabanel

351

October 19.. St. René Goupil
October 19... St. John de Lalande
October 24... St. Anthony Mary Claret
November 3... St. Martin de Porres
November 13[7]...................................... St. Frances Xavier Cabrini
November 17.................................... Bl. Rose Philippine Duchesne
November 17... Bl. Roch González
November 17.. Bl. Alphonse Rodríguez
November 17.. Bl. John de Castillo
December 14 .... Bl. Frances Shervier

1. The days assigned for the feasts or memorials of some of these saints and blessed were changed several times while this book was being printed. The calendar given here has been corrected, as of January 1, 1973, to conform to the Roman Calendar for the United States of America.

2. Bl. Angela of Foligno in the Franciscan Calendar on this day has been moved for the United States to January 6.

3. In the Roman Calendar these martyrs of Nagasaki are included among the companions of St. Paul Miki.

4. Bl. Louis Flores is included among the companions of Bl. Alphonse Navarette.

5. These martyrs of Japan are included among the companions of Bl. Apollinaris Franco.

6. St. Peter of Alcantara in the Franciscan Calendar on this day has been moved for the United States to October 21.

7. St. Didacus of Alcalá in the Franciscan Calendar on this day has been moved for the United States to November 7.

Appendix IV

Saints and Blessed Who Were Born
or Died or Lived in the Americas

A. Born in the Americas

1571: St. Philip of Jesus (Mexico City)
1576: Bl. Roch González (Asunción, Paraguay)
1579: St. Martin de Porres (Lima, Peru)
1580: Bl. Bartholomew Gutiérrez (Mexico City)
1586: St. Rose of Lima (Lima, Peru)
1618: St. Mariana of Jesus (Quito, Ecuador)
1758: Bl. Andrew Grasset de St. Sauveur (Montreal, Canada)
1771: Bl. Marie Marguerite d'Youville (Varennes, Canada)
1774: Bl. Elizabeth Ann Seton (New York City)

B. Died in the Americas

1600: Bl. Sebastian de Aparicio (Puebla, Mexico)
1606: St. Turibius de Mogrovejo (Saña, Peru)
1610: St. Francis Solano (Lima, Peru)
1628: Bl. John de Castillo (Asunción, Río Grande do Sul, Brazil)
1628: Bl. Alphonse Rodríguez (Todos Santos, Río Grande do Sul, Brazil)
1642: St. René Goupil (Auriesville, New York)
1645: Bl. John Masías (Lima, Peru)
1646: St. Isaac Jogues (Auriesville, New York)
1646: St. John de Lalande (Auriesville, New York)
1648: St. Anthony Daniel (Ontario, Canada)
1649: St. John Brébeuf (Ontario, Canada)
1649: St. Gabriel Lalemant (Ontario, Canada)
1649: St. Charles Garnier (Ontario, Canada)
1649: St. Noel Chabanel (Ontario, Canada)
1654: St. Peter Claver (Cartagena, Colombia)
1700: Bl. Marguerite Bourgeoys (Montreal, Canada)
1852: Bl. Rose Philippine Duchesne (St. Charles, Missouri)
1860: Bl. John N. Neumann (Philadelphia, Pennsylvania)
1917: St. Frances X. Cabrini (Chicago, Illinois)

C. Lived in the Americas

	1562-1569:	St. Louis Bertrand (Colombia)
c.	1566-1569:	Bl. Ignatius Azevedo (Brazil)
c.	1580-1602:	Bl. Louis Flores (Mexico)
	1581-1583:	St. Peter Baptist Blásquez (Mexico)
	1581-1583:	St. Francis de San Miguel (Mexico)
	1585-1596:	Bl. Peter Manrique de Zúñiga (Mexico)
c.	1592-1593:	St. Martin de Aguirre (Mexico)
c.	1592-1593:	St. Francis Blanco (Mexico)
c.	1599-1618:	Bl. Bartholomew Laurel Días (Mexico)
	1608-1611:	Bl. Richard Trouvé of St. Anne (Mexico)
c.	1614-1618:	Bl. Vincent Ramírez de San José (Mexico)
	1614-1618:	Bl. Louis Sasada (Mexico)
	1614, 1617-1618:	Bl. Louis Sotelo (Mexico)
	1614, 1617-1618:	Bl. Louis Baba (Mexico)
	1851-1857:	St. Anthony Mary Claret (Cuba)
	1863-1868:	Bl. Frances Schervier (United States)

Appendix V

American Candidates for Sainthood

BESIDES the twenty-three Blessed of the Americas, who are candidates for canonization, there is a large number of others whose cause of beatification has been introduced in Vatican City or at least in the dioceses where they lived and died. To some of these the title "Venerable" has been given inasmuch as their causes have advanced to the stage in which the heroic nature of their virtues has been recognized or at least the examination of their heroic life of virtue has made some progress. The latter we shall list in alphabetical order in the first place, and then the others who are called "Servants of God."

Venerable

Ailion (or de Dios), Ven. Nicholas. A priest who died in Lima, Peru, in 1618. His cause was introduced in Rome in 1699. A decree to proceed with the final phase of his beatification was issued in 1704.

Bardesio, Ven. Peter (1641-1700). A Franciscan lay brother who died in Chile. Three times his cause was interrupted; but in 1912, the ordinary and apostolic processes were approved once more and the cause was resumed.

Betancurt (or Bethencourt), Ven. Peter of St. Joseph (1626-1667). A member of the Third Order Secular of St. Francis and the founder of the Bethlehemite Brothers, who died in Guatemala. His cause was introduced in 1771, and his virtues have been declared heroic.

López, Ven. Gregory. A hermit who died in Mexico in 1596. His virtues were declared heroic in 1770.

Margil de Jesús, Ven. Anthony (1657-1726). A Franciscan priest who was an outstanding missionary in Central America, Mexico and Texas. He founded five missions in Texas, including the famous Mission San José in San Antonio (1720). He died in Mexico City, and his tomb is in the cathedral. His cause was introduced in 1769, and in 1796 his writings were approved. On July 31, 1863, the year of Texas Independence, the title of Venerable was conferred on him.

355

María de Jesus, Ven. (1579-1637). A Conceptionist Poor Clare, who died at Puebla de los Angeles, Mexico. The decree concerning her heroic practice of all the virtues was issued in 1785.

Marie de l'Incarnation, Ven. (1599-1672). Born in Tours, France, she became the first superior of the Ursulines in Quebec City, Canada. She died in Quebec.

Namuncurá, Ven. Zepherin. A young Araucano Indian of the rugged Argentinian pampas who bore pain, anguish and even death to bring Christianity to his people. He died in Rome on May 11, 1905; Pope Paul VI named him Venerable in June, 1972.

Palafox y Mendoza, Ven. John de. Bishop of Puebla de los Angeles, Mexico, where he died in 1659. By 1777, the investigation of his heroic virtues had commenced; and in 1852 this investigation was resumed.

Tekakwitha, Ven. Kateri (Catherine) (1656-1680). The Indian maiden called the "Lily of the Mohawks." Born at present Auriesville, New York, she was baptized at the age of twenty, and a year later fled to Caughnawaga, near Montreal, where she died. Her cause was introduced in Rome in 1939, and her practice of the virtues was declared heroic in 1943.

Urraca, Ven. Peter. A priest of the Mercederian Order, who died in Lima, Peru, in 1657. The examination of his heroic life of virtue was begun in 1816.

Servants of God

Aguilar y Seixas, S. of G. Francis. As bishop of Michoacán, Mexico, he died in 1678. The informative process concerning his life was opened in 1860.

Andreis, S. of G. Felix de (1778-1820). A native of Italy and a member of the Congregation of the Mission, he came to the United States in 1816 and established the Vincentians in the country. He built St. Mary's Seminary, the oldest institution of higher learning west of the Mississippi River. He died in St. Louis, Missouri. His cause was introduced in 1918.

Avellaneda, S. of G. Mariano. Priest of the Missionary Sons of the Immaculate Heart of Mary, who died in 1915. His writings were approved in 1952.

Baraga, S. of G. Frederic (1797-1868). For thirty-seven years he was a missionary to the Indians of Michigan and Wisconsin, and became the first bishop of Marquette, Michigan. The preliminary process was begun in 1933.

Bentivoglio, S. of G. Mary Magdalene (1834-1905). A Poor

Clare nun who introduced her order into the United States, founding the first separate convent in Omaha in 1882. She died at Evansville, Indiana. A decree approving her writings was issued in 1940.

Camacho, S. of G. Francis. He devoted himself to the care of the sick in hospitals, and died in Peru in 1698. His writings were approved in 1881, and his cause was officially introduced in Rome in 1953.

Castillo, S. of G. Francisco del. A Jesuit priest in Peru, who died in 1673. His writings were found to be free of all errors in Christian doctrine in 1704, and preliminary steps were taken to examine the heroic nature of his virtues in 1912.

Catalá, S. of G. Magín (1761-1830). Born in Spain, he entered the Franciscan Order and served Mission Santa Clara, California, for thirty-six years. He died and was buried at this mission. Preliminary steps toward his beatification were taken in 1909; and his writings were approved in 1911. He is known as "the Holy Man of Santa Clara."

Cieplak, S. of G. John (1857-1926). Archbishop of Vilna, Poland. The Communists condemned him to death in Moscow in 1923, commuted the sentence to ten years' imprisonment, and in 1924 released him provided he would leave. He came to the United States the same year and died two years later in Passaic, New Jersey. The examination of his cause was begun in Rome in 1952.

Columbus, S. of G. Christopher (1451-1506). The discoverer of the New World, who died as a Franciscan tertiary. His cause has been listed for a long time among those which are in the hands of the Franciscan Postulator General in Rome.

Demjanovich, S. of G. Miriam Teresa (1901-1927). Born in Bayonne, New Jersey, she was a member of the Sisters of Charity of St. Elizabeth, Convent Station, New Jersey. The diocesan processes were completed in 1954.

Drexel, S. of G. Katherine (1858-1955). She was born in Philadelphia and was the daughter of international banker Francis A. Drexel. Before and after founding the Sisters of the Blessed Sacrament of Cornwells Heights, Pennsylvania, she spent more than twenty million dollars of her own money for mission work among the Indians and blacks of the United States. The Sacred Congregation for the Causes of Saints approved her writings in 1974.

Esquiú, S. of G. Mamert (1826-1883). Franciscan bishop of Córdoba, Argentina. The ordinary processes having been completed, the Sacred Congregation of Rites began to study his cause in 1947.

Galvão, S. of G. Antonio de Santa Anna (1739-1822). Franciscan priest, whose cause was presented by the archdiocese of São Paulo, Brazil, to the Roman authorities in 1949.

Garcia Acosta, S. of G. Andres Filomeno (1800-1853). Franciscan lay brother who died in Santiago, Chile. The apostolic process was started in Rome in 1930.

Guerin, S. of G. Theodora (1798-1856). Founder of the Sisters of Providence of Indiana at St. Mary-of-the-Woods in 1840. The Sacred Congregation of Rites gave its approval to her writings in 1940.

Ibarguren, S. of G. Saturnino. Jesuit priest who died in 1927 in Barranquilla, Colombia. His writings received approval in 1946.

Jansoone, S. of G. Frederick (1834-1916). Franciscan priest who died in the diocese of Trois Riviérès (Three Rivers), Canada. The apostolic process was opened in Rome in 1950.

Kopp, S. of G. Marianne (1838-1918). A member of the Sisters of the Third Franciscan Order Minor Conventuals of Syracuse, New York, since 1862, she died on the island of Molokai after serving the lepers for thirty years. With the approval of the Sacred Congregation for the Causes of Saints the preliminary investigation of her life and virtues was begun in 1974.

La Palma, S. of G. John Martin de. A Franciscan priest of Colombia. He was born at La Palma, near Bogotá, served as a missionary on the banks of the Magdalena River and the Tolima area, and was known for many miracles. His cause has been taken to Rome.

Loras, S. of G. Mathias (1792-1858). First bishop of Dubuque, Iowa. When he was consecrated in 1837, his diocese included all the Wisconsin territory, extending from Missouri to Canada and from the Mississippi to the Pacific. Preliminary steps to introduce his cause were begun in 1937.

Marcet, S. of G. Peter. A lay brother of the Missionary Sons of the Immaculate Heart of Mary, who died in Santiago, Chile, in 1870. The ordinary informative process was begun in 1951.

Masia, S. of G. Joseph Mary (1815-1902). Franciscan bishop of Loja, Ecuador. His cause of beatification was begun in 1902.

Mayoral, S. of G. Peter. A Jesuit priest who died in Paraguay in 1724. The ordinary process began in 1910.

Meri Alfaro, S. of G. Louis Philip. An Oratorian priest of Mexico. His cause of beatification was introduced in 1829.

Miguel, S. of G. Brother. A Christian Brother who died in 1910 at Premiá de Mar, Ecuador. His writings were approved in 1930, and five years later his cause was officially begun in Rome.

Molina, S. of G. María Mercedes de Jesús. Founder of the Institute of the Sisters of St. Mariana of Jesus, who died in 1883 at

Riobamba, Ecuador. The decree for the introduction of her cause was issued in 1946.

Monteagudo, S. of G. Ana de los Angeles. A Dominican nun who died in 1686. Introduced in 1817, her cause was confirmed as a valid one in 1918.

Moreno Díaz, S. of G. Ezechiel (1843-1906). Born in Spain, he was an Augustinian missionary in the Philippines before he came to Colombia in 1888 and became bishop of Pasto. In 1906 he returned to Spain because of poor health and died there the same year. Preparatory steps for the investigation of his heroic practice of virtues were taken in 1947.

Mosquera, S. of G. Emmanuel Joseph (1800-1853). Archbishop of Bogotá, Colombia. Born at Popayán, Colombia, the archbishop was banished by the Congress from the country in 1852, at which time his own brother was president of the republic. He spent eight months in New York City, and died at Marseilles, France, while on the way to Rome. Preliminary steps for the introduction of his cause have been taken in Bogotá.

Paz y Figueroa de San José, S. of G. María Antonia. An unmarried lay person who lived in her own home and died in Buenos Aires, Argentina, in 1799. Her cause was officially introduced in Rome in 1917.

Perdomo y Borrero, S. of G. Ismael (1872-1950). Born at Gigante, Colombia, he became archbishop of Bogotá in 1928 and died in 1950. The investigation for the introduction of his cause was still of a local character in 1956.

Pro, S. of G. Michael August (1891-1927). Jesuit priest of Mexico, who ministered to thousands during one of the persecutions of the Church. He was unjustly accused of being involved in a plot to assassinate President Obregon and shot to death by the police. His cause was begun in Rome in 1952.

Reynaud, S. of G. Paul Emilian. A Franciscan priest who died as a martyr in 1862 at the hands of the Chimanos Indians of Bolivia. The title of "Venerable" has, it seems, been bestowed on him popularly, not officially.

Rolón de San José, S. of G. Camila. Founder of the Poor Sisters of St. Joseph in Buenos Aires, Argentina, who died in 1913. The informative process was opened in 1952.

Rosal del Sagrado Corazón de Jesús, S. of G. María Encarnación (1815-1886). Founder of the Congregation of the Bethlehemite Sisters in Guatemala, her native land. She has been compared with St. Margaret Mary Alacoque. The ordinary informative process was begun in 1917.

Sarobe, S. of G. Pius (1885-1910). A Franciscan priest, who died at Huancayo, Peru. His cause was introduced in Rome in 1947.

Seelos, S. of G. Francis Xavier (1819-1867). A Redemptorist missionary in Pittsburgh and New Orleans. Steps were taken to introduce his cause in Rome in 1912.

Serra, S. of G. Juniper (1713-1784). Franciscan missionary in Mexico, including Lower California, and founder of the first nine missions in California. He died and was buried at San Carlos Mission, Carmel. Preparations to present his cause began in 1934; and in 1950 the apostolic process opened in Rome.

Simón y Rodenas, S. of G. Francis. A Spanish Capuchin Franciscan, who was consecrated bishop of Santa Marta, Colombia, and died at Barranquilla in 1904. The cause of his beatification has been taken to Rome.

Vera, S. of G. Jacinto. Bishop of Montevideo, Uruguay, who died in 1881. The ordinary informative process was begun in 1949.

Villaseca, S. of G. Joseph Mary. Priest and founder of the Campañía Missionera de San José, who died in 1910 in Mexico. In 1939, the ordinary informative process was launched.

Yerovi, S. of G. José María de Jesús (1819-1867). Born in Quito, Ecuador, he joined the Franciscans and became archbishop of Quito in 1866. Introduced in 1947, his cause advanced in 1956 to the investigation of his heroic practice of the virtues.

118 Martyrs in the United States

The cause of the beatification and canonization of the early missionary martyrs of the United States was launched at the annual meeting of the hierarchy of the country in November, 1930.

Bishop John M. Gannon of Erie presented a motion that "the bishops in annual conference assembled petition the Holy See that there be introduced one cause for the beatification and canonization of the early missionaries who were put to death for the faith in what is now United States territory." After the motion had been seconded by Archbishop Rudolph A. Gerken of Santa Fe and then discussed, it was passed unanimously.

A mere petition was not sufficient, and so Bishop Gannon appointed a committee of historians to draw up a martyrology listing the martyrs, containing brief accounts of the martyrdom of each, and indicating the sources of information. By the end of summer in 1941, this document was ready. It listed 116 martyrs. Bishop Gannon obtained the approval and blessing of the Apostolic Delegate, Archbishop Amleto G. Cicognani; and Cardinal

Dennis Dougherty of Philadelphia, senior member of the American hierarchy, in the name of all the bishops signed the Latin petition which was sent with the martyrology to Cardinal Carolo Salotti, Prefect of the Sacred Congregation of Rites. Subsequently two more names were added, making a total of 118 martyrs. The following is a list of these in chronological order, indicating year, name and place, i.e., the present states, where the martyrs died.

1542 — Father John de Padilla, O.F.M. — Kansas
1542 —Father (or Bro.) John de la Cruz, O.F.M. (?) — N.M.
1542 —Brother Louis Descalona de Ubeda, O.F.M. — N.M.
1549 — Father Diego de Peñalosa, O.P. — Florida
1549 — Brother Fuentes, O.P. — Florida
1549 — Father Louis Cancer de Barbastro, O.P. — Florida
1553 — Father Diego de la Cruz, O.P. — Texas
1553 — Father Hernando Mendez, O.P. — Texas
1553 — Father John de Mena, O.P. — Texas
1553 — Father John Ferrer, O.P. — Texas
1566 — Father Peter de Martínez, S.J. — Florida
1571 — Father Louis de Quiros, S.J. — Virginia
1571 — Gabriel de Solís, S.J. — Virginia
1571 — Baptista Méndez, S.J. — Virginia
1571 — Father John Baptist de Segura, S.J. — Virginia
1571 — Christopher Redondo, S.J. — Virginia
1571 — Brother Peter Linares, S.J. — Virginia
1571 — Brother Gabriel Gómez, S.J. — Virginia
1571 — Brother Sancho Zeballos, S.J. — Virginia
1581 — Father John de Santa María, O.F.M. — New Mexico
1582 — Father Francis López, O.F.M. — New Mexico
1582 — Brother Augustine Rodríguez, O.F.M. — New Mexico
1597 — Father Peter de Corpa, O.F.M. — Georgia
1597 — Father Blaise de Rodríguez, O.F.M. — Georgia
1597 — Father Michael de Añón, O.F.M. — Georgia
1597 — Brother Anthony de Badajoz, O.F.M. — Georgia
1597 — Father Francis de Berascola, O.F.M. — Georgia
1631 — Father Peter de Ortega, O.F.M. — New Mexico
1631 — Father Peter Miranda, O.F.M. — New Mexico
1631 — Father Dominic de Saraoz, O.F.M. — New Mexico
1632 — Father Francis Letrado, O.F.M. — New Mexico
1632 — Father Martin de Arvide, O.F.M. — New Mexico
1633 — Father Francis Porras, O.F.M. — New Mexico
1639 — Father Diego de San Lucas, O.F.M. — New Mexico
1647 — An unnamed Franciscan — Florida
1647 — An unnamed Franciscan — Florida

1647 — An unnamed Franciscan — Florida
1661 — Father René Menard, S.J. — Wisconsin
1672 — Father Peter Avila y Ayala, O.F.M. — New Mexico
1675 — Father Alonso Gil de Avila, O.F.M. — New Mexico
1680 — Father Gabriel de la Ribourde, O.F.M. — Illinois
1680 — Father Anthony de Mora, O.F.M. — New Mexico
1680 — Brother John de la Pedrosa, O.F.M. — New Mexico
1680 — Bartholomew Naranjo, Indian — New Mexico
1680 — Father John Bernal, O.F.M. — New Mexico
1680 — Father Dominic de Vera, O.F.M. — New Mexico
1680 — Father Ferdinand de Velasco, O.F.M. — New Mexico
1680 — Father Emmanuel Tinoco, O.F.M. — New Mexico
1680 — Father John Baptist Pio, O.F.M. — New Mexico
1680 — Father Thomas de Torres, O.F.M. — New Mexico
1680 — Father Louis de Morales, O.F.M. — New Mexico
1680 — Brother Anthony Sánchez de Pro, O.F.M. — N.M.
1680 — Father Mathias Rendon, O.F.M. — New Mexico
1680 — Father Francis Lorenzana, O.F.M. — New Mexico
1680 — Father John de Talabán, O.F.M. — New Mexico
1680 — Father Joseph de Montesdoca, O.F.M. — New Mexico
1680 — Father John de Jesús, O.F.M. — New Mexico
1680 — Father John del Val, O.F.M. — New Mexico
1680 — Father Luke Maldonado, O.F.M. — New Mexico
1680 — Father Joseph de Figueroa, O.F.M. — New Mexico
1680 — Father Joseph de Trujillo, O.F.M. — New Mexico
1680 — Father Joseph de Espeleta, O.F.M. — New Mexico
1680 — Father Augustine de Santa María, O.F.M. — N.M.
1689 — Father Zénobe Membré, O.F.M. — Texas
1689 — Father Maxim Le Clerq, O.F.M. — Texas
1689 — Father Chefdeville, S.S. — Texas
1690 — Stephen Tegananokoa, Indian — New York
1692 — Frances Gonannhatenha, Indian — New York
1692 — Margaret Garangouas, Indian — New York
1696 — Father Francis Corvera, O.F.M. — New Mexico
1696 — Father Anthony Moreno, O.F.M. — New Mexico
1696 — Father Francis Casañas, O.F.M. — New Mexico
1696 — Father Joseph de Arbizu, O.F.M. — New Mexico
1696 — Father Anthony Carbonel, O.F.M. — New Mexico
1696 — Father Louis Sánchez, O.F.M. — Florida
1697 — Father Christopher Plunkett, O.F.M. Cap. — Virginia
1702 — Father Nicholas Foucault — Mississippi
1704 — Father John Parga Arraiyo, O.F.M. — Florida
1704 — Brother Mark Delgado, O.F.M. — Florida
1704 — Anthony Enixa, Indian — Florida

1704 — Amador Cuipa Feliciano, Indian — Florida
1704 — Father Manuel de Mendoza, O.F.M. — Florida
1704 — Father Dominic Criado, O.F.M. — Florida
1704 — Father Tiburcio Osorio, O.F.M. — Florida
1704 — Father Augustine Ponce de León, O.F.M. — Florida
1706 — Father John Francis Buisson de St. Cosme — La.
1706 — Father Constantine Delhalle, O.F.M. — Michigan
1708 — Father James Gravier, S.J. — Alabama
1715 — Father Leonard Vatier, O.F.M. — Wisconsin
1718 — Brother Louis de Montesdoca, O.F.M. — Texas
1720 — Father John Mínguez, O.F.M. — Nebraska
1721 — Brother Joseph Pita, O.F.M. — Texas
1724 — Father Sebastian Rale, S.J. — Maine
1729 — Father Paul du Poisson, S.J. — Mississippi
1729 — Father John Souel, S.J. — Mississippi
1730 — Father Gaston — Illinois
1736 — Father John Peter Aulneau, S.J. — Michigan
1736 — Father Anthony Senat, S.J. — Mississippi
1736 — Commander Peter d'Artiquette — Mississippi
1736 — Captain Francis Marie Bissot de Vincennes — Miss.
1736 — Captain Louis Dailebout de Coulogne — Mississippi
1736 — Captain Louis Charles du Tisne — Mississippi
1736 — Captain Francis Mariauchau d'Esgly — Mississippi
1736 — Captain Peter Anthony de Tonty — Mississippi
1736 — Captain Louis Groston de St. Ange, Jr. — Mississippi
1749 — Father Francis Xavier Silva, O.F.M. — Texas
1752 — Father Joseph Francis Ganzabal, O.F.M. — Texas
1758 — Father Alonso Giraldo de Terreros, O.F.M. — Texas
1758 — Father Joseph Santiesteban, O.F.M. — Texas
1775 — Father Louis Jayme, O.F.M. — California
1781 — Father John Marcellus Díaz, O.F.M. — California
1781 — Father Joseph Matthias Moreno, O.F.M. — California
1781 — Father Francis Hermenegild Garcés, O.F.M. — Cal.
1781 — Father John Anthony Barreneche, O.F.M. — Cal.
1812 — Father Andrew Quintana, O.F.M. — California
1834 — Father Joseph Anthony Díaz de León, O.F.M. — Tex.
1872 — Father Francis of Bassost, O.F.M. Cap. — California
1886 — Archbishop Charles J. Seghers — Alaska

Father Peter de Corpa and Companions

Since the death of the five martyrs of Georgia in 1597 (mentioned in the preceding list) appeared to be a plain case of martyr-

363

dom in the strict sense, it was proposed in 1950 that a separate cause of beatification be introduced for them without further delay. For this reason, on July 11, 1950, the writer was appointed pro-postulator; and on September 16, the task of gathering all available historical documents concerning the life and death of these martyrs was assigned to a commission of three Franciscans: Father Alexander Wyse, Father Ignatius Omaechevarria, and the author, Father Marion A. Habig.

Since the original documents were in the archives of Spain, Father Omaechevarria made authentic copies and forwarded them to Rome. Later he published them in a printed monograph: *Martires de Georgia, Informes y relaciones sobre su muerte* (Madrid, 1955).

Inasmuch as Father Peter de Corpa and his four companions gave their lives in defense of Christian monogamous marriage, they were regarded as true martyrs as soon as the facts became known. After a careful investigation of the circumstances of their death had been made, the superiors of the Franciscan Custody of Santa Elena de la Florida made the following official statement in a letter to the Spanish king, dated October 16, 1612:

"Although the Indians did not martyr the friars for the faith [directly], it is certain that they martyred them because of the law of God which the friars taught them. This is the reason they gave and which they attest today, since they realize their sin. . . . It is known in this land that since the death of these holy friars this people [the Guale Indians] has become docile and mild-mannered."

Noteworthy is the coincidence that the martyrs of Georgia died in the same year in which the protomartyrs of Japan were crucified at Nagasaki.

Although the cause of the Georgia martyrs has not as yet been formally introduced in Rome, we still entertain the hope that this will be done eventually. As champions of the sanctity of Christian marriage, they would indeed be timely heavenly patrons in this day and age when a barrage of attacks is made upon the laws of the Church. Privately, of course, we may even now invoke the intercession of these martyrs. Such a practice will also very greatly promote the cause of their beatification.

Notes of Each Chapter and Appendix V

CHAPTER 1

The most complete biography of St. Isaac Jogues is Francis Talbot's *Saint among Savages* (New York and London, 1935), 466 pages. John J. Wynne's *The Jesuit Martyrs of North America* (New York, 1925) is an excellent account of all eight canonized martyrs; and he makes it clear that the so-called Récollets of New France were Franciscans, something most other historians have failed to do. The first chapter (pp. 1-41) in *Pioneer Priests of North America, 1642-1710*, vol. I (Among the Iroquois), by T. J. Campbell (New York, 1908) is a biography of Father Isaac Jogues. *The Jesuit Relations*, with English translations, edited by R. G. Thwaites, were published in Cleveland, 1896-1901.

CHAPTER 2

Of the many lives of Mother Seton and her own writings which have been published we list the following in the alphabetical order of the authors' names: Barberey, Madame de, *Elizabeth Seton*, published in French in Baltimore, 1879, and translated into English by J. B. Code (New York, 1927). Burton, K., *His Dear Persuasion: The Life of Elizabeth Ann Seton* (New York, 1940). Danemarie, J., *Anne-Elizabeth Seton* (Paris, 1938). Dirvin, J. I., *Mrs. Seton: Foundress of the American Sisters of Charity* (New York, 1962). Feeney, L., *An American Woman: Elizabeth Seton* (New York, 1938). Melville, A. M., *Elizabeth Bayley Seton, 1774-1821* (New York, 1960). O'Neil, M. C., *Mother Elizabeth Ann Seton* (Emmitsburg, Md., 1940). Regis, Sister Mary, *Virgin Soil* (Boston, 1942). Seton, E. A., *Letters of Mother Seton to Mrs. Juliana Scott*, edited by J. B. Code, 2nd edn. (New York, 1960). Seton, E. A., *Memoirs, Letter, and Journal of Elizabeth Seton*, edited by Archbishop Robert Seton, 2 vols. (New York, 1869). Simone Seramur, Clare, *Courageous Calling: A Biographical Novel* (Elizabeth Ann Seton) (New York, 1961). White, C. I., *Life of Elizabeth A. Seton* (Baltimore, 1879). Revised edn. (Garden City, N.Y., 1949).

CHAPTER 3

Five biographies of Bl. Rose Philippine have been published in English: *History of Mother Duchesne,* a translation by Fullerton of Baunard's French life (Roehampton, England, 1879); *Mother Philippine Duchesne,* by Mother M. Erskine (New York, 1926); *Blessed Rose Philippine Duchesne,* by Mother Keppel (New York, 1940); *Heart of Oak,* by T. Gavan Duffy (St. Louis, 1940); and *Philippine Duchesne,* by Mother L. Callan (Westminster, Md., 1957). The last mentioned is to a great extent an autobiography, inasmuch as it contains numerous letters written by Mother Duchesne, who had a facile pen.

CHAPTER 4

The first life of Bishop Neumann was written in German by his nephew Father John Berger, who came to Philadelphia in 1857 and joined the Redemptorists two years later. An English translation by Grimm was published in New York, 1884. Since then three other biographies have appeared in English: a *Short Life,* by Magnier (St. Louis, 1897); M. J. Curley, *Venerable John Neumann, C.SS.R.* (Baltimore, Md., 1952); and W. Frean, *Blessed John Neumann: The Helper of the Afflicted* (Ballarat, Victoria, Australia, 1963).

CHAPTER 5

A German life of Bl. Frances Schervier written by Father Ignatius Jeiler, O.F.M., a book of 480 pages, was first published in 1893 and again in 1897, in 1912 and in 1927; and an English translation by Father Bonaventure Hammer, O.F.M., *The Venerable Mother Frances Schervier* (St. Louis, Mo.) was published in 1895. The third edition of the latter appeared in 1924 and can be found in some libraries.

A shorter German biography by Bruno Gossens, O.F.M. Cap., 150 pages, was published in Munich in 1932; and a very short abridgment of it (64 pages), now out of print and rare, is *The Venerable Servant of God Mother Frances Schervier, Foundress of the Congregation of the Sisters of the Poor of St. Francis,* by Father Ferdinand B. Gruen, O.F.M., Ph. D. (New York, 1935).

A pamphlet life by Roland Burke, O.F.M., *Fire upon the Earth, The Story of Frances Schervier and Her Sisters* (30 pages) was published in 1951, and has been reprinted, by the Franciscan Sisters of the Poor. Short biographies are also contained in two other private publications of the Franciscan Sisters of the Poor: *Centenary Souvenir, 1845-1945, Congregation of the Sisters of the Poor of St. Francis* and *In Love with Christ Poor: The Story of the Franciscan Sisters of the Poor, 1858-1959*, compiled from the Annals of the Congregation (469 pages) by Sister M. Pauline, S.F.P., Provincial House of St. Clare, Cincinnati, Ohio.

CHAPTER 6

An English biography, *Mother Cabrini*, by E. J. McCarthy, was published in Chicago in 1937. Following the decree of canonization, three excellent lives appeared: A Benedictine Dame of Stanbrook, England, *Frances Xavier Cabrini, the Saint of the Emigrants* (1944); L. P. Borden, *Francesca Cabrini: Without Staff or Scrip* (New York, 1945); T. Maynard, *Too Small a World* (Milwaukee, 1945); and F. P. Keyes, *Mother Cabrini, Missionary to the World* (New York, 1959). Cf. also A. G. Cicognani, *Sanctity in America*, 3rd edn. (Paterson, N. J., 1945); and M. A. Habig, *The Franciscan Book of Saints* (Chicago, 1959).

CHAPTER 7

A more detailed account of the Martyrs of Huronia will be found in J. J. Wynne, *The Jesuit Martyrs of North America*. Cf. also C. LeClercq, *First Establishment of the Faith in New France*, tr. by J. G. Shea, 2 vols. (New York, 1881). W. and E. M. Jury, *Sainte-Marie among the Hurons* (1953). F. X. Talbot, author of *A Saint among the Savages* (St. Isaac Jogues), has also written *A Saint among the Hurons* (St. John de Brébeuf). E. J. Pratt, *Brébeuf and His Brethren* (a blank-verse epic poem of 66 pages) (Detroit, 1942).

CHAPTER 8

There are several English lives of Bl. Marguerite Bourgeoys: Margaret Mary Drummond, The *Life and Times of Marguerite Bourgeoys* (Boston, 1907); E. F. Butler, *Life of the Ven. Marguerite Bourgeoys* (New York, 1932); and Katherine Burton, *Valiant Voyager* (Milwaukee, 1964). An English life of Bl. Marguerite

Bourgeoys, by Sister St. I. Doyle, was published in 1940; and an English version of Y. Charron, *Mère Bourgeoys* appeared in 1950.

CHAPTER 9

A French biography of Bl. Marie Marguerite by Faillon was published at Ville Marie (Montreal) in 1852, and another by Jetté at Montreal in 1900. An English life, *Hands of the Needy*, by M. P. Fitts (New York, 1950), was approved for the beatification of Bl. Marie Marguerite. The article in the old *Catholic Encyclopedia*, XV (1912), pp. 736-737, is more detailed than the one in the *New Catholic Encyclopedia;* but the latter is based on Fitts' biography. Cf. also the article in *The Apostle* (Detroit), January, 1969, pp. 16-18, by Sister Teresa Margaret, O.C.D.

CHAPTER 10

The sources of our information concerning Blessed Andrew Grasset is a booklet of thirty pages, illustrated, but without a picture of the martyr: Olivier Maurault, curé of Notre Dame, *Le Bienheureaux André Grasset de Saint Sauveur et sa famille* (Montreal, 1927).

CHAPTER 11

The *Autobiography* of St. Anthony Claret is available in an English translation by L. J. Moore (Compton, Calif., 1945). Several biographies of the saint have likewise appeared in English. We enumerate them in the order of their publication: E. Sugranes, *Venerable Anthony W. Claret* (San Antonio, Texas, 1921); Claretian Missionaries, *The Modern Apostle, Blessed Anthony M. Claret* (Compton, Calif., 1934); J. Echevarría, *Reminiscences of Blessed Anthony Mary Claret, Archbishop and Founder* (Compton, Calif., 1938); D. Sargent, *The Assignments of Antonio Claret* (New York, 1948); Father Thomas, *Saint Anthony Mary Claret, A Sketch of His Life and Works* (Chicago, 1950); Fanchon Royer, *Saint Anthony Claret, Modern Prophet and Healer* (New York, 1957).

The sources for this chapter are the same as those mentioned in the notes for Chapter 13. To these we can now add an interesting little book of 106 pages by Helene Magaret, published in Milwaukee in 1962 and entitled: *Felipe, Being the little known history of the only canonized saint born in North America.*

CHAPTER 13

The best account of the Protomartyrs of Japan is in T. Uyttenbroeck's *Early Franciscans in Japan* (Himeji, Japan, 1958), pp. 1-33. Cf. also his *Bina Generosi Apostolatus Saecula in Japonia, 1549-1650 et 1844-1945* (Tokyo, n.d.) and *The Franciscans in the Land of the Rising Sun* (Tokyo, 1957).

See also S. M. Botero-Restrepo, *Los Sesenta y Tres Santos Americanos* (Medellin, Colombia, 1956), pp. 136-151; L. de Clary, *Lives of the Saints and Blessed of the Three Orders of St. Francis,* 4 vols. (Taunton, England, 1885-1887), I, 160-223; M. A. Habig, *In Journeyings Often* (St. Bonaventure, N. Y., 1953), pp. 243-251, and *The Franciscan Book of Saints* (Chicago, 1959), pp. 81-84; *Historia Missionum Ordinis Fratrum Minorum,* I (Rome, 1967), 197-202, 219-222, 235-236; F. P. Keyes, *The Land of Stones and Saints* (Garden City, N. Y., 1957), pp. 228-288. The last mentioned is a good detailed life of St. Peter Baptist.

Most of the other historians who have written about these martyrs have done so from a prejudiced viewpoint and have misrepresented the advent of the first Franciscans to Japan and their missionary work, even after the martyrs were canonized, for instance, F. V. Williams, *The Martyrs of Nagasaki* (1956), pp. 23 and 27, and even *The Catholic Directory of Japan* (1958) p. ii. It has been proved altogether false that St. Peter and his companions violated a decree of the Holy See when they entered Japan or that they spoiled the work of the Jesuits by their imprudent zeal and their failure to conform themselves to the missionary accommodation practiced by the Jesuits.

A. Butler et al., *Lives of the Saints,* II (February), pp. 86-87, devotes only a page and a half to the martyr-saints of Japan and does not even mention the names of these saints except those of St. Peter Baptist and the three Jesuits. A revised and somewhat shortened edition of the twelve-volume set of Butler's *Lives of the Saints,* edited by H. Thurston and D. Attwater, was published in four volumes (New York, 1956) — mentioned hereafter as *Butler's*

Lives, 4 vols. This edition (I, 259-260) at least gives the names of the Franciscan companions of St. Peter Baptist.

Since an article in *Our Sunday Visitor*, March 9, 1969, "The Martyrs of Nagasaki," by C. Stevens, repeats the old accusations against St. Peter Baptist and his confreres, it will be well to point out some of its statements which have been shown to be false by contemporary Spanish and Japanese documents. It is not true that when the Franciscans arrived in 1593, the *daimyo* Hideyoshi "tolerated Christianity only because of his admiration for Valignano" the Jesuit superior. The fact is that six years before the friars came, that is in 1587, Hideyoshi had issued an edict of exile against the Jesuits then in Japan, and they had gone underground (T. Uyttenbroeck, *Early Franciscans in Japan*, p. 4).

It is not true that "their [the Franciscans'] complete lack of understanding of the Japanese situation brought them into frequent conflict with the Japanese authorities." St. Peter Baptist and his companions came to Japan as ambassadors of the Spanish Philippines in 1593, concluded a pact of friendship with Hideyoshi, and received permission to remain. The dictator even contributed to their maintenance and remained friendly towards them until the *San Felipe* was wrecked (*ibid.*, pp. 8-9). He did not object to their charitable and missionary activities; and it was out of consideration for them that he again allowed the Jesuits to remain in Japan (*ibid.*, p. 16). Furthermore, in December, 1594, St. Peter Baptist consulted the Jesuit vice-provincial in Nagasaki, received from him clearly outlined directives, and ordered his friars to conform to them (*ibid.*, p. 12).

It is not true that the Franciscans' effort to save the *San Felipe* and its cargo through Japanese intermediaries, as was just, infuriated Hideyoshi. It was the lies of his personal physician, the former *bonze* Jaquin, which turned the fickle tyrant against the friars and caused him to pronounce the death sentence upon them and their Japanese helpers (*ibid.*, p. 20). And so it is incorrect to say that "in many ways, the martyrdom was unnecessary."

CHAPTER 14

At least sixteen Spanish, Italian and Latin lives of Bl. Sebastian have been written and printed; but so far there is no book-length English biography. There is a delightful account of Bl. Sebastian's life-story in Charles F. Lummis' *Flowers of Our Lost Romance* (Boston and New York, 1929), pp. 50-87. Father León de Clary also tells the story at some length in *Lives of the Saints and*

Blessed of the Three Orders of St. Francis, I, 313-319. Cf. also M. A. Habig, *Franciscan Book of Saints*, pp. 133-135; *Butler's Lives*, 12 vols., II, 349-351; 4 vols., III, 533-534; and S. M. Botero-Restrepo, *Los Sesenta y Tres Santos Americanos* (Medellin, Colombia, 1956), pp. 153-164.

CHAPTER 15

The main sources used for the biographical sketch of Bl. Richard Trouvé in Chapter 15 are: T. Uyttenbroeck, *Early Franciscans in Japan*, pp. 34-131, especially pp. 106-107; León de Clary, *op. cit.*, III, pp. 124-178, especially pp. 138-140; S. M. Botero-Restrepo, *op. cit.*, pp. 138-140. In M. A. Habig, *In Journeyings Often*, cf. pp. 251-260 (with a list of the 26 canonized martyrs of 1597 on p. 258, and one of the 45 beatified Franciscan martyrs of the early seventeenth century on pp. 259-260).

CHAPTER 16

The sources are the same as for Father Richard Trouvé, Chapter 15, especially T. Uyttenbroeck, *op. cit.*, p. 106; L. de Clary, *op. cit.*, III, pp. 140-141; S. M. Botero-Restrepo, *op. cit.*, pp. 211-212.

CHAPTER 17

Our account of Bl. Peter is based principally on T. Uyttenbroeck, *Early Franciscans in Japan*, especially p. 107, and *Bina Generosi Apostolatus Saecula in Japonia*, p. 140; S. M. Botero-Restrepo, *op. cit.*, pp. 175-179; and A. Thoonsen, *Santos da America* in *O Santuario de S. Antonio* (Divinopolis, Brazil, 1937-1939). He is not mentioned by name in A. Butler et al., *Lives of the Saints*, nor in D. Attwater, *A Dictionary of the Saints* (London and New York, 1942). However, he is listed, and the principal dates of his life are given, in F. G. Holweck, *A Biographical Dictionary of the Saints* (St. Louis and London, 1924), p. 805.

CHAPTER 18

The sources are the same as for Bl. Peter Manrique de Zúñiga

(Chapter 17). In *Dominican Saints* (Washington, D. C., 1921), pp. 428-432, the names are given of the 109 companions of Bl. Alphonse Navarette. The latter became a martyr in 1617. Eight of his Dominican companions died in the Great Martyrdom, September, 1622, only a month after the death of Bl. Louis Flores: five at Nagasaki on September 10 (Bl. Francis Morales, Bl. Angelo Orsucci, Bl. Alphonse de Mena, Bl. Joseph of St. Hyacinth, and Bl. Hyacinth Orfanel), and three at Omura on September 12 (Bl. Thomas Zumárraga of the Holy Spirit and two novices).

CHAPTER 19

Our principal sources for Bl. Louis Sotelo, Bl. Louis Sasada and Bl. Louis Baba, and the other martyrs mentioned are the same as for Chapter 17, especially T. Uyttenbroeck, *Early Franciscans in Japan*, pp. 54-68, 83-84, and 112-115, and *Bina Generosi Apostolatus Saecula*, pp. 99-100 and 142-143; S. M. Botero-Restrepo, *op. cit.*, pp. 212-214, 216-217, and 220-228.

CHAPTER 20

The sources are the same as for Chapter 17. See especially T. Uyttenbroeck, *Early Franciscans in Japan*, pp. 115-117, and S. M. Botero-Restrepo, *op. cit.*, pp. 115-117. It seems that Bl. Gaspar and Bl. Mary Vaez (Vaz, Vos) were Koreans by birth, but had been living in Japan for some time before they became Christians.

CHAPTER 21

The sources are the same as for Chapter 17, especially T. Uyttenbroeck, *Bina Generosi Apostolatus Saecula*, p. 146ff., and *Early Franciscans in Japan*, pp. 119-125; León de Clary, *op. cit.*, III, 173-176; A. Thoonsen, op. cit.; S. M. Botero-Restrepo, *op. cit.*, pp. 60-63. *Butler's Lives*, 4 vols., (II, 451) merely mentions the name of Bl. Bartholomew Gutiérrez.

CHAPTER 22

Father Bertrand Wilberforce, O.P., wrote an English life of his patron saint, *The Life of St. Lewis Bertrand*, (London, 1882), which is based on one written shortly after the death of the saint by one of his novices, Father V. J. Antist, and printed in 1582-1583. The English biography has been translated into several modern languages. A good shorter life of 40 pages is in *Dominican Saints* (Washington, D. C., 1921), pp. 338-357. Cf. also Butler et al., *Lives of the Saints*, IX (London, 1941), pp. 118-122.

According to the chronology indicated in *Dominican Saints*, which we have followed, St. Louis Bertrand resided in Valencia during his whole life except the three years at Albayda (1557-1560), seven and a half years in the New World including his voyages to and from Cartagena, Colombia (1562-1569), and three years at San Onofre — a total of thirteen and a half years. He served as master of novices, not for thirty, but for about ten years (1551-1557; 1560-1562; 1573-1575); and he was engaged in the preaching apostolate in Spain for about twenty-two years (1550-1562; 1570-1580).

CHAPTER 23

The first English biography, *St. Peter Claver, Apostle of the Negroes*, by J. R. Slattery, was published in Philadelphia in 1893. Arnold Lunn's *A Saint in the Slave Trade* (New York, 1935) is an excellent work. The latest life is that of Angel Valtierra, *Peter Claver*, (Westminster, Md., 1960). *Butler's Lives*, 4 vols., III, pp. 519-524. M. Farnum, *Street of the Half Moon* is a fictional account of the life of St. Peter Claver.

CHAPTER 24

The best English biography of St. Mariana is contained in the second part of F. P. Keyes' *The Rose and the Lily* (New York, 1961), pp. 151-230. There is also an English version of Father Botero's Italian and French *Life of Blessed Mary Anne of Jesus* (sic). *Saint Mariana of Jesus, Lily amid Thorns*, by Anna C. Pertsch, has appeared serially in *Fatima Findings* (1967). Cf. also Botero-Restrepo, *op. cit.*, pp. 35-45.

CHAPTER 25

An early life of St. Toribio, by Juan Francisco de Valladolid, was printed in Spanish and Italian. The latter was published in

Rome in 1655: *Vita del servo di Dio D. Toribio Alfonso Mogrovejo Arcivescovo di Lima*. Another is that of Francisco Antonio de Montalvo, *El sol de Nuevo Mundo ideado y compuesto en las esclarecidas operaciones del bienaventurado Toribio arzobispo de Lima* (Rome, 1683). A later life is that by Father Cyprian de Herrera. The most comprehensive work on St. Toribio are the four volumes of D. G. Irigoyen, *Santo Toribio: Obra escrita con motivo del tercer centenario de la muerte del Santo Arzobispo de Lima* (Lima, 1906). Among the many sources used by the writer for the sketch given here, are S. M. Botero-Restrepo, *op. cit.*, pp. 162-168, and *Butler's Lives*, 4 vols., II, 176-178.

CHAPTER 26

The first English book-length life of St. Francis Solano published seems to have been F. Windeatt's *Song in the South* (New York and St. Meinrad's, Ind., 1946). Since then another has appeared, namely Fanchon Royer's *St. Francis Solanus, Apostle to America* (Paterson, N.J., 1955). *Saint Francis Solano, Apostle of Argentina and Peru* (Paterson, N. J., 1942) is a pamphlet life by M. A. Habig. Cf. also León de Clary, *The Lives of the Saints and Blessed of the Three Orders of St. Francis*, II, 509-522; *Butler's Lives*, 4 vols., III, 93-95; and Botero-Restrepo, *op. cit.*, pp. 90-108.

CHAPTER 27

A life of St. Martin de Porres by J. C. Kearns was published in 1950. Cf. also N. Georges, ed., *With Bl. Martin* (New York, 1945) and *Fifteenth Anniversary Book, Bl. Martin Guild* (New York, 1950). *Lad of Lima*, by M. F. Windeatt (New York, 1943) and *St. Martin de Porres and the Mice* (Paterson, N. J.) by E. K. Betz, are biographies of St. Martin for the young. Cf. also Botero-Restrepo, *op. cit.*, pp. 66-71.

Some of the earlier biographical sketches of Brother Martin erroneously gave the year 1569 as the date of his birth instead of 1579; that his mother was an Indian instead of a black, and that he was beatified on October 29 instead of August 8, 1837.

CHAPTER 28

The first English life of St. Rose of Lima seems to have been the one in the Oratorian series edited by Father Faber, which was a translation from the French of J. B. Feuillot. In 1899 and again in 1913 a biography by F. M. Capes, entitled *The Flower of the New World*, was published in New York. A good short life was included in *Dominican Saints* (Washington, D. C., 1921), pp. 381-408. Since then several excellent lives have appeared in various works by well-known authors: M. T. Munro, *A Book of Unlikely Saints* (New York, 1943), pp. 80-130; S. Maynard, *Rose of America* (London, 1944); T. Maynard, *Saints of Our Times* (Image Books); F. P. Keyes, *The Rose and the Lily* (New York, 1961), pp. 51-150; S. Kaye-Smith, *Quartet in Heaven* (Garden City, N. Y., 1962). There is also a life of St. Rose for children by M. F. Windeatt, entitled *Angel of the Andes.*

CHAPTER 29

The principal source used for our biographical sketch of Bl. John Masías is Father S. M. Botero-Restrepo's *Los Sesenta y Tres Santos Americanos* (Medellin, Colombia, 1956), pp. 125-129, and Father Adolpho Thoonsen's *Santos da America* (Divinopolis, Minas Gerais, Brazil, 1937-1939). There is a short account of the life of Bl. John Masías also in *Butler's Lives*, 4 vols., III, 593-594.

CHAPTER 30

Sources used were S. M. Botero-Restrepo, *op. cit.*, pp. 131-134; A. Thoonsen, *Santos da America* (Divinopolis, 1937-1939); *Butler's Lives*, 4 vols., III, 112-113.

CHAPTER 31

A copy of the documents of the episcopal inquiry made a few months after the death of Bl. Roch González and his two companions was found in the twentieth century in Argentina. A detailed history of the martyrs and their martyrdom is contained in J. M. Blanco, *Historia documentada de la Vida y glorioso Muerte de los PP. Roque González, etc.* Cf. also H. Thurston, "The First Beatified Martyr of Spanish America," in *The Catholic Historical Review*, XX, no. 4 (January, 1935), 371-383; S. M. Botero-Restrepo, *op. cit.*, pp. 55-58 and 230; and *Butler's Lives*, 4 vols., IV, 376-377.

CHAPTER 32

The long list of the principal sources for this chapter is contained in the notes and bibliographies of the writer's articles and studies on which the chapter is based. These articles appeared in *Studia Mariana* of the Commissio Marialis Franciscana in Rome, vols. VII and IX; in the series of the International Pontifical Marian Academy entitled *Virgo Immaculate,* vol. XIV, and another series of the same Academy, *Maria et Ecclesia,* vol. XI; in *The Marian Era* (eleven volumes, 1960-1974, Chicago) of which the writer has served as editor; and in *American Ecclesiastical Review,* vols. CXXXI and CXXXII (Washington, 1954).

CHAPTER 33

Besides the sources indicated at the end of the preceding chapter, mention should be made of J. B. Carol, ed., *Mariology,* Vol. III (Milwaukee, 1961), especially pp. 326-352; J. L. Cassidy, *Mexico, Land of Mary's Wonders* (Paterson, N. J., 1958); and Titas Narbutas, *Marian Shrines of the Americas* (New York, 1968). The latter contains short historical sketches of the principal pilgrimage shrines of our Lady in all the Americas.

CHAPTER 34

In addition to the books and studies mentioned for Chapters 32 and 33, the sources for this chapter include especially the well-known histories by Father Z. Engelhardt, Father Maynard Geiger, and C. E. Castañeda; also E. L. Hewett and R. G. Fisher, *Mission Mounuments of New Mexico* (Albuquerque, 1943), M. A. Habig, *The Alamo Chain of Missions* (Chicago, 1968) and *San Antonio's Mission San José* (San Antonio and Chicago, 1968). Further details concerning some of the Marian shrines mentioned will be found in the eleven volumes of *The Marian Era* and F. B. Thornton, *Catholic Shrines in the United States and Canada* (New York, 1954).

Appendix V

The principal sources for this Appendix are the following: S. M. Botero-Restrepo, *Los Sesenta y Tres Santos Americanos:*

"Catalogus ac Status Causarum Beatificationis Servorum Dei et Canonizationis Beatorum Ordinis Fratrum Minorum quae apud S. R. Congregationem vel Curias ordinarias tractantur" in *Acta Ordinis Fratrum Minorum*, vol. 76, no. 3 (May, 1957), pp. 139-157; A. G. Cicognani, *Sanctity in America*, 3rd edn. (1945); J. M. Gannon et al., *The Martyrs of the United States of America, Preliminary Studies Prepared by the Commission for the Cause of Canonization and Related Essays*, xviii plus 196 pages, privately published, Erie, Pa., 1957; M. A. Habig, *Heroes of the Cross*, 3rd edn. (1947); M. A. Habig, M. Geiger and A. Chavez, *Historia Missionum Ordinis Fratrum Minorum*, vol. III (Rome, 1968); pp. 406-408.

Bibliography

Abbott, W. M., ed. *The Documents of Vatican II*. New York, 1966.

Attwater, D. *A Dictionary of Saints*. New York, 1938, 1942.

Betz, E. K. *St. Martin de Porres and the Mice*. Paterson, N. J.

Borden, L. P. *Francesca Cabrini: Without Staff or Scrip*. New York, 1945.

Botero-Restrepo, S. M. *Los Sesenta y Tres Santos Americanos*. Medellin, Colombia, 1956.

Burton, K. *His Dear Persuasion: The Life of Elizabeth Ann Seton*. New York, 1904.

Burton, K. *Valiant Voyager* (Bl. Marguerite Bourgeoys). Milwaukee, 1964.

Butler, A. et al. *Lives of the Saints*. 12 vols. London, 1926-1942. The work was revised by H. Thurston; (vols. I and II), H. Thurston and N. Lesson; (vols. III-VI), H. Thurston and D. Attwater; (vols. VII-XII), and was published 1926-1937; and some of the volumes at least were reprinted 1937-1941, and again in 1942. Another printing in four volumes appeared in 1956.

Butler, E. F. *Life of Ven. Marguerite Bourgeoys*. New York, 1932.

Callan, L. *Philippine Duchesne: Frontier Missionary of the Sacred Heart, 1769-1852*. Westminster, Md., 1957.

Campbell, T. J. *Pioneer Priests of North America, 1642-1710*. 2 vols. Vol. I (Among the Iroquois). New York, 1908.

Capes, F. M. *The Flower of the New World* (St. Rose of Lima). New York, 1899 and 1913.

Cicognani, A. G. *Sanctity in America*. 3rd edn. Paterson, N.J., 1945.

Claretian Missionaries. *The Modern Apostle: Blessed Anthony M. Claret*. Compton, Calif., 1934.

Code, J. B., tr. *Elizabeth Seton* (from the French of Madame de Barbery). New York, 1927.

Code, J. B., ed. *Letters of Mother Seton to Mrs. Juliana Scott*. 2nd edn. New York, 1960.

Code, J. B. *Great American Foundresses*. New York, 1929.

Curley, M. J. *Anne-Elizabeth Seton*. Paris, 1938.

Dehey, E. T. *Religious Orders of Women in the United States*. Hammond, Ind., Chicago, New York, 1913.

Dirvin, J. I. *Mrs. Seton, Foundress of the American Sisters of Charity*. New York, 1962.

Dominican Novices. *Dominican Saints*. Washington, D. C., 1921.

Drummond, M. M. *The Life and Times of Marguerite Bourgeoys*. Boston, 1907.

Duffy, T. G. *Heart of Oak* (Bl. Rose Philippine Duchesne). St. Louis, Mo., 1940.

Echevarria, J. *Reminiscences of Blessed Anthony Mary Claret, Archbishop and Founder*. Compton, Calif., 1938.

Erskine, M. *Mother Philippine Duchesne*. New York, 1926.

Feeney, L. *An American Woman: Elizabeth Seton.* New York, 1938.

Fitts, M. P. *Hands to the Needy* (Bl. Marie Marguerite d'Youville). New York, 1950.

Frean, W. *Blessed John Neumann: The Helper of the Afflicted.* Ballaret, Victoria, Australia, 1963.

Fullerton, tr. *History of Mother Duchesne* (from the French of Baunard). Roehampton, England, 1879.

Gannon, J., et al. *The Martyrs of the United States of America.* Erie, Pa.

Grimm, tr. *Life of John N. Neumann* (from the German of J. Berger). New York, 1884.

Habig, M. A. *Saint Francis Solano, Apostle of Argentina and Peru* (24 pp.). Paterson, N. J., 1942.

Habig, M. A. *In Journeyings Often: Franciscan Pioneers in the Orient.* St. Bonaventure, N.Y., 1953.

Habig, M. A. *Heroes of the Cross: An American Martyrology.* 3rd edn. Paterson, N. J., 1947.

Habig, M. A. *The Franciscan Book of Saints.* Chicago, 1959.

Habig, M. A. *Franciscan Pictorial Book One.* Chicago, 1963.

Habig, M. A. and A. J. Nimeth. *Franciscan Pictorial Book Two.* Chicago, 1966.

Hallack, C., and P. F. Anson. *These Made Peace: Studies in the Lives of the Beatified and Canonized Members of the Third Order of St. Francis.* London and Paterson, N. J., 1957.

Holland, C. C., tr. *St. Martin de Porres: Apostle of Charity* (translation of a life by G. Cavallini). St. Louis, Mo., 1963.

Holweck, F. G. *A Biographical Dictionary of the Saints.* St. Louis, Mo., and London, 1924.

Kaye-Smith, S. *Quartet in Heaven.* Garden City, N. Y., 1962.

Kempf, C. *The Holiness of the Church in the Nineteenth Century: Saintly Men and Women of Our Own Times* (from the German of F. Breymann). New York, 1916.

Keppel, Mother. *Blessed Rose Philippine Duchesne.* New York, 1940.

Keyes, F. P. *The Land of Stones and Saints.* Garden City. N.Y., 1957.

Keyes, F. P. *Mother Cabrini, Missionary to the World.* New York, 1959.

Keyes, F. P. *The Rose and the Lily: The Lives and Times of Two South American Saints.* New York, 1961.

Lappin, P. M. *Bury Me Deep.* Huntington, Ind., 1974.

León (Clary), Fr. *Lives of the Saints and Blessed of the Three Orders of St. Francis* (translation of the French *Aureole Seraphique).* 4 vols., Taunton, England, 1885-1887.

Lummis, C. F. *Flowers of Our Lost Romance.* Boston and New York, 1929.

Margaret, H. *Felipe: Being the little known history of the only canonized saint born in North America.* Milwaukee, Wis., 1962.

Magnier. *A Short Life of John N. Neumann.* St. Louis, Mo., 1897.

Maurault, O. *Le Bienheureux André Grasset de Saint Sauveur et sa famille.* Montreal, Can., 1927.

Maynard, T. *Too Small a World: The Life of Francesca Cabrini.* Milwaukee, Wis., 1945.

Maynard, S. *Rose of America*. London, 1944.

McCarthy E. J. *Mother Cabrini*. Chicago, 1937.

Melville, A. M. *Elizabeth Bayley Seton, 1774-1821*. New York, 1960.

Moore, L. J., tr. *Autobiography of Antonio M. Claret*. Compton, Calif., 1945.

Munro, M. T. *A Book of Unlikely Saints*. New York, 1943.

Nevins, A. J. *Our American Catholic Heritage*. Huntington, Ind., 1973.

O'Neil, M. C. *Mother Elizabeth Ann Seton*. Emmitsburg, Md., 1940.

Peters, C. *Lives of the Saints for Boys and Girls*. Paterson, N. J., 1966.

Pratt, E. J. *Brébeuf and His Brethren*. Detroit, Mich., 1942.

Roemer, T. *The Catholic Church in the United States*. St. Louis, Mo., and London, 1950.

Royer, F. *St. Francis Solanus, Apostle to America*. Paterson, N. J., 1955.

Royer, F. *Saint Anthony Claret, Modern Prophet and Healer*. New York, 1957.

Regis, Sister M. *Virgin Soil* (Bl. Elizabeth Ann Seton). Boston, 1942.

Sargent, D. *The Assignments of Antonio Claret*. New York, 1948.

Schnusenberg, A., ed. *Historia Missionum Ordinis Fratrum Minorum*, I (Asia Centro-Orientalis et Oceania). Rome, 1966.

Seton, R. ed. *Memoirs, Letter and Journal of Elizabeth Seton*. 2 vols., New York, 1869.

Shea, J. G. tr. *First Establishment of the Faith in New France* (from the French of C. LeClercq). 2 vols. New York, 1881.

Simone Seramur, Clare. *Courageous Calling: A Biographical Novel* (Elizabeth Ann Seton). New York, 1961.

Slattery, J. R. *St. Peter Claver, Apostle of the Negroes*. Philadelphia, 1893.

Sugranes, E. *Venerable Anthony M. Claret*. San Antonio, Texas, 1921.

Talbot, F. *Saint Among Savages: The Life of Isaac Jogues*. New York and London, 1935.

Thomas, Fr. *Saint Anthony Mary Claret: A Sketch of His Life and Works*. Chicago, 1950.

Thoonsen, A. *Santos da America*. A series of articles which appeared in *O Santuario de S. Antonio*, Published monthly at Divinopolis, Minas Gerais, Brazil, 1937-1939.

Thwaites, R. G., ed. *The Jesuit Relations*. Cleveland, 1896-1901.

Uyttenbroeck, T. *Bina Generosi Apostolatus Saecula in Japonia, 1549-1650 et 1844-1945*. Tokyo, n.d.

Uyttenbroeck, T. *The Franciscans in the Land of the Rising Sun*. Tokyo, 1957.

Uyttenbroeck, T. *Early Franciscans in Japan*. Himeji, Japan, 1958.

Valtierra, A. *Peter Claver*. Westminster, Md. 1960.

Wilberforce, B. *The Life of St. Lewis Bertrand*. London, 1882.

White, C. I. *Life of Elizabeth A. Seton*. Baltimore, 1879. Revised edn., Garden City, N. Y., 1949.

Windeatt, M. F. *Song in the South* (St. Francis Solano). New York and St. Meinrad's, Ind., 1946.

Windeatt, M. F. *Angel of the Andes* (St. Rose of Lima).New York, 1944.

Windeatt, M. F. *Lad of Lima* (St. Martin de Porres). New York, 1942.

Wynne, J. J. *The Jesuit Martyrs of North America*. New York, 1925.

INDEX

383